Paths to Successful Development

Personality in the Life Course

Edited by

Lea Pulkkinen and Avshalom Caspi

CAMBRIDGE
UNIVERSITY PRESS

PUBLISHED BY THE PRESS SYNDICATE OF THE UNIVERSITY OF CAMBRIDGE
The Pitt Building, Trumpington Street, Cambridge, United Kingdom

CAMBRIDGE UNIVERSITY PRESS
The Edinburgh Building, Cambridge CB2 2RU, UK
40 West 20th Street, New York, NY 10011-4211, USA
477 Williamstown Road, Port Melbourne, VIC 3207, Australia
Ruiz de Alarcón 13, 28014 Madrid, Spain
Dock House, The Waterfront, Cape Town 8001, South Africa

http://www.cambridge.org

© Cambridge University Press 2002

First published 2002

Printed in the United Kingdom at the University Press, Cambridge

Typeface Plantin 10/12 pt.   *System* LaTeX 2$_\varepsilon$ [TB]

A catalogue record for this book is available from the British Library.

ISBN 0 521 80048 x hardback
ISBN 0 521 80483 3 paperback

Contents

v

Contributors

LARS R. BERGMAN, University of Stockholm, Sweden

JOCHEN BRANDTSTÄDTER, University of Trier, Germany

AVSHALOM CASPI, Institute of Psychiatry, King's College London, UK and University of Wisconsin, USA

ROBERT CROSNOE, University of North Carolina, USA

NANCY EISENBERG, Arizona State University, USA

GLEN H. ELDER, JR., University of North Carolina, USA

RICHARD A. FABES, Arizona State University, USA

KARIN GROSSMANN, University of Regensburg, Germany

KLAUS E. GROSSMANN, University of Regensburg, Germany

IVANNA K. GUTHRIE, Arizona State University, USA

GERBERT J. T. HASELAGER, University of Nijmegen, The Netherlands

JUTTA HECKHAUSEN, University of California, Irvine, USA

LINDA JUANG, University of Jena, Germany

KATJA KOKKO, University of Jyväskylä, Finland

BRETT LAURSEN, Florida Atlantic University, USA

MARSHA MAILICK SELTZER, University of Wisconsin, USA

JARI-ERIK NURMI, University of Jyväskylä, Finland

JOHAN ORMEL, University of Groningen, The Netherlands

LEA PULKKINEN, University of Jyväskylä, Finland

SAMUEL P. PUTNAM, University of Oregon, USA

MARK REISER, Arizona State University, USA

MATTHIAS REITZLE, University of Jena, Germany

RICHARD J. ROSE, Indiana University, USA

MARY K. ROTHBART, University of Oregon, USA

CAROL D. RYFF, University of Wisconsin, USA

RON H. J. SCHOLTE, University of Nijmegen, The Netherlands

RAINER K. SILBEREISEN, University of Jena, Germany

BURTON H. SINGER, Princeton University, USA

MARCEL A. G. VAN AKEN, University of Utrecht, The Netherlands

CORNELIS F. M. VAN LIESHOUT, University of Nijmegen, The Netherlands

VICKIE WILLIAMS, Florida Atlantic University, USA

MONIKA WINTER, University of Regensburg, Germany

PETER ZIMMERMANN, University of Regensburg, Germany

Personality and paths to successful development: an overview

Lea Pulkkinen and Avshalom Caspi

Research traditions in developmental psychology vary with respect to how much emphasis they give to successful development. Historically, most studies of personality development have been biased by the goal of seeking to understand maladjustment and behavioral problems, such as anxiety or aggression, and have tended to overlook the study of pathways to successful outcomes. Whereas the study of problem behavior is clearly oriented toward predicting, explaining, and preventing social and clinical problems, the study of successful development is made more difficult because the end point (success) is more elusive and thus more difficult to operationalize and to promote.

To study successful personality development one must first have a way of thinking about the course of lives and a way of assessing how adaptational processes are patterned over time. We can identify three general approaches to this conceptual problem: growth models, life-span models, and life-course models. Each of these social-developmental approaches provides a framework for understanding adaptational processes and the coherence of personality development by focusing on the distinctive ways individuals organize their behavior to meet new environmental demands and developmental challenges.

Growth and stage models

Growth models of personality development are not homogeneous in their orientation, but are based on different traditions and conceptual backgrounds. For example, humanistic theories of personality development are best known for emphasizing the potential for positive development. People can take charge of their lives and direct them toward creativity and self-actualization which involves self-fulfillment and the realization of one's potential (Maslow, 1954). In contrast, psychoanalytically oriented models tend to emphasize the growth of ego through age stages. Integrity is the goal of successful development in Erikson's (1950) theory, as well as in Loevinger's (1997) model of ego development and in the model of Labouvie-Vief (e.g., Labouvie-Vief, Hakim-Larson, DeVoe, and Schoeberlein, 1989) which integrates Piaget's theory of cognitive development with emotions and social relations. Erikson's theory covers eight stages across the life-span. Each stage involves a crisis or an age-specific challenge that should be satisfactorily resolved for optimal development. The theory states that a successful resolution of each crisis results in the refinement of a predominantly positive quality, such as trust in infancy. The psychosocial crises to be solved in adulthood concern intimacy versus isolation, generativity versus stagnation, and integrity versus despair. Common virtues or ego skills such as hope, will, purpose, and skill in childhood, fidelity in adolescence, and love, care, and wisdom in adulthood emerge as successful outcomes of the crises. Development is based on successful resolution of psychological crises leading finally to integrity in old age.

The passage from one developmental stage to another is also central to Levinson's work (1978, 1986), who has studied what he calls "life structures": things that a person finds important in work and love, as well as the values and emotions that make these important. Life structures are subjected to change during transitional periods when people reappraise and restructure important things in their lives. According to Levinson, people spend about half their adult lives in transitional periods.

Sanford (1962), another psychodynamically influenced theorist, described a fully developed person as one characterized by high degrees of both differentiation and integration. Specifically, the fully developed person has a rich and varied impulse life, a broad and refined conscience, a strong sense of individuality, and a balance of control and expression of needs. As for when people reach this stage, Sanford placed the development of impulse control in adolescence and the development of ego, or the controlling function of personality (e.g., maturity), in adulthood. In both cases, Sanford did not presuppose that personality ever stopped changing: "The highly developed person is always open to new experience, and capable of further learning."

Life-span models

Research on life-span personality development is concerned with three major influence systems (Baltes, Lindenberger, and Staudinger, 1998): (1) age-graded influences (e.g., education) which shape individual development in relatively normative ways; (2) history-graded influences (e.g., wars) which make development different across historical periods; and (3) non-normative influences (e.g., accidents) which may have powerful effects on an individual's development. Life-span development theories hold that psychological functioning is not fixed at a certain age. Rather, "during development, and at all stages of the life span, both continuous (cumulative) and discontinuous (innovative) processes are at work" (Baltes, 1987, p. 613). Development is defined as "selective age-related change in adaptive capacity" (Baltes, Staudinger, and Lindenberger, 1999, p. 479) and special attention is given to the developing person's contribution to the creation of his or her own development (Brandtstädter, 1998). Individuals steer their physical, cognitive, social, and personality development by constructing strategies for coping with various developmental challenges, by setting goals, and by making choices. According to Brandtstädter (this volume), such intentional self development over the life span is geared to the realization and maintenance of normative representations that individuals construct of themselves and their future.

The function and significance of goals and choices in successful development is especially apparent beyond childhood, and several chapters in this volume are explicitly concerned with these topics in their efforts to study successful development. Pulkkinen, Nurmi, and Kokko (this volume) discuss how individuals steer their development by setting goals and making choices as responses to developmental challenges. On the one hand, personal goals reflect major age-graded transitions and normative demands. On the other hand, individual differences in personal goals reflect motivational orientations, such as security seeking or aiming at personal growth, which result in intraindividual coherence in goal patterns. With data from the Jyväskylä Longitudinal Study of Personality and Social Development, Pulkkinen and her colleagues show that some personal goals are so pervasive that they operate as unifying life themes that define long-term successful and unsuccessful development.

An agentic conception of human nature is also central in Heckhausen's work on control. Heckhausen (this volume) proposes that humans strive to maximize primary control of their environment throughout life. However, control capacities undergo radical changes and losses and individuals have to disengage from unattainable goals and manage their own emotional responses to such loss experiences. This type of control that is directed at the internal world of the individual is referred to as secondary control. Heckhausen shows how the age-normative structure of life-course transitions allows individuals to anticipate decremental changes in the opportunities to attain developmental goals. For example, an individual can increase primary control striving when approaching "developmental deadlines" (e.g., union formation, health-maintenance in old age) and use secondary control to compensate for potential negative affect and self-evaluation associated with failure to meet or resolve developmental deadlines successfully.

Brandtstädter's work (this volume) on intentional self-development is also striking in its appreciation of the tension between gains and losses in life-span development. His chapter documents that successful development hinges on the interplay between, on the one hand, activities through which individuals assimilate the actual course of personality development to their goals and, on the other hand, processes through which goals are accommodated to the feasible range.

Although life-span models do not articulate what is success, some commentators have noted that developmental models that emphasize freedom of individual decision and action are plagued by a Western bias associated with an individualistic cultural base (Kagitcibasi, 1988). There is a clear need for cultural psychologists to engage life-span researchers in testing the limits of the developmental models that have been advanced. Still, the models that have been put forth are exciting because they articulate hypotheses about how individuals at different junctures in their lives struggle to derive meaning from and make sense of life events, and of their part in these events.

Life-course models

Especially beyond childhood the study of successful adaptation becomes more complicated, and it may be that a purely psychological approach is insufficient for the study of personality development as the individual increasingly negotiates social roles defined by the culture. Whereas life-span theories specify the temporal order of life stages, such as childhood, adolescence, and adulthood, life-course researchers tend to emphasize social-role demands at different ages. Social trajectories are influenced by four factors (Elder, 1998). First, they are influenced by human agency, the choices that persons make about their own lives. Second, they are influenced by the timing of life-course events in relation to other events in an individual's life. Third, they are influenced by linked lives, because social changes are expressed in an individual's life through the experiences of related others. Finally, they are influenced by historical changes. Life-span and life-course models are complementary. Biological changes across the life span and social demands across the life course define typical life events and social roles in people's lives. Indeed, some psychological researchers have found it useful to adopt a sociocultural perspective and to conceive of the life course as a sequence of culturally-defined, age-graded roles that the individual enacts over time (Caspi, 1987; Helson, Mitchell, and Moane, 1984).

Helson introduced the concept of a "social clock project" as a framework for studying life-span development. The concept of a social clock focuses attention on the age-related life schedules of individuals in particular cultures and cohorts, and organizes the study of lives in terms of patterned movements into, along, and out of multiple role-paths such as education, work, marriage, and parenthood. In this fashion, the life course can be charted as a sequence of social roles that are enacted over time, and adaptational processes can be explored by investigating the ways different persons select and perform different social-cultural roles. In her 30-year longitudinal study of female college seniors, who were first studied in 1958-60, Helson examined the personality antecedents and consequences of adherence to a Feminine Social Clock (FSC) and a Masculine Occupational Clock (MOC). For example, women who adhered to the FSC were earlier in life characterized by a desire to do well and by a need for structure; women in this birth cohort who adhered to a MOC were earlier in life more rebellious and less sensitive to social norms. Helson *et al.* (1984, p. 1079) were thus able to identify "culturally salient need-press configurations through time" and to show predictable and meaningful relations between personality and behavior in different social settings at different ages.

Several chapters in this book either explicitly or implicitly adopt a sociocultural approach in their efforts to study successful development. The chapters by Laursen and Williams and by Silbereisen, Reitzle, and Juang tackle the adolescent age period and examine how youth create sense out of their place in the larger world. Laursen and Williams (this volume) explore the role of ethnic identity, a personally and politically-charged topic that is also a profound source of strength. The authors conceive of ethnic identity as a personality variable that shapes the nature and course of successful adolescent adjustment, and describe how ethnic identity offers an important mechanism through which minority adolescents cope with the tension between the inner self and the psychological environment of the majority culture. Silbereisen and his colleagues have capitalized on a "natural experiment" – the unification of Germany during the 1990s – to examine how historical changes shape the nature of adolescent transitions.

The chapters by Elder and Crosnoe and by Ryff, Singer, and Seltzer tackle a different point in the life course (midlife and old age) in order to examine the pathways to and the mechanisms in successful adjustment. Elder and Crosnoe draw on data from the Terman Study, begun in 1922, to explore how young-adult personality profiles shape the subsequent life course of men, in terms of their family life, civic involvement, career, and health trajectories. What is most remarkable is the emergence of such wide variations in life-outcomes, and in the successful negotiation of adult roles, despite the advantages enjoyed by all study participants by virtue of their intellectual prowess. Ryff and her colleagues provide an overview of their exciting research program where they track how different life challenges, both normative and non-normative, influence psychological well being. Included here are experiences of mid-life parenting, caregiving, and community relocation in old age. The authors conclude with a summary of their recent studies that link cumulative profiles of adversity and advantage to cumulative stress physiology. This work successfully links qualitative and quantitative methods as well as research on the mind and body.

One criticism of research on successful development, as studied by life-course researchers, is that it may be too value-laden and too culture-bound. What, for example, is the difference between conforming to social expectations vs. successfully performing socially-valued roles? There is also a serious epistemological issue with which life-course researchers must deal: how is it possible to move from historically specific findings to a more general understanding of life-course processes? At least one historian (Zuckerman, 1993) has argued that the coupling of developmental psychology and history represents a "dangerous liaison" because it is unclear whether psychologists are willing to abandon their quest for lawlike predictions.

Bouchard (1995) correctly argued that a purely sociocultural perspective on the life course "ignores the fact that life-histories themselves are complex evolved adaptations," and suggests that an evolutionary perspective may complement the sociocultural perspective by exploring how personality variation is related to those adaptively-important problems with which human beings have had to repeatedly contend. Evolutionary psychology thus focuses attention on the coherence of behavioral strategies that people use in, for example, mate selection, mate retention, reproduction, parental care, kin investment, status attainment, and coalition building (Buss, 1999). It focuses research on the genetically-influenced strategies and tactics that individuals use for survival and reproduction. An evolutionary perspective on successful life-course development could thus offer a fusion of concerns in evolutionary theory, behavior genetics, and demography (Stearns, 1992). For example, using the evolutionary perspective, Draper and Belsky (1990) and Gangestad and Simpson (1990) have offered intriguing hypotheses about personality characteristics and reproductive strategies that facilitate adaptations in different environments at different ages. Although these and other specific models have not yet been tested in the context of longitudinal studies of personality development – and are not represented in this volume – they show the promise of evolutionary psychology for organizing longitudinal-developmental data on patterns of successful development.

Ormel (this volume) tackles this problem from a somewhat different perspective and introduces social production function (SPF) theory as a heuristic for studying successful development. The theory attempts to integrate the various strengths of psychological theories and economic consumer/household production theories. It identifies two ultimate goals that all humans seek to optimize (physical well-being and social well-being) and five instrumental goals by which they are achieved (stimulation, comfort, status, behavioral confirmation, affection). The core notion of SPF theory is that people choose and substitute instrumental goals so as to optimize the production of their well-being, subject to constraints in available means of production.

How do personality differences shape successful development?

Whether one adopts a life-span or a life-course perspective, the question remains: what role do individual differences in personality play in mastering different social-developmental tasks across the course of life? The starting point for such work should be a system for describing individual differences in personality dispositions and temperamental traits. This is not to suggest that these psychological constructs are the only way to study the contribution of personality differences to successful development. Indeed, motivational concepts in personality are better represented in much of the research on adult development. We do think, however, that an exciting bridge to understanding the making of success will derive from advances in the measurement of temperament and personality traits and types.

Over the past 15 years, the intensity and productivity of psychological research on the dimensionality of adult personality has been phenomenal (Lubinski, 2000), and has influenced research in diverse fields such as organizational behavior, psychiatry, and genetics. An emerging consensus points to the existence of five important factors: Extraversion (active, assertive, enthusiastic, outgoing), Agreeableness (generous, kind, sympathetic, trusting), Conscientiousness (organized, planful, reliable, responsible), Neuroticism (anxious, self-pitying, tense, worrying), and Openness to Experience (artistic, curious, imaginative, having wide interests). Each superfactor covers a broad domain of individual differences and includes a number of more specific personality dimensions or facets (John and Srivstava, 1999). Some developmental researchers have noted that this Five-Factor Model of personality does not provide a theory of personality (Block, 1995), which is correct to the extent that most personality taxonomies are focused on describing regularities in behavior rather than examining dynamic and developmental processes. Other critics have noted that researchers interested in the Five-Factor Model have not paid attention to issues of personality development (Pervin, 1994). Indeed, whereas the study of personality structure in adulthood has influenced research on adult development and aging, the study of personality structure in childhood has been all but neglected (McCrae and Costa, 1990). But these are criticisms of what has been done, not of what can be accomplished.

An especially important area of integration involves efforts to connect existing models of infant and child temperament with studies of adult personality structure (Clark and Watson, 1999). What are normally understood as personality traits may be aspects of temperament differentiated in the course of life experience. But, surprisingly, there has been virtually no contact between child psychologists who study temperament and personality psychologists who are concerned with personality differences (Diener, 2000; Shiner, 1998). Halverson and colleagues (1994) have made a strong case that research on life-span personality development will remain unintegrated unless child psychologists begin to study the structure of personality. Research linking temperament to the development of personality will be facilitated by two parallel achievements: the development of a consensual system for describing the structure of personality differences in adulthood, as noted earlier, and the development of such a system for temperamental traits.

In the domain of temperament, conceptual reviews and factor-analytic studies have identified several "consensus" dimensions of infant and childhood temperament that might show influences on later developmental outcomes (Martin, Wisenbaker, and Huttunen, 1994; Rothbart and Bates, 1998). In the present volume, and in relation to the study of successful development, the chapters by Rothbart and Putnam and by Eisenberg, Fabes, Guthrie, and Reiser help to clarify several key definitional issues. For example, some researchers cling to the notion that temperament can only be assessed in the young infant and that temperament cannot be shaped by experience. However, as the two chapters in this book make clear, the key definitional component of temperament is not that it is immune from experience nor that it can be measured only in the first few months of life; rather, the key is that behaviors observed and measured should reliably index individual differences in children's characteristic style of approach and response to the environment.

Rothbart and Putnam (this volume) define temperament as "constitutionally based individual differences in reactivity and self-regulation, influenced over time by heredity and experience." Reactivity refers to the excitability, responsivity, or arousability of the behavioral and physiological systems of the individual, and self-regulation refers to the behavioral processes that modulate this reactivity. Importantly, Rothbart and Putnam note that such temperament differences develop and they are not immune to experience. Recent research shows that infants' temperament is shaped by experience even before birth (e.g., fetal nutrition, fetal substance exposure, daylight during pregnancy). Moreover, behavioral genetic studies have established that individual differences in temperament, measured even during the first year of life, are only partially heritable and are influenced significantly by unique environmental events (Plomin and Caspi, 1999), suggesting that younger age of measurement does not guarantee that temperament is purely "constitutional." The chapter by Rothbart and Putnam, along with related important research (e.g., Kochanska, 1997; Bates, Pettit, Dodge, and Ridge, 1998), points to the important ways in which socialization experiences – with parents and with peers – can shape emergent social competencies and psychological adjustment.

Eisenberg and her colleagues (this volume) provide an overview of their ongoing efforts to differentiate theoretically and empirically among the various aspects of both emotionality and emotional regulation, which are core concepts in practically every model of temperament and personality. The authors propose that individual differences in children's emotionality and regulation predict children's emerging social skills and the quality of their peer relationships. Specifically, they show that children high in emotional intensity and low in attentional and behavioral regulation experience numerous problems in their interactions with peers and in peer relationships, whereas children high in regulation typically function extremely well in their social worlds.

It is possible that a purely dimensional approach may yield confusing developmental portraits because orthogonal dimensions of temperament and personality conceal distinct types of children and adults who are characterized by unique configurations. Person-centered research may offer a promising approach for the study of paths to successful development, as demonstrated by Block (1971) and Pulkkinen (1996). The person-centered approach identifies types of individuals based on their particular configuration of attributes, and thus provides a bridge between purely nomothetic research (which emphasizes the attributes on which all individuals differ) and idiographic research (which emphasizes the unique patterning of attributes within an individual). It aims at a more holistic view of personality which "emphasizes the close dependency of individual functioning and individual development on the social, cultural, and physical characteristics of the environment" (Magnusson and Stattin, 1998, p. 686).

In this volume, the person-centered approach is utilized in the research conducted by Elder and Crosnoe, by Pulkkinen, Nurmi, and Kokko, and by Ryff, Singer, and Seltzer, but it is Van Aken and his colleagues who take on most directly the challenge of providing a person-centered structural model that could act as a complement to the variable-centered models of temperament and personality that currently dominate research on personality development across the life-span. Van Aken and his colleagues report findings from several of their own studies that point to the existence of a replicable typology of personality types in childhood and adolescence. The three types that are repeatedly identified are labelled Resilient, Overcontrolled, and Undercontrolled. At various ages in childhood and adolescence, the types differ in the quality of their psychological functioning and social relationships. Van Aken and his colleagues point to various ways in which transactions between personality characteristics and social relationships lead to different developmental outcomes. Overall, Resilients have the most favourable relationships, both in terms of perceived support and in terms of peer acceptance. Overcontrolled and Undercontrolled report similarly low social support, and are less accepted and more often rejected by their peers. They differ, however, in their psychological functioning, with Overcontrollers tending toward internalizing problems and Undercontrollers toward externalizing problems. As the authors note, in addition to their own work, over the past decade other independent investigators have identified similar personality types in different parts of the Western world using different data sources and different statistical procedures. The convergence across studies is not perfect, and more typological research needs to be done before anything close to a comprehensive, generalizable personality typology can be said to exist. Nevertheless, at this point, these three types are good candidates to become an integral part of any generalizable personality typology and they can be used effectively to guide future developmental studies of personality development (Mervielde and Asendorpf, in press). But this is just a starting point, and the chapter by Bergman offers a sober appraisal of the methodological challenges that lie ahead, on the road to research about paths to successful development.

It should be emphasized that any personality taxonomy, whether of traits or types, is an evolving classification system whose purpose is to integrate and guide research. Rather than foreclose or forestall new approaches to the study of personality structure and development, any such system must remain flexible and be willing to accommodate new empirical information. Most important, it should be noted that our concern is less about the number of factors or types, but with whether the nomological net surrounding personological constructs can be harnessed in the service of better understanding of how people become able to master their environment and the social-developmental tasks they encounter, as lovers, workers, parents, and civic-minded citizens.

Ultimately, whether one chooses to employ variable-centered models or person-centered models, it is important to note that temperament traits and personality predispositions can influence successful and maladaptive life outcomes in four different ways: as risk factors, vulnerability factors, protective factors, and as resources. *Risk* factors are predictors of problems in adaptation. Risk generally refers to elevated probabilities of undesired outcomes among members of a group who have one or more of these characteristics in common. *Vulnerability* refers to an individual's susceptibility to negative developmental outcomes that can occur under high-risk conditions. While a risk factor has a general negative effect (main effect) on outcomes, a vulnerability factor has little effect at low risk but a deterimental effect at high risk (Tiet *et al.*, 1998). The term *protective* factor refers to individual (or environmental) characteristics that correlate with or predict good outcomes in children at risk. A protective factor has a buffering effect at high risk but no effect at low risk. Protective factors differ from *resource* factors in that a resource factor has beneficial effects whether at low or high risk.

Beginning in early life, temperament traits and personality predispositions shape developmental pathways through three basic transactional processes. Reactive transactions occur when different individuals exposed to the same environment experience it, interpret it, and react to it differently. Evocative transactions occur when an individual's personality evokes distinctive responses from others. Proactive transactions occur when individuals select or create (consciously or not) environments of their own. It should be clear, then, that temperament and personality traits are not static, non-developmental conceptions of personality. Rather, these constructs refer to individual differences in the tendency to behave, think, and feel in certain consistent ways. They are organizational constructs that influence (through behavioral, cognitive, and affective means) how individuals organize themselves to meet new environmental demands in new developmental settings. These same processes also enable an individual's personality to influence the life course itself. In particular, person-environment transactions can produce two kinds of consequences in the life course: cumulative consequences and contemporary consequences. Cumulative consequences describe the process wherein personality characteristics "select" individuals into environments that further strengthen predispositions. Interactional consequences describe the process wherein personality characteristics are strengthened by the reciprocal responses that they elicit from others.

An important challenge for research on personality and successful development is to trace personality variables through a succession of social-developmental changes in order to understand how they shape adaptation. Essentially what is needed is a good road map on which the effects of early characteristics can be charted and studied (van Lieshout, 2000). A good illustration of this type of thinking is contained in the chapter by Grossman, Grossman, Winter, and Zimmerman (this volume). Although their concern is with the adaptive significance of early attachment relationships, their approach can inform students of personality development irrespective of the individual-difference variables under consideration. The authors provide an overview of attachment theory and then summarize findings from their long-term study of attachment relationships from birth to young adulthood. The early measures focused on maternal sensitivity to the child in the first few years of life and on the quality of early attachment relationships. Subsequent assessments included both behavioral observations and language representations of attachment relationships at age six years (e.g., responses to projective separations), 16 years (e.g., attachment representations), and 22 years (e.g., current attachment relationship strategies). The findings from this longitudinal study – with its innovative measurement strategies – provide intriguing hints about how early experiences in one age-normative developmental task shape successful outcomes in subsequent age-normative developmental tasks (see also Waters, Hamilton, and Weinfeld, 2000).

Sroufe and his colleagues (1979; Sroufe, Carlson, and Shulman, 1993) have used a similar strategy to study adaptational processes. By outlining the tasks and milestones that can be expected in the course of development, from infancy through adolescence, they have designed assessment procedures that capture the organization of behavior in different developmental periods. Longitudinal data show that continuity across development can be discerned in children's adaptational profiles with respect to the challenges they face at each developmental phase. This general approach enables Sroufe and his colleagues to confer conceptual coherency on their findings that individuals who are securely attached as infants later explore their environments as toddlers (Matas, Arend, and Sroufe, 1978), are less dependent on their teachers in the preschool years (Sroufe, Fox, and Pancake, 1983), attain higher sociometric status and display greater competence in peer relations in late childhood (Urban et al., 1991), and appear to establish appropriate cross-sex relationships in adolescence (Sroufe et al., 1993). Invariant behavior patterns do not emerge in these findings. Instead, the findings point to people's predictable and meaningful ways of relating to and shaping the environment in different social settings at different ages.

An equally important challenge is to identify the right types of research designs that can enable behavioral scientists to identify how personality variables shape adaptation and how psychosocial influences shape the course of personality development (Rutter, Pickles, Murray, and Eaves, in press). The chapters by Rose and by Caspi in this volume show that genetic and epidemiological strategies, which are often thought to be used only by those interested in pathology and disease, are relevant to the study of development more generally, and are especially useful in uncovering different sources of influence at key points in the life course, be it in friendship formation, in educational attainment, or in adjustment to the world of work. We are reminded that methods are tools in the service of answering questions and, in the quest to understand how personality shapes the life course, methodological inclusiveness is a virtue and a necessity.

ACKNOWLEDGMENTS

The production of this book was supported by a conference on "Personality in the Life Course" held in Finland in August 1999 and financed by the Academy of Finland (Finnish Centre of Excellence Programme No. 40166).

REFERENCES

Baltes, P. B. (1987). Theoretical propositions of life-span developmental psychology: on the dynamics between growth and decline. *Developmental Psychology,* 23, 611–26.

Baltes, P. B., Lindenberger, U., and Staudinger, U. M. (1998). Life-span theory in developmental psychology. In W. Damon (Editor-in-Chief) and R. M. Lerner (Volume Editor), *Handbook of child psychology,* New York: Wiley. Volume 1, 1029–43.

Baltes, P. B, Staudinger, U. M., and Lindenberger, U. (1999). Lifespan psychology: theory and application to intellectual functioning. *Annual Review of Psychology,* 50, 471–507.

Bates, J. E., Pettit, G. S., Dodge, K. A., and Ridge, B. (1998). The interaction of temperamental resistance to control and restrictive parenting in the development of externalizing behavior. *Developmental Psychology,* 34, 982–95.

Block, J. (1971). *Lives through time.* Berkeley, CA: Bancroft Books.

Block, J. (1995). A contrarian view of the five-factor approach to personality description. *Psychological Bulletin,* 117, 187–215.

Bouchard, T. J. Jr. (1995). Longitudinal studies of personality and intelligence: a behavior genetic and evolutionary psychology perspective. In D. Saklofske and M. Zaidner (eds.), *International handbook of personality and intelligence.* New York: Plenum Press.

Brandtstädter, J. (1998). Action perspectives on human development. In W. Damon (Editor-in-Chief) and R. M. Lerner (Volume Editor), *Handbook of Child Psychology* (5th edn.): *Theoretical models of human development*, New York: Wiley. Volume 1, 807–63.

Buss, D. M. (1999). Human nature and individual differences: the evolution of human personality. In L. A. Pervin and O. P. John (eds.), *Handbook of personality theory and research*. New York: Guilford, 31–56.

Caspi, A. (1987). Personality in the life course. *Journal of Personality and Social Psychology*, 53, 1203–13.

Clark, L. A., and Watson, D. (1999). Temperament: a new paradigm for trait psychology. In Pervin and John, 399–423.

Diener, E. (2000). Introduction to the special section on personality development. *Journal of Personality and Social Psychology*, 78, 120–21.

Draper, P., and Belsky, J. (1990). Personality development in evolutionary perspective. *Journal of Personality*, 58, 141–61.

Elder, G. H., Jr. (1998). Life-course and human development. In W. Damon (Editor-in-Chief) and R. M. Lerner (Vol. Ed.), *Handbook of child psychology*, vol. 1: *Theoretical models of human development*. New York: Wiley, 939–91.

Erikson, E. H. (1950). *Childhood and society*. New York: Norton.

Gangestad, S. W., and Simpson, J. A. (1990). Toward an evolutionary history of female sociosexual variation. *Journal of Personality*, 58, 69–96.

Halverson, C. F., Jr., Kohnstamm, G. A., and Martin, R. P. (eds). (1994). *The developing structure of temperament and personality from infancy to adulthood*. Hillsdale, NJ: Lawrence Erlbaum.

Helson, R., Mitchell, V. and Moane, G. (1984). Personality and patterns of adherence and nonadherence to the social clock. *Journal of Personality and Social Psychology*, 46, 1079–96.

John, O. P., and Srivstava, S. (1999). The Big Five trait taxonomy: history, measurement, and theoretical perspectives. In L. A. Pervin and O. P. John (eds.). *Handbook of personality theory and research*. New York: Guilford, 102–38.

Kagitcibasi, C. (1996). *Family and human development across cultures: a view from the other side*. Hillsdale, NJ: Lawrence Erlbaum.

Kochanska, G. (1997). Multiple pathways to conscience for children with different temperaments: from toddlerhood to age 5. *Developmental Psychology*, 33, 228–40.

Labouviev-Vief, G., Hakim-Larson. J., DeVoe, M., and Schoeberlain, S. (1989). Emotions and self-regulation: a life-span view. *Human development*, 32, 279–99.

Levinson, D. J. (1978). *The seasons of a man's life*. New York: Knopf.

(1986). A conception of adult development. *American Psychologist*, 41, 3–13.

Loevinger, J. (1997). Stages of personality development. In R. Hogan, J. Johnson, and S. Briggs (eds.), *Handbook of personality psychology*. San Diego, CA: Academic Press, 199–208.

Lubinski, D. (2000). Scientific and social significance of assessing individual differences: sinking shafts at a few critical points. *Annual Review of Psychology*, 51, 405–44.

Magnusson, D., and Stattin, H. (1998). Person-context interaction theories. In W. Damon (Editor-in-Chief) and R. M. Lerner (Vol. Ed.), *Handbook of child psychology*, vol. 1: *Theoretical models of human development*, New York: Wiley, 685–759.

Martin, R. P., Wisenbaker, J., and Huttunen, M. (1994). Review of factor analytic studies of temperament measures based on the Thomas-Chess structural model: implications for the Big Five. In Halverson, Kohnstamm, and Martin, 157–72.

Maslow, A. (1954). *Motivation and personality*. New York: Harper.

Matas, L. Arend, R., and Sroufe, L. A. (1978). Continuity of adaptation in the second year: the relationship between quality of attachment and later competence. *Child Development*, 49, 547–56.

McCrae, R. R., and Costa, P. T., Jr. (1990). *Personality in adulthood*. New York: Guilford.

Mervielde, I., and Asendorpf, J. (In press). Variable-centered and person-centered approaches to childhood personality. In S. E. Hampson (ed.), *Advances in personality psychology*. London: Routledge, Vol. 1.

Pervin, L. A. (1994). A critical analysis of current trait theory. *Psychological Inquiry*, 5, 103–13.

Plomin, R., and Caspi, A. (1999). Behavioral genetics and personality. In L. A. Pervin and O. P. John (eds.). *Handbook of personality theory and research*. New York: Guilford, 251–76.

Pulkkinen, L. (1996). Female and male personality styles: a typological and developmental analysis. *Journal of Personality and Social Psychology*, 70, 1288–306.

Rothbart, M. K., and Bates, J. E. (1998). Temperament. In W. Damon (Series Editor) and N. Eisenberg (Volume Editor), *Handbook of child psychology: social, emotional, and personality development*. New York: Wiley, Vol. 3, 105–76.

Rutter, M., Pickles, A., Murray, R., and Eaves, L. M. (In review). Testing hypotheses on specific environmental risk mechanisms for psychopathology. Unpublished manuscript, Institute of Psychiatry, London.

Sanford, R. N. (1962). *The American college*. New York: Wiley.

Shiner, R. L. (1998). How shall we speak of children's personalities in middle childhood? A preliminary taxonomy. *Psychological Bulletin*, 124, 308–32.

Sroufe, L. A. (1979). The coherence of individual development. *American Psychologist*, 34, 834–41.

Sroufe, L. A., Carlson, E., and Shulman, S. (1993). Individuals in relationships: development from infancy through adolescence. In D. C. Funder, R. D. Parke, C. Tomlinson-Keasey, and K. Widaman (eds.), *Studying lives through time*. Washington, DC: American psychological Association, 315–42.

Sroufe, L. A., Fox, N., and Pancake, V. (1983). Attachment and dependency in developmental perspective. *Child Development*, 54, 1615–27.

Stearns, S. C. (1992). *The evolution of life histories*. New York: Oxford University Press.

Tiet, Q. Q., Bird, H. R., Davies, M., Hoven, C., Cohen, P., Jensen, P. S., and Goodman, S. (1998). Adverse life events and resilience. *Journal of American Academy of Child and Adolescent Psychiatry*, 37, 1191–200.

Urban, J., Carlson, E., Egeland, B., and Sroufe, L. A. (1991). Patterns of individual adaptation across childhood. *Development and Psychopathology*, 3, 445–60.

Van Lieshout, C. (2000). Lifespan personality development: self-organizing goal-oriented agents and developmental outcome. *International Journal of Behavioral Development*, 24, 276–88.

Waters, E., Hamilton, C. E., and Weinfeld, N. S. (2000). The stability of attachment security from infancy to adolescence and early adulthood: general introduction. *Child Development*, 71, 678–83.

Zuckerman, M. (1993). History and developmental psychology, a dangerous liaison: a historian's perspective. In G. H. Elder, J. Modell, and R. D. Parke (eds.), *Children in time and place: Developmental and historical insights.* New York: Cambridge University Press, 230–40.

Part I

Temperament and emotion regulation

1   Temperament and socialization

Mary K. Rothbart and Samuel P. Putnam

Traditional approaches to successful development have focused almost entirely on socialization practices expected to lead to optimal outcomes. An implicit assumption of much research on achievement (e.g., McClelland, Atkinson, Clark, and Lowell, 1953), altruism (e.g., Hoffman, 1975), and morality (e.g., Bandura, 1977), for example, has been that parental and societal influences affect all children in a similar manner. More recent work, however, indicates that different children may respond to similar socialization efforts in predictably divergent ways, with the individual characteristics of the child influencing pathways to both successful and maladaptive outcomes. Characteristics of the child may also determine whether intervention is needed, as well as the strategies chosen by adults to influence change. Temperament research allows us to study interactions between individual and environmental influences, because it describes processes evident early in life from which social adaptations to environmental conditions develop. Whereas the child's personality will include skills, habits, and cognitive structures shaped through interaction with the environment, temperament provides the biological basis upon which these structures are built.

In this chapter, a brief introduction to temperament is presented and data from our laboratory on the developmental structure of temperament are discussed. We then review links between dimensions of temperamental variability and mechanisms of socialization. We propose that three broad temperamental systems: surgency, negative affectivity (including facets of fear and anger/frustration), and effortful control, can be seen early in life and are influential in the development of personality. In this discussion, interactions between temperament and environment that may lead to successful social development are highlighted.

Definitions of temperament

We have defined temperament as constitutionally based individual differences in reactivity and self-regulation, influenced over time by heredity and experience (Rothbart and Bates, 1998; Rothbart and Derryberry, 1981). Temperament develops; much behavior during the early months can be seen as reactive either to immediate stimulus events or to endogenous internal changes. Later, however, more directly self-regulatory systems, including inhibitory aspects of fear and the attentional flexibility of effortful control, will develop to modulate this reactivity (Rothbart and Derryberry, 1981). We return later to these developing self-regulatory processes.

Our definition of temperament is more inclusive than several prior interpretations of the construct, including Gordon Allport's (1961) emotionality-based definition as "the characteristic phenomena of an individual's emotional nature, including his susceptibility to emotional stimulation, his customary strength and speed of response, the quality of his prevailing mood, these phenomena being regarded as dependent upon constitutional make-up" (p. 34). In our view, and in agreement with Thomas and Chess (1977), individual differences in activity and attention also have an important place within the temperament domain. Our view nevertheless goes beyond Thomas and Chess' (1977) definition of temperament as behavioral style, in that we emphasize the content of children's emotional, attentional, and activity-related characteristics as well.

Questionnaire findings

Temperament in infancy

Until recently, the domain of temperament has chiefly been seen as including the nine dimensions of individuality identified by Thomas, Chess and their colleagues in the New York Longitudinal Study (NYLS) over 30 years ago. These include Activity Level, Mood, Approach/ Withdrawal, Adaptability, Intensity, Threshold, Distractibility, Attention Span/Persistence, and Rhythmicity. This set of characteristics was identified through a content analysis of parent interviews describing the behavior of their infants aged two to six months (Thomas, Chess, Birch, Herzig, and Korn, 1963).

In our initial research (Rothbart, 1981), we set out to develop a parent-report questionnaire to assess Thomas and Chess' dimensions, along with characteristics Diamond (1957) had identified as showing temperamental variability in other animal species. We also assessed characteristics identified as heritable in human behavioral genetics research, and positive affect, which had been the focus of our early research (Rothbart, 1973). Over 450 parents were asked to act as informants about their infants' reactions (Rothbart, 1981). In developing the Infant Behavior Questionnaire (IBQ), we tried to avoid asking parents to make global judgments about events that had happened some time ago. Instead, we asked parents how frequently certain behaviors had occurred in specified contexts across the past week. For example, "When put in the bath water, how often did the baby kick and splash? When meeting a stranger, how often did the baby cry?" Parents responded using seven-point scales ranging from never, through about half the time, to always.

One of the most interesting findings from our early questionnaire research was that items comprising some of Thomas and Chess' NYLS dimensions did not co-vary as had been expected (Rothbart, 1981). For example, in the parents' reports, a child who was intense in smiling and laughter was not necessarily intense in fear or frustration, and a child rhythmic in bowel habits was not necessarily rhythmic in sleeping. The covariation of item scores across different response modalities proved to be so low that it was not possible to construct psychometrically sound scales for Intensity, Threshold, or Rhythmicity. Moreover, on the Adaptability scale, only items referring to soothability clustered together. We were thus left with six unipolar scales. The first three assessed reactivity of separable affective systems (fear, frustration, and positive affect). The other three included a dynamic aspect of negative affect (soothability), a duration of orienting scale that combined items from Thomas and Chess' Distractibility and Attention Span scales, and a scale containing items indicative of overall activity level. The original IBQ (Rothbart, 1981) thus aggregated item scores across a range of situations and eliciting conditions to yield scale scores with high internal reliability for Activity Level, Smiling and Laughter, Fear, Distress to Limitations (frustration), Soothability, and Duration of Orienting (attentional persistence).

In our review of empirical studies of the structure of infant temperament (Rothbart and Mauro, 1990), these scales showed considerable similarity to factors that had emerged from other researchers' item-level analyses of NYLS-based scales (e.g., Sanson, Prior, Garino, Oberklaid, and Sewell, 1987; Bohlin, Hagekull, and Lindhagen, 1981). These similar dimensions are particularly intriguing because characteristics of fear, frustration/anger, positive reactivity/incentive motivation, and the orienting aspects of attention have been evolutionarily conserved and are present in non-human species (Panksepp, 1998; Rothbart, Derryberry, and Posner, 1994).

We have now also revisited the IBQ (the IBQ-R; Gartstein and Rothbart, in preparation), writing additional scales to assess infant forms of reactivity and self-regulation that we have explored at older ages. In addition to the six scales listed above, the following eight scales were found to possess satisfactory reliability and validity: Approach (rapid approach, excitement, and positive anticipation of pleasurable activities), Cuddliness (enjoyment and molding of the body to being held by a caregiver), Falling Reactivity (rate of recovery from peak distress, excitement, or general arousal), High Intensity Pleasure (enjoyment of situations involving high intensity stimuli), Low Intensity Pleasure (enjoyment of situations involving low intensity stimuli), Perceptual Sensitivity (detection of slight or low intensity stimuli from the external environment), Sadness (negative affect and diminished energy related to personal suffering, physical state, disappointment, and object loss), and Vocal Reactivity (vocalization during daily activities).

Particularly intriguing are the results of factor analysis investigating higher-order relationships among these fourteen scales. We have now carried out factor analyses for the full sample of 360 three- to twelve-month-old infants and also separately for three- to eight-month-olds and nine- to twelve-month-olds. In these analyses, as well as other factor analyses reported in this chapter, we have used principal axis factoring with oblique rotation of the extracted factors. For the full sample, scales with primary loadings on the first factor included Activity Level, Smiling and Laughter, High-Intensity Pleasure, Perceptual Sensitivity, Approach, and Vocal Reactivity. This factor, which we have labeled Surgency, appears similar in content to adult personality dimensions of Extraversion and Positive Emotionality. It also demonstrates high loadings for an orienting scale (Perceptual Sensitivity) that in adult research has been linked to the personality trait of Openness (Rothbart, Ahadi, and Evans, 2000). The second factor was defined by positive loadings for Distress to Limitations, Fear, Sadness, and a negative loading for Falling Reactivity. The relations among different forms of negative affect shown in this factor are similar to the broad adult dimensions of Negative Emotionality and Neuroticism. Finally, the third factor was defined by loadings for Duration of Orienting, Low-Intensity Pleasure, Soothability, and Cuddliness, with a substantial secondary loading for Smiling and Laughter. These scales appear to index both orienting tendencies and capacities to enjoy and to be comforted by low-intensity stimulation. We have tentatively named this factor Affiliation/Orienting.

Temperament in toddlerhood

In recent years, our additions to Goldsmith's Toddler Behavior Assessment Questionnaire (TBAQ; Goldsmith, 1996) have led to development of a highly differentiated interim instrument for the measurement of temperament in toddlers, which we refer to as the Early Childhood Behavior

Questionnaire, or ECBQ. This measure, unlike the IBQ-R, contains separate scales for shyness and non-social fear. Additional scales found in the toddler measure, but not the IBQ-R, are based on children's growing ability to effortfully control their attention and behavior. These scales include Inhibitory Control (capacity to plan and to suppress inappropriate action), Attention Shifting (capacity to shift from one activity to another), Attention Focusing (capacity to maintain attention on tasks) and Impulsivity (speed of response initiation). Additional scales included on the ECBQ include Positive Anticipation (excitement in anticipation of expected pleasurable activities) and Discomfort (negative affect related to sensory qualities of stimulation).

To date, we have collected toddler data for 166 of the 360 children whose parents had filled out the IBQ-R. The ages of these children at the time of completion of the ECBQ ranged from 18- to 30-months. Factor analysis of the instrument yielded three factors showing some similarity to those found among infants. A Surgency factor with primary loadings for Activity Level, High-Intensity Pleasure, Impulsivity, and Positive Anticipation and secondary loadings for Perceptual Sensitivity and (negatively) Shyness emerged. A Negative Affectivity factor was characterized by high loadings for Fear, Discomfort, Sadness, Shyness, Anger/Frustration, and (negatively) Soothability. As in infants, Cuddliness and Low-Intensity Pleasure have primary loadings on a third factor. In toddlers, however, the third factor is further defined by the self-regulatory scales of Attention Focusing, Attention Shifting, Inhibitory Control, and Perceptual Sensitivity, with secondary contributions from Soothability, and (negatively) Anger/Frustration. We have labeled this factor Effortful Control. In both infants and toddlers, high scores on the third factor, Affiliation/Orienting for infants and Effortful Control for toddlers, are associated with low levels of Negative Affectivity (see Table 1.1). Low-intensity and calming social stimulation may decrease infants' negative emotionality, and effortful control may also serve that function in toddlers.

In our sample of 166 children, we also examined stability and predictability from infancy through toddlerhood. As can be seen in Table 1.1, Surgency and Negative Affectivity were both significantly positively correlated across the two ages. In addition, the infant Affiliation/Orienting and toddler Effortful Control factors were positively related. Interestingly, the Effortful Control factor in toddlers was also predicted by infant Surgency, although infant Affiliation/Orienting was not related to toddler Surgency. In addition, when infant Surgency and Affiliation/Orienting were entered as predictors of Effortful Control using multiple regression, both of the infant factors were significant. This finding suggests an important role

Table 1.1 *Concurrent and longitudinal correlations between broad infant (IBQ-R) and toddler (ECBQ) factors*

	Infant factors[a]			Toddler factors[b]		
	Surgency	Negative affectivity	Affiliation/ orienting	Surgency	Negative affectivity	Effortful control
Infant factors[a]						
Surgency	–	.11	.32*	.36*	.10	.45*
Negative affectivity		–	−.26*	.02	.50*	−.10
Affiliation/orienting			–	.02	−.09	.40*
Toddler factors[b]						
Surgency				–	.02	.03
Negative affectivity					–	−.22*
Effortful control						–

Note: IBQ-R Surgency = mean of activity level, smiling and laughter, high-intensity pleasure, approach, and vocal reactivity scales. IBQ-R negative affectivity = mean of distress to limitations, fear, sadness and reverse-scored falling reactivity scales. IBQ-R affiliation/orienting = mean of duration of orienting, low-intensity pleasure, soothability, and cuddliness scales. ECBQ surgency = mean of impulsivity, high-intensity pleasure, activity level, and positive anticipation scales. ECBQ negative affectivity = mean of fear, discomfort, sadness, frustration, shyness, and reverse-scored soothability scales. ECBQ effortful control = mean of attention shifting, low-intensity pleasure, inhibitory control, cuddliness, attention focusing, and perceptual sensitivity scales.
[a] $n = 360$.
[b] $n = 166$.
* $p < .05$.

for early Surgency in the development of self-regulatory abilities. One possibility is that children who are highly attuned to rewarding aspects of the environment may call on such cues in the service of controlling their attention and behavior. Although more research is required to address this possibility, this finding casts new light on the relationship between positive approach tendencies and self control.

Temperament in preschool and middle childhood

The Children's Behavior Questionnaire (CBQ) was designed to measure temperament characteristics of preschool and early school age children (Rothbart, Ahadi, Hershey, and Fisher, in press). Dimensions assessed by the CBQ derived from those identified in our adult research (Derryberry and Rothbart, 1988), and from dimensions of temperament already measurable in infancy (Rothbart, 1981), and toddlerhood (Goldsmith, 1996).

Because the ECBQ was strongly based on the CBQ, the two instruments share the majority of their scales. Cuddliness, included on the toddler measure but not the CBQ, reflects our recent interest in systems of affiliation. Smiling and Laughter, appearing on the CBQ, was omitted from the ECBQ, in favor of more situation-specific scales measuring positive affect.

Structurally, the 15 scales of the CBQ reliably cluster into three large factors similar to two of those found in infants, and three of those found in toddlers. The first, labeled Surgency/Extraversion, is defined primarily by loadings for the scales of Impulsivity, High Intensity Pleasure, Activity Level, and, loading negatively, Shyness, with substantial loadings for the Positive Anticipation and Smiling and Laughter scales. It is similar to the Surgency factors identified in infancy and childhood and to the broad adult factor of Extraversion. Although the Positive Anticipation scale loads on this factor as expected, it also consistently loads on a second factor, Negative Affect. A relation between positive anticipation and negative affect would be consistent with Panksepp's (1998) suggestion that unsuccessful reward-related activities may activate anger and frustration.

A second large factor, Negative Affectivity, is defined primarily by loadings for the scales of Sadness, Discomfort, Anger/Frustration, Fear, and, loading negatively, Falling Reactivity/Soothability. This pattern of loadings is consistent with the broad dimension of Negative Affectivity/ Neuroticism found in adult investigations of personality structure and also seen in the infant and toddler data. The third broad dimension, Effortful Control, is defined primarily by loadings for Inhibitory Control, Attentional Focusing, Low Intensity Pleasure, and Perceptual Sensitivity. These characteristics appear to share the child's voluntary regulation of attention and behavior, along with aspects of perceptual and reward sensitivity. We have suggested that Effortful Control may be developmentally related to the broad dimension of Conscientiousness/Constraint/Superego Strength/Psychoticism identified in other structural models of personality (Ahadi and Rothbart, 1994).

Results of a recent investigation to map these temperament dimensions onto Big Five personality factors in adults support the hypothesized connections put forward above (Rothbart, Ahadi et al., 2000). Adult subjects completed the Adult Temperament Questionnaire (Evans and Rothbart, 1999) as well as the minimarker measure of the Big Five (Saucier, 1994). The Adult Temperament Questionnaire yielded a four-factor structure including dimensions similar to those found in children as well as a fourth factor labeled Orienting Sensitivity. As expected, temperamental and Big Five Extraversion were positively correlated, temperamental Negative

Affectivity was related to Big Five Neuroticism, and Effortful Control was linked to Conscientiousness. In addition, Orienting Sensitivity was associated with the personality construct of Intellect/Openness.

In the factor structure of our scales, the broad groupings of Surgency and Negative Affectivity can be seen in infancy and beyond, whereas Effortful Control, appearing in toddlerhood and during the childhood period, may be a precursor to Conscientiousness in adults. Our research team is currently collecting temperament data in adolescents to further test the robustness of these dimensions (Ellis and Rothbart, in preparation). Preliminary findings indicate a similar factor pattern, with the addition of a fourth factor similar to the Orienting Sensitivity factor found in our adult temperament measure.

Developmental studies

Having introduced these temperament variables, we are now able to address the early development of temperament in more detail. Wherever possible in this review, we cite research investigating interactions between temperament and socialization in child development. The idea that the temperamental predispositions do not directly determine developmental outcomes, but occur in interaction with the environment is not a new one. Thomas and Chess (1977; Thomas, Chess, and Birch, 1968) emphasized the notion of "goodness of fit," arguing that adaptive and maladaptive patterns of behavior were determined by the match between an individual's temperament and the demands of specific contexts. Wachs (Wachs and Gandour, 1983; Wachs and Gruen, 1982) elaborated on this theme, using the term "organismic specificity" to describe the differential effects that similar environments may have on temperamentally dissimilar children.

Despite the theoretical importance of interactional effects, relatively few examples of interactions can be found in the empirical literature. There are at least two reasons for this scarcity. First, there have been few testable models of temperament/environment interactions. For instance, although Thomas and Chess provided case studies exemplifying mismatches between the child and environment, more general conceptions of what constituted a good or poor fit were not specified. A second reason is methodological. Studies relating caregiver and child behavior often measure the two constructs concurrently, resulting in ambiguity about causal direction, a problem compounded when the sole source of information for parenting practices and temperament is parent report. In addition, when researchers have used independent sources of information and uncovered separable effects of temperament and parenting for a given outcome, many have not taken the additional step of testing for multiplicative relations between the two, whereas others have included multiplicative effects without first statistically controlling for main effects (Rothbart and Bates, 1998; Sanson and Rothbart, 1995). In our review, we include recent studies we believe to be exemplary in their demonstration of interactions between temperament and the environment.

Positive affect and approach (surgency/extraversion)

We have noted above continuities from infancy to adulthood of a surgency dimension including activity level, impulsivity, and positive affect in response to highly stimulating situations. Appetitive motivational systems underlying positive affect and motor activity have also been proposed within a number of neurological theories (e.g., Depue and Collins, 1999; Gray, 1992; Panksepp, 1998). Individual differences in surgency appear to be based on sensitivity to cues of reward and manifested as orientation to and exploration of novelty, as well as expressions of positive affect. When rewards are blocked, high levels of surgency may also result in aggressive actions to overcome obstacles.

In observational studies, behavior indicative of surgency can be observed by the age of two to three months, in a cluster of reactions including vocal activity, motor movement, and positive affect (Kistiakovskaia, 1965). We have assessed surgency using laboratory observation and questionnaire measures in a longitudinal study of infants at the ages of three, six, ten, and thirteen months (Rothbart, Derryberry, and Hershey, 2000). Infants were videotaped during presentation of non-social (e.g., small squeezable toys, a mechanical dog, a rapidly opening parasol) and social stimuli (e.g., experimenter's speech, a peek-a-boo game). Smiling and laughter to these stimuli were coded for latency, intensity, and duration, and these ratings were aggregated into positive affect scores. Behavioral approach was assessed through infants' latency to grasp low intensity toys, and activity level was measured via 13-month-olds' movement among toys distributed across a grid-lined floor. Activity level was positively related to parent-reported Smiling and Laughter, negatively related to Fear, and associated with more rapid laboratory approach to the toys (Rothbart, Derryberry et al., 2000).

Individual differences in approach become increasingly salient as motor control develops over the first year. We have successfully separated approach and inhibition tendencies by measuring infants' latencies to grasp two sets of toys, one set familiar and low in intensity, the other novel and intense (Rothbart, 1988). Rate of approach to the low-intensity toys was expected to be governed chiefly by appetitive, but not inhibitory tendencies, and was found to be related to smiling and laughter. In addition, individual differences in approach to the low-intensity toys were stable from six to thirteen months. In contrast, response to the more intense toys was believed to involve input from both the behavioral approach and inhibition systems. Because the inhibition system undergoes rapid development over the second half of the first year, we predicted and found that latencies to approach the novel toys increased from six to ten months, were not stable from six to thirteen months, and were related to fear at six, ten, and thirteen months (Rothbart, 1988).

Individual differences in surgency can also be seen in infants' positively toned activity level. For instance, although activity level occurring in conjunction with negative affect during early infancy is related to later inhibition (Kagan and Snidman, 1991), the combination of high motor activity and positive affect is associated with bold behavior in later childhood (Calkins, Fox, and Marshall, 1996). Activity level as an aspect of surgency can be seen even in the earliest days of life, so long as the measure is separated from distress-related activity: Korner *et al.* (1985) found levels of non-distress motor activity in the neonate to be a predictor of high approach scores at ages four–eight years.

We have documented stability of approach tendencies from infant laboratory assessments through seven years in a small sample of children (Rothbart, Derryberry *et al.*, 2000). Children who exhibited rapid approach during infancy through their short latencies to grasp low-intensity toys were high in parent-rated Positive Anticipation and Impulsivity, and low in Sadness at seven years. Positive affect, measured both with the IBQ and in the laboratory, was predictive of seven-year Positive Anticipation and Impulsivity. Although our more highly reactive IBQ Activity Level measure was not related to the later measures, more intentional locomotion observed in the laboratory predicted high Positive Anticipation, Impulsivity, and low Sadness at seven years.

Stability in approach behavior has been found in other studies as well. Putnam (1999) found approach at 12 months, measured via latencies to reach for low-intensity objects, to predict surgency during a battery of laboratory tasks at two years. Pedlow, Sanson, Prior, and Oberklaid (1993) found parent-reported approach to be stable from infancy through eight years. Long-term stability of surgency has also been reported by Caspi and Silva (1995), who found that children rated by experimenters as high on approach at three years of age described themselves as impulsive, spontaneous, careless, and reckless at age eighteen.

The self-description of low levels of caution and planfulness among high-surgency individuals in Caspi and Silva's report suggests that approach tendencies may hold some risk. Our data are supportive of this idea: children showing short latencies to grasp low-intensity toys in the laboratory were described at age seven as showing greater Impulsivity, Anger/Frustration and Aggression, and lower Attentional Focusing and Inhibitory Control. In addition, activity level observed at 13 months predicted negative affect dimensions such as Anger/Frustration, Aggression, and low Soothability/Falling Reactivity. These findings suggest that, in addition to contributing to positive emotionality, strong approach tendencies may contribute to externalizing problems as well (Derryberry and Reed, 1994; Rothbart, Ahadi, and Hershey, 1994). Also supporting an association between surgency and a lack of self-control are multiple studies relating sensation seeking to externalizing difficulties in school-aged children and young adolescents (e.g., Arnett, 1995; Frick, O'Brien, Wotton, and McBurnett, 1994; Gabel, Stabler, Born, Shindledecker, and Bowden, 1994; Kafry, 1982; Russo et al., 1993).

More positive aspects of surgency can be seen in the relation between infant positive affect and scores on the Bayley scales of development (see review by Matheny, 1989). A meta-analysis of school-age children has found positive interest to compose approximately 10 percent of variance connected with achievement (Schiefele, Krapp, and Winteler, 1992). Finally, Putnam (1996) found high levels of self-reported sensation seeking, a form of surgency that has typically been studied in adults, to be associated with low levels of internalizing behaviors in a sample of five-year-old boys.

Because traditional research and theory on temperament has tended to consider approach/positive affect and withdrawal/negative affect as opposite poles of a single continuum and often focused on withdrawal, there have been very few examples in the literature referring to interactions between surgency and parenting. One study addressing an aspect of surgency, however, is Wachs' (1987) examination of the development of mastery motivation. Relations between social interaction and mastery behavior differed for toddlers who were rated by parents as being either high or low in activity level. For 12-month old infants who were low in activity, high levels of parent mediation (object naming) were associated with more advanced object mastery. In contrast, when children were highly active, similar caregiver behaviors were related to lower mastery of the environment. Similar results were reported by Gandour (1989), who found exploration competency in 15-month-olds to be promoted by maternal attention focusing among children who were low in activity level, whereas attention focusing was associated with lower exploration scores for highly active children.

Contemporary resources for new parents often mention activities such as pointing out and naming objects as a tool for aiding intellectual development. The results of Wachs (1987) and Gandour (1989), however, suggest that, whereas children low in surgency may not seek out or actively explore new stimuli and thus would benefit from parental direction, this may not be the case for children higher in temperamental approach. For such children, the well-intentioned focusing of attention by parents may actually distract the child and interfere with his/her active learning process.

Temperamental surgency thus appears to represent both liabilities and assets for the developing child. Pathways to beneficial and detrimental outcomes are not likely to be direct ones. Rather, they are influenced by the developmental environment and by interactions with other components of temperament. We now consider the second broad dimension of temperament: negative affectivity.

Negative affect: fear and frustration

Although the negative emotions often fall into the same broad factors in factor analyses of temperament and personality, fear and frustration contain unique, as well as common, origins. In our longitudinal research, infants' distress to situational elicitors of fear (novel, intense, and unpredictable stimuli) and frustration (placement of attractive toys out of reach or behind a Plexiglass barrier) were coded, and between six and thirteen months we found that fear and frustration in the laboratory were increasingly uncorrelated. Fox (1989) has also reported dissociations between fear and frustration: frustration to arm restraint at five months was related more to 14-month approach than to withdrawal from strangers and novel events (indicators of fear). Lemery, Goldsmith, Klinnert, and Mrazek (1999) have found that parent-report measures from three to eighteen months loaded on separate (but correlated) factors representing fear and anger-distress, and separate fear and frustration factors are commonly identified in infancy research (see review by Rothbart and Mauro, 1990).

Temperament and environment interactions have often been studied using temperamental dimensions based on general negative emotionality. A number of these studies do not distinguish between components of fear and anger, relying instead on overall dimensions of infant/child difficultness. For instance, Wachs (1987) found that the number of persons in the home was not related to the mastery behavior of easy infants, but was negatively related to the performance of difficult children. Similar findings were reported by Sanson, Oberklaid, Pedlow, and Prior (1991) in a sample of children aged four–five. Although difficult temperament status alone was only slightly related to elevated incidence of problem behaviors, when this temperamental variable was considered in combination with

low socio-economic status, poor mother-child relationship, or mothers'
perception of the child as difficult, substantially stronger prediction of
both externalizing and internalizing problems was obtained. A final example of this recurrent pattern are the results of Maziade (1989), who found
temperamentally difficult children were not particularly likely to have developed behavior disorders at seven years of age unless they were raised in
an environment characterized by poor family functioning. These findings
fit within Sameroff and Chandler's (1975) developmental model in which
possibly negative constitutional factors may be ameliorated through positive transactions within the family or exacerbated through dysfunctional
patterns of interaction.

Frustration The appropriateness of making an additional distinction between frustration/anger and fear can be seen in their differing patterns of developmental relationships. In our research, laboratory frustration observed at six and ten months predicted seven year Anger/
Frustration, as well as other components of negative affectivity, including high Discomfort, low Soothability, and high Guilt/Shame (Rothbart,
Derryberry et al., 2000). Infant frustration in the laboratory was also
related to seven year surgency, as reflected in high CBQ Activity Level,
Positive Anticipation, Impulsivity, Aggression, and High Intensity Pleasure. IBQ Frustration predicted later Positive Anticipation, High Intensity Pleasure, Impulsivity, and low Sadness. The only relation found between infant frustration and childhood fear was a negative one, between
early IBQ Frustration and later Fear. These relations again suggest a link
between anger/frustration and approach tendencies. Conceptually replicating our findings are results reported by Lemery et al. (1999), who
found that distress-anger was positively related to activity level, whereas
fear and activity level were independent.

In a study of temperament/socialization interaction, Bates, Pettit,
Dodge, and Ridge (1998) examined resistant temperament as it inter-
acted with restrictive parenting style in the development of externalizing
difficulties. Resistant temperament includes aspects of both surgency and
negative affectivity. As discussed above, approach tendencies may lead to
high frustration and aversive behaviors when goals are blocked. Bates
et al. (1998) suggest that resistance to control may also be linked to
deficiencies in effortful control. Parental restrictive control referred to
behaviors meant to stop or punish the child such as negative commands,
removing objects, scolding, and spanking. In two separate samples of
elementary school children, resistant temperament was more strongly related to externalizing problems when parents were low in restrictive control than when parents were highly controlling. This relation was found

whether infant temperament ratings were made retrospectively or concurrently, and whether teacher- or mother-rated outcomes were predicted.

Implications of resistant temperament for possible externalizing difficulties are clear. The findings of Bates *et al.* (1998) indicate, however, that parents may modify the relationship between early resistance and later problem behavior. Bates and his colleagues suggest that for a child high in resistance to control, parents who are consistently restrictive may shape the child's responsivity to socially-imposed limits. For children low in resistance, lower amounts of parental control may allow the child opportunities for autonomy, allowing the child to learn to meet social demands independently.

Fear Late in the first year, infants begin to demonstrate their fear in inhibited approach to unfamiliar and intense stimuli. Once fearful inhibition is established, individual differences in the relative strength of approach versus inhibition in novel or intense situations appear to be relatively enduring aspects of temperament (see review by Rothbart and Bates, 1998). When motor inhibition is incorporated into the fear reaction, a differentiation of fear and frustration may result. Although frustration can invigorate approach tendencies (Newman, 1987), fear involves a more consistent inhibition of approach. Fear can thus be seen to serve an important, yet relatively reactive, form of regulatory control, and we have identified it as one of the major control systems in the developing child (Derryberry and Rothbart, 1997; Rothbart, 1989; Rothbart and Bates, 1998). Fearful inhibition is surely adaptive, in that it helps protect the infant from inadvertent approach responses to stimuli that may be dangerous. It is also a system well adapted to early socialization, in that it is related to sensitivity to punishment and the internalization of guilt reactions (Dienstbier, 1984; Kochanska, 1993; Kochanska, DeVet, Goldman, Murray, and Putnam, 1994).

As with approach tendencies, fear-related inhibition shows considerable stability across childhood and even into adolescence (Kagan, 1998). Longitudinal research indicates stability of fearful inhibition from two to four years (Lemery *et al.*, 1999), two to eight years (Kagan, Reznick, and Snidman, 1988), and from the preschool period to age eighteen (Caspi and Silva, 1995). In our longitudinal sample (Rothbart, Derryberry *et al.*, 2000), both observed laboratory and IBQ fear predicted CBQ Fear and Shyness at seven years. Fear also predicted later Sadness and Low Intensity (non-risk taking) Pleasure. Neither IBQ nor laboratory fear measures predicted Frustration/Anger in childhood.

A good deal of work on temperamental fear has emphasized its possible role in the development of maladaptive behavior patterns such as social withdrawal (Rubin and Asendorpf, 1993). Other sources, however, support our view of fear as affording possibly beneficial control over approach-related problem behaviors. In our studies, high laboratory fear at 13 months predicted low Positive Anticipation, Impulsivity, Activity Level, and Aggression at age seven. These relationships are consistent with models such as Gray and McNaughton's (1996), where an anxiety-related behavioral inhibition system inhibits an approach-related behavioral activation system. Dominance of the surgency/approach system over behavioral inhibition has been proposed as an underlying mechanism for a variety of clinical disorders including attention deficit disorder (Quay, 1988), mania (Depue, Krauss, and Spoont, 1987; Fowles, 1988), drug abuse (Cloninger, 1987a) and histrionic, passive-aggressive, and explosive personality disorders (Cloninger, 1987b).

Additional findings provide evidence of the beneficial aspects of fear. Pliszka (1989) found children with concurrent ADHD and anxiety to show reduced impulsivity relative to those with ADHD alone, and aggressiveness appears to decrease between kindergarten and first grade for children who show internalizing patterns of behavior (Bates, Pettit, and Dodge, 1995). A recent study found that a group of children who were uninhibited at 21 months of age exhibited greater levels of delinquent and aggressive behavior at 13 years than did adolescents who were inhibited as toddlers (Schwartz, Snidman, and Kagan, 1996). In our longitudinal study, we found evidence that infants with greater fear had higher parent-reported empathy and guilt/shame and lower aggression during childhood (Rothbart *et al.*, 1994).

In an impressive body of work connecting temperament, parenting and successful social development, Kochanska (1991, 1995, 1997) found temperamental fearfulness to be a source of both main and interaction effects in children's developing internalization of the rules of conduct. Kochanska's model of moral development was influenced by a theory advanced by Hoffman (1983) and Dienstbier (1984). Prior to Hoffman, fear and anxiety had been strongly implicated in the development of moral conduct. Hoffman modified this view by positing that gentle socialization techniques would elicit an optimal level of arousal, allowing the child to effectively encode the parental message. In contrast, more power-assertive forms of discipline would produce higher arousal and distress, interfering with the socialization message and leading the child to attribute their compliance to external, rather than internal, causes. Dienstbier further contributed to this framework by proposing that temperamentally fearful children would be more responsive to gentle discipline strategies, given their intrinsically high levels of arousal.

An initial study by Kochanska (1991) provided empirical support for these ideas. Temperamental fearfulness was assessed in the laboratory when children were between eighteen months and three and a half years of age. Maternal discipline strategies were determined using both observational and self-report measures. When these children were seen again five to six years later, their internalized conscience was measured through their completion of narratives focusing on various moral dilemmas. Consistent with expectations, there was a main effect for fear, in that fearful children showed higher levels of conscience. In addition, Kochanska (1991) found support for the proposed interaction between fearfulness and parenting. For temperamentally fearful children, rearing techniques that were low in power assertion (i.e., authoritative or democratic strategies such as rational guidance, empathy induction, and open expression of affect) were associated with high levels of conscience at the later age, whereas highly power assertive techniques (i.e., authoritarian practices including physical punishment, prohibitions, and discouragement of emotion expression) were related to low levels of internalized conscience. In contrast, among children who were relatively fearless, socialization was not consistently related to later conscience.

Kochanska's later work (e.g., Kochanska, 1995, 1997) built upon her earlier effort both methodologically and theoretically. Conscience in toddlers and preschoolers was operationalized through children's observed compliance with maternal requests and refusal to "cheat" on games or touch a forbidden object when unsupervised, and expression of empathic and prosocial themes to projective stories. Measurement of maternal discipline was similarly expanded: observations of mother behavior were made in two challenging laboratory contexts and a large battery of self-report measures were used to assess socialization attitudes and practices. As in the earlier (Kochanska, 1991) study, discipline based on low power assertion was successful in promoting moral conduct and orientation at three and four years of age in fearful, but not relatively fearless, children. This interactional relation, however, had largely disappeared by the time the children were five years old, perhaps due to the increasing influence of other sources of socialization such as peers or to the greater regulative function of effortful control, discussed later in this chapter.

An alternative pathway to conscience was proposed and supported for children low in fear. In reference to the work of Maccoby (1983), who indicated the importance of responsive and positive parent–child interaction for internalization of the parents' agenda, Kochanska (1995) suggested that this type of cooperative relationship may be especially influential in the development of conscience among fearless children. To examine this possibility, two different aspects of positive mother–child orientation were measured: children's attachment security was assessed via Q-sort, and maternal responsiveness to the child was coded from videotapes of naturalistic interactions. These aspects of mothering were not found to be related to morality in fearful children. For children who were relatively fearless, however, security of attachment was associated with the ability to refrain from cheating and to adopt prosocial themes in response to hypothetical moral dilemmas when they were four years old. Observed maternal responsiveness was successful in promoting these positive outcomes at five years for fearless, but not fearful, children (Kochanska, 1997).

Kochanska's findings indicate that motivational characteristics of individual children can be used to help parents guide parenting techniques. Children high in anxiousness respond strongly to gentle discipline, which elicits sufficient amounts of fear to allow the child to effectively internalize their parent's goals. This strategy is relatively ineffective for children who are less motivated by fear. In contrast, temperamentally fearless children appear to be motivated more strongly by reward than by punishment and thus respond more strongly to parenting efforts based on positive anticipation.

This interpretation evokes an additional theoretical and empirical issue. Might the children identified as fearless in the work of Kochanska also be high on surgency? Since surgency is believed to be based in sensitivity to reward, the effectiveness of reward-based socialization for these children suggests that this may indeed be the case. It has long been reasoned that approach/withdrawal behavior can be considered a function of two separate, opposed systems (Schnierla, 1959). Although the continuous nature of approach/withdrawal has typically been emphasized in psychological research (including that of Kochanska), our work (Rothbart, 1988; Putnam, 1999) suggests that it is possible to disentangle reward-oriented approach from fear-based withdrawal. Future work separating the two tendencies in order to investigate temperament/socialization interactions may prove fruitful.

In this section, we have discussed some of the beneficial aspects of fear. The fact that fear can be directed toward a positive outcome may seem paradoxical, in that fear is often viewed as maladaptive. As was the case for surgency, however, this is consistent with our view that any given behavioral profile may contain both costs and benefits (Rothbart, 1982; Sanson and Rothbart, 1995). The motor inhibition associated with fear may aid in the constraint of impulsivity or, alternatively, it may lead to rigid over-controlled patterns of behavior that can limit the individual's experiences (Block and Block, 1980; Kremen and Block, 1998). Similarly, as suggested above, although surgency may in some cases lead to difficulty in controlling aggressive urges, in other cases this same mechanism can motivate exploration and triumph over obstacles to achievement. The expression of these relatively reactive aspects of temperament may be in large part determined by the activity of a third, less reactive, component of temperament: effortful control.

Effortful control

Temperamental effortful control, based on the executive attention system, makes major contributions to successful social development (Kochanska, Murray, and Harlan, 2000; Posner and Rothbart, 1998). Individuals high in effortful control are able to voluntarily regulate their emotional state by deploying their attention, and can suppress initial reactive tendencies to conform to situational demands successfully. As described above, the ECBQ and CBQ contain a broad factor of Effortful Control which is distinct from Surgency and Negative Emotionality. In addition, we have uncovered relationships between the abilities to focus attention, restrain dominant impulses, and shift attention in adults (Derryberry and Rothbart, 1988). Although a factor likely to be based on effortful control (Conscientiousness) often emerges in models of adult personality (Digman, 1990), our conceptualization of attention in relation to behavioral control is relatively recent and goes beyond definitions limiting temperament to individual differences in emotional experience and expression (e.g., Allport, 1961; Goldsmith and Campos, 1982).

Indicators of effortful control first appear late in the first year in the form of infants' ability to inhibit and correct the course of visually controlled movement (Posner and Rothbart, 1998; Ruff and Rothbart, 1996). During the infancy and preschool periods, attentional capacities can be seen in the ability to inhibit forbidden behaviors. Kochanska and her colleagues, for example, recently reported relations in nine-month-olds between focused attention and voluntary restraint from touching a prohibited toy (Kochanska, Tjebkes, and Forman, 1998).

The effortful control system continues to develop during early childhood, becoming more sophisticated as children develop the use of language-based forms of regulation. Using a Stroop-like marker task, we have recently documented rapid improvement between 27 and 36 months in children's ability to inhibit a dominant response in order to execute a nondominant response in a conflict situation (Gerardi-Caulton, 1998; Posner and Rothbart, 1998). Individual differences in this skill appear to reach beyond the laboratory, because children who perform well are also described by their parents as more skilled at attentional control, less impulsive, and less prone to frustration reactions. Using a very similar task with adults, Derryberry and Reed (1999) have found that individuals who perform well in a conflict task tend to be low in anxiety and high on self-reported attentional control.

Kochanska and her associates have devised a series of innovative methods to assess effortful control throughout early childhood (Kochanska, Murray, Jacques, Koenig, and Vandegeest, 1996; Kochanska, Murray, and Coy, 1997; Kochanska, Murray, and Harlan, 2000). In addition to delay-of-gratification tasks and a Stroop-like procedure which requires the recognition of small shapes hidden within a dominant large shape, they measure children's ability to slow down motor activity (draw a line slowly), suppress initiated responses (go-no-go games), and lower the voice. Beginning at age two and a half, children's performance becomes highly consistent across these tasks, suggesting they are measuring an underlying process that develops over time.

Once effortful control has been established, it appears to be relatively stable throughout the preschool period, childhood, and adolescence. Kochanska found nine-month measures of attentional and behavioral control to predict compliance to maternal demands at 14 months and performance on a battery of effortful control tasks at 22 months, but these relations were relatively modest. In the later preschool years, however, individual differences in inhibitory control as measured by the tasks listed above, become remarkably consistent, with internal consistency coefficients as high as .42 from 22 to 33 months and .65 from 46 to 65 months (Kochanska et al., 1998; Kochanska et al., 2000). The stability findings of Mischel and colleagues are also impressive: the duration of time preschool children were able to wait for a physically present reward predicted parent-reported attentiveness, ability to concentrate, and control of negative emotions assessed over a decade later (Mischel, 1983; Shoda, Mischel, and Peake, 1990).

We would expect effortful control to be linked to other important competencies such as sensitivity and understanding in social relationships, regulation of antisocial behavior, critical thinking skills, problem solving skills, flexibility in the application of information-processing strategies, and facility in the use of resources for learning and problem solving. Many of these skills require flexibility in thinking and the use of mental strategies such as planning and error detection related to executive function (Posner and Rothbart, 1998). Other skills are related to the development of personality characteristics that promote positive interactions with others. We now consider research related to these connections.

In our research, six- to seven-year-old children high in Effortful Control were also high in Empathy, Guilt/Shame, and low in Aggressiveness (Rothbart et al., 1994). Eisenberg and her colleagues have also found that four- to six-year-old boys with good attentional control tend to deal with anger by using nonhostile verbal methods rather than overt aggressive methods (Eisenberg, Fabes, Nyman, Bernzweig, and Pinulas, 1994). Effortful control may support empathy by allowing attention to the thoughts and feelings of others without becoming overwhelmed by one's own distress. Similarly, Guilt/Shame in six- to seven-year-old children is positively related to Effortful Control and Negative Affectivity (Rothbart *et al.*, 1994). Negative emotionality may contribute to guilt by providing the individual with strong internal cues of discomfort, increasing the probability that the cause of these feelings is attributed to an internal rather than external cause (Dienstbier, 1984; Kochanska, 1993). Effortful control may further contribute by providing the flexibility needed to notice these feelings and relate them to feelings of responsibility for one's own actions and possible negative consequences for another (Derryberry and Reed, 1994, 1996).

Recent findings by Kochanska provide further evidence of the powerful role played by effortful control in the development of social competencies (Kochanska *et al.*, 1996, 1997, 1998, 2000). In two separate samples, this work has documented both concurrent and longitudinal relations between effortful control and a host of positive outcomes, including children's committed compliance to parental agendas, morality, and regulation of emotion.

Kochanska *et al.* (1996) measured young children's internalization of standards using a number of tasks. Children were observed in situations in which they were asked to refrain from touching a prohibited toy, to complete an unpleasant task, or to keep from "cheating" in games while not under surveillance by parents or experimenters. High levels of both toddler and preschool effortful control were concurrently related to a lack of misbehavior in both the observational tasks and maternal ratings. In addition, effortful control during toddlerhood was predictive of internalization at preschool age. A follow-up of these children at age five showed children high on effortful control as toddlers continuing to exhibit higher levels of internalization. In addition, when given hypothetical dilemmas contrasting selfish and helping acts, children high on effortful control were more likely to respond with prosocial answers (Kochanska *et al.*, 1997).

An especially exciting finding in Kochanska *et al.* (2000) concerns possible parental influence on effortful control. In response to previous research showing relations between sensitive, responsive parenting and child qualities similar to effortful control, it was reasoned that this aspect of parenting may promote effortful control in young children. Maternal responsivity assessed at 22 months, using measures of promptness, sensitivity, engagement and acceptance, was associated with higher levels of effortful control at both 22 and 33 months. Importantly, the effects of parenting were found to contribute significantly even after regressing out earlier temperamental attention and effortful control.

Findings of environmental influences upon effortful control are consistent with recent work in comparative psychology. Rumbaugh and Washburn (1996; Rumbaugh, Richardson, and Washburn, 1989) have developed a set of computer-based tasks which promote the development of attentional skills in rhesus monkeys and chimpanzees. As well as improving the skills of non-human primates in Stroop-like tasks, this training also appears to lower aggressiveness and facilitate social interaction (Washburn, personal communication, 1999). We are currently adapting this battery for use with toddlers to investigate whether effortful control can be enhanced in humans through attention training.

Summary and future directions

In this chapter, we have indicated the contribution made by temperament to successful life-course trajectories. Recent work has shown that dimensions of temperament observed in infancy and childhood can be seen as the potential core of aspects of personality found in later development. We have argued that emotional and motivational dimensions of positive affect/surgency and negative affect/neuroticism may lead to either beneficial or detrimental outcomes to society and the individual. We have also reviewed a growing body of literature examining ways in which temperament moderates and is moderated by socializing influences in the prediction of outcomes. The landmark work of Kochanska and others studying temperament/environment interactions should be viewed as the genesis of an exciting new era of work. We hope that new efforts will build upon previous findings of direct relations between temperament, socialization, and social outcomes by focusing on these indirect routes to success. Future efforts may also determine techniques for promoting appropriate forms of surgency and using effortful control capacities to successfully control fear and anger. Following these directions, research on temperament and socialization can move toward greater understanding of alternative pathways to successful development.

REFERENCES

Ahadi, S. A., and Rothbart, M. K. (1994). Temperament, development, and the Big Five. In C. F. Halverson Jr, G. A. Kohnstamm, and R. P. Martin (eds.), *The developing structure of temperament and personality from infancy to adulthood*. Hillsdale, NJ: Lawrence Erlbaum, 189–207.

Ahadi, S. A., Rothbart, M. K., and Ye, R. M. (1993). Children's temperament in the US and China: similarities and differences. *European Journal of Psychology*, 7, 359–77.

Allport, G. W. (1961). *Pattern and growth in personality*. New York: Holt.

Arnett, J. (1995). Developmental contributors to adolescent reckless behavior. Poster presented at the biennial meeting of the Society for Research on Child Development, Indianapolis, Indiana, March, 1995.

Bandura, A. (1977). *Social learning theory*. Englewood Cliffs, NJ: Prentice-Hall.

Bates, J. E., Pettit, G. S., and Dodge, K. A. (1995). Family and child factors in stability and change in children's aggressiveness in elementary school. In J. McCord (ed.), *Coercion and punishment in long-term perspectives*. New York: Cambridge University Press.

Bates, J. E., Pettit, G. S., Dodge, K. A., and Ridge, B. (1998). Interaction of temperamental resistance to control and restrictive parenting in the development of externalizing behavior. *Developmental Psychology*, 34 (5), 982–95.

Block, J. H., and Block, J. (1980). The role of ego-control and ego-resiliency in the organization of behavior. In W. A. Collins (ed.), *Minnesota Symposium on Child Psychology*. Hillsdale, NJ: Erlbaum, Vol. XIII, pp. 39–101.

Bohlin, G., Hagekull, B., and Lindhagen, K. (1981). Dimensions of infant behavior. *Infant Behavior and Development*, 4, 83–96.

Calkins, S. T., Fox, N. A., and Marshall, T. R. (1996). Behavioral and physiological antecedents of inhibited and uninhibited behavior. *Child Development*, 63, 1456–72.

Caspi, A., and Silva, P. A. (1995). Temperamental qualities at age three predict personality traits in young adulthood: longitudinal evidence from a birth cohort. *Child Development*, 66, 486–98.

Cloninger, R. C. (1987a). Neurogenetic adaptive mechanisms in alcoholism. *Science*, 236, 410–16.

Cloninger, R. C. (1987b). A systematic method for clinical description and classification of personality variants. *Archives of General Psychiatry*, 44, 573–88.

Depue, R. A., and Collins, P. F. (1999). Neurobiology of the structure of personality: dopamine, facilitation of incentive motivation, and extraversion. *Behavioral and Brain Sciences*, 22 (3), 491–569.

Depue, R. A., Krauss, S. P., and Spoont, M. R. (1987). A two-dimensional threshold model of seasonal bipolar affective disorder. *Psychopathology: An interactional perspective. Personality, psychopathology, and psychotherapy*. Orlando, FL, USA: Academic Press, Inc. 95–123.

Derryberry, D., and Reed, M. A. (1994). Temperament and the self-organization of personality. *Development and Psychopathology*, 6, 653–76.

Derryberry, D., and Reed, M. A. (1996). Regulatory processes and the development of cognitive representations. *Development and Psychopathology*, 8, 215–34.

Derryberry, D., and Reed, M. A. (1999). *Individual differences in attentional control: adaptive regulation of response interference*. Manuscript submitted for publication.

Derryberry, D., and Rothbart, M. K. (1988). Arousal, affective and attentional components of temperament. *Journal of Personality and Social Psychology*, 55, 958–66.

Derryberry, D., and Rothbart, M. K. (1997). Reactive and effortful processes in the organization of temperament. *Development and Psychopathology*, 9, 633–52.

Diamond, S. (1957). *Personality and temperament*. New York: Harper.

Dienstbier, R. A. (1984). The role of emotion in moral socialization. In C. E. Izard, J. Kagan, and R. B. Zajonc (eds.), *Emotions, cognition, and behavior.* Cambridge University Press, 484–514.

Digman, J. M. (1990). Personality structure: emergence of the five-factor model. *Annual Review of Psychology,* 41, 417–40.

Eisenberg, N., Fabes, R. A., Nyman, M., Bernzweig, J., and Pinulas, A. (1994). The relations of emotionality and regulation to children's anger-related reactions. *Child Development,* 65, 109–28.

Ellis, L. K., and Rothbart, M. K. (In preparation). Revision of the Early Adolescent Temperament Questionnaire.

Fowles, D. C. (1988). Psychophysiology and psychopathy: a motivational approach. *Psychophysiology,* 25, 373–91.

Fox, N. A. (1989). Psychophysical correlates of emotional reactivity during the first year of life. *Developmental Psychology,* 25, 364–72.

Fox, N. A., and Davidson, R. J. (1988). Patterns of brain electrical activity during facial signs of emotion in 10-month-old infants. *Developmental Psychology,* 24 (2), 230–6.

Frick, P. H., O'Brien, B. S., Wotton, J. M., and McBurnett, K. (1994). Psychopathy and conduct problems in children. *Journal of Abnormal Psychology,* 103 (4), 700–17.

Gabel, S., Stabler, J., Born, J., Shindledecker, R., and Bowden, C. L. (1994). Sensation seeking in psychiatrically disturbed youth: relationship to biochemical parameters and behavior problems. *Journal of the American Academy of Child and Adolescent Psychiatry,* 33 (1), 123–9.

Gandour, M. J. (1989). Activity level as a dimension of temperament in toddlers: its relevance for the organismic specificity hypothesis. *Child Development,* 60, 1092–98.

Gartstein, M. A., and Rothbart, M. K. (in preparation). Infant behavior questionnaire – revised: a fine-grained approach to assessment of temperament in infancy.

Gerardi-Caulton, G. (1998). *Measuring executive attention in the third year of life: a new task and its relation to the development of self-regulation.* Manuscript submitted for publication.

Goldsmith, H. H. (1996). Studying temperament via construction of the Toddler Behavior Assessment Questionnaire. *Child Development,* 67, 218–35.

Goldsmith, H. H., and Campos, J. J. (1982). Toward a theory of infant temperament. In R. N. Emde and R. J. Harmon (eds.), *Advances in developmental psychology.* Hillsdale, NJ: Erlbaum, 231–283.

Goldsmith, H. H., and Campos, J. J. (1986). Fundamental issues in the study of early temperament: the Denver Twin Temperament Study. In M. H. Lamb and A. Brown (eds.), *Advances in developmental psychology.* Hillsdale, NJ: Erlbaum.

Gray, J. A., and McNaughton, N. (1996). The neuropsychology of anxiety: reprise. In D. A. Hope (ed.), *Nebraska Symposium on Motivation: Perspectives on anxiety, panic, and fear.* Lincoln, NE: University of Nebraska Press, 43, 61–134.

Hoffman, M. L. (1975). Altruistic behavior and the parent-child relationship. *Journal of Personality and Social Psychology,* 31, 937–43.

Hoffman, M. L. (1983). Affective and cognitive processes in moral internalization. In E. T. Higgins, D. Ruble, and W. Hartup (eds.), *Social cognition and social development: a sociocultural perspective*. New York: Cambridge University Press, 236–74.

Kafry, D. (1982). Sensation seeking of young children. *Personality and Individual Differences*, 3, 161–6.

Kagan, J. (1998). Biology and the child. In W. S. E. Damon and N. V. E. Eisenberg (eds.), *Handbook of child psychology: social, emotional and personality development* (5th edn.), vol. 3: *Social, emotional and personality development*, New York: Wiley, 177–235.

Kagan, J., Reznick, J. S., and Snidman, N. (1988). Biological bases of childhood shyness. *Science*, 240, 167–73.

Kagan, J., and Snidman, N. (1991). Temperamental factors in human development. *American Psychologist*, 46, 856–62.

Kistiakovskaia, M. I. (1965). Stimuli evoking positive emotions in infants in the first months of life. *Soviet Psychology and Psychiatry*, 3, 39–48.

Kochanska, G. (1991). Socialization and temperament in the development of guilt and conscience. *Child Development*, 62, 1379–92.

Kochanska, G. (1993). Toward a synthesis of parental socialization and child temperament in early development of conscience. *Child Development*, 64, 325–47.

Kochanska, G. (1995). Children's temperament, mothers' discipline, and security of attachment: multiple pathways to emerging internalization. *Child Development*, 66, 597–615.

Kochanska, G. (1997). Multiple pathways to conscience for children with different temperaments: from toddlerhood to age five. *Developmental Psychology*, 33, 228–40.

Kochanska, G., DeVet, K., Goldman, M., Murray, K., and Putnam, S. P. (1994). Maternal reports of conscience development and temperament in young children. *Child Development*, 65, 852–68.

Kochanska, G., Murray, K., and Coy, K. C. (1997). Inhibitory control as a contributor to conscience in childhood: from toddler to early school age. *Child Development*, 68, 263–77.

Kochanska, G., Murray, K. T., and Harlan, E. T. (2000). Effortful control in early childhood: continuity and change, antecedents, and implications for social development. *Developmental Psychology*, 36, 220–32.

Kochanska, G., Murray, K., Jacques, T. Y., Koenig, A. L., and Vandegeest, K. A. (1996). Inhibitory control in young children and its role in emerging internalization. *Child Development*, 67, 490–507.

Kochanska, G., Tjebkes, T. L., and Forman, D. R. (1998). Children's emerging regulation of conduct: restraint, compliance, and internalization from infancy to the second year. *Child Development*, 69, 1378–89.

Korner, A. F., Hutchinson, C. A., Koperski, J., Kraemer, H. C., Berkowitz, R. I., and Agras, W. S. (1985). Relation between neonatal and later activity and temperament. *Child Development*, 52, 83–90.

Kremen, A. M., and Block, J. (1998). The roots of ego-control in young adulthood: links with parenting in early childhood. *Journal of Personality and Social Personality*, 75, 1062–75.

Lemery, K. S., Goldsmith, H. H., Klinnert, M. D., and Mrazek, D. A. (1999). Developmental models of infant and childhood temperament. *Developmental Psychology*, 35, 189–204.

Maccoby, E. E. (1983). Let's not over-attribute to the attribution process: comments on social cognition and behavior. In E. T. Higgins, D. Ruble, and W. Hartup (eds.), *Social cognition and social development: a sociocultural perspective*. New York: Cambridge University Press, 356–70.

Matheny, Adam P., Jr. (1989). Temperament and cognition: relations between temperament and mental test scores. In G. A. Kohnstamm, J. E. Bates, and M. K. Rothbart (eds.), *Temperament in Childhood*, New York: John Wiley and Sons, 263–82.

Maziade, M. (1989). Should adverse temperament matter to the clinician? In G. A. Kohnstamm, J. E. Bates and M. K. Rothbart (eds.) *Temperament in childhood*, New York: John Wiley and Sons, 421–35.

McClelland, D. C., Atkinson, J. W., Clark, R. A., and Lowell, E. L. (1953). *The achievement motive*. New York: Appleton-Century-Crofts.

Mischel, W. (1983). Delay of gratification as process and as person variable in development. In D. Magnusson and V. P. Allen (eds.), *Human development: an interactional perspective*, New York: Academic Press, 149–65.

Newman, J. P. (1987). Reaction to punishment in extraverts and psychopaths: implications for the impulsive behavior of disinhibited individuals. *Journal of Research in Personality*, 21, 464–80.

Panksepp, J. (1998). *Affective Neuroscience*. New York: Oxford.

Pedlow, R., Sanson, A. V., Prior, M., and Oberklaid, F. (1993). The stability of temperament from infancy to eight years. *Developmental Psychology*, 29, 998–1007.

Pliszka, S. R. (1989). Effect of anxiety on cognition, behavior, and stimulant response in ADHD. *Journal of the American Academy of Child and Adolescent Psychiatry*, 28, 882–7.

Posner, M. I., and Rothbart, M. K. (1998). Attention, self-regulation and consciousness. *Philosophical Transactions of the Royal Society of London B*, 353, 1915–27.

Putnam, S. P. (1996). *Self-reported sensation seeking in a sample of first-born, five-year-old males*. Unpublished masters thesis, Pennsylvania State University.

Putnam, S. P. (1999). *Behavioral approach at two years: early antecedents, emergent structure, and cardiac contributions*. Unpublished doctoral dissertation, Pennsylvania State University.

Quay, H. C. (1988). Attention deficit disorder and the behavioral inhibition system: the relevance of the neuropsychological theory of Jeffery A. Gray. In L. M. Bloomindale (ed.). *Attention deficit disorder*. Oxford: Pergamon Press, Vol. III, 176–86.

Rothbart, M. K. (1973). Laughter in young children. *Psychological Bulletin*, 80, 247–56.

Rothbart, M. K. (1981). Measurement of temperament in infancy. *Child Development*, 52, 569–78.

Rothbart, M. K. (1982). The concept of difficult temperament: a critical analysis of Thomas, Chess, and Korn. *Merill-Palmer Quarterly*, 28 (1), 35–40.

Rothbart, M. K. (1988). Temperament and the development of inhibited approach. *Child Development*, 59, 1241–50.

Rothbart, M. K. (1989). Temperament and development. In G. A. Kohnstamm, J. E. Bates, and M. K. Rothbart (eds.), *Temperament in childhood*, New York: John Wiley and Sons, 187–247.

Rothbart, M. K., Ahadi, S. A., and Evans, D. E. (2000). Temperament and personality: origins and outcomes. *Journal of Personality and Social Psychology*, 78 (1), 122–35.

Rothbart, M. K., Ahadi, S. A., and Hershey, K. L. (1994). Temperament and social behavior in childhood. *Merrill-Palmer Quarterly*, 40, 21–39.

Rothbart, M. K., Ahadi, S. A., Hershey, K., and Fisher, P. (in press). *Investigations of Temperament at 3-7 Years: the Children's Behavior Questionnaire*. Manuscript submitted for publication.

Rothbart, M. K., and Bates, J. E. (1998). Temperament. In W. S. E. Damon and N. V. E. Eisenberg (eds.), *Handbook of child psychology: social, emotional and personality development* (5th edn.), vol. 3: *Social, emotional and personality development*. New York: Wiley, 105–76.

Rothbart, M. K., and Derryberry, D. (1981). Development of individual differences in temperament. In M. E. Lamb and A. L. Brown (eds.), *Advances in developmental psychology*, Hillsdale, New Jersey: Erlbaum, 1, 37–86.

Rothbart, M. K., Derryberry, D., and Hershey, K. (2000). Stability of temperament in childhood: laboratory infant assessment to parent report at seven years. In V. J. Molfese and D. L. Molfese (eds.), *Temperament and personality development across the life span*. Mahwah, NJ: Erlbaum, 85–119.

Rothbart, M. K., Derryberry, D., and Posner, M. I. (1994). A psychobiological approach to the development of temperament. In J. E. Bates and T. D. Wachs (eds.), *Temperament: individual differences at the interface of biology and behavior*. Washington, DC: American Psychological Association, 83–116.

Rothbart, M. K., and Mauro, J. A. (1990). Questionnaire approaches to the study of infant temperament. In J. W. Fagen and J. Colombo (eds.), *Individual differences in infancy: reliability, stability and prediction*. Hillsdale, NJ: Erlbaum, 411–29.

Rubin, K. H., and Asendorpf, J. B. (1993). *Social withdrawal, inhibition, and shyness in childhood*. Hillsdale, NJ: Erlbaum.

Ruff, H. A., and Rothbart, M. K. (1996). *Attention in early development: themes and variations*. New York: Oxford University Press.

Russo, M. F., Stokes, G. S., Lahey, B. B., Christ, M. A. G., McBurnett, K., Walker, J. L., Lobber, R., Stouthamer-Lobber, M., and Green, S. M. (1993). A sensation seeking scale in children: further refinement and psychometric development. *Journal of Psychopathology and Behavioral Assessment*, 15, 69–86.

Sameroff, A. J. and Chandler, M. J. (1975). Reproductive risk and the continuum of caretaking causality. In F. Horowitz (ed.) *Review of child development research*, University of Chicago Press, 4, 187–244.

Sanson, A., Oberklaid, F., Pedlow, R., and Prior, M. (1991). Risk indicators: assessment of infancy predictors of pre-school behavioral maladjustment. *Journal of Child Psychology and Psychiatry*, 32 (4), 609–26.

Sanson, A. V., Prior, M., Garino, E., Oberklaid, F., and Sewell, J. (1987). The structure of infant temperament: factor analysis of the Revised Infant Temperament Questionnaire. *Infant Behavior and Development*, 10, 97–104.

Sanson, A., and Rothbart, M. K. (1995). Child temperament and parenting. In M. Bornstein (ed.) *Handbook of parenting*. Hillsdale, NJ: Erlbaum.

Schiefele, A., Krapp, A., and Winteler, T. (1992). Interest as a predictor of academic achievement: a meta-analysis of research. In K. A. Renninger, S. Hidi, and A. Krapp (eds.), *The role of interest learning and development*. Hillsdale, NJ: Erlbaum, 183–212.

Schnierla, T. C. (1959). An evolutionary and developmental theory of biphasic processes underlying approach and withdrawal. In M. R. Jones (ed.), *Nebraska Symposium on Motivation*. Lincoln, NE: University of Nebraska Press, 7, 1–42.

Schwartz, C. E., Snidman, N., and Kagan, J. (1996). Early childhood temperament as a determinant of externalizing behavior in adolescence. *Development and Psychopathology*, 8, 527–37.

Shoda, Y., Mischel, W., and Peake, P. K. (1990). Predicting adolescent cognitive and self-regulatory competencies from preschool delay of gratification: identifying diagnostic conditions. *Developmental Psychology*, 26, 978–86.

Thomas, A., and Chess, S. (1977). *Temperament and development*. New York: Brunner/Mazel.

Thomas, A., Chess, S., and Birch, H. G. (1968). *Temperament and behavior disorders in children*. New York University Press.

Thomas, A., Chess, S., Birch, H. G., Herzig, M. E., and Korn, S. (1963). *Behavioral individuality in early childhood*. New York University Press.

Wachs, T. D. (1987). Specificity of environmental action as manifest in environmental correlates of infants' mastery motivation. *Developmental Psychology*, 23, 782–90.

Wachs, T. D., and Gandour, M. J. (1983). Temperament, environment, and six-month cognitive-intellectual development: a test of the organismic specificity hypothesis. *International Journal of Behavioral Development*, 6, 135–52.

Wachs, T. D., and Gruen, G. (1982). *Early experience and human development*. New York: Plenum.

2 The role of emotionality and regulation in children's social competence and adjustment

Nancy Eisenberg, Richard A. Fabes,
Ivanna K. Guthrie and Mark Reiser

The topic of regulatory processes, especially emotion-related regulation, has emerged as a major focus of psychological interest in the last decade. This seems to be especially true in developmental and clinical psychology, probably because of the role of emotion and its regulation in developmentally important outcomes such as social competence and adjustment. Indeed, emotion-related regulation is a critical aspect of individual functioning because it likely contributes to nearly all domains of human functioning and behavior, including the quality of individuals' interactions with others, the social appropriateness of overt behavior, and the nature of experienced emotion. Consequently, emotion-related regulation, through its effects on behavior and emotional experience, influences others' perceptions of an individual and the individual's self-related cognitions and evaluations. For example, children who are especially unregulated in their peer interactions are likely to be rejected by their peers, which can affect future opportunities for learning about socially competent behavior, willingness to stay in school with peers, self-related evaluations, and adjustment (e.g., problems with anxiety or depression; e.g., Parker and Asher, 1987, 1993; Parker, Rubin, Price, and DeRosier, 1995). Thus, emotion-related regulation in the early years is likely to influence the course of development across the life-span. For these reasons, knowledge about emotion-related regulation is important not only for a basic scientific understanding of social and emotional development, but also for work aimed at preventing and remediating problem behaviors and promoting adaptive coping and socially competent behavior across the life-course.

Emotionality and emotion-related regulation as individual difference variables

Individual differences in emotionality and related regulatory capacities play a major role in most theories and models of temperament (e.g.,

Goldsmith and Campos, 1982; Rothbart and Bates, 1998) and personality (e.g., in the Big Five constructs of neuroticism and conscientiousness). As for other aspects of temperament, emotionality and regulation of reactivity are believed to be facets of functioning that are relatively stable over time and feed into adult personality (Caspi, 1998; Rothbart and Bates, 1998). As such, they would be expected to have substantial implications for individual differences in social competence and adjustment in both childhood and adulthood.

Consistent with this perspective, numerous investigators have examined and discussed the role of individual differences in regulation and/or emotional reactivity in both social competence and externalizing behaviors such as aggression and delinquency (Caspi, 1998; Eisenberg and Fabes, 1992; Pulkkinen, 1982; Rothbart and Bates, 1998). This research usually has been guided by the assumption that children (or adults) who express inappropriate emotion and cannot regulate their expression of emotion or their emotion-related behavior generally are less adjusted and behave in a less competent manner in social interactions than do people who are less emotional and more regulated. More specific hypotheses and theorizing in work on this topic generally reflect variations and nuances in investigators' definitions and operationalizations of the constructs of emotionality and regulation.

Conceptions of emotionality and regulation

In our ongoing research, we have been trying to differentiate, conceptually and empirically, among various aspects of both emotionality and regulation and to examine their relations to social outcomes in childhood. Our basic assumption is that when people become emotionally overaroused in social contexts, their social behavior (and psychological functioning) is compromised. Thus, it is important to examine aspects of temperament or personality that contribute to the likelihood of this sort of emotional dysregulation.

Emotionality

In regard to emotionality, it is likely that both the frequency and intensity of individuals' typical emotional responding contribute to their social competence and adjustment. In temperament and personality research, the constructs of reactivity (Rothbart, 1989), emotional or affective intensity (Eisenberg and Fabes, 1992; Larsen and Diener, 1987), valence of emotion (positive or negative; Watson, Clark, and Tellegen, 1988), and type of negative emotion (e.g., sadness, fear; Goldsmith and Rothbart,

1991; Rothbart, Ahadi, and Hershey, 1994) have been discussed. However, in many studies, researchers have not made distinctions among various types of negative (or positive) emotions, and sometimes intensity of positive versus negative emotions has not been differentiated (e.g., Buss and Plomin, 1984; Eysenck, 1967; Larsen and Diener, 1987; Watson *et al.*, 1988). A notable exception is the distinction among different types of negative emotions such as anger/frustration, fear, and sadness in some temperament measures developed relatively recently (Goldsmith and Rothbart, 1991; Rothbart *et al.*, 1994). Sometimes intensity of emotion has been differentiated from frequency of occurrence of emotions (e.g., Larsen and Diener, 1987), but more often measures have tapped frequency and, to some degree, intensity of emotionality. Probably both frequency and intensity of emotion are important to consider in predicting quality of social functioning, as are valence of emotion and the type of negative emotion (e.g., externalizing versus internalizing).

Emotion regulation

Although definitions of emotion regulation vary, they tend to contain some common elements. Campos and colleagues hypothesized that emotion regulation can take place at three general loci: at the level of sensory receptors (input regulation), at central levels where information is processed and manipulated (central regulation), and at the level of response selection (labelled output regulation; Campos, Mumme, Kermoian, and Campos, 1994). Somewhat in the same vein, Thompson (1994) argued that, "Emotion regulation consists of the extrinsic and intrinsic processes responsible for monitoring, evaluating, and modifying emotional reactions, especially their intensive and temporal features, to accomplish one's goals" (pp. 27–8).

Definitions such as these are quite broad, in that they include monitoring, modulating, and changing internal mental and physiological states, as well as actions that have effects in the external world. Rather than include so many processes under the rubric of "emotion regulation," we find it heuristically useful to differentiate between the regulation of internal processes or physiological states and the regulation of behavioral reactions associated with, or resulting from, internal states. Thus, we define *emotion regulation* as the process of initiating, maintaining, modulating, or changing the occurrence, intensity, or duration of internal feeling states and emotion-related physiological processes, often in the service of accomplishing one's goals (Eisenberg, Fabes, Guthrie, and Reiser, 2000). We have argued that emotion regulation often is achieved through effortful management of attention (e.g., attention shifting and focusing, cognitive distraction or emotion-focused coping) and through cognitive processes that affect the interpretation of situations (e.g., positive cognitive restructuring), as well as through neurophysiological processes (see Rothbart, Posner, and Hershey, 1995; Thompson, Flood, and Lundquist, 1995). Much of emotion regulation occurs once an emotion is elicited. However, individuals can also regulate their emotion by choosing and shaping situations so that optimal emotional responding is likely and through attending to and interpreting events in ways that foster optimal emotional responding before it actually occurs (Gross, 1999). People who can regulate their emotional reactivity in social or nonsocial contexts through allocating attention appear to be emotionally modulated, less prone to negative emotion and better able to delay gratification (Bridges and Grolnick, 1995; Buss and Goldsmith, 1998; Derryberry and Rothbart, 1988; Mischel and Mischel, 1983; Rothbart, Ziaie, and O'Boyle, 1992; Rusting and Nolen-Hoeksema, 1998; also see Kochanska, Coy, Tjebkes, and Husarek, 1998). It is likely that the neural processes labeled executive functioning (Newman and Wallace, 1993) in the anterior attention network that are believed to be involved in control of attention contribute to emotion regulation (see Frick, 1998; Rothbart *et al.*, 1995).

Emotion-related behavioral regulation

While and once emotion is elicited, it often is expressed in facial or gestural reactions, or through overt behaviors such as verbal or physical aggression. We define emotion-related behavioral regulation as the process of initiating, maintaining, inhibiting, modulating, or changing the occurrence, form, and duration of behavioral concomitants of emotion. Thus, emotion-related behavioral regulation, which for brevity is labeled behavioral regulation, includes control of facial and gestural reactions and other overt behaviors that stem from, or are associated with, internal emotion-related psychological or physiological states and goals (Eisenberg *et al.*, 2000). Behavioral regulation is tapped by some temperament researchers who assess inhibition or activation control, that is, the abilities to voluntarily inhibit or activate behavior (e.g., Derryberry and Rothbart, 1988). In addition, clinical, developmental, and personality theorists frequently have discussed constructs such as self-regulation, constraint, or ego control, which involve the ability to modulate the behavioral expression of impulses and feelings (Block and Block, 1980; Kochanska, 1993; Kopp, 1982; Tellegen, 1985). Problem-focused or instrumental coping – that is, attempts to manage a stress-inducing and emotion-eliciting context through processes such as planning and active problem solving – could also be considered an aspect of emotion-related behavioral regulation, although it may prove useful to distinguish between the regulation of the expression, communication, or release of emotion and attempts to alter an emotion-eliciting context (Eisenberg and Fabes, 1992; Sandler, Tein, and West, 1994).

Emotion regulation and emotion-related behavioral regulation obviously are intimately related. Behavioral regulation is affected by internal emotion-related processes; moreover, the consequences of behavioral regulation frequently might influence the course of internal emotion-related processes and states, and modify subsequent emotion-related cognitive or physiological processes. Moreover, it is likely that some processes can serve as a mechanism for both emotional regulation or behavioral regulation. For example, effortful inhibition of behavior obviously is part of emotion-related behavioral regulation, but it also could be used to decrease exposure to a stimulus (e.g., a child may cease approaching a novel and somewhat scary toy) and, thereby, can be used in the service of reducing emotional arousal. Nonetheless, emotion regulation and emotion-related regulation refer to somewhat different processes, at least at a conceptual level.

Prediction of outcomes from emotionality and regulation

Our view is that individual differences in emotionality and regulation jointly contribute to the prediction of numerous aspects of social functioning, including socially appropriate behavior, popularity with peers, adjustment, shyness, sympathy and prosocial behavior. In some cases the contributions of emotionality and regulation are additive; in other cases, one might predict interactive or moderating effects.

A key distinction in thinking about the relation of regulation to developmental outcomes may be between voluntary or effortful regulation and involuntary (or less voluntary) control. Well-adjusted, regulated children would be expected to be relatively high in the ability to voluntarily control their attention and behavior as needed to respond in an adaptive manner. Mary Rothbart has defined *effortful* control as "the ability to inhibit a dominant response to perform a subdominant response" (Rothbart and Bates, 1998, p. 137). Effortful control involves both attentional regulation (e.g., the ability to voluntarily focus attention as needed), and behavioral regulation, or the ability to inhibit or activate behavior as appropriate. In contrast to effortful types of regulation, there are aspects of control, or the lack thereof, that often seem to be involuntary or so automatic that they are not usually under voluntary control. These might include some types of impulsivity or, at the other extreme, very low impulsivity as in highly inhibited children who appear overcontrolled due to their timidity and lack of flexibility when dealing with novel objects, situations, and people.

Eisenberg, Fabes, and colleagues have developed a preliminary heuristic model of the ways in which emotion and regulation jointly predict social competence and adjustment (Eisenberg and Fabes, 1992; Eisenberg *et al.*, 2000). In this model, they outlined expected relations of social functioning with degree of negative emotionality and three styles of regulation – highly inhibited, undercontrolled, and optimally regulated. Undercontrolled individuals are hypothesized to be low in effortful emotional and behavioral regulation, including inhibitory, attentional, and activational control, high in impulsivity, and low in adaptive problem-focused coping behavior. Optimally regulated individuals are high in various modes of adaptive, effortful regulation, including attentional control, inhibitory control, and activation control (the ability to get oneself to do things that one might not be motivated to do, e.g., do a difficult task), but not overcontrolled due to involuntary mechanisms. *Highly inhibited* individuals are expected to be high in involuntary behavioral inhibition (often labeled behavioral inhibition in the temperament literature, e.g., inhibition to novelty, rigidity of behavior), low to average in effortful inhibitory control, low in activation control, low to moderate in attentional regulation (lower in attention shifting than attention focusing), and low in constructive instrumental or problem-focused strategies. Individuals high in involuntary behavioral inhibition tend to be constrained in their behavior; consequently, they may be viewed as behaviorally regulated by others, even if their inhibition is not voluntary. In our view, highly inhibited individuals are overcontrolled behaviorally, but their inhibition usually is involuntary (and may be tapped by very low scores on impulsivity, more so than high scores on effortful inhibitory control).

In general, we expect optimally regulated individuals, regardless of their level of negative emotionality, to exhibit constructive behavior, social competence, and low levels of problems with adjustment. In contrast, undercontrolled people, who are low in a variety of modes of regulation, are expected to be prone to externalizing problems and to be viewed as low in social competence. Undercontrolled people who are *also* high in intensity and frequency of negative emotion are predicted to be especially out of control and predisposed to reactive, that is, emotion-based, aggression, as well as other externalizing behaviors driven by unregulated emotion. Undercontrolled individuals who are low in negative emotionality also would be expected to be low to moderate in social competence, but especially inclined to calculated or covert externalizing problems (e.g., theft) that are less emotionally driven. Highly inhibited individuals who also are predisposed to intense and frequent negative emotions are expected to be susceptible to internalizing problems such as fearfulness, anxiety, depression, and social withdrawal (see Weinberger and Schwartz, 1990). In contrast, those individuals low in negative emotionality but highly inhibited are hypothesized to be low to average in social competence, to engage in some social withdrawal due to a nonfearful tendency to be alone (rather than social anxiety; Eisenberg, Fabes, and Murphy, 1995), and to exhibit an average level of internalizing emotional reactions. However, because Chinese children who are shy, have sensitive feelings, and are cautious and inhibited in their behavior they are viewed as socially competent and as leaders by teachers and are liked by their peers (Chen, Rubin, and Li, 1995a,b; Chen, Rubin, and Sun, 1992), we recognize that cultural factors may influence the social functioning of highly inhibited children.

The empirical work supporting these predictions is reviewed in some detail elsewhere (Eisenberg *et al.*, 2000). However, it is important to note that other researchers have identified groups of children who appear to fall into the underregulated, highly inhibited, and optimally inhibited groupings discussed above. For example, Hart, Hofmann, Edelstein, and Keller (1997) and Robins, John, Caspi, Moffitt, and Stouthamer-Loeber (1996), in studies of Icelandic school children and European-American and African-American adolescent boys, respectively, identified three groups of children based on adults' ratings: well adjusted, undercontrolled, and overcontrolled. Newman, Caspi, Moffitt, and Silva (1997) identified similar groups of New Zealand three-year-olds based on their behavior during a testing session (although they identified five groups). The well-adjusted children generally were resilient, self-assured, and not emotionally labile. In two studies (Hart *et al.*, 1997; Newman, Schmitt, and Voss, 1997), they also were attentionally and/or behaviorally regulated and not overcontrolled or undercontrolled. (In Robins *et al.*'s sample, emotionality and regulation were less evident in the characteristics of these children). The adjusted children continued to do well over time (Hart *et al.*, 1997; Newman *et al.*, 1997). The undercontrolled individuals were low in attentional and behavioral regulation, active, and sometimes irritable and impulsive. They were prone to externalizing problem behaviors in later adolescence or adulthood or concurrently (Hart *et al.*, 1997; Newman *et al.*, 1997; Robins *et al.*, 1996). Newman *et al.*'s undercontrolled three-year-olds had attention problems and Hart *et al.* found that undercontrolled children developed concentration problems later in adolescence (it was not clear if they had attentional problems in elementary school; Hart *et al.*, 1997). The highly inhibited children were shy, fearful, and socially constrained in childhood (Newman *et al.*, 1997). Overcontrolled children were prone to internalizing problems (Robins *et al.*, 1996), were more likely to be socially withdrawn as adolescents (Hart *et al.*, 1997), and exhibited relatively few social strengths in early adulthood (Newman *et al.*, 1997).

The items used to classify children into personality groups in these studies included ratings of a wide variety of social behaviors and both regulation and emotionality. Thus, the investigators did not examine individual differences in regulation and emotionality *separate* from one another, their social consequences, or other personality characteristics. Nonetheless, the pattern of findings in these studies is consistent with the notion that children have different characteristic styles of regulation that are associated with long-term adjustment and social competence.

In addition, there is a growing body of work demonstrating linear relations between relatively high regulation and social competence or low externalizing problems, even when information on regulation and outcome variables has not been obtained from the same source and when behavioral measures of regulation were obtained (e.g., persistence on a task or delay of gratification; Block and Block, 1980; Colder and Chassin, 1997; Eisenberg *et al.*, 1993; Eisenberg *et al.*, 1996; Krueger, Caspi, Moffitt, White, and Stouthamer-Loeber, 1996; Kyrios and Prior, 1990; Lynam, 1997; Oosterlaan and Sergeant, 1996; Rothbart *et al.*, 1994). Similarly, attentional regulation has been associated with high social competence (Eisenberg *et al.*, 1993; Eisenberg, Guthrie *et al.*, 1997) and low problem behavior (Eisenberg, Fabes, Nyman, Bernzweig, and Pinuelas, 1994; Eisenberg, Guthrie, *et al.*, in press), as has a composite of effortful behavioral and attentional regulation (Eisenberg *et al.*, 1995; Rothbart *et al.*, 1994). Problems in attentional regulation, as tapped by measures of executive cognitive functioning, have been linked to both conduct disorders (Moffitt, 1993) and psychopathy (O'Brien and Frick, 1996; Patterson and Newman, 1993). Moreover, behavioral underregulation has been positively related to externalizing problems in clinic referred children, whereas ego overcontrol (rigid control and high inhibition) and low resiliency have been associated with internalizing problems (Huey and Weisz, 1997). Externalizing problems have been related to children's impulsivity and low attentional regulation even when items that were confounded across measures were removed from the questionnaires used to assess externalizing problems and temperamental emotionality and regulation (Lengua, West, and Sandler, 1998).

In regard to emotionality, high intensity and/or frequency of negative emotionality have been associated with low social competence (Eisenberg *et al.*, 1993, 1994; Eisenberg, Fabes, *et al.*, 1997), externalizing problem behavior (e.g., Eisenberg, Fabes, Guthrie, *et al.*, 1996; Rothbart *et al.*, 1994; Stice and Gonzales, 1998), and adolescent substance abuse/use

(Chassin, Pillow, Curran, Molina, and Barrera, 1993; also see Caspi, Moffitt, Newman, and Silva, 1996), although relations between childhood negative emotion and adults' substance use can be complex (see Pulkkinen and Pitkänen, 1994). Temperamental/personality negative emotionality also has been linked to shyness (Asendorpf, 1987; Eisenberg, Shepard, *et al.*, 1998; Eisenberg *et al.*, 1995; Leary, 1986) and internalizing problems (Caspi, Henry, McGee, Moffitt, and Silva, 1995; Teglasi and MacMahon, 1990). Although measures of internalizing and negative emotionality often contain similar items (Sanson, Prior, and Kyrios, 1990), there is initial evidence that the aforementioned relations are not due primarily to confounding of items across assessment instruments (Lengua *et al.*, 1998).

In our laboratory, we have been particularly interested in the additive and multiplicative effects of emotionality and regulation on social competence and problem behaviors. Rothbart and Bates (1998) noted the lack of research on the prediction of adjustment from temperament X temperament interactions, but suggested that such interactions were likely to prove important. Consistent with their suggestion, investigators have found that composite scores including measures of both emotionality and regulation predict quality of social behavior over time. For example, Caspi *et al.* (1995) found that a composite labeled "Lack of Control," including irritability, restlessness, short attention span, and negativism, predicted conduct disorders and antisocial behavior at ages 13 and 15, and low competence (social and otherwise) at 15. Individuals classified as undercontrolled at age three years were also, at age 18, relatively undercontrolled and aggressive (Caspi and Silva, 1995). Similarly, Pulkkinen and Hämäläinen's (1995) measure of weak self-control at age 14, which contained a combination of impulsivity, attentional regulation, and moodiness (is impulsive, lacks concentration, changes mood), predicted criminal offenses at 20 years of age and degree of criminal behavior at age 32. Although these findings are of great interest, it is impossible to determine if the predictive power of the composite measures was due to either emotionality or regulation (and not both), to additive effects of both emotionality and regulation, or to nonlinear, multiplicative effects of regulation and emotionality (i.e., to the interaction of regulation and emotionality).

In research on alcohol and substance use, there is initial evidence of interaction effects. Colder and Chassin (1997) found that impulsive adolescents who also were prone to low levels of positive affectivity were higher in alcohol use and impairment. However, negative emotionality, albeit positively related to alcohol use, did not interact with impulsivity to predicting alcohol use. Impulsivity did moderate the relation of depression to alcohol use, such that depressed, impulsive adolescents drank more heavily than depressed, nonimpulsive adolescents or nondepressed adolescents (Hussong and Chassin, 1994).

In our laboratory, we have found interactions between regulation (behavioral or both attentional and behavioral) and negative emotionality (intensity and/or frequency) when predicting both social competence (Eisenberg, Fabes *et al.*, 1995, 1997) and externalizing problem behavior (Eisenberg *et al.*, 1996). Most of the initial findings were for concurrent data and indicated that regulation is especially important for predicting high social competence or low levels of externalizing behavior when children are prone to experience intense and/or frequent negative emotions. Regulation is a poorer predictor of outcomes for children who are not prone to negative emotions; well regulated children are relatively socially competent and low in externalizing problems whether or not they are prone to negative emotionality.

Finally, there are theoretical reasons to expect some quadratic relations between regulation and children's social competence and externalizing behavior. Up to a point, behavioral regulation is likely to enhance social competence in a linear fashion. However, people characterized by overcontrol (often due to very high involuntary behavioral inhibition) probably are not as socially skilled as individuals who are moderately high in involuntary control (although they may not be as low in social functioning as underregulated individuals).

Few researchers have examined the quadratic effects of measures of emotionality/regulation on socially relevant outcomes. Shedler and Block (1990) found a linear, but not quadratic, relation between ego control (a measure of behavioral regulation) and marijuana use, with use increasing with undercontrol. Eisenberg, Fabes, Guthrie *et al.* (1996) obtained some quadratic relations between mothers' and fathers' reports of ego control and parental reports of boys' problem behavior. In general, low ego control (undercontrol) was positively associated with high problem behavior; moderate and high levels of ego control predicted lower levels of externalizing problem behavior and did not differ much from one another (although overcontrol was associated with somewhat less problem behavior). With the same sample, Eisenberg, Guthrie *et al.* (1997) found a quadratic (as well as linear) relation between adults' reports of children's behavioral regulation or control (ego control) and ego resiliency. Teacher-reported resiliency was highest at moderate levels of control, in comparison to low or high levels. Parents' reports of resiliency were lowest for children low in control and higher and similar for children moderate or high in control. Thus, the relation between regulation and social behavior probably is not always linear.

In summary, there is a growing body of work concerning the role of individual differences in emotionality and regulation in quality of social functioning. However, much of this work has merely established concurrent correlations between measures of emotionality or regulation and social functioning and some of the research has involved measures obtained from a single reporter. Moreover, constructs of emotionality and regulation sometimes have not clearly differentiated from other constructs (e.g., social competence) or from one another. Thus, research focused on different kinds of emotionality and regulation, and their prediction of quality of social functioning over time, is scarce and needed. As part of this effort, it seems worthwhile to examine multiplicative relations between aspects of emotionality and regulation when predicting outcomes at a later point in time. Especially sparse are studies in which longitudinal effects are examined while controlling for initial levels of outcome variables. In the next section of this chapter, we report some new findings bearing on this issue.

Recent empirical findings

In this chapter, we emphasize findings from two recent studies pertaining to the prediction of socially competent behavior from individual differences in emotionality and regulation, and briefly mention a few other relevant findings.

Prediction of young children's sociometric status over time

In a study of four- to six-year-olds, change in sociometric status was predicted from teacher- or peer-reported negative emotionality and regulation/coping across two semesters of school (Time 1(T1) and Time 2(T2); Maszk, Eisenberg, and Guthrie, 1999). The focus was on concurrent and especially longitudinal prediction. Due to the relatively small sample size, there was little power for testing interaction effects.

Participants were 74 middle-class children (82 percent Euro-American) enrolled in preschool, daycare, or kindergarten classes and their teachers. Teachers and aides completed measures of children's coping, intensity of emotionality (mostly negative), regulation, and aggression at T1 and T2 near the end of each semester. The time between the T1 and T2 data collection was about five months.

The measure of regulation was a subset of items from Kendall and Wilcox's self-regulation scale (1979); items tap primarily behavioral regulation. Coping was assessed with a measure in which teachers reported how children would respond in a sequence of scenarios about everyday social conflicts (similar to Eisenberg *et al.*, 1993). Two analytically derived composite scores were used in the analyses: (a) *constructive coping*, including cognitive restructuring, low aggressive coping, and instrumental coping, and (b) *emotional venting coping*, including venting of emotion to get attention and seeking emotional support. Emotional intensity was assessed with a measure that taps intensity of negative emotions and general emotional intensity (i.e., intensity of emotion, with valence unspecified; Eisenberg *et al.*, 1996). Aggression was assessed with teachers' reports of children's proactive ("this child coerces other children into doing things for him or her") and reactive ("when this child has been teased or threatened, he or she gets angry easily and strikes back") aggression, as well as peers' reports of fighting.

Children's sociometric status was assessed in individual sessions near the end of both semesters. Each child sorted photographs of peers in his or her classroom into one of three piles according to the degree to which the child liked to play with each peer. Pictures of smiling, neutral, and frowning faces were used to designate each pile. Peer nominations for children who fit the descriptions of "cries the most," as well as "fights the most" and "gets angry the most," also were obtained at these times (Price and Dodge, 1989).

Sociometric status was significantly related across time, $r(67) = .46$, $p < .001$, as were teachers' or peers' ratings of emotionality, regulation, coping, and aggression. Peer social status at T2 was positively correlated with teachers' ratings of regulation and constructive coping from both semesters, and negatively related to children's emotional intensity, emotional coping (only at T2), aggression (albeit $p < .07$ at T2), and peer-nominated anger, crying, and fighting (albeit $p < .08$ for fighting at T2). There were no sex differences in the correlations; partialing age or sex had little effect on the correlations.

Regression analyses were computed to determine whether measures of emotionality and regulation at T1 and T2 predicted a child's sociometric status at T2 beyond prediction based on the child's social status at T1. In two separate regressions, average peer social status at T1 was entered in the first step, and the significant emotionality/regulation predictors for either T1 or T2 were entered on the second step. Measures of aggression and fighting were not included in this analysis because they were considered measures of social behavior, not regulation or emotionality.

After entering T1 peer social status ratings, T1 teachers' reports of regulation, emotional intensity, and constructive coping, and peer nominations for angry and crying as a group accounted for an additional 19 percent of the variance in T2 social status. When each T1 predictor was entered by itself on the second step (without controlling for the other predictors) after entering T1 social status, emotional intensity, regulation, constructive coping, peer-nominated anger and crying were all at least marginally significant predictors of T2 social status.

For the regression analysis including T2 predictors, measures of emotionality and regulation accounted for 16 percent additional variance in T2 social status. When predictors were entered individually on step 2 rather than as a group in separate regressions, emotional intensity, regulation, constructive coping, and peer nominated anger and crying all were at least marginally significant predictors of T2 social status. Thus, peers' and teachers' ratings of children's emotionality/regulation predicted social status at T2 above and beyond the variance accounted for by T1 social status.

In another set of regressions, we examined whether T1 measures of emotionality and regulation (including coping) predicted T2 social status when the effects of analogous T2 measures of regulation/emotionality were controlled. These analyses tested whether T1 emotionality/ regulation predicted T2 social status solely by virtue of its correlation with emotionality/regulation at T2 or whether T1 emotionality/regulation provided some prediction of T2 social status independent of any effect mediated through T2 emotionality/ regulation. Separate regressions were computed for each of the T1 predictors. The T2 value of a given predictor was entered on the first step of the equation predicting T2 social status; the T1 value of the predictor was entered on the next step.

T1 emotional intensity and constructive coping did not predict T2 social status once the effect of the analogous measure at T2 was controlled. However, T1 regulation and peer nominations of both anger and crying were at least marginally significant predictors of T2 social status on step 2 when controlling on step 1 for T2 values of the same variable. Thus, these three variables provided some prediction of T2 social status that was not mediated through consistency in the given measure over time.

In additional regression analyses, we assessed the prediction of T2 emotionality and regulation from T1 social status after controlling for T1 emotionality/regulation. These analyses were computed to test the plausibility of T1 social status producing change in emotionality/regulation at a later time (in contrast to the reverse direction of causality). There was no evidence of early social status predicting later emotionality/regulation after earlier regulation and emotionality were taken into account with the exception of peer-rated anger. Finally, we examined whether aggression mediated the relation of emotionality/regulation to later social status; it did not.

In summary, in this study, social status at T2 was positively related to teacher-reported regulation and constructive coping and negatively related to emotional intensity, as well as peer-reported anger and crying. Measures of regulation and emotionality accounted for additional variance in T2 social status after controlling for initial social preference. In contrast, initial (T1) social status infrequently predicted subsequent regulation and emotionality after controlling for scores on initial emotionality/regulation. Thus, emotionality/regulation predicted future social status whereas social status did not appear to account for changes in emotionality and regulation over time. The data, albeit correlational, were consistent with the conclusion that changes in children's sociometric status were due to the effects of individual differences in emotionality and regulation. Given children with low sociometric status are at risk for externalizing behaviors, delinquency, internalizing behavior, and dropping out of school (Bierman and Wargo, 1995; Boivin, Hymel, and Bukowski, 1995; Coie, Terry, Lenox, Lochman, and Hyman, 1995; Ollendick, Weist, Borden, and Greene, 1992; see Rubin, Bukowski, and Parker, 1998), any effects of individual differences in emotionality and regulation on sociometric status may have significant long-term implications for children.

Additive and multiplicative effects: longitudinal prediction of social competence

We also have examined the longitudinal relations of dispositional regulation and emotionality to social competence with a larger sample of unselected school children (Eisenberg, Fabes, Guthrie et al., 1996: see Eisenberg et al., 2000). The sample of approximately 80 percent Euro-American children varied considerably in socioeconomic status. At the initial assessment of 199 children in kindergarten to third grade, teachers and peers reported on children's peer status and social skills or, for peers, prosocial behavior. The primary caregiving parent (usually mothers) and teachers also provided information on children's attentional regulation (shifting and focusing), ego control (i.e., reflecting, in part, behavioral regulation; see Block and Block, 1980), and ego resiliency (resourceful adaptation to changing circumstances and contingencies, flexible use of the available repertoire of coping strategies, the ability to rebound from stress; see Block and Block, 1980). In addition, children played a puzzle box game in which their persistence rather than cheating while doing a puzzle for a prize was assessed; this measure was viewed as an index of behavioral regulation (see Eisenberg, Guthrie et al., 1997).

Two years later, most of the same measures were readministered, although we could not get peer reports of social functioning. We used structural equation modeling procedures, and included measures of regulation, emotionality, and social competence from both time periods in the model. We examined several issues: (a) whether attentional and behavioral regulation were different and separate latent constructs, (b) if the relations among regulation, emotionality, and social competence were the same at both ages, (c) if the effects of regulation on social competence were mediated by children's resiliency, (d) if the relations of regulation to resiliency were moderated by individual differences in negative emotionality, and (e) if the effects on T2 social competence came through regulation/emotionality or needed to move from T1 to T2 through paths directly between T1 and T2 social competence. Emotional regulation was operationalized as parents' (usually mothers') and teachers' reports of attention shifting and attention focusing. Behavioral regulation was measured with parents' and teachers' reports of ego control (Block and Block, 1980) and children's persistence on a difficult task toward a prize when they could cheat to finish it. We expected regulation to predict resiliency, which in turn was expected to predict social functioning – in this case, popularity with peers and socially appropriate/prosocial behavior as reported by peers and teachers. However, we expected these relations to be stronger for children high in negative emotionality because regulation is more important for those children (see Eisenberg, Guthrie *et al.*, 1997, for the T1 structural equation model, which is highly similar to the combined T1/T2 model presented below).

The best fitting model (based on $n = 142$ due to missing data) included separate latent constructs for attentional regulation and behavioral regulation at both times, each of which provided unique prediction of social competence (see Figure 2.1). At T1 and T2, the effects of attentional (i.e., emotional) control on social status and socially appropriate behavior were mediated by resiliency. In addition, at T1 only, the path from attentional control to resiliency, albeit significant for children high and low in negative emotionality, was higher for children prone to negative emotion (this path did not differ in significance for children high versus low in negative emotionality at T2). Thus, children who could regulate their attention appeared to be resilient in stressful contexts and, perhaps as a consequence, were better liked by peers and viewed as socially appropriate or prosocial by teachers and peers. However, level of attentional control was particularly important for predicting social functioning for children prone to negative emotion at T1.

At both T1 and T2, the effects of behavioral regulation on social functioning were not mediated by resiliency. Rather, individual differences in behavioral regulation were directly related to socially appropriate behavior (but not peer status). Moreover, this direct effect held only for children high in dispositional negative emotionality. Behavioral regulation

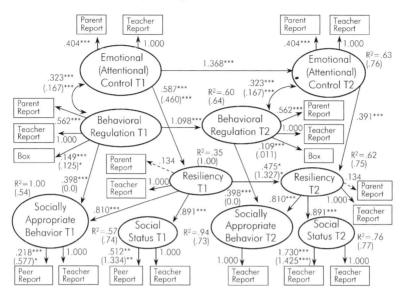

Figure 2.1 Prediction of social status and socially appropriate behavior from dispositional regulation and emotionality: moderating and mediating effects.

Note: Dotted lines represent nonsignificant paths at $p > .05$ both for children high and low in negative emotionality. Unstandardized coefficients for children high in negative emotionality are not in parentheses; unstandardized coefficients for children low in negative emotionality are in parentheses. If one coefficient is presented, this parameter was constrained to be equal across children high and low in negative emotionality. Values on curved lines with double-headed arrows are unstandardized covariances between the two connected constructs.

Adapted from Eisenberg *et al.* (2000) in *Journal of Personality and Social Psychology*, 78, p. 152. American Psychological Association.

was particularly important for children likely to experience negative emotions because they have more frequent and intense emotions to manage emotions that can undermine their social behavior.

The paths from behavior regulation to socially appropriate behavior were equivalent in strength at T1 and T2, as were the paths from resiliency to indexes of social competence. The lagged effects (i.e., the paths across time for the same variable) were significant for attentional control, behavioral regulation, and resiliency for both high and low negative emotionality children. However, adding paths from T1 to T2 social competence did not improve the fit of the model, which suggests that dispositional emotionality and regulation were sufficient for the prediction of T2 social competence without including the direct effect of earlier level of social competence (Eisenberg *et al.*, 2000).

The quadratic relations between measures of behavioral regulation and resiliency that were found at T1 and discussed previously were not significant at T2. They may have disappeared because some of the most unregulated children were lost from the sample at T2, so the sample was less diverse in important ways than at T1.

In summary, both attentional regulation and behavioral regulation predicted aspects of social competence, although the patterns of their relations differed somewhat. In addition, children's resiliency mediated the effects of their attentional regulation on social competence and negative emotionality moderated some of the relations such that regulation was a better predictor of social competence for children prone to negative emotions. Thus, we have documented the importance of examining moderational and mediational relations and of considering various levels or types of regulation and emotional reactions when assessing relations of emotionality and regulation to socially competent behavior over time.

Other findings

In other recent work we have additional evidence of multiplicative effects. For example, in the same sample just discussed (Eisenberg, Guthrie *et al.*, 2000), we have found that individual differences in regulation and negative emotionality also predict externalizing problems at two different ages, two years apart. Additive effects were obtained at both ages (i.e., both attentional control and behavioral regulation predicted problem behaviors), even at T2 when the effects of T1 problem behavior were taken into account. In addition, the relation of attentional regulation (but not behavioral control) to externalizing problem behaviors was moderated, such that regulation was a better predictor of low problem behavior for children high in negative emotionality. Moderational effects provided better prediction than solely linear effects and the pattern of relations was obtained at T2 even when children's level of externalizing behavior at T1 was taken into account.

In another longitudinal study, emotionality and regulation were used to predict children's shyness, an aspect of internalizing behavior (Eisenberg, Shepard *et al.*, 1998). We obtained parents' and teachers' reports of children's shyness at ages 6–8, 8–10, and 10–12. Data on teacher- and parent-reported regulation, emotionality, and coping were available at the same ages and at age 4–6. In general, adult- reported shyness appeared to be positively related to internalizing negative emotion, primarily within a context (at home or at school, albeit sometimes over time). Shyness was not related to externalizing emotionality (e.g., anger), but was associated with low positive emotionality. Teachers viewed shy children as low in attentional control (attention shifting and focusing); if anything, parents tended to view their shy children as somewhat high in attention focusing. In general, parent-rated shyness (but not teacher-rated shyness) was associated with adults' reports of high behavioral regulation/low impulsivity (combined).

We also expected children low in attentional control but prone to intense and frequent internalizing emotions to be especially high on rated shyness. Such children would be likely to experience negative emotions and would have difficulty regulating them because they were not skilled at controlling their attention. This interaction effect was obtained for parental reports of children's attentional shifting and internalizing negative emotion (e.g., fear, sadness, and physiological reactivity) at age 4–6 when predicting parent- and teacher-reported shyness at age 6–8 and parent-reported shyness at age 8–10. Such interactions were not found for teachers or at age 10–12, perhaps because our measure of internalizing emotion at later ages was briefer and did not contain many items related to fear or physiological reactivity. The sample size was relatively small in this study, so interaction effects had to be fairly strong to be detected. These findings, albeit obtained at only some time periods and for maternal reports of regulation/emotionality, provide initial evidence of importance of the multiplicative effects of temperament/personality when predicting internalizing problems. Moreover, the results demonstrate the importance of differentiating between internalizing and externalizing types of emotions.

Finally, in a new sample that we are following longitudinally, we are finding that different negative emotions relate differently to externalizing behavior and an aspect of internalizing behavior (social withdrawal). Social withdrawal was used as the index of internalizing behavior problems to avoid the confounding of items on the measures of emotionality and the depression/anxiety subscale of internalizing behavior on the Child Behavior Checklist (Achenbach, 1991; Achenbach and Edelbrock, 1986). For example, we found that sadness is somewhat more characteristic of socially withdrawn children whereas proneness to anger characterizes children prone to externalizing problems (or the combination of internalizing and externalizing problems). These data are consistent with Rothbart and Bates' (1998) assertion that specific temperament dimensions relate in a differentiated way to internalizing and externalizing problems, with early inhibition more closely related to later internalizing problems and early unmanageability linked to later externalizing problems. It is likely that different negative emotions relate differently to social competence, with anger predicting low social competence (Eisenberg, Fabes *et al.*, 1999) and fear predicting social inhibition in some social contexts (Kagan, 1997; Kagan, Snidman, and Arcus, 1998). The role of different negative emotions, alone and in combination with various modes of regulation, in predicting different components of social competence and adjustment is a topic that is in the rudimentary stages of investigation.

Summary

It is clear that temperamental emotionality and regulation, which un-doubtedly are components of personality, contribute to children's social competence with peers, as well as their behavioral problems. Recent longitudinal work is consistent with the conclusion that individual differences in emotionality and regulation predict important outcomes in later childhood, adolescence, and adulthood. Moreover, it appears that emotionality and regulation, albeit correlated, provide some unique prediction of social competence and problem behavior, and sometimes interact in predicting quality of children's social functioning. Longitudinal work using repeated measures of central constructs over time and structural equation modeling procedures will be useful for testing hypotheses about causality over substantial periods of time. This is the best way, short of experimental studies, for determining whether temperamental or personality differences in children's emotionality and regulation actually engender differences in their social competence and adjustment later in life.

ACKNOWLEDGMENT

This research was supported by grants (1 R01 HH55052 and R01 MH60838) and a Research Scientist Award (K05 M801321) from the National Institute of Mental Health.

REFERENCES

Achenbach, T. M. (1991). *Manual for the Child Behavior Checklist/4-18 and 1991 Profile*. Burlington, VT: University of Vermont Department of Psychiatry.
Achenbach, T. M., and Edelbrock, C. (1986). Manual for the Teacher's Report Form. Burlington, VT: University of Vermont.
Asendorpf, J. B. (1987). Videotape reconstruction of emotions and cognitions related to shyness. *Journal of Personality and Social Psychology*, 53, 542–9.
Bierman, K. L., and Wargo, J. B. (1995). Predicting the longitudinal course associated with aggressive-rejected, aggressive (nonrejected), and rejected (nonaggressive) status. *Development and Psychopathology*, 7, 669–82.

Block, J. H., and Block, J. (1980). The role of ego-control and ego-resiliency in the organization of behavior. In W. Andrew Collins (ed.), *Development of cognition, affect, and social relations. The Minnesota Symposia on Child Psychology.* Hillsdale, NJ: Erlbaum 13, 39–101.

Boivin, M., Hymel, S., and Bukowski, W. M. (1995). The roles of social withdrawal, peer rejection, and victimization by peers in predicting loneliness and pressed mood in children. *Development and Psychopathology,* 7, 765–85.

Bridges, L. J., and Grolnick, W. S. (1995). The development of emotional self-regulation in infancy and early childhood. In N. Eisenberg (ed.), *Review of Personality and Psychology.* Newbury Park: Sage.

Buss, A. H., and Plomin, R. (1984). *Temperament: early developing personality traits.* Hillsdale, NJ: Erlbaum.

Buss, K. A., and Goldsmith, H. H. (1998). Fear and anger regulation in infancy: effects on the temporal dynamics of affective expression. *Child Development,* 69, 359–74.

Campos, J. J., Mumme, D. L., Kermoian, R., and Campos, R. G. (1994). A functionalist perspective on the nature of emotion. In N. A. Fox (ed.), *The developmental of emotion regulation: biological and behavioral considerations. Monographs of the Society for Research in Child Development,* 59 (Serial No. 240, 284–303).

Caspi, A. (1998). Personality development across the life course. In W. Damon (Series Editor) and N. Eisenberg (Volume Editor.), *Social, emotional and personality development. Handbook of child psychology.* New York: Wiley, 3, 311–88

Caspi, A., Henry, B., McGee, R. O., Moffitt, T. E., and Silva, P. A. (1995). Temperamental origins of child and adolescent behavior problems: from age 3 to age 15. *Child Development,* 66, 55–68.

Caspi, A., Moffitt, T. E., Newman, D. L., and Silva, P. A. (1996). Behavioral observations at age 3 years predict adult psychiatric disorders. *Archives of General Psychiatry,* 53, 1033–39.

Caspi, A., and Silva, P. A. (1995). Temperamental qualities at age three predict personality traits in young adulthood: longitudinal evidence from a birth cohort. *Child Development,* 66, 486–98.

Chassin, L., Pillow, D. R., Curran, P. J., Molina, B. S. G., and Barrera, M. J. (1993). Relation of parental alcoholism to early adolescent substance use: a test of three mediating mechanisms. *Journal of Abnormal Psychology,* 102, 3–19.

Chen, X., Rubin, K. H., and Li, B. (1995a). Social and school adjustment of shy and aggressive children in China. *Development and Psychopathology,* 7, 337–49.

Chen, X., Rubin, K. H., and Li, B. (1995b). Social functioning and adjustment in Chinese children: a longitudinal study. *Developmental Psychology,* 31, 531–9.

Chen, X., Rubin, K. H., and Sun, Y. (1992). Social reputation and peer relationships in Chinese and Canadian children: a cross-cultural study. *Child Development,* 63, 1336–43.

Coie, J., Terry, R., Lenox, K., Lochman, J., and Hyman, C. (1995). Childhood peer rejection and aggression as predictors of stable patterns of adolescent disorder. *Development and Psychopathology,* 7, 697–713.

Colder, C. R., and Chassin, L. (1997). Affectivity and impulsivity: temperament risk for adolescent alcohol involvement. *Psychology of Addictive Behaviors*, 11, 83–97.

Derryberry, D., and Rothbart, M. K. (1988). Arousal, affect, and attention as components of temperament. *Journal of Personality and Social Psychology*, 55, 958–66.

Eisenberg, N., and Fabes, R. A. (1992). Emotion, regulation, and the development of social competence. In M. S. Clark (ed.), *Review of personality and social psychology; Emotion and social behavior*. Newbury Park, CA: Sage, 14, 119–50.

Eisenberg, N., Fabes, R. A., Bernzweig, J., Karbon, M., Poulin, R., and Hanish, L. (1993). The relations of emotionality and regulation to preschoolers' social skills and sociometric status. *Child Development*, 64, 1418–38.

Eisenberg, N., Fabes, R. A., Guthrie, I. K., Murphy, B. C., Maszk, P., Holmgren, R., and Suh, K. (1996). The relations of regulation and emotionality to problem behavior in elementary school children. *Development and Psychopathology*, 8, 141–62.

Eisenberg, N., Fabes, R. A., Guthrie, I. K., and Reiser, M. (2000). Dispositional emotionality and regulation: their role in predicting quality of social functioning. *Journal of Personality and Social Psychology*, 78, 136–57.

Eisenberg, N., Fabes, R. A., and Murphy, B. (1995). The relations of shyness and low sociability to regulation and emotionality. *Journal of Personality and Social Psychology*, 68, 505–17.

Eisenberg, N., Fabes, R. A., Murphy, B. C., Shepard, S., Guthrie, I. K., Mazsk, P., Poulin, R., and Jones, S. (1999). Prediction of elementary school children's socially appropriate and problem behavior from anger reactions at age 4 to 6. *Journal of Applied Developmental Psychology*, 20, 119–42.

Eisenberg, N., Fabes, R. A., Murphy, M., Maszk, P., Smith, M., and Karbon, M. (1995). The role of emotionality and regulation in children's social functioning: a longitudinal study. *Child Development*, 66, 1360–84.

Eisenberg, N., Fabes, R. A., Nyman, M., Bernzweig, J., and Pinuelas, A. (1994). The relations of emotionality and regulation to children's anger-related reactions. *Child Development*, 65, 109–28.

Eisenberg, N., Fabes, R. A., Shepard, S. A., Murphy, B. C., Guthrie, I. K., Jones, S., Friedman, J., Poulin, R., and Maszk, P. (1997). Contemporaneous and longitudinal prediction of children's social functioning from regulation and emotionality. *Child Development*, 68, 642–64.

Eisenberg, N., Guthrie, I. K., Fabes, R. A., Reiser, M., Murphy, B. C., Holmgren, R., Maszk, P., and Losoya, S. (1997). The relations of regulation and emotionality to resiliency and competent social functioning in elementary school children. *Child Development*, 68, 367–83.

Eisenberg, N., Guthrie, I. K., Fabes, R. A., Shepard, S., Losoya, S., Murphy, B., Jones, S., Poulin, R., and Reiser, M. (2000). Prediction of elementary school children's externalizing problem behaviors from attentional and behavioral regulation and negative emotionality. *Child Development*, 71, 1367–82.

Eisenberg, N., Shepard, S. A., Fabes, R. A., Murphy, B. C., and Guthrie, I. K. (1998). Shyness and children's emotionality, regulation, and coping:

contemporaneous, longitudinal, and across context relations. *Child Development*, 69, 767–90.

Eysenck, H. J. (1967). *The biological basis of personality*. Springfield, IL: Charles C. Thomas.

Frick, P. J. (1998). Callous-unemotional traits and conduct problems: applying the two-factor model of psychopathy to children. In D. J. Cooke *et al.* (eds.), *Psychopathy: Theory, research and implications for society*. Amsterdam: Kluwer Academic Publishers, 161–87.

Goldsmith, H. H., and Campos, J. J. (1982). Toward a theory of infant temperament. In R. N. Emde and R. J. Harmon (eds.), *The development of attachment and affiliative systems*. New York: Plenum, 161–93.

Goldsmith, H. H., and Rothbart, M. K. (1991). Contemporary instruments for assessing early temperament by questionnaire and in the laboratory. In A. Angleitner and J. Strelau (eds.), *Explorations in temperament*. New York: Plenum Press, 249–72.

Gross, J. J. (1999). Emotion and emotion regulation. In L. A. Pervin and O. P. John (eds.), *Handbook of personality: Theory and research* (2nd edn.). New York: Guilford, 525–52.

Hart, D., Hofmann, V., Edelstein, W., and Keller, M. (1997). The relation of childhood personality types to adolescent behavior and development: a longitudinal study of Icelandic children. *Developmental Psychology*, 33, 195–205.

Huey, S. J., and Weisz, J. R. (1997). Ego control, ego resiliency, and the five-factor model as predictors of behavioral and emotional problems in clinic-referred children and adolescents. *Journal of Abnormal Psychology*, 106, 404–15.

Hussong, A. M., and Chassin, L. (1994). The stress-negative affect model of adolescent alcohol use: disaggregating negative affect. *Journal of Studies in Alcohol*, 55, 707–18.

Kagan, J. (1997). Temperament and the reactions to unfamiliarity. *Child Development*, 68, 139–43.

Kagan, J., Snidman, N., and Arcus, D. (1998). Childhood derivatives of high and low reactivity in infancy. *Child Development*, 69, 1483–93.

Kendall, P. A. and Wilcox, L. E. (1979). Self-control in children: development of a rating scale. *Journal of Consulting and Clinical Psychology*, 47, 1020–9.

Kochanska, G. (1993). Toward a synthesis of parental socialization and child temperament in early development of conscience. *Child Development*, 64, 325–47.

Kochanska, G., Coy, K. C., Tjebkes, T. L., and Husarek, S. J. (1998). Individual differences in emotionality in infancy. *Child Development*, 64, 375–90.

Kopp, C. B. (1982). Antecedents of self-regulation: a developmental perspective. *Development Psychology*, 18, 199–214.

Krueger, R. F., Caspi, A., Moffitt, T. E., White, J., and Stouthamer-Loeber, M. (1996). Delay of gratification, psychopathology, and personality: is low self-control specific to externalizing problems? *Journal of Personality*, 64, 107–29.

Kyrios, M., and Prior, M. (1990). Temperament, stress and family factors in behavioural adjustment of 3–5-year-old children. *International Journal of Behavioral Development*, 13, 67–93.

Larsen, R. J., and Diener, E. (1987). Affect intensity as an individual difference characteristic: a review. *Journal of Research in Personality*, 21, 1–39.

Leary, M. R. (1986). Affective and behavioral components of shyness: implications for theory, measurement, and research. In W. H. Jones, J. M. Cheek, and Briggs, S. R. (eds.), *Shyness: Perspectives on research and treatment*. New York: Plenum Press, 27–38.

Lengua, L. J., West, S. G., and Sandler, I. N. (1998). Temperament as a predictor of symptomatology in children: addressing contamination of measures. *Child Development*, 69, 164–81.

Lynam, D. R. (1997). Pursuing the psychopathy: capturing the fledgling psychopath in a nomological net. *Journal of Abnormal Psychology*, 106, 425–38.

Maszk, P., Eisenberg, N., and Guthrie, I. K. (1999). Relations of children's social status to their emotionality and regulation: a short-term longitudinal study. *Merrill-Palmer Quarterly*, 45, 468–92.

Mischel, H. N., and Mischel, W. (1983). The development of children's knowledge of self-control strategies. *Child Development*, 54, 603–19.

Moffitt, T. E. (1993). The neuropsychology of conduct disorder. *Development and Psychopathology*, 5, 135–51.

Newman, D. L., Caspi, A., Moffitt, T. E., and Silva, P. A. (1997). Antecedents of adult interpersonal functioning: effects of individual differences in age 3 temperament. *Developmental Psychology*, 33, 206–17.

Newman, J. P., Schmitt, W. A., and Voss, W. D. (1997). Impact of motivationally neutral cues on psychopathic individuals: assessing the generality of the response modulation hypothesis. *Journal of Abnormal Psychology*, 106, 563–75.

Newman, J. P., and Wallace, J. F. (1993). Diverse pathways to deficient self-regulation: implications for disinhibitory psychopathology in children. *Clinical Psychology Review*, 13, 699–720.

O'Brien, B. S., and Frick, P. J. (1996). Reward dominance: associations with anxiety, conduct problems, and psychopathy in children. *Journal of Abnormal Child Psychology*, 24, 223–39.

Ollendick, T. H., Weist, M. D., Borden, M. C., and Greene, R. W. (1992). Sociometric status and academic, behavioral, and psychological adjustment: a five-year longitudinal study. *Journal of Consulting and Clinical Psychology*, 60, 80–7.

Oosterlaan, J., and Sergeant, J. A. (1996). Inhibition in ADHD, aggressive, and anxious children: a biologically based model of child psychopathology. *Journal of Abnormal Child Psychology*, 24, 19–36.

Parker, J. G., and Asher, S. R. (1987). Peer relations and later personal adjustment: are low-accepted children at risk. *Psychological Bulletin*, 102, 357–89.

Parker, J. G., and Asher, S. R. (1993). Friendship and friendship quality in middle childhood: links with peer group acceptance and feelings of loneliness and social dissatisfaction. *Developmental Psychology*, 29, 611–21.

Parker, J. G., Rubin, K. H., Price, J. M., and DeRosier, M. E. (1995). In D. Cicchetti and D. Cohen (eds.), *Developmental psychopathology, risk, disorder, and adaptation*. New York: Wiley, vol. 2, 96–161.

Patterson, C. M., and Newman, J. P. (1993). Reflectivity and learning from aversive events: toward a psychological mechanism for the syndromes of disinhibition. *Psychological Review*, 100, 716–36.

Price, J. M. and Dodge, K. (1989). Reactive and proactive aggression in childhood: relations to peer status and social context dimensions. *Journal of Abnormal Child Psychology*, 17, 455–71.

Pulkkinen, L. (1982). Self-control and continuity from childhood to late adolescence. In P. B. Baltes and O. Brim, Jr. (eds.), *Life-span development and behavior*. New York: Academic Press, vol. 4, 63–105.

Pulkkinen, L., and Hämäläinen, M. (1995). Low self-control as a precursor to crime and accidents in a Finnish longitudinal study. *Criminal Behaviour and Mental Health*, 5, 424–38.

Pulkkinen, L., and Pitkänen, T. (1994). A prospective study of the precursors to problem drinking in young adulthood. *Journal of Studies on Alcohol*, 55, 578–87.

Robins, R. W., John, O. P., Caspi, A., Moffitt, T. E., and Stouthamer-Loeber, M. (1996). Resilient, overcontrolled, and undercontrolled boys: three replicable personality types. *Journal of Personality and Social Psychology*, 70, 157–71.

Rothbart, M. K. (1989). Biological processes of temperament. In G. A. Kohnstamm, J. Bates, and M. K. Rothbart (eds.), *Handbook of temperament in childhood*. New York: Wiley, 77–110.

Rothbart, M. K., Ahadi, S. A., and Hershey, K. L. (1994). Temperament and social behavior in childhood. *Merrill-Palmer Quarterly*, 40, 21–39.

Rothbart, M. K., and Bates, J. E. (1998). Temperament. In W. Damon (Series Editor) and N. Eisenberg (Volume Editor), *Handbook of child psychology. Social, emotional, personality development*. New York: Wiley, vol. 3, 105–76.

Rothbart, M. K., Posner, M. I., and Hershey, K. L. (1995). In D. Cicchetti and J. D. Cohen (eds.), *Developmental psychopathology: theory and methods*. New York: Wiley, vol. 1, 315–40.

Rothbart, M. K., Ziaie, H., and O'Boyle, C. G. (1992). Self-regulation and emotion in infancy. *New Directions in Child Development*, 55, 7–23.

Rubin, K. H., Bukowski, W., and Parker, J. G. (1998). Peer interactions, relationships, and groups. In W. Damon (Series Editor) and N. Eisenberg (Volume Editor), *Handbook of child psychology: social, emotional, and personality development* (5th edn.), vol. 3: *Social, emotional and personality development*, 77–110, New York: Wiley.

Rusting, C. L., and Nolen-Hoeksema, S. (1998). Regulating responses to anger: effects of rumination and distraction on angry mood. *Journal of Personality and Social Psychology*, 74, 790–803.

Sandler, I. N., Tein, J., and West, S. G. (1994). Coping, stress and the psychological symptoms of children of divorce: a cross-sectional and longitudinal study. *Child Development*, 65, 1744–63.

Sanson, A., Prior, M., and Kyrios, M. (1990). Contamination of measures in temperament research. *Merrill-Palmer Quarterly*, 36, 179–92.

Shedler, J., and Block, J. (1990). Adolescent drug use and psychological health: a longitudinal inquiry. *American Psychologist*, 45, 612–30.

Stice, E., and Gonzales, N. (1998). Adolescent temperament moderates the relation of parenting to antisocial behavior and substance use. *Journal of Adolescent Research*, 13, 5–31.

Teglasi, H., and MacMahon, B. H. (1990). Temperament and common problem behaviors of children. *Journal of Applied Developmental Psychology*, 11, 331–49.

Tellegen, A. (1985). Structures of mood and personality and their relevance to assessing anxiety, with an emphasis on self-report. In A. H. Tuma and J. D. Maser (eds.), *Anxiety and anxiety disorders*. Hillsdale, NJ: Erlbaum, 681–706.

Thompson, R. A. (1994). Emotional regulation: a theme in search of definition. *Monographs of the Society for Research in Child Development*, 59 (Serial No. 240), 25–52.

Thompson, R. A., Flood, M. F., and Lundquist, L. (1995). Emotion regulation: its relations to attachment and developmental psychopathology. In D. Cicchetti and S. L. Toth (eds.), *Emotion, cognition, and representation. Rochester Symposium on Developmental Psychopathology*, University of Rochester Press, vol. 6, 261–99.

Watson, D., Clark, L. A., and Tellegen, A. (1988). Development and validation of brief measures of positive and negative affect: the PANAS Scales. *Journal of Personality and Social Psychology*, 54, 1063–70.

Weinberger, D. A., and Schwartz, G. E. (1990). Distress and restraint as super-ordinate dimensions of self-reported adjustment: a typological perspective. *Journal of Personality*, 58, 381–417.

Part II

Formation of social relationships

3 Attachment relationships and appraisal of partnership: from early experience of sensitive support to later relationship representation

Klaus E. Grossmann, Karin Grossmann, Monika Winter and Peter Zimmermann

Introduction

Part of Bowlby's developmental writing focused on the accumulation of empirical evidence towards the most far-reaching hypothesis provided by psychoanalysis, namely, that the mother-child relationship has profound influences on the psychological development of the child well into adulthood (Bowlby, 1969/82, 1973, 1979). Bowlby saw a strong relationship between an individual's experience with his parents and his later capacity to make affectional bonds (Bowlby, 1987). The major goal of this chapter is not only to provide support for the viewpoint that attachments are a life-long concern, but also to argue for the influence of the child's early attachment experiences and representations on his or her later partnership representations. In support of this argument, we will demonstrate three pathways from infancy to young adulthood that point in the direction of the quality of later partnership representation. They are as follows: a) maternal sensitivity turned out to be a strong predictor even from the earliest assessments on; b) attachment assessments in childhood and adolescence but not in infancy predicted later partnership representation; and c) assessments of discourse quality about attachment issues made a unique contribution to the prediction of later partnership representation. The three pathways were closely interrelated suggesting that the roots of adult partnership representation can be found in interactive assessments, in discourse, or in standard assessments of attachment. We will base our argument on the extensive empirical evidence provided by our Bielefeld longitudinal project in northern Germany, specifically focused on birth to young adulthood (Grossmann, Grossmann, Spangler, Suess, and Unzner, 1985; Grossmann and Grossmann, 1991; Grossmann, Grossmann, and Zimmermann, 1999).

Ainsworth's concept of maternal sensitivity provided the basis for understanding the role of the attachment figure beyond that of organizing the infant's and child's emotional and behavioral responses (Grossmann and Grossmann, 1991). Specifically, the concept opened the interest in how relationships within the family contribute substantially to the child's successful peer relationships at any age (Sroufe, Egeland, and Carlson, 1999). In her famous Baltimore study, Mary Ainsworth and her coworkers demonstrated that the quality of maternal sensitivity, cooperation, and acceptance predicted the infant's developing attachment security (Ainsworth, Bell, and Stayton, 1974). Ainsworth's definition of maternal sensitivity reflected alertness to infant signals, appropriate interpretation of response, promptness of response, flexibility of attention and behavior, appropriate level of control, and negotiations of conflicting goals. All of these behaviors reflect love and portray a mother who respects her baby as a separate, active, and autonomous person whose wishes and activities have a validity of their own (Ainsworth, Blehar, Waters, and Wall, 1978). The importance of sensitivity for any tender and cooperative partnership seems to be self-evident. Maternal sensitivity can be shown to provide the child with a model of relationships that the child is likely to adopt within his or her own later relationships. Our longitudinal study started as a partial replication of the Baltimore study. However, we chose to follow 49 families with no discernible social, emotional, medical, or economical risk from the birth of the children until the age of 22.

Direct observations of early mother-infant interaction have provided access to testing the basic idea that emotional pre-dispositions may be shaped by the quality of the responses to the infant's signals and behavioral expressions. Through interactions with the infant, caregivers learn about the individuality of the infant and the infant learns to anticipate the individual behavioral style of the caregiver. Of course, there are great individual differences between infants as well as caregivers. Mastering interaction competence is the very foundation of the various qualities of attachment and is a task of matching two individuals to one another who at the onset of their relationship are unknown to each other. The development of a good "understanding" of each other far transcends behavioral dispositions. It accounts for biologically and experientially based individual differences, including temperament. The concept of "good understanding of each other" is central to our longitudinal study. Assessments of "maternal sensitivity and valuing attachment" constitute our first pathway of longitudinal variables tested to predict partnership representation.

The second pathway relies on standard assessments of qualities of attachment ages 1, 6, and 16. Using a controlled observational mini-drama called the Strange Situation Procedure (SSP), Ainsworth (1964) assessed infants' attachment behavior strategies towards their mothers after two brief separations, thus testing infants' treatment of their mother as a secure base. We subjected the infants in our study to the Strange Situation Procedure with their mothers and fathers during their second year of life. Later assessments of attachment security and quality included the widely accepted projective Separation Anxiety Test for the six-year-olds (Main, Kaplan, and Cassidy, 1985; see also Solomon and George, 1999) and the Adult Attachment Interview (George, Kaplan, and Main, 1984) for the 16-year-olds. Findings from these assessments as predictors of later partnership representation constitute the variables of our second pathway, labeled "quality of child attachment and representation."

The third pathway contains variables that index the quality of discourse about attachment issues. These variables were created in order to assess internal working models of attachment (Bowlby, 1973, Bretherton, 1999), using new methods of assessing the quality of discourse at ages 6, 10, and 16. The background to these new methods will be elaborated briefly in order to highlight our unique approach to studying attachment from childhood on.

Narratives came to the field of attachment about 15 years ago via the seminal paper by Main, Kaplan, and Cassidy (1985). This shift from interactive behavioral observations, as the method of choice for assessing attachment security, to linguistic assessments, was called "a move to the level of representation." Discourse is communication of thought with words. In attachment research, it usually means communicating feelings and thoughts (reflections) with words about attachment experiences. Discourse about attachment issues indicates whether the speaker verbally demonstrates access to his own emotions as related to significant life events, particularly attachment experiences. It is assumed that the ability to establish an internal working model of self as worthy of help and of others as willing to help (Bowlby, 1973) is based on early attachment experiences. These experiences need discourse about the child's accompanying emotions as the child grows older (Bowlby, 1979). Narrative coherence in discourse is given when verbal and emotional representations match. Coherence develops when the adult who talks to the child about daily matters (Nelson, 1999) also sensitively notices the child's emotions, interprets them correctly, and responds to them promptly and appropriately, verbally as well as non-verbally. Whereas appropriate discourses may also result in coherent narratives about attachment issues, inappropriate discourses are likely to result in distorted narratives about attachment experiences. At the discourse level, Grice (1975) defines coherence in terms of quality, quantity, manner, and relevance of discourse in conversation. A coherent narrative communicates feelings, memories, and thoughts clearly and without contradiction. In intelligence research, coherence refers to a concordance between internal coherence and external correspondence (Sternberg, 1997), implying that a coherent representation must fit reality in order to be psychologically adaptive. Neglected by intelligence research but central to attachment research, including our own, is the organization of emotions as the main foundation of internal coherence.

Important questions arise from the hypothesis that pre- and extra-lingual emotional attachment experiences need to be incorporated discursively into a meaning system as represented by language. Some of the new questions in attachment research are as follow: is it possible to overcome insecure attachment experiences in early childhood by sensitive discourse with reliable trusted figures? Most therapists have answered this question affirmatively. Can insensitive discourse in later life overshadow secure early childhood experiences? Research in clinical application of attachment theory will strive to answer these and other related questions (Grossmann, K. E., 1999). They may turn out to be pivotal to studying risk and protective factors as well as the sequel of traumatic events in the lives of individuals (van der Kolk, 1998). Methods to assess quality of discourse about attachment using stories or age-appropriate interviews were developed by our research group.

An overall regression analysis will be presented in Figure 3.1. However, regression analyses resulted in only major associations at the expense of the more subtle ones. Thus, the longitudinal relationships of Pathway 1 are presented in Figure 3.2, viz., "maternal sensitivity and valuing attachment." The longitudinal relationships for Pathway 2 are presented in Figure 3.3, viz., "quality of child attachment and representation." The longitudinal relationships for Pathway 3 are presented in Figure 3.4, viz., "quality of discourse about attachment issues." Figures 3.5a and 3.5b show how the three pathways are related to each other. Figure 3.5a shows the relationship between the standard assessments of the quality of child attachment and representation and the variables of the other two pathways. Figure 3.5b shows the relationship between Pathway 1, viz., "maternal sensitivity and valuing attachment," and Pathway 3, viz., "quality of discourse about attachment issues." Finally, Figure 3.6 augments the data for mothers with some new findings for the early father-child relationship (Grossmann, K. Grossmann, Fremmer-Bombik, Kindler, Scheuerer-Englisch, and Zimmermann, in prep.). Data on the father's role for the attachment development of the child are rare in attachment research (Grossmann, Grossmann, and Zimmermann, 1999), most likely because of Bowlby's original psycho-analytic inclination to concentrate mainly on mothers. In our study, the predictive power of the early toddler-father interactive quality during play rivals that of early maternal sensitivity. Both contribute uniquely to their children's development of partnership representation security, as well as to the quality of discourse about partnership.

The Bielefeld Longitudinal Attachment Study from birth to young adulthood

Sample and data collection

The findings presented in this chapter are part of a 22-year longitudinal study. It started in 1976 in Bielefeld, a middle size city in northern Germany. The Bielefeld Longitudinal Study is an ongoing study of attachment and socio-emotional development of children in families with no discernible risk at time of recruitment (Grossmann, K. *et al.*, 1985). The original sample consisted of 49 families, 26 boys and 23 girls. Parents were recruited in the hospital and gave consent to participate just prior to the birth of the focal child (in 1976/77). Healthy pregnancy at birth and German as the mother's native tongue were specific criteria for recruitment (for details see Grossmann, K. and Grossmann, K. E., 1991). All agreed to subsequent home visits. Most of the families were quite traditional in their division of labor; mothers were primarily responsible for home and children, and fathers were in all but three families the sole financial providers of the family. Thirty-eight young adults still participated at age 21/22. The age of fathers at the time of birth ranged from 19 to 46 years and the age of mothers ranged from 18 to 42 years.

Twenty-six fathers had completed at least some basic level education (Hauptschule plus apprenticeship). Another five had completed at least level "A" high school (Abitur) and yet another two had a university degree by the time of the child's second birthday. By the age of 22, 13 of the children studied had obtained more education than their fathers and 15 had obtained more education than their mothers. Only four children had an educational level below that of their parents. Most young adults (27 out of 38) still lived at home and only one person was married.

With the exception of the hospital observations at birth, the Strange Situations, and the recent assessments at age 21/22, all observations, interviews, and other data collections were done in the homes of the families. Independent collections of data were acquired by sending new research teams to the families at each subsequent visit, each new team unfamiliar with any of the previous data collected.

Our study started with a replication and extension of the Baltimore study conducted by Mary Ainsworth and her co-workers (Ainsworth, *et al.*, 1978). Table 3.1 presents an overview of the children's ages at the

Table 3.1 *The ages of the children at which data collection was done. Selected groups of variables that represent parental sensitivity, quality of children's attachment behavior and representations, and children's quality of discourse about attachment issues*

Children's ages at data collection in the Bielefeld Longitudinal Study

Children's ages in years at assessments

0	1	2	3*	6	10	16	22

Actual years of assessment

76	77	78	79	82	86	92	98

0: Newborn behavioral organization; maternal sensitivity and tenderness to the newborn

2, 6, 10 months: Maternal sensitivity; paternal involvement and responsiveness; maternal discourse about relationship to child

12, 18 months: Infant quality of attachment to mother and father

2 years: Maternal and paternal sensitivity and appropriate challenges during interactive play; maternal discourse about relationship to child

3 years: Maternal and paternal sensitivity and appropriate challenges during interactive play; maternal discourse about relationship to child

6 years: Projective measurement of child attachment security (SAT); attachment representation of mother and father (AAI)

10 years: Interview assessment of child attachment security and parental support; parental discourse about relation to child

16 years: Adolescents' attachment representation (AAI); interview assessment of parental support; social rejection task; life events as potential risk factors

22 years: Current relationship interview, Adult attachment interview, Current adaptation assessments

*Data not used in the present context

various times of data collection, of the actual years the data collection took place, and of the kinds of variables that were assessed and that are relevant to this chapter.

Lengthy home visits and observations of mother's and father's sensitivity to the child's communication were the core elements of our longitudinal study. During the first year, we visited the families when the focal child was two, six, and ten months old, for three to five hours on each occasion. The intent was to assess maternal sensitivity on a regular basis over extended periods of time (Grossmann *et al.*, 1985). Later assessments of attachment quality to both parents followed. At the beginning of attachment research, assessments of the child-father attachment relationship were either missing or the father-child relationship was not considered to have the same salience as the mother-child attachment relationship. Beside the assessment of attachment quality, we extended our database by including father-child-interaction measures parallel to those assessed with mothers. When assessing interactive quality during joint play in toddlerhood we combined sensitive responsiveness and supportive challenges into a single measurement of play sensitivities for mothers as well as fathers. Father's play sensitivity emerged as a pivotal variable within the child-father attachment relationship, more so than the index of quality of attachment as assessed in the strange situation procedure (Grossmann, K. *et al.*, in prep.). Based on our wider view of attachment (Grossmann, K. E. and Grossmann, K., 1990) we explored whether the two parents contribute uniquely to the child's attachment development. Maternal sensitivity seems to relate more to the infant's secure base behavior system whereas fathers' sensitivity seems to relate more to the child's exploratory behavior system (Grossmann, K. E., Grossmann, K., and Zimmermann, 1999). Some of the central findings regarding the influence of the father's play sensitivity will be presented in addition to the results for the mother-child relationship (for further details see Grossmann, K. *et al.*, in prep.).

The conceptual strategy of data analysis

The conceptual frame for presenting our longitudinal data is based on the three perspectives of attachment theory outlined in the introduction. The variables used make up the three main conceptual pathways are assumed to lead to differences in partnership representations in young adulthood. The pathways are (1) assessments of maternal sensitivity, (2) assessments of the child's attachment organization, and (3) assessments of the child's discourse quality about attachment or relationship related topics. Details of the procedures and measures will be presented accordingly.

Maternal sensitivity assesses the mother's reactions to the infant's and child's emotional expression of needs, especially attachment needs from early on. Maternal sensitivity to the infant's communication is seen as a mediator between the infant's internal state and its experience of competence in achieving its goals. Maternal sensitivity to infant attachment signals functions primarily to achieve a coherent internal organization of attachment emotions in the child (Sroufe and Waters, 1977). The function of the attachment figure as an external organizer of the child's emotions is based on predictability, goal-oriented partnership, and appropriate responsiveness. The infant's attachment behavioral system is assumed to be pre-set by phylogenetic propensities in the service of protection (Bowlby, 1969). In addition, maternal sensitivity is an expression of the mother's state of mind regarding the value of attachments (Grossmann, K., Fremmer-Bombik, Rudolph, and Grossmann, 1988) and it supports the development of a secure quality of attachment. Bowlby (1973) argued that continuous support and emotional availability of parents is prerequisite to the development of a resilient personality. Thus, the influences of maternal sensitivity will not only be tested as single predictors at each age but will also be tested as composite scores, including the experienced sensitivity of the years before. In addition, maternal valuing of attachment is included, as assessed in the AAI (Geore, Kaplan & Main, 1985). In this chapter, the pathway of variables relating to maternal sensitivity as an external organization of the child's attachment behavioral system is labeled "maternal sensitivity and valuing of attachment."

Secure attachment organization assesses psychological security which is the prime state to be achieved through the communication and sensitivity of the attachment figures. Differences in the availability of the attachment figure, his or her sensitivity, acceptance, and cooperation will result in different organizations of the child's attachment system and strategies of attachment behavior. The strategies assessed at any age are thought of as the result of past attachment experiences. In addition, they are indications of expectations based on prior experiences that have developed into internal working models of self and relevant others. Variables that indicate the pathway of measurements of attachment security are reported by the label "quality of child attachment and attachment representation."

The third conceptual pathway introduced here is assessed via the analysis of discourse about salient social relationships. Coherent appraisal of one's own and of others' motives, the way solutions for social conflicts are presented, and whether subjects have access to their own emotional states in social interactions represent the underlying functionality of internal working models. Mental representation of the organization of emotions and emotional appraisals can be expressed in language (Harris, 1999). These representations develop within autobiographies, which are generally based on narratives (Nelson, 1999). Carefully conducted interviews about attachment can reflect the child's or adolescent's state of mind, as derived from reflections about his or her expectancies within attachment or social relationships. Assessments of the children's and adolescents' "quality of discourse about attachment issues" make up the third pathway of our current analysis.

Procedures and assessments of the longitudinal outcome and predictor variables

The central theme of this chapter is based on describing the connection between developmental influences and the pathways guiding representations of partnership in early adulthood. The assessment of partnership representation at age 22 will be presented first, followed by a presentation of the predictor variables along the three conceptual pathways.

Security of partnership representation and quality of discourse about partnership in young adulthood

During a six to seven-hour-long visit to the university lab, 38 young adults (ages 21 and 22) completed an array of procedures spanning from tests of verbal associations and experimental priming procedures (Maier, 2000), questionnaires, and other interviews (Winter, in prep.) to the Adult Attachment Interview (AAI) (Strasser, in prep.).

The young adults were interviewed with the *Partnership Representation Interview*. The interview was conducted in a style paralleling the Adult Attachment Interview with semi-structured questions. The German interview is based on the Current Relationship Interview developed by Crowell and Owens (1998) and adapted for use with young adults. The third author conducted all interviews. The interviewer's familiarity with the protocol was ensured by a pilot study. The interviewer asked the young adults to describe the most important of any recent romantic relationships that had lasted at least three months. Thirty-three of the young adults acknowledged having had a recent romantic relationship as such.

The young adults were asked to describe their romantic partnership. They were asked to recall specific times when they had been upset, hurt, jealous, or ill, and to recall whether they had experienced separations from the partner, threats, and/or feelings of confinement or rejection by the partner. The issues of mutual willingness to ask for support and accept support as well as being aware of the partner's emotional needs were recurrent during the interview. How decisions were made and disagreements resolved were further additional topics. Other questions required subjects to integrate specific experiences with the partner into a more general understanding of the relationship. For instance, the interviewer asked the young adults to describe how the partnership had influenced them, how they related their experiences with previous romantic partners to this partner, and to describe their hopes and fears regarding this partnership. Interviews were videotaped.

The third author developed the Partnership Representation Q-set in order to assess from the videotapes both the person's discourse and information processing style regarding partnership within a romantic relationship. The Q-sort methodology allows raters to integrate several aspects of partnerships into a descriptive pattern evaluating the state of mind of the individual with respect to partnership. Some of the aspects integrated are information processing, emotion regulation, and partnership strategies across multiple domains, including depictions of self in relation to the partner. Prototypical Q-sorts for secure, dismissing, and enmeshed mental representations, with respect to romantic relationships, were formed in order to assess the degree to which a particular representation of partnership was characteristic for that specific interview. Criterion Q-sorts for the three prototypes were established by ten attachment researches in Regensburg, all with profound knowledge of attachment theory and familiarity with the conceptual coding system of the Adult Attachment Interview. The mean inter-rater reliability for the three prototypes was .80, with a range of .73–.91. Q-sort items were formulated based on some of the following concepts: the secure base phenomenon described by Waters (1997); the qualitative functioning of relationships with aspects such as the partner's loving, involvement, or rejection as used in the Current Relationship Interview (Owens *et al.*, 1995), the Marital Q-set (Kobak, 1989) and the Adult Attachment Interview Q-set as used to assess coherency and integration of experiences (Kobak, 1993). The Q-sort items were pilot-tested and revised for this study. Two independent raters viewed the videotaped interview and provided a Q-sort description, distributing 100 items into nine categories ranging from the most characteristic (9) to least characteristic (1). The Partnership Representation Q-sort has a forced bell-shaped distribution with only five items in the two extreme categories and 18 items in the category neither characteristic nor uncharacteristic (5).

The secure partner representation prototype closely paralleled our conception of a secure strategy in infancy and adulthood. It describes a person who values an intimate relationship as a reliable source of comfort, who functions as a secure base to the partner, and who has an easy access to partnership-related thoughts and feelings. Applying Main and Goldwyn's (1984) concepts for the analysis of an interview transcript, a person with a secure partnership representation is able to communicate about the experiences in a partnership in a smooth, coherent way without denying unfavorable aspects (Hesse, 1999). The prototypic secure person expresses affection openly and gives many lively examples of a warm and mutually supporting romantic partnership, i.e. the person has a working model of the partner as available and of the self as efficacious in their romantic partnership. On the other hand, the most decisive items of a dismissing partnership representation were as follows: idealization of the partnership, i.e., giving a very positive view of the relationship at a general level that was either unsupported or contradicted by actual memories; avoiding emotional themes and thoughts relevant to a goal-corrected partnership; no perception of the partner as available or as a source of comfort; and instrumental but not emotional support considered necessary and sought or given. The discourse of a dismissing partnership representation is characterized by a low degree of emotional openness and coherence.

A prototypic enmeshed partnership representation is characterized by oscillation between positive and negative evaluations of the relationship. Emotional topics are "ruminated" upon, and a longing for more closeness and indications of the person's fear of not having their needs met by the partner are central in the narrative. Low coherence is also characteristic of an enmeshed partnership representation, i.e., the young adult has difficulties in acknowledging and integrating contradictory experiences. Other discourse features of an enmeshed partnership representation are confused and angry narratives and lacking meta-monitoring, such as extensive descriptions of details and failure to notice contradictions within the interview.

Each videotaped interview was rated by two raters who were blind to all other measures in the study. The raters independently sorted each interview and their ratings were combined to form a composite Q-description. The average composite reliability on the videotapes was .76, with a range from .43 to .86. For each interview, the similarity with each of the three prototypes is calculated by correlations, which serve as raw scores thus resulting in continuous scores ranging from +1 to −1. Since dismissing partnership representation strongly correlates negatively with a secure partnership representation, only results for the latter will be presented here.

Most subjects varied in the degree to which the least characteristic items of the enmeshed prototype were endorsed. Only four subjects showed positive scores for an enmeshed partnership representation whereas the majority received negative scores. Whereas positive scores would have implied a great need of care, clinging, and fears of being rejected, low to moderately negative scores mainly represent the formal aspects of an enmeshed narrative. This can be described by the following Q-sort items: lack of coherence, the interviewed person is judged unable to focus on one topic, the person offers contradictory descriptions, the person does not show meta-monitoring, and the person has no insight into his or her own patterns of behavior or appraisals. Consequently, for this sample, the scores were re-labeled as representing "discourse quality" and scores were inverted. Thus, high scores on this prototype indicate a high quality of disourse. The prototype secure partnership representation correlated positively ($r = .40$; $p < .05$) with the prototype discourse quality.

Measurements along the pathway of maternal sensitivity and valuing of attachment relationships

Measures at different ages of the children were consolidated in order to test how continuous maternal sensitivity and support, from infancy through adolescence, influences partnership representation at age 22. Mothers' attachment representation was included as well.

Based on lengthy home observations at ages two, six, and ten months (Grossmann, K. et al., 1985), maternal sensitivity was rated from written protocols and yielded an average rating for the first year. Ainsworth quantified the home observations of mother-infant interactions along four dimensions of maternal behavior. These dimensions are described and labeled as "sensitivity versus insensitivity to the baby's communications," "co-operation versus interference," "acceptance versus rejection," and "availability versus ignoring and neglect." The inclusive nine-point rating scales serve to describe maternal behavior that facilitates harmonious interaction with the infant and thus promotes the development of a secure attachment relationship (Ainsworth, Bell, and Stayton, 1974). For this presentation we focus on the ratings of maternal sensitivity only.

At ages two and six years, mother-child play was observed and rated for maternal sensitivity and appropriately challenging support. The nine-point scale "maternal sensitivity to the infant's signals and communications" as defined by Ainsworth, Bell, and Stayton (1974), was either used without modification or, for older children, was transformed into a "sensitive" and challenging interactive play (SCIP) scale (see p. 95; Grossmann, K. et al. in prep.).

Mothers' attachment representation was assessed using the Adult Attachment Interview (AAI, George et al., 1985), when the children were six. The AAI is an open interview based on a well-structured guideline of 16 questions. It addresses attachment-related autobiographical memories from childhood, general descriptions and evaluations of the person's relationships with his/her attachment figures, specific supportive or contradicting memories in attachment relevant situations (e.g. separations, rejection), evaluations of the influence of the attachment history on personality, and descriptions of current relationships with attachment figures. In addition, participants are asked to evaluate their memories from their current perspective. The interviews were transcribed verbatim at a later point. Classifications of attachment representations that value attachments (secure) or dismiss their importance (insecure), were derived using a method developed by Fremmer-Bombik, Rudolph, Veit, Schwarz, and Schwarzmeier (1989), which was based on an early version of Main and Goldwyn's (1984) system for analyzing the AAI. In addition to the validity shown in the transgenerational concordance between mothers' attachment representations and their infants' attachment organizations, we were the first to find that mothers with secure attachment representations indeed had been more sensitive to their infants' communication during the first year (Grossmann, K. *et al.*, 1988).

When the child was age ten, mothers were interviewed about their relationship to him/her. Mothers who respected and valued their child, who were aware of their child's emotional and social needs, and who did not reject their child's wishes for closeness or for autonomy, received a high rating on maternal sensitivity and support (Scheuerer-Englisch, 1989). At age 16, the adolescents were given a current parent relationship interview. Their report as to what degree their mother was sensitive, supportive, and emotionally available was rated on a five-point scale (Zimmermann, 2000).

Nested scores were created from the measures of sensitivity and support from infancy to adolescence. In order to include mothers' attachment representations as a measure of their valuation of attachment, a dichotomous variable, subjects were grouped by median split for each of the variables along the path "maternal sensitivity and valuing attachment" into high (scored 1) or low (scored 0) sensitivity at each specific age of the child. Maternal sensitivity at age one and two was combined, leading to a possible range from zero to two. The nested scores for ages 6, 10, and 16 capture the child's experience of maternal sensitivity and continuity of support.

Measurements of the quality of childhood attachment and attachment representation

Children were observed with their mothers in the Strange Situation Procedure at 12 months. Attachment categories (ABC) were derived by using standard procedures (Ainsworth *et al.*, 1978). Infants were grouped into secure vs. insecure. Disorganized attachment patterns ($n = 6$) were disregarded in the present analysis.

At age six, the Separation Anxiety Test (SAT, Klagsbrun and Bowlby, 1976) was administered to the children as a projective assessment of attachment security. Researchers have previously used this projective technique when assessing the children's working models of self as worthy of help and attachment figures as supportive and willing to give help (Bretherton and Munholland, 1999). The SAT features a series of six photographs of children undergoing separation. Sessions are videotaped and transcribed. A rating scale for attachment security was developed, based on the work of Main and colleagues (1985). Attachment security was defined in accordance with the following suggestion of Bowlby (1979): a child who is certain of his parent's acceptance and support is not only capable of tolerating ambiguous feelings towards them, but is also confident in his or her ability to control those feelings without having to deny them. The children's attachment security was rated on a seven-point scale. A high score was given if a child spoke about negative feelings in response to severe separations but not to mild separations, if the non-verbal expressions were congruent with the content of the verbal responses, and if the child volunteered a constructive perspective or positive solution for the situation, i.e. requesting help from trusted others, given that the parents were not present (Geiger, 1991, see also Grossmann, K. E., and Grossmann, K., 1991).

The adolescents were given the Adult Attachment Interview (AAI) at age 16. Transcripts were rated and classified using the AAI-Q-Sort method (Kobak, 1993). This method results in continuous scores for the AAI-dimensions "secure," "dismissing," and "preoccupied" attachment representation, as well as for the dimension "deactivation of attachment relevant thoughts and feelings" (Zimmermann, 1999; Zimmermann and Grossmann, 1997). Each interview was sorted by two raters blind to any previous findings about the families and personally trained by Main. If their agreement was less than .59, the ratings of a third rater was included. Intercoder reliability (Spearman-Brown) was r = .78 with a range from r = .61 to r = .91.

Measurements of the quality of discourse about attachment issues

Children need to be able to tell stories and comply with an interviewer before their quality of discourse can be evaluated. Thus, assessments of children's working models at a verbal level started at age six.

The Separation Anxiety Test given at age six was analyzed separately because the children's ability to talk about the sources of their own and their parents' emotions and motives can be assessed from the separation stories of this projective assessment. A standard set of open questions concerning the feelings of the child, his/her coping with separation, and his/her social support, was asked for each of the six pictures on the test. The children's discourse about these issues was rated on a five-point scale, viz., "clarity of motives." Responses from the children regarding what they do when parents are away ranged from seeking support of others or securing the availability of the parents via telephone to destroying household items, getting lost and starving, and/or imagining a permanent separation with the parent. These kinds of answers were rated on a five-point scale, viz., "perspectives for actions" (Aimer and Müller, 1998). At age ten, children were interviewed about the support they expected from their parents using episodes of daily life (Scheuerer-Englisch, 1989). Again, the scales "clarity of motives" and "perspectives for actions" were used to evaluate the responses of the children. At age 16, the adolescents were confronted with five hypothetical stories about social rejection or social failure (Zimmermann, 1999). These stories were read to the adolescents and covered topics such as being abandoned by one's dance partner at a ball or not being invited to a friend's birthday party, etc. Afterwards, they were asked specifically: 1) what they would think in such a situation and how they would explain the situation (attribution), 2) how they would react in such a situation (behavior strategy), and 3) how they would feel and why they would feel that way (access to personal feelings).

The answers were transcribed and rated on the following three scales for each story, combined over all five stories. *Flexibility of attribution* assessed the subject's flexibility when thinking about the explanations of the situation. *Flexibility of behavior* assessed whether the adolescents reported only one solution for the situation (e.g. "I will never talk to them again") or whether they generated a range of different alternatives, depending on the situation. *Access to Personal Feelings* assessed whether subjective feelings in the situations were reported with a clear quality and intensity, and whether they could explain why they felt the way they did. Transcripts of the five social rejection stories were rated by an independent rater, blind to other results of the study. Inter-rater reliability was high with concordance of 88 percent (kappa .89) for the scale *flexibility of attribution*, 100 percent (kappa .97) for the scale *flexibility of behavior*, and 96 percent (kappa .80) for the scale *access to personal feelings*. All three scales describe parts of the adaptation process (Lazarus, 1991). An overall mean score for the three z-transformed scales was computed to assess *Flexibility of Response to Social Rejection* and was included in the regression analysis. In a broader context this was conceptualized by Zimmermann (1999) as adaptive emotion regulation.

Predictability of partnership representation in young adulthood: interpretation of longitudinal relationships

Findings will be presented as graphic overviews without exact numbers and without details regarding the methods of statistical analyses. The study of the 22-year-olds was conducted very recently. After the analysis of the Current Relationship Interview had been completed, longitudinal relationships to earlier variables were tested. The exact strategy of data analysis and results will be published later (Winter, in prep.). Our presentation at this time will address the theme of finding the pathways to partnership representation in young adulthood.

The longitudinal relationships are presented in four parts. First, variables along the three paths "maternal sensitivity and valuing attachment," "quality of child attachment and representation," and "quality of discourse about attachment issues" are shown in their relationship to partnership representation security and the quality of discourse about partnership over an age span of 22 years (Figure 3.1). Second, the direct contributions of each of the variables, along the three pathways, to 22 year outcome variables are shown in Figures 3.2, 3.3, and 3.4. Third, Figures 3.5a and 3.5b demonstrate the intercorrelations among the variables between and within the three pathways. Fourth, Figure 3.6 gives a picture of the fathers' contributions in comparison with mothers' from the first two years to the partnership representation of the young adults. Analysis of the multitude of variables contributing to the child-father relationship are currently in progress (Grossmann, K. *et al.*, in prep.; Kindler, 2001).

Overview and results of a multiple regression analysis

Figure 3.1 presents an integrative overview of the contribution of the three different sources of influence of attachment experiences and their organization within the child to the prediction of two outcome variables at age 22 based on a multiple regression analysis. The young adults' quality of discourse about their partnership was strongly predicted by the composite index of maternal sensitivity and valuing attachment, from the age of six. Young adults, who had experienced a mother who was sensitive to her preverbal as well as verbal young child and who valued attachments, had a coherent discourse about their partnership that gave evidence of self reflection and respect for the partners' autonomy as well as their attachment needs. Sensitive response to a young child's signals and communication seems to enhance the ability to reflect on his/her own feelings and motives as young adults. Further, it enhances the ability to take into account his/her partner's feelings and motives and to relate these reflections coherently in a question-guided discourse. The intermediate steps between early experience and later discourse quality will be specified in subsequent figures.

Secure partnership representation at age 22 was most strongly predicted by the composite index of continuous maternal sensitivity until 16 years and by the adolescents' flexibility of thoughts and responses to vignettes of social rejection (Flexibility of Response to Social Rejection). However, these two predictor variables were strongly correlated (Figure 3.5b). Partnership representation security was also predicted by the children's security of response to the Separation Anxiety Test which, in turn, was predicted by the infants' quality of attachment to the mother. Thus, the young adults who described a secure partnership, implying a willingness to help and accept help when in distress, and who gave many lively examples of warm and mutually supporting partnerships, had experienced a more sensitive mother throughout their first 16 years, were flexible when confronted with social rejection, and, as six-year-olds, had shown a secure attachment representation in response to stories of separation from parents.

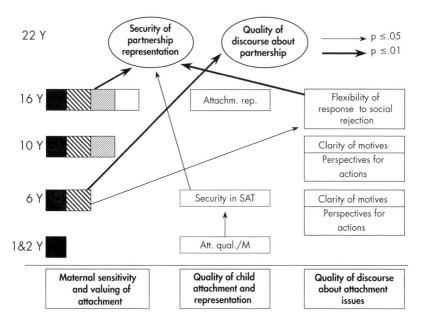

Figure 3.1 Main predictors of partnership representation

Longitudinal correlation with the outcome measures

Figure 3.2 focuses on the direct relationships between maternal sensitivity, as assessed during the first year and at ages 2, 6, 10, and 16, and the young adult's secure partnership representation and quality of discourse about partnership at age 22. The findings shown in this graph support the most central thesis of attachment theory as proposed by Bowlby (1987, 58): "*There is a strong causal relationship between an individual's experience with his parents and his later capacity to make affectional bonds, ...*" Our findings suggest that children who have experienced a sensitive mother, and, as we shall see, a sensitive father, develop into adults who themselves are sensitive to their partner's attachment needs and value attachment relationships. It is interesting to note, on the individual level, that the two young adults with the highest ratings on security of partnership representation had experienced a mother that was highly sensitive throughout the first 16 years. The mean sensitivity score of their mothers was high with low variance between the assessments. The maternal sensitivity index at each assessment age was related to security of partnership representation as well as to quality of discourse about partnership at age 22. Most remarkable, although expected by attachment theory, maternal sensitivity to the preverbal child significantly predicted by itself the quality of discourse at age 22. The influence of maternal sensitivity to the developing child's mental representation of close relationships will be discussed in the last section of this chapter.

Figure 3.3 presents the correlation between the children's attachment behavior strategies in infancy, childhood and adolescence and the outcome measures of the quality of partnership representation at age 22. Quality of attachment to mother at 12 months was significantly related to the child's security as assessed with the SAT at six years. The child's security at age six, in turn, predicted security of partnership representation at age 22 (see also Figure 3.1). In our longitudinal study, infant quality of attachment to mother as assessed in the strange situation procedure was not related to adolescent attachment representation at age 16 (Zimmermann, Fremmer-Bombik, Spangler and Grossmann, 1997). Stability of quality of attachment from infancy (SSP) to young adulthood (AAI) is still a controversial issue. However, at the correlative level, there was a modest relationship between adolescent attachment representation (AAI) at age 16 and young adults' security of partnership representation six years later. Adolescents with a more secure and less dismissing state of mind regarding attachment tended to receive higher scores for security in their partnership representation.

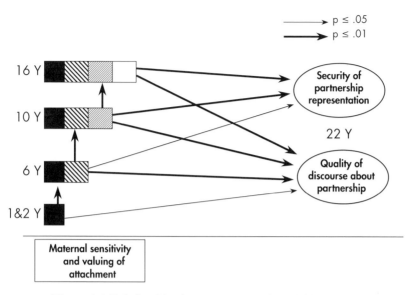

Figure 3.2 Relationships between maternal sensitivity and valuing of attachment and children's later partnership representation

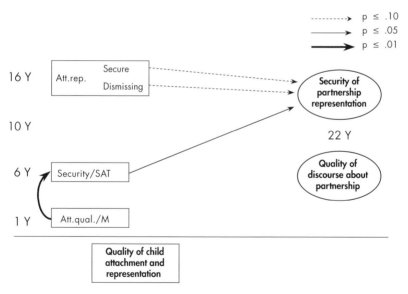

Figure 3.3 Relationship between quality of child attachment and adult partnership representation

The interview questions about attachment issues resemble each other in all of the assessments of attachment security. The questions deal with attachment feelings and responses to separations, goal-corrected partnership orientation in evaluating interactions, and the value placed on joint goals in comparison to individual goals. Still, attachment quality and attachment representations are not necessarily stable characteristics from ages 6, 16, to 22. During this period, children's cognitive capacities develop greatly and experientially based changes are quite possible. For example, 25 percent of the children had experienced a loss of a parent through divorce or death by the age of 16. Yet, the direct influence of *early* maternal sensitivity and attachment security at age six remained significant.

The predictive correlation between the variables within the pathway "quality of discourse about attachment issues" at ages 6, 10, and 16, and the partnership assessment measures at age 22, are shown in Figure 3.4. This figure is more detailed because the discourse variables from ages six and ten, although related, do not show the same prediction to partnership variables from age 22. The six-year-old's reflectivity over his/her own motives and feelings, rated on the scale "clarity of motives,"

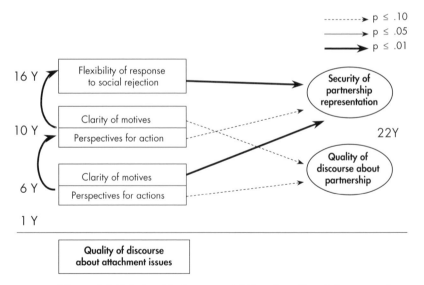

Figure 3.4 Relationship between childhood quality of discourse about attachment and adult partnership representation

predicted later security of partnership representation. However, ratings on the same scale at age ten were only modestly related to later quality of discourse about partnership. The opposite was found for the scale "perspectives for actions." Here, ratings at age six were only modestly related to quality of discourse about partnership at age 22, but ratings at age ten were clearly related to security of partnership representation at age 22. Only preliminary interpretations can be made as of now. Compared to the findings for the predictive power of maternal sensitivity, the assessments of discourse quality at ages six and ten were less predictive of later discourse quality at age 22. We assume that the development of discourse quality about partnership is less an individual developmental progression and more a result of dyadic communication (see Grossmann, 1999). However, when assessments were closer in time, direct relationships were found between qualities of discourse. The adolescents who scored high on the measure flexibility of response to social rejection were more likely to have secure discourse about partnership at age 22. In turn, the flexibility of the adolescents had its roots in their discourse quality at earlier ages.

Interrelations among predictor variables

The next two figures show the interrelations among the predictor variables. Measurements of attachment qualities of the child from infancy to adolescence are shown at the center of Figure 3.5a. The relationship between maternal sensitivity during the first year and infant-mother quality of attachment has previously been documented (Grossmann, K. *et al.*, 1985). The predictive relationship from infant-mother attachment quality to maternal sensitivity and valuing of attachments at the six-year assessment is mainly due to the age six index being a composite of the quality of maternal attachment representation and three maternal sensitivity indices at ages one, two, and six. Maternal sensitivity during infancy was strongly related to quality of maternal attachment representation assessed at age six, and both were highly correlated with quality of infant-mother attachment. Thus, the early mother-child variables formed a close net. As expected, children's security assessed with the SAT was closely related to the six-year-olds' quality of discourse about attachment issues, mainly because the SAT was the basis for both analyses. Quality of discourse relied solely on the transcripts of the children's verbal responses, whereas the security rating included the non-verbal reactions as rated from the video recordings. Although they were assessed with three different interviews, all measures were intercorrelated at age 16. The adolescents' state

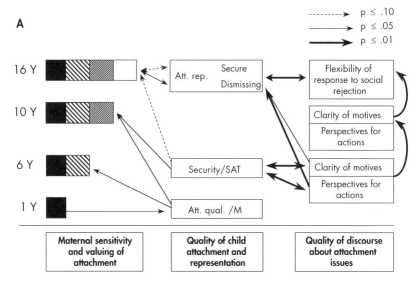

Figure 3.5a Relationships between child attachment security and maternal sensitivity as well as quality of discourse

of mind regarding attachment (AAI) was related to their representations of the current availability of their mothers as well as to their flexibility of response to social rejection. An additional finding was the prediction from quality of discourse at age six to security of attachment representation at age 16 (see Figure 3.5a).

Maternal sensitivity was related to the children's quality of discourse about attachment issues at all ages (Figure 3.5b). Maternal sensitivity to the preverbal infant and toddler predicted flexibility of responses to social rejection in adolescence. This specific assessment of adolescent quality of discourse had its roots in all maternal sensitivity indices.

The definition of maternal sensitivity, as given by Ainsworth *et al.* (1974), may provide an explanation. A mother who is attentive to the communications of her child, i.e., who interprets them correctly and responds appropriately, seems to help the child know his/her own feelings and motives and help put them into words. By talking about the feelings of rejection that may occur during many daily interactions, a sensitive mother explains her own motives, acknowledges the child's feelings, and may give reasons why the child's feelings of rejection often are unjustified. Sensitive mothers can take the child's perspective and help him/her understand the perspective of others, including herself (Meins, 1999).

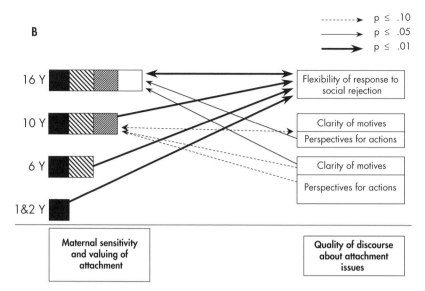

Figure 3.5b Interrelations between maternal sensitivity and valuing attachment and children's quality of discourse

The contribution of fathers' sensitivity to quality of partnership representation in young adulthood

During the 22 years of the study, we tried to include the fathers as much as possible. However, the division of labor was quite traditional in these families and fathers felt less responsible for care giving. Thus, fewer fathers than mothers participated in the assessments across the years. Still, a sufficient number of fathers were observed with their children during the early assessments. Only one set of data from the longitudinal analyses of the child-father relationship assessments is presented in the current chapter. Further analyses have been conducted (Grossmann, K. *et al.*, in prep.; Kindler, 2001) At age 24 months, 47 father-child pairs were observed in a ten-minute play session with a creative play material, Playdoh. Fathers were scored for their sensitivity and gentle challenging interactive play behavior with the toddler using a newly constructed inclusive nine-point rating scale of sensitive and challenging interactive play (SCIP scale, Grossmann, K. *et al.*, in prep.). The SCIP scale is defined to assess sensitivity to the child's attachment signals, support for the child's exploratory behaviors, careful scaffolding, as well as gentle challenges to the child's competencies. Bowlby gave equal importance to parental support of the child's exploratory needs as to the child's attachment needs.

"Complementary in importance to a parent's respect for a child's attachment desires is respect for his desire to explore and gradually to extend his relationships both with peers and with other adults" (Bowlby, 1987, p. 58). Our results show that fathers' play sensitivity, as assessed with the SCIP scale, is a pivotal variable for the child's attachment development (Grossmann, K. *et al.*, in prep.).

Figure 3.6 shows the set of findings relevant to the current presentation. Security of partnership representation as well as quality of discourse about partnership at age 22 was directly rooted in the fathers' early play sensitivity with their toddlers as was maternal sensitivity to the pre-school child. The fathers' play sensitivity was also predictive of the adolescents' attachment representations. We interpret these findings in light of the role of fathers as supporters of the child's desire to explore. Our new concept of security of exploration is elaborated in Grossmann, K. E. *et al.* (1999). By being sensitive and by gently challenging the child's cognitive and social competence during joint play, while, at the same time, attending to the child's expressions of need for reassurance and sympathy, the fathers' role may be to foster autonomy within relatedness. Fathers seem to complement the mothers' role in the domain of the child's exploratory

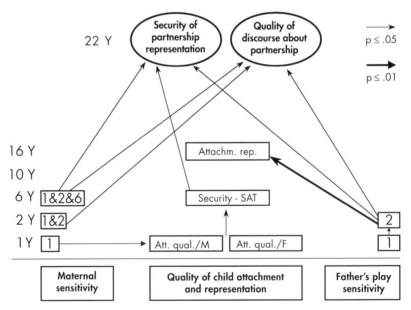

Figure 3.6 Roots of adult partnership representation in early parental sensitivity

system. Both parents' sensitivities are core contributions to the development of attachment security. As more findings emerge, the unique role of the fathers' play sensitivity for the child's emerging regard for close relations will become more evident.

Discussion: the origins of the capacity to make affectional bonds

Attachment and biological anthropology

The Bielefeld Longitudinal Study of attachment development began in the middle 1970s. Attachment research at that time was only concerned with infancy and measurements of quality of attachment were available only for the infancy period. We were hoping for a prosperous development of attachment research as our participants grew older. The development has been richer than we could have imagined. There are two overriding features of attachment theory. 1. It is an open theory; 2. It is primarily an inductive theory. As an open theory, it invites observations based on a general hypothesis about biological and psychological adaptation. The biological adaptation of a species, based on genetic selection, constitutes the phylogenetic roots of attachment. Attachment behavior occurs in the young of almost all species of mammals. Protection is the set-goal of infants in seeking and maintaining proximity to the attachment figure. It brings about a feeling of security and is associated with a reduction of stress hormones (Spangler and Schieche, 1998). Such behaviors are "pre-selected" and have survival value. Attachment behaviors are, in Bowlby's (1969) terms, environmentally stable. Genetic propensities transform differently into phenotypic expressions, depending on environmental influences. Compared to our present environment, environmental features have been necessarily different during most of our previous human evolutionary adaptation period. However, the match between the attachment figure's sensitivity and the infant's communicative competence for the development of highly individualized attachment relationships remains crucial. This match still carries most of the elements of the roots of psychological security which, in humans, developed from simple mammalian measures of protecting the young in the service of inclusive fitness. This part of attachment theory is firmly grounded in biological anthropology. On the physiological level, the attachment behavioral system operates, in infants, primarily in the mid-brain. The corresponding parental care giving system has been referred to as "intuitive parenting" by Papousek and Papousek (1987).

Maternal sensitivity as organizing the child's emotional communication: attachment and cultural anthropology

From early on, attachment figures' sensitivity to the infant's signals shape the expression and communication of his/her emotional needs. The richest communicative development is achieved by subtle, prompt, and appropriate responses to the infant's signals by the interactive partner. The responses are usually accompanied by vocal melodies relating emotions to the infant. All interactions, whether sensitive or not, are responses that acknowledge or ignore the infant's wishes and that interpret them correctly or incorrectly from his/her viewpoint. The infant experiences pre-verbally whether he has been understood and appropriately responded to or not. Eventually, verbal responses by the attachment figures begin to carry meaning. Through words, the child eventually learns, in addition to the already existing experiences at the procedural level, to understand emotions as a valuable appraisal system needing interpretation (Grossmann, K. E., 1999). In this manner, negative emotions may eventually become integrated into a clear goal oriented plan to remedy the causes of the bad feelings. This integration of negative emotions into a communicative strategy starts rather early, e.g., in the case of an infant who is angrily protesting his mother's departure. If the mother understands the infant's anger as a signal of insecurity, she will come back to reassure him and may provide him with another secure base. Thus, the infant's angry expression of distress becomes functional in the service of gaining proximity or security. However, if the mother interprets the infant's anger as aggression, she may choose to ignore or reject his/her distress. Under such circumstances, the infant's anger may become dysfunctional because the goal of proximity and security is not achieved and anger lingers on. Appropriate discourses with the verbal child about such associations between inner feeling states and attachment figures' (as well as other people's) responses will make the child's attachment experiences available for reflections and understanding at the level of conscious language (Harris, 1999). This process is part of the cultural anthropology aspect of attachment theory. This background will serve to elucidate the multiple influences of early pre-verbal and later discursive "external" organization of emotions and behavior in terms of "maternal sensitivity and valuing attachment."

Development of attachment behavior strategies and attachment representation

Measurements of quality of attachment in infancy as assessed in the Strange Situation Procedure, in childhood, by using projective presentations of separations, or starting in adolescence by conducting the Adult Attachment Interview, were central to the rapid development of attachment research. However, it should not be forgotten that attachment theory is much richer and needs more creative research than demonstrating links between only a few attachment measures. As an open theory patterned after behavioral biology, its strength lies in generating hypotheses by observing and comparing attachment relevant events. As we could demonstrate, our inductive measures, sensitivity and valuing attachment on the one side and quality of discourse on the other, yielded a much richer harvest than the few traditional attachment measures. Attachment theory, as a special way of thinking about human development, may guide attachment research much better than any particular already existing methodology.

Development of discourse about attachment issues

Learning through discourse takes much longer and needs more effort on the part of the child and the caretaker than can be achieved by maternal sensitivity alone. Discourse is the most important way of establishing firm connections between internal coherence and external correspondence. This is not only valid in the realm of formal knowledge and intelligence (Sternberg, 1997), but particularly important for linking pre- and extra-verbal experiences within attachment relationships to their underlying emotions and behaviors. Mental links have to be formed between the reaction patterns of the attachment figures and the child's emotional and other experiences. In the Adult Attachment Interview, for example, a person may report about a miserable childhood but at the same time and in a goal-corrected manner find coherent and non-hostile justifications for her or his parents' behaviors. Thus, related emotions can be acknowledged and dealt with appropriately. This mental representation of attachment is classified as "earned secure" within the Adult Attachment Interview coding system (Hesse, 1999).

In our longitudinal study, first indications of clarity of motives and an orientation toward solutions, i.e. integration of negative emotions into a goal-corrected strategy, came about at age six (see Figures 3.4, 3.5a, 3.5b). Interrelations between ages 6, 10, and 16 were highly significant. At age 16, access to one's own feelings was well established in many subjects and correlated highly with security of partnership representation and quality of discourse about partnership at age 22. Of course, it is not words alone that bring about security in partnership representation in young adulthood. Our data suggest that there is a continuum between early organization of emotions through maternal sensitivity and the integration of this organization into a coherent narrative representation of the self in an attachment relationship.

The father's role in his child's attachment development

Fathers have been a neglected group in attachment research. Those few researchers who have assessed infant-father patterns of attachment have mostly found weaker but parallel effects in comparison to the effects of mothers' influences (Belsky, 1999). However, the role of fathers for child development is different in many ways (Parke and Buriel, 1998). We found many and strong longitudinal relationships between the ages of 2 and 16 when, instead of relying on the Strange Situation Procedure as the core assessment of the child-father relationship, we assessed the father's support of the child's desire for exploration and his sensitive behaviors towards the child's new competencies (Grossmann, K. *et al.*, in prep.). In this sample, we found a direct correlation between the play sensitivity of fathers with their two-year-old toddlers, the mental representation of attachment of their 16-year-old children, and the partnership representation of the same children at age 22. Our findings suggest that fathers' sensitive play and supportive challenges are just as important as the sensitivity of mothers to attachment signals of the infant and child. Both seem to provide a decisive contribution to the development of children's relationship representation. In line with our findings, we like to think that there may be a gender difference in parents' impact on the development of the overall mental security of their child. Together, both lay the developmental foundation of secure attachment development. According to our observations, both invest in their children's need for security and protection by responding to their need for a secure base and to their desire for exploration. Without the attachment person's availability, support, and cooperation the child's exploration has been shown to be less elaborate and less concentrated (Carew, 1980, Ainsworth and Bell, 1970). Our data suggest that secure partnership representations are based on both parents and that mothers and fathers contribute differently to that development.

Conclusion

The Current Relationship Interview is the first set of data of the 22-year-olds presently available to us. Further data sets are being analyzed. Attachment theory as an open theory requires new ways of thinking and assessments influenced by biological and cultural anthropology which, if we are lucky, should help us to discover new aspects of attachment development (Grossmann, K.E. and Grossmann, K., 1984). We have introduced a number of new measurements along three pathways to a secure partnership representation. The strong interrelations presented here suggest that these measures add to the central body of attachment theory. However, our most important goal is to provide solid data reflecting a strong causal relationship between an individual's experience with his or her parents and the later capacity to make affectional bonds, as Bowlby (1987) suggested. Trevarthen stresses the importance of "older and wiser brains" for an integration of emotional organization and cognitive representation across the life span (Trevarthen, 1987a, b). Now, there is additional empirical support for this notion. Our longitudinal results suggest that discoursive elaboration with engaged parents or other mindful attachment figures is important for the development of coherent and psychologically secure internal working models of self and others. Thus, attachment research has been able to provide a secure base for understanding an important aspect of an "experiential perspective on the ontogenesis of psychological complexity" (Csikszentmihalyi and Rathunde, 1998). We believe we have provided some insight into how attachment experiences, throughout the years of immaturity, come to have an impact on a young adult's "state of mind" with regard to his/her affectional partnerships.

ACKNOWLEDGMENTS

The Bielefeld Longitudinal Study has repeatedly been funded by Deutsche Forschungs-Gemeinschaft. Decisive funding in crucial phases of risk and increased uncertainty came from Koehler-Stiftung München, which is gratefully acknowledged. We especially thank Kerstin Stöcker for her competent and well-organized data analyses and graphic presentations.

REFERENCES

Aimer, B., and Müller, C. (1998). Die Entwicklung von adaptiven Perspektiven im sprachlichen Diskurs von 6 und 10jährigen Kindern. Zusammenhänge von 0–10 Jahren (Birgit Aimer). Zusammenhänge von 6–16 Jahren (Christina Müller) (The development of adaptive perspectives in discourse of 6 and 10 year old children: Correlations from 0 to 10 years (Birgit Aimer). Correlations from 6 to 16 years (Christina Müller)). Unpublished Dilpom Thesis. Institut für Psychologie, Universität Regensburg.

Ainsworth, M. D. S. (1964). Pattern of attachment behavior shown by the infant in interaction with his mother. *Merrill-Palmer Quarterly*, 10, 51–8.

Ainsworth, M. D. S. and Bell, S. M. (1970). Attachment exploration, and separation: illustrated by the behavior of one-year-olds in a strange situation. *Child Development*, 41, 49–67.

Ainsworth, M. D. S., Bell, S. M., and Stayton, D. J. (1974). Infant-mother attachment and social development: "Socialization" as a product of reciprocal responsiveness to signals. In P. M. Richards (ed.), *The integration of a child into a social world*, Cambridge University Press, 99–135.

Ainsworth, M. D. S., Blehar, M. C., Waters, E., and Wall, S. (1978). *Patterns of attachment. A psychological study of the strange situation*, Hillsdale, NJ: Lawrence Erlbaum Associates.

Belsky, J. (1999). Interactional and contextual determinants of attachment security. In J. Cassidy, and P. R. Shaver (eds.). *Handbook of attachment theory and research*, New York: Guilford Press, 249–64.

Bowlby, J. (1969/82). *Attachment and loss*, London: Hogarth Press, vol. 1 Attachment.

Bowlby, J. (1973). *Attachment and loss*, New York: Basic Books, vol. 2 Separation: anxiety and anger.

Bowlby, J. (1979). *The making and breaking of affectional bonds*, London: Tavistock Publications.

Bowlby, J. (1987). Attachment. In R. L. Gregory (ed.), *The Oxford companion to the mind*, Oxford University Press, 57–8.

Bretherton, I., and Munholland, K. A. (1999). Internal working models in attachment relationships: a construct revisited. In J. Cassidy, and P. R. Shaver (eds.), *Handbook of attachment theory and research*, New York: Guilford Press, 89–114.

Carew, J. (1980). Experience and the development of intelligence in children at home and in day care. *Monographs of the Society for Research in Child Development*, 45.

Crowell, J., and Owens, G. (1998). Current Relationship Interview and Scoring System. Unpublished manuscript. State University of New York at Stony Brook.

Csikszentmihalyi, M., and Rathunde, K. (1998). The development of the person: an experiential perspective on the ontogenesis of psychological complexity. In W. Damon (Editor-in-Chief), and R. M. Lerner (Vol. Ed.), *Handbook of child psychology*, vol. 1: *Theoretical models of human development*, 635–84. New York: John Wiley and Sons, Inc.

Fremmer-Bombik, E., Rudolph, J., Veit, B., Schwarz, G., and Schwarzmeier, I. (1989). Regensburger Auswertemethode des Adult Attachment Interviews (The Regensburg method of analyzing the Adult Attachment Interview). Unpublished manuscript. Universität Regensburg.

Geiger, U. (1991). Reaktionen sechsjähriger Kinder in imaginären Trennungssituationen (Reactions of six-year-olds in pictured separation situations). Diplomarbeit. Universität Regensburg.

George, C., Kaplan, N., and Main, M. (1984). Adult Attachment Interview Protocol. Unpublished manuscript, University of California at Berkeley.

Grice, H. P. (1975). Logic and conversation. In P. H. Cole, and J. L. Moran (eds.), *Syntax and semantics*. New York: Academic Press, vol. III, Speech acts, 41–58.

Grossmann, K., Fremmer-Bombik, E., Rudolph, J., and Grossmann, K. E. (1988). Maternal attachment representations as related to patterns of infant-mother attachment and maternal care during the first year. In R. A. Hinde, and J. Stevenson-Hinde (eds.), *Relationships within families*, Oxford Science Publications, 241–60.

Grossmann, K., and Grossmann, K. E. (1991). Newborn behavior, early parenting quality and later toddler-parent relationships in a group of German infants. In J. K. Nugent, B. M. Lester, and T. B. Brazelton (eds.), *The cultural context of infancy*, Norwood: Ablex, vol. II, 3–38.

Grossmann, K., Grossmann, K. E., Fremmer-Bombik, E., Kindler, H., Scheuerer-Englisch, H., and Zimmermann, P. (in prep.). The uniqueness of the child-father attachment relationship: fathers' sensitive and challenging play as the pivotal variable in a 16-year longitudinal study.

Grossmann, K., Grossmann, K. E., Spangler, G., Suess, G., and Unzner, L. (1985). Maternal sensitivity and newborns' orientation responses as related to quality of attachment in northern Germany. In I. Bretherton, and E. Waters (eds.), *Growing points in attachment theory and research. Monographs of the Society for Research in Child Development*, 50, 233–56.

Grossmann, K. E. (1999). Old and new internal working models of attachment: the organisation of feelings and language. *Attachment and Human Development*, 1, 253–69.

Grossmann, K. E. and Grossmann, K. (1984). Discovery and proof in attachment research. Commentary to M. Lamb, R. M. Thompson, W. Garner, E. L. Charnov and D. Estes, Security of infantile attachment as assessed in the strange situation – its study and biological interpretation. *The Behavioral and Brain Science*, 7, 154–5.

Grossmann, K. E. and Grossmann, K. (1990). The wider concept of attachment in cross-cultural research. *Human Development*, 33, 31–47.

Grossmann, K. E., and Grossmann, K. (1991). Attachment quality as an organizer of emotional and behavioral responses in a longitudinal perspective. In C. M. Parkes, J. Stevenson-Hinde, and P. Marris (eds.), *Attachment across the life cycle*, London/New York: Tavistock/Routledge, 93–114.

Grossmann, K. E., Grossmann, K., and Zimmermann, P. (1999). A wider view of attachment and exploration: stability and change during the years of immaturity. In J. Cassidy, and P. R. Shaver (eds.), *Handbook of attachment: theory, research, and clinical applications*, New York: Guilford Press, 760–86.

Harris, P. (1999). Individual differences in understanding emotion: the role of attachment status and psychological discourse. *Attachment and Human Development*, 1, 307–24.

Hesse, E. (1999). The adult attachment interview. Historical and current perspectives. In J. Cassidy, and P. R. Shaver (eds.). *Handbook of attachment: theory, research, and clinical applications*, New York: Guilford Press, 395–433.

Kindler, H. (2001). PhD. Thesis, Department of Psychology, University of Regensburg.

Klagsbrun, M., and Bowlby, J. (1976). Responses to separation from parents: a clinical test for young children. *British Journal of Projective Psychology*, 21, 7–21.

Kobak, R. R. (1989). The marital Q-set. University of Delaware. Unpublished manuscript.

Kobak, R. R. (1993). The attachment interview Q-sort. University of Delaware. Unpublished manuscript.

Lazarus, R. S. (1991). Progress on a cognitive-motivational-relational theory of emotion. *American Psychologist*, 46, 819–34.

Maier, M. (2000). Subliminales Priming frühkindlicher Bindungserfahrungen und Bindungsrepräsentationen im jungen Erwachsenenalter. Experimentelle Überprüfung eines Kontinuitätsmodells (Subliminal priming of early childhood. Attachment quality and attachment representation in young adults. Experimental test of a continuity model). Unpublished doctoral dissertation. Institut für Psychologie, Universität Regensburg.

Main, M., and Goldwyn, R. (1984). Adult attachment classification and rating system. Unpublished manuscript, University of California, Berkeley.

Main, M., Kaplan, N., and Cassidy, J. (1985). Security in infancy, childhood, and adulthood: a move to the level of representation. In I. Bretherton, and E. Waters (eds.), *Growing points in attachment theory and research.* Monographs of the Society for Research in Child Development, 50, 66–106.

Meins, E. (1999). Sensitivity, security, and internal working models: bridging the transmission gap. *Attachment and Human Development*, 1, 325–42.

Nelson, K. (1999). Representations, narrative development, and internal working models. *Attachment and Human Development*, 1, 239–51.

Owens, G., Crowell, J. A., Pan, H. and Treboux, D. (1995). The prototype hypothesis and the origins of attachment working models: adult relationships with parents and romantic partners. *Monographs of the Society for Research in Child Development*, vol. 60(2–3), 216–33.

Papousek, H., and Papousek, M. (1987). Intuitive parenting: a dialectic counterpart to the infant's integrative competence. In J. D. Osofsky (ed.), *Handbook of infant development*, 2nd edn., New York: Wiley, 669–720.

Parke, R. D., and Buriel, R. (1998). Socialization in the family: ethnic and ecological perspectives. In W. Damon (Editor-in-Chief), and N. Eisenberg (Vol. Ed.), *Handbook of child psychology* (5th edn.), vol. 3: *Social, emotional, and personality development*, 463–552. New York: Wiley.

Scheuerer-Englisch, H. (1989). Das Bild der Vertrauensbeziehung bei zehnjährigen Kindern und ihren Eltern: Bindungsbeziehungen in längsschnittlicher und aktueller Sicht (Representations of trust-relationships in ten-year-olds and their parents: attachment relationships in longitudinal and concurrent perspectives). Unpublished doctoral dissertation, Universität Regensburg.

Solomon, J., and George, C. (1999). The measurement of attachment security in infancy and childhood. In J. Cassidy and P. R. Shaver (eds.). *Handbook of attachment: theory, research and clinical applications*, New York: Guilford Press, 287–316.

Spangler, G., and Schieche, M. (1998). Emotional and adrenocortical responses of infants to the strange situation: The differential function of emotional expression. *International Journal of Behavioral Development*, 22, 681–706.

Sroufe, L. A., Egeland, B., and Carlson, E. A. (1999). One social world: the integrated development of parent-child and peer relationships. In W. A. Collins and B. Laursen (eds.), *The Minnesota Symposia on Child Psychology*, Mahwah, NJ: Lawrence Erlbaum Associates, vol. 30, 241–61.

Sroufe, L. A., and Waters, E. (1977). Attachment as an organizational construct. *Child Development*, 48, 1184–99.

Sternberg, R. J. (1997). The concept of intelligence and its role in lifelong learning and success. *American Psychologist*, 52, 1030–7.

Strasser, Karin (in prep.). Bindungsrepräsentationen bei jungen Erwachsenen: Längsschnittliche Zusammenhänge (Attachment representation in young adults: Longitudinal correlations). Unpublished Doctoral Dissertation. Universität Regensburg.

Trevarthen, C. (1987a). Brain development. In R. L. Gregory (ed.), *The Oxford companion to the mind*, Oxford University Press, 101–10.

Trevarthen, C. (1987b). Mind in infancy. In R. L. Gregory (ed.), *The Oxford companion to the mind*, Oxford University Press, 362–8.

Van der Kolk, B. A. (1998). Zur Psychologie und Psychobiologie von Kindheitstraumata (The psychology and psychobiology of developmental trauma). *Praxis der Kinderpsychologie und Kinderpsychiatrie*, 47, 19–35.

Winter, M. (in prep.). Attachment relationships and partnership representations from 0 to 22 years (working title). Unpublished doctoral dissertation. Universität Regensburg.

Zimmermann, P. (1999). Structure and functions of internal working models of attachment and their role for emotion regulation. *Attachment and Human Development*, 1, 291–306.

Zimmermann, P. (2000). L'attachement à l'adolescence: mesure, développement et adaptation (Attachement in adolescence: Development, assessment, and adaptation). In S. Larose, G. M. Tarabulsy, D. R. Pederson & G. Moran (Eds.). *Attachement et développement*, Quebec University Press, 181–204.

Zimmermann, P., Fremmer-Bombik, E., Spangler, G. and Grossmann, K. E. (1997). Attachment in adolescence: a longitudinal perspective. In W. Koops, J. B. Hoeksma and D. C. van den Boom (eds.), *Development of interaction and attachment: traditional and non-traditional approaches*, Amsterdam: North-Holland, 281–292.

Zimmermann, P. and Grossmann, K. E. (1997). Attachment and adaptation in adolescence. In W. Koops, J. B. Hoeksma, and D. C. van den Boom (eds.), *Development of interaction and attachment: traditional and non-traditional approaches*, Amsterdam: North-Holland, 271–280.

4 How do adolescents select their friends? A behavior-genetic perspective

Richard J. Rose

Introduction

Friendships serve important functions for both children and adults. Across the life-span, the dynamics of friendship are complex (Hartup and Stevens, 1997; 1999) and, as yet, poorly understood. Two observations are well established: an absence of friends characterizes those who seek clinical intervention for personal problems, and good adjustment is associated with having a social network of friends. It is less certain whether friends directly contribute to our well-being, or whether well-adjusted persons find it easier to make and keep friends. Regardless, friendships provide children and adolescents with experiences that facilitate growth of social competence, providing functions critical to development of self-concept and serving as resources of emotional support, buffering against life stress (Price, 1996). Indeed, recent evidence suggests that only for children without mutual best friends does victimization predict bad behavioral outcomes; peer friendships appear to be crucial in preventing escalating cycles of peer abuse (Hodges, Malone and Perry, 1997; Hodges, Boivin, Vitaro and Bukowski, 1999). Friendship relations are implicated in children's social and emotional growth, influencing children's school adaptations, adjustment to major life transitions, and the acquisition of social skills and values (Bukowski, Newcomb, and Hartup, 1996). The developmental significance of friendships includes who one's friends are, as well as the stability and quality of those friendship relationships across time. And, because the identity of one's friends accounts for more outcome variance than whether one has friends (Hartup and Stevens, 1997), it is important to study the qualitative features of friendship selection.

There is much evidence that those who are friends are behaviorally similar. Such similarities arise from three sources: demographic propinquity, within which similar individuals are brought into contact with one another; selection processes, through which we select as friends those who are similar to ourselves; and socialization processes, by which we become similar to our friends by interacting with them. This chapter assumes that similarity is important to attraction and that selection choices are embedded in assortative processes; those processes have been characterized as complex, "about which relatively little is known" (Hartup and Stevens, 1997). Because research from behavior-genetics (e.g., Kendler, 1997) suggests that each of us plays a role in creating our own social environment, friendship choices made by young adolescent twins, as studied in this report, may inform us about assortative processes in friendship selection.

Recent behavioral research on adolescent friendship is guided by the fundamental hypothesis that we like those who are similar to ourselves. It must be more complex than that, for with age, children become more particular about their friendship choices and, although the number of friends does not necessarily increase with age, the number of reciprocated friendships does, as children increasingly restrict their nominations of friends to peers who, in turn, like them (Aboud and Mendelson, 1996). Nonetheless, a simple similarity-attraction hypothesis offers a framework for a twin study of friendship selection, for, if we like those who are like ourselves, twin children should make concordant friendship selections. This chapter reports that they do.

A substantial body of research literature reveals significant behavioral similarity among members of adolescent friendship dyads. As already acknowledged, propinquity contributes to such similarity, for adolescents have opportunities to befriend only those with whom they can interact, and regional, community, and neighborhood influences on behavior will create similarities in adolescent affiliations formed within those environments. But effects other than propinquity have been documented in research studies over the past six decades. Children and adolescents like those who are similar to themselves. And once formed, friendships among children and adolescents foster shared experiences that enhance the initial similarities that led to attraction and affiliation. Two seminal papers, published more than two decades ago, emphasized that similarities among adolescents may result from either or both selection and socialization, and the two processes are separable, conceptually and empirically. Selection processes lead to assortative pairing: adolescents purposefully select as their friends those already similar on attributes of importance to them. Attributes important in the similarity $\rightarrow$ attraction process will change with developmental age and may be modulated by sex, cohort, and culture. Selection is complemented by socialization: behavioral homogeneity among adolescent friends results also from socialization processes in which individuals who associate, regardless of initial similarity, reciprocally influence each other to enhance their concordance. The two seminal papers in this research area (Cohen, 1977; Kandel, 1978a) argued that selection and socialization are not mutually exclusive. Each can play a role at different points in the process of friendship formation, its maintenance and its dissolution. Both papers suggested that selection, as well as socialization, is important as an underlying cause of behavioral similarity among adolescent friends.

Cohen (1977) evaluated behavioral homogeneity across 18 questionnaire measures (e.g., frequency of smoking, drinking, dating, and church attendance) in all members of school cliques that were identified by asking high school students to name same-sex students with whom they associated most frequently. Analyses, carried out over time on characteristics of stable, new, and former members of surviving and new cliques, permitted the conclusion that similarity prior to clique formation was the most important contributor to the behavioral similarities observed. Results from Kandel's analysis (1978a) led to similar conclusions. She studied three types of dyads at two points in time: friendship pairs remaining stable from Time 1 to Time 2, those that dissolved by Time 2, and dyads that became new friends by Time 2. Distinctions could then be made between friendship pairs who remain stable over time, newly formed pairs, and pairs of former friends. Kandel's results revealed that adolescents coordinate their choices of friends by their behaviors, particularly so with regard to substance use. The general conclusions from these two influential papers are very much like earlier data collected on heterosexual dating couples: prior similarity for behaviors and attitudes influences interpersonal attraction and contributes to lasting relationships, documented by the finding that, early in their formation, friendships that dissolve are less similar than friendships that endure.

Actual similarity in adolescent friendships

There are now a number of published studies that have assessed actual similarity among adolescent friendship dyads in real-life relationships. These contrast with laboratory studies of similarity → attraction (Bryne and Griffitt, 1973), in which individuals are given controlled information about fictitious strangers to assess how variation in behavioral similarity influences attraction; the laboratory studies establish, in children and adults, a linear relationship between attraction and similarity, but they are of uncertain generalizability to real-life relationships which require us to seek information about strangers and evaluate similarity to self (Aboud and Mendelson, 1996). Studies of actual friendship similarity are particularly relevant to the twin study data we here report, so we selectively review some of these studies to provide a context for our own analyses.

We begin with one of the earliest studies of the role of behavioral similarity in friendship formation. It was reported by Challman (1932), in observational study of three and four year-old nursery school children; the study was intended to assess what factors, other than propinquity, influence friendship formation in early childhood. Friendship indices were created from the frequency with which each of the 33 sampled children was found in a group with every other child during free play; friendship was treated as a continuous variable in which every child had some degree of friendship and social affiliation with each of the 32 others. A major finding was the very strong influence of same-sex matching on affiliation; even among these very young children, nearly all social associations were conditioned by same-sex matching. That finding is a pervasive one among older children and young adolescents, although, quite obviously, in later adolescence, interest in the opposite sex emerges, as revealed in research and celebrated in song. From our perspective, the most interesting result from Challman's early study was the influence of the children's similarity for sociality, an index of cooperative behavior, in their friendship formation. Correlations between similarity for sociality and friendship associations were much stronger than those found for measured IQ or other behavioral variables.

One of the largest studies of adolescent friendship formation was reported by Kandel (1978b), who studied nearly 1,900 adolescent best-school-friend dyads among students from five public high schools, grades 9–12. Each student identified his or her best friend in the school (with no requirement that the friend be in the same grade or classroom), and consistent with other research, the nominated best-school-friends were predominantly (91 percent) of the same sex. The friendships were of some duration, most of three years or more. The highest similarities in these friendship dyads were for school grade (kappa = .84), sex (.81), ethnicity (.66), age (.64), and, among the behaviors measured, marijuana use (.40) and frequency of smoking (.34) and drinking (.25), as illustrated in Figure 4.1. Kandel (1978b) makes the interesting observation, without reporting details, that the overall observed behavioral similarity was higher in reciprocated friendships than in friendships that were not reciprocated. The conclusion reached in this study, like that offered by Cohen, is that similarity is an important, perhaps critical, variable in adolescent attraction.

In a more recent report, Kandel and colleagues (Kandel, Davies, and Baydar, 1990) present data from another large sample of adolescent best-school-friend dyads. Again, high school students were asked to nominate their best friend in school. Again, by far, most of these dyads were same-sex. And, the best school friend was the best friend overall for about

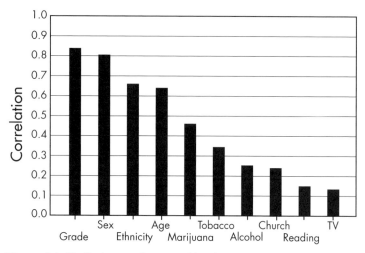

Figure 4.1 Similarity on demographic characteristics and behaviors within adolescent friendship dyads; characteristics shown in the figure include the school, grade, sex, ethnicity, and age of the adolescents, their use or abstinence from marijuana, tobacco, and liquor, frequency of attending religious services and leisure time spent in reading or watching TV. Data from Kandel, 1978, Table 1.

80 percent of the adolescents studied. The amount of observed similarity for substance use was high. The cross-sectional weighted kappas among the adolescent friendship dyads were all significant and typically ranged from .25 to .45 for use of cigarettes, alcohol, sedatives, stimulants, and other substances. Kandel and her colleagues conclude that dyads form *because* of similarity, and dyads then grow to be more similar over time. This now-familiar argument is set within a newer context – the thematic perspective of developmental behavior genetics that people create their own environments. With development, children gain control over the contextual environments in which they live their lives, and, by late adolescence, they join peer groups and form friendships to their liking – if not always to that of their parents! Kandel and colleagues conclude that there is a general tendency to seek out individuals similar to oneself, but suggest, without evidence, that not everyone shares this tendency to the same degree. Is this so? And if so, why? Why should there be individual differences in the strength of the similarity → attraction relationship? What is the origin of such individual differences? Further, individual differences in susceptibility to similarity in the formation of peer groups can be but half the story; there must be individual differences, as well, in

susceptibility to socialization effects subsequent to peer affiliation. What is *their* origin? Questions surrounding peer formation and peer influence during adolescence are many and provocative (Urberg, 1999), but answers await future research.

Such questions assume much importance in the growing research literature on the influence of selection and socialization with specific reference to health habits in friendship choices made by adolescents. Much of this research has specific reference to adolescent smoking and drinking, and the research is typically framed within evidence that substance use by an adolescent's peers powerfully predicts an adolescent's own use. Thus, Fisher and Bauman (1988) provide evidence of the impact of selection, as well as socialization, in formation of adolescent-friend relationships. These authors point out that although selection and socialization are not mutually exclusive, and both may well contribute to the observed similarity found in adolescent friendships, the two processes do imply different descriptions of the causal relationship between an adolescent's behavior and that of his/her peers. Socialization implies a direction of effect from friend to adolescent. In contrast, selection suggests that the source of similarity is 'within' the adolescent. Fisher and Bauman focused on patterns of smoking and drinking and tested the socialization hypothesis of a strong, positive association between a friend's behavior and change in an adolescent's behavior. Specifically, they tested whether abstinent adolescents with friends who are smokers or drinkers are more likely than those with non-user friends to initiate smoking or drinking over a period of time. Conversely, the socialization hypothesis predicts that smokers with non-smoking friends will more likely quit than will smokers whose friends are also smokers. In contrast, the selection model predicts that changes in friendship status will be related to the adolescent subject's own behavior. The behavior of newly acquired friends will be similar to that of the adolescent, such that subjects who are non-users are more likely than users to acquire a non-user friend. Similarly, users are more likely than non-users to choose other users to be their new friends. Studying large samples of school-age subjects in a longitudinal design, Fisher and Bauman (1988) concluded that the acquisition of friends "is determined to a great extent by the similarity between friend and subject", for their data offer stronger evidence of similarity $\rightarrow$ attraction than for affiliation $\rightarrow$ similarity. Figure 4.2 illustrates some of their results; 97 percent of baseline non-smokers, against 37 percent of baseline smokers, acquired non-smoking friends on follow-up. Friendship selection of users and non-users of beer and liquor were similarly directed by initial similarity. Ennett and Bauman (1994), report parallel results using social network analysis to identify adolescent cliques.

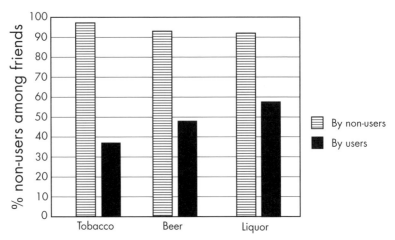

Figure 4.2 Tobacco and alcohol use attributed to friends acquired by adolescents who, themselves, were non-smokers/non-drinkers or smoking/drinking adolescents; for tobacco, 97% of non-smokers, but 37% of smokers, acquired a non-smoking friend. Data from Fisher and Bauman, 1988.

Finally, another recent study (Tolson and Urberg, 1993) offers an important replication of Kandel's work. This sample, like that of Kandel, was large – more than 2,300 students in grades 8 and 11 from thirteen public and private schools, and, interestingly, ethnic minority students comprised about one-third of the sample. Each student nominated two same-grade, same-school best friends and, consistent with earlier work, 94 percent of the matched dyads were of the same sex, and 88 percent were of the same ethnicity. Overall, about 44 percent of the friendship dyads were reciprocated, with each member selecting the other. The measures, taken from an existent data set, were associated with adolescent smoking (abstinence/use and frequency of smoking among users) and its risk factors (attitudes toward smoking and importance of peer involvement). Adolescent friendship dyads were significantly similar on all measures, with the highest intra-class correlation (0.58) for ever having smoked. Evidence of greater behavioral similarity among the reciprocated relationships was inconsistent across measures and ethnic groups.

Perceived similarity in adolescent friendships

The studies of *actual* similarity reviewed above can be contrasted with studies of *perceived* similarity. Adolescents perceive themselves to be similar to their friends. There are a number of studies in which adolescents are assessed on targeted behaviors, and the adolescents are then asked to attribute to their peers (or best friends) the same behaviors. Thus, a design in recent research literature in substance abuse has compared attributed similarity in peer use of tobacco and alcohol among adolescent subjects who differ in their own smoking and drinking patterns. In a variation on this design, parents describe the frequency of substance use in their adolescent children and then attribute substance use to their children's close friends. These studies of perceived similarity are subject to systematic biases, for adolescents over-estimate their similarity to their friends (Urberg, 1999), and parents' descriptions of their children's peers are prone to a similar bias.

Twin studies of perceived similarity of peers

Of direct relevance to this chapter are two recent studies, using genetically-informative designs, of perceived similarity among adolescents' peers. In one study, Grant and her colleagues (Grant, Bucholz, Madden, Slutske, and Heath, 1998) acknowledge that peer substance use is so predictive of an adolescent's own use that one must ask: how do adolescents become involved with peers who smoke and drink? Do genetic dispositions actively influence peer-selection? If so, data from peer attributions of monozygotic (MZ) and dizygotic (DZ) twins should reveal that fact. A sample of >400 pairs of twin sisters, at mean age 18, were asked to describe what proportion of their friends smoke and drink; results showed that both MZ and DZ twin sisters attributed substantial similarity in smoking and drinking patterns to their friends, a result suggesting large effects arising from the twins' shared environments, with no significant or consistent evidence of genetic effects. Of course, adolescent twin sisters will share many common friends, may not distinguish personal from shared friends, and, as already noted, may systematically bias reports of their friends' behavior. Another genetically-informative study of perceived similarity was reported by Manke, McGuire, Reiss, Hetherington, and Plomin (1995), who compared parents' perceptions of their adolescent children's peer groups; the sample included >700 same-sex sibling pairs, ages 10–18, comprised of MZ and DZ twins, full siblings, and step-siblings. The varying levels of genetic relationship within these several sibships (unity for MZ twins, one-half for full siblings, one-quarter for half-siblings and zero for unrelated siblings) offer unusual and informative analyses. The parents of each sibling pair rated the peer group of both of their children on adjective scales intended to measure delinquency, popularity, and college orientation of each child's peers. Correlations across all types of related siblings were significant, and, within step families, were as high for half-siblings as for full siblings. These are not unexpected findings, given that the correlations are based on a single rater in which each parent rates the peer group of both siblings. Bias in the ratings enhances all sibling correlations, inflating estimates of both genetic and familial-environmental effects on peer selection, if parents perceive peers of their children to be more similar than they are, and if that biased perception is greater for parents of MZ twin children. With those caveats in mind (caveats acknowledged by Manke *et al.*, 1995), the pattern of results suggests that both genetic and shared environmental influences may affect adolescent peer formation.

We have obtained new data on perceived similarity of peer substance use from a large population-based sample of Finnish twins at age 16 (Rose, Kaprio, Winter, Koskenvuo, and Viken, 1999). The sample included 5,400 twins from five consecutive birth cohorts who were sequentially enrolled into the study, over 60 months of baseline testing, as they reached age 16. The twins self-reported smoking and drinking behaviors were assessed, and the twins attributed to their peers what proportion used tobacco, liquor, and beer with questionnaire items similar to those used by Grant *et al.* (1998) in their study of twin sisters. The pattern of correlations yields answers to several questions: do adolescent twins, at age 16, assort with friends they describe as similar to themselves in patterns of smoking and drinking? The non-surprising answer, obtained from correlations of twin individuals and their peers, is positive, and correlations are very consistent across twins of both sexes and all five twin types; e.g., correlations between a twin's self-reported frequency of intoxication with the drinking attributed by that adolescent twin to his or her peers range from .37 to .44 across the five twin types (MZ and DZ twin brothers, MZ and DZ twin sisters, and brother-sister DZ twin pairs). Perceived similarity of *individual* twins to their peers does not vary with zygosity. But what of the similarity of the *peers of co-twins*? A much more interesting question: do MZ co-twins attribute greater similarity to their peers than do DZ co-twins? Results shown in Figure 4.3, which plots correlations for the proportion of peers drinking alcohol attributed by co-twins of the five twin types, suggest that they do. The proportions of peers to whom drinking is attributed by MZ twin sisters (FMZ in the Figure) correlate .72; for DZ twin sisters (FDZ), the comparable correlation is .61. The correlation for MZ twin brothers is .61; that for DZ twin brothers is .50, and, for the 925 brother-sister (opposite-sex DZ or OSDZ) twins who affiliate with gender-matched peers, peer drinking correlates but .28. These results suggest very large effects from the twins' shared experiences, their common friends, and their reciprocal

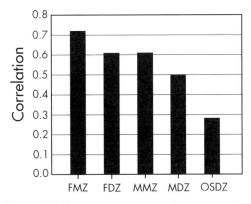

Figure 4.3 Correlations between frequency of substance use reported by 16-year-old Finnish twins and the frequency of substance use they attribute to their peers. Data from *FinnTwin16* (Rose *et al.*, 1999).

interactions with one another. The correlations suggest only modest effects from shared genes. Brother-sister pairs likely share far fewer friends, and they may accurately attribute greater disparity in drinking patterns to their separate and sex-stratified friends. Frequency of drinking patterns among adolescent same-sex DZ (SSDZ) twins are significantly more similar than those of brother-sister (OS) DZ pairs, just as drinking patterns of MZ co-twins are significantly more similar than those of SSDZ twin pairs. So, MZ co-twins are more alike in their own patterns of drinking, and they attribute greater drinking similarity to their peers. Of course, the peers of MZ co-twins may actually be more alike. Or is it only that the twins perceive them so? With data from another, ongoing study of Finnish twins, we sought an answer.

A twin study of actual similarity

We know of no previous investigation of actual peer similarity using a genetically-informative design. We report first results from such an investigation here, using data from a second Finnish twin study, in which baseline data were collected at ages 11–12. For a subset of twins in the study, the baseline assessment included a standardized, school-based peer-nomination of behavior (Pulkkinen, Kaprio, and Rose, 1999) made of twins and their classmates; using the peer nomination data, we explored genetic contributions to friendship choice by studying behavioral resemblance among nominated best-school-friends of 1,150 twin children.

The data are from an on-going longitudinal twin study we call *FinnTwin12* (Rose, 1998). The subjects are from five consecutive birth cohorts of Finnish twin children enrolled into the study, with postal questionnaires, at age 11. In the winter and spring of the following year, the year in which the twin subjects reached age 12, intensively studied subsets were appraised in school-based assessments, including a peer nomination procedure in which all pupils in all classrooms containing one (or both) targeted twins engaged in a 33-item behavioral rating process. For each of the behavioral attributes, each child in the classroom was asked to nominate classmates who best fit that attribute. No mention was made of the fact that the twins in the class were the focus of our study. The last of the 33 items asked each child to nominate two classmates for the question: "Who are your best friends?". With data from that item, we identified the nominated best friends of monozygotic and dizygotic twin children and asked three questions:

(1) Are MZ co-twins more likely to nominate one another and/or common classmates as their best friends?
(2) Do twins identify as their best friends, classmates who are behaviorally similar to themselves?
(3) In dyads formed from the best friends of co-twins, are there greater similarities in peer-ratings of the best friends of MZ twins?

Our initial analyses offer affirmative answers to all three questions.

Subjects

From 1994 through 1998, Finnish families with twins born in the years 1983 through 1987 were identified from Finland's Central Population Registry, and, in the autumn of the year in which the twins reached age 11, the families were sequentially invited to participate in the study by completing questionnaires; ~87 percent of identified families did so. Parents completed a family questionnaire that concerned the twins' childhood development and medical history and requested permission to contact the schools attended by their twin children enabling us to carry out peer ratings. Consent was obtained from ~93 percent of respondent families. Selection for inclusion in the intensively-studied sub-sample, for which peer ratings were sought, was made randomly from families for about half of all subjects, and the random sub-sample was enriched with "at risk" twins, selected on the basis of parental scores on an alcohol screening test. Peer nominations were conducted in school. Permission from school principals was obtained in 99 percent of the cases. Peer nomination data were obtained from 953 twin pairs, enrolled in 1,002 classrooms throughout

Finland, and those classes included >25,000 pupils who participated in the peer nomination procedures. For the analyses of friendship selection here reported, we excluded brother-sister twins, all twin pairs in which the co-twins were not in the same classroom, pairs of uncertain zygosity, and pairs for whom data on the twins' friendship choices were missing; these exclusions left a sample of 1,150 twins who formed 575 same-sex twin pairs, 306 MZ and 269 DZ.

Measures, variables, and procedures

The peer nomination instrument was developed explicitly for this study as a multidimensional inventory of children's social behavior. Core items for the instrument were developed in the earlier longitudinal research of Lea Pulkkinen (1987) from a set of items originating in her own work and from earlier instruments developed by others. The final version of the Multidimensional Peer Nomination Inventory (MPNI) used in this study was created after a series of pilot studies. Peer nominations were made in classroom settings under supervision of a research staff member. Except for the first two and the last of the 33 items, the inventory was presented in a mixed order. Each pupil was given a pad with 33 pages; the first two items, which asked the child to identify him or herself and to indicate which classmates were absent from the classroom on that day, provided practice with the task-demands of the method. All pages were similar; each page included the given names of all students in the class, divided by gender and presented, within gender, in alphabetical order. All questions (e.g., "Which of your classmates may hurt other kids when they are angry, for instance, by hitting, kicking, or throwing things at them?") were read aloud by the research assistant; the pupils responded by crossing out the names of those classmates who engage in the behavior described. For all but the first two and the last item, pupils were asked to nominate three female and three male classmates who best fit the described behavior of each item. Each pupil in the class received some number of nominations for each item, and these were expressed as a percentage, a ratio of received nominations to the maximum number that pupil could have received.

Factor analysis of the MPNI (Pulkkinen, Kaprio, and Rose, 1999) identified three factors. The first, Behavioral Problems, is loaded by items for hyperactivity-impulsiveness, aggression, and inattention. The second factor, loaded by constructiveness, social activities, and compliance, is labeled Adjustment. The third factor, comprised of items for anxiety and depression, is identified as Emotional Problems. In the analyses here reported, we focus on correlations of these three factor scales in peer ratings of twin-friend dyads and for dyads formed by the non-common friends of co-twins from all same-sex twin pairs of known zygosity schooled in the same classroom.

Results

The 1,150 individual twins identified 2,240 best classmate friends; of these, 296 (13.2 percent) were nominations of the co-twin. Because twins were not prohibited from nominating one another and because, as expected, some did so, we first asked: do more MZ than DZ twins nominate one another as (one of) their best classmate friends? The answer, suggestively although not significantly, is yes: 182 of the 612 MZ twins (29.7 percent) but only 114 of the 538 DZ twins (21.2 percent) chose their co-twin as one of their best classmate friends.

We next asked: do MZ co-twins tend to nominate, with greater frequency than do DZ co-twins, common classmates as their best friends? Or, conversely, are DZ co-twins more likely to form networks of best classmate friends that have no commonality? Table 4.1 provides answers. The proportion of 12-year-old twins that nominate neither common classmate friends, nor one another, as best friends is 3.6× greater among DZ twin sisters than among MZ twin sisters, and 1.5× greater among DZ than MZ twin brothers. Conversely, one can ask what proportion of twin pairs, again of differing twin types, share *both* a common friend, *as well as* the co-twin. These pairs have the greatest overlap in their network of friends, for they share one another and the same classmate as their best friends. The second column of Table 4.1 lists these proportions; these "most alike" friend networks characterize more than one-quarter of MZ

Table 4.1 *Best friend networks of 12 year-old twins*

Twin type[a]	N	Percent least alike[b]	Percent most alike[c]
FMZ	156	8.8	29.4
MMZ	126	17.8	25.0
FDZ	150	32.0	19.5
MDZ	143	26.7	13.7

Notes: [a]FMZ/MMZ = female/male monozygotic twin pairs; FDZ/MDZ = female/male dizygotic twin pairs
[b]Pairs in which co-twins nominate neither common classmate nor one another as best friend
[c]Pairs sharing both common classmates and one another as best friends

Table 4.2 *Correlations of peer-related behavior for all twin-friend dyads*

Type	N dyads[a]	Behavior problems	Emotional problems	Adjustment
Girls	1098	0.42[b]	0.44	0.39
Boys	1112	0.28	0.42	0.26
All	2210	0.35	0.46	0.33

Notes: [a]All possible twin-friend dyads after exclusion of twin-twin dyads
[b]$p < .01$ for all correlations

pairs, but only ~15 percent of DZ twin pairs. Clearly, at age 11-12, the networks of best classmate friends of MZ co-twins more likely include one another and more likely include common classmates than do those of DZ co-twins.

The third, and more interesting, question asks: how do twins choose their classmate friends? Do twins like those who are like themselves? To address it, we formed all possible dyads of each individual twin and that twin's nominated classmate friends. The correlations of peer-nominated behavior for these twin-friend dyads are given in Table 4.2 for the three factor scales of the MPNI. Correlations for all three scales are highly significant for twin-friend dyads among both boys and girls. The correlations in Table 4.1 are inflated by the fact that 13 percent of the dyads are of twins and their co-twins. But we included those dyads to ensure that the correlations reported in Table 4.1 reflect the *actual* behavioral similarity of twins' friendship relations as rated by their classmates.

Clearly, individual 12-year-old twins choose as their best friends, classmates who are behaviorally similar to themselves. The correlations in Table 4.2 offer evidence that similarity in actual behavior, as assessed by peers, is an influential factor in friendship selection, evidence that 12-year-old Finnish children like those who are behaviorally like themselves. Interestingly, twin-friend correlations are consistently higher for twin girls than twin boys, not only for the three factor scales of the MPNI shown in Table 4.2, but for all of the individual scales which comprise these factors. Perhaps at this age, when girls are more psycho-sexually mature than boys and often given more social responsibility as a result, assortative pairing is more characteristic of girls' friendship selections.

Finally, the question of most interest: do the nominated best friends of all twins exhibit behavioral similarity and are friends of MZ co-twins more behaviorally alike than those of DZ co-twins? What is the actual similarity, as rated by classmate peers, of twins' best friends? To answer that question, we restricted the nominated friends to independent dyads, requiring that each twin nominate a classmate not nominated by the co-twin, to yield a direct test of the influence of shared genes and shared family environments in active friendship selection. If there is assortative pairing, the independent classmate friends nominated by co-twins will be significantly alike. And, if assortative pairing is influenced by genetic dispositions, friends of MZ co-twins will be more alike than those of DZs. Of course, samples for MZ twin sisters will be smaller, given the restriction that the co-twins must nominate separate classroom friends, and fewer MZ twin sisters do so. We used all dyads created by the twins' friendship selections, such that a twin pair could generate four dyads for the analysis, if neither co-twin nominated one another, but both nominated two classmates, sharing none; conversely, a twin pair that nominated one another and a common classmate did not contribute to this analysis.

Results for the three factor dimensions of the MPNI are shown in Table 4.3. The most striking result is that classmates rate the friends of both MZ and DZ twin sisters as significantly alike for emotional problems (anxiety and depression). That result suggests that age 12 girls assortatively select as their friends, girls whose levels of depression and anxiety are similar to their own. The friends of MZ twin sisters are significantly correlated also in peer ratings of behavioral problems (hyperactivity-impulsiveness, aggressiveness, and inattention). Correlations of the independent friends of twin brothers are lower, and none achieve significance. Perhaps, as suggested by the lower correlations found in male twin-friend dyads, assortative pairing is less influential among boys at this age. Collapsing on gender, three of the six correlations of behavioral similarity among twins' independent classroom-best-friends achieve significance. Although the magnitude of these correlations is modest, they represent

Table 4.3 *Correlations for MPNI scale scores among friendship dyads of twins*

Type	N dyads[a]	Behavior problems	Emotional problems	Adjustment
FMZ	81	0.27[b]	0.34[b]	0.11
FDZ	121	0.14	0.27[b]	−0.01
MMZ	122	0.10	0.05	0.09
MDZ	153	0.15	0.10	−0.03
All MZ	203	0.15[b]	0.15[b]	0.09
All DZ	274	0.04	0.19[b]	−0.01

Notes: [a]Number of dyads formed from all possible pairings of best friends of both twins in each pair; co-twins and common classmate friends excluded
[b] $p < .05$

the first direct evidence of assortative pairing in behavioral ratings by classmate peers.

These results, documenting some significant resemblance of twins' friendship choices, are consistent with the inference of active selection processes in friendship formation. Those selection processes may be conditioned by both genetic dispositions and shared environmental experience. With larger samples, more incisive analyses can be made, in approaches we sketch below.

Assortative mating and assortative pairing

Our results are, quite obviously, preliminary; we offer them as an illustration of a research approach, rather than as a definitive empirical story. Limitations of sample size, particularly the very limited number of independent best-friend dyads of MZ co-twins, constrain these initial analyses. But our full sample adds 255 brother-sister twin pairs in common classes and 100 pairs of co-twins schooled in separate classrooms; twins in separated classes are highly informative, for their nominated classmate friends are, necessarily, different individuals, and they are rated by independent classroom raters in different classroom contexts. The present results offer but a promissory note on the potential utility of studying friendship selection among adolescent twins. We conclude by sketching that potential, placing the analyses of assortative pairing within a discussion of earlier research on assortative mating.

Studying friendship selection by adolescent twins and assessing the actual similarities of twins' friends can inform us on processes by which selection leads to attraction and affiliation. We suggest that assortative pairing in same-sex adolescent friendships parallels assortative mating of adult men and women. Married spouses are behaviorally alike, with correlations ranging as high as 0.5 for verbal IQ (Nance, Corey, Rose, and Eaves, 1981) and religious values (Schooley, 1936) to a range of 0.15 to 0.45 for major personality dimensions (Buss, 1984). These behavioral correlations observed among spouses, like those observed in adolescent friendship dyads, may arise from selection or socialization, from assortative mating and selective pairing of couples at courtship/marriage, or from cumulative socialization effects of shared lives thereafter. How can we resolve these effects? Marriages of twins offer one approach, for these marriages create four correlations of interest in evaluating selection and socialization processes. The correlations are first, that between the twins; second, the marital correlation of husband and wife; third, the correlation of a twin and the spouse of the co-twin; fourth, the correlation between the spouses of the two twins. Elsewhere (Nance, Corey, and

Eaves, 1980; Nance *et al.*, 1981), expected values of these correlations were described by genetic and environmental path models to partition the correlations into causal elements and assess concordant assortation. Here, we note only that comparisons of interest can distinguish selection from socialization. In the case of MZ twins, comparing correlations between husband and wife with those between twin and co-twin's spouse provides a measure of the contribution of the common home environment to the observed marital correlation. Husband and wife share a household environment that twin and spouse of the co-twin do not.

Analogously, we can compare the resemblance between twins and their friends with that of twins and their co-twins' friends. The first dyads share social experiences that the second dyads do not; if socialization effects contribute to friendship resemblance, the correlations should differ. If socialization effects are large, as some posit they are for, say, substance use, dyads sharing social experience should exhibit substantially greater resemblance.

A second comparison of interest is that between each co-twin and that twin's friends with that between the independent friends of the co-twins; the comparison offers a measure of concordant assortation. If twins are assortatively pairing, their independent friends will resemble one another as much as the twins resemble their own friends. Figure 4.4 suggests these several relationships within the friendship associations of twins. Although our available data may not be an adequate match for the potential of

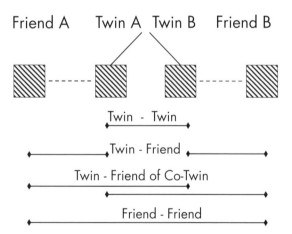

Figure 4.4 Illustration of the four correlations created by the relationships of co-twins to their friends

this design, given few MZ co-twins at age 12 who have independent classmate friends, we will add brother-sister twin pairs and focus on co-twins schooled in separate classrooms, in efforts to conduct analyses that exploit the analytic strategies suggested in Figure 4.4. Results of such analyses should enhance understanding of selection processes in adolescent friendship formation and the role of friendship in life-course development (Hartup and Stevens, 1997).

Summary

Selection, as well as socialization, contributes to the behavioral similarities observed in adolescent friendships. We like those who are like ourselves, and the salient similarities for social selection are behavioral, as well as demographic. To assess processes of friendship selection, we studied similarities attributed by 16-year-old co-twins to their peers, finding that monozygotic (MZ) co-twins attributed greater similarity to their peers' smoking and drinking patterns than did dizygotic (DZ) twins. We then studied overlap in classmate friendship choices made by 12-year-old twins and evaluated peer-rated behavioral similarities of the twins' classmate friends. MZ twins more often than DZ twins identified each other and common classmates as their best friends, and classmates rated the friends of MZ twins more alike than the friends of DZ twins. Our results suggest that active selection processes influence adolescent affiliations: the greater similarity of MZ co-twins leads them to choose, as their friends, classmates who are more similar to one another. Marital choices of adult twins have informed the study of assortative mating among adults; analogously, developmental studies of friendship selection by adolescent twins will inform processes, and consequences, of assortative pairing during behavioral development.

ACKNOWLEDGMENTS

The Finnish twin-family research described in this paper has been conducted in collaboration with Lea Pulkkinen, University of Jyväskylä, and Jaakko Kaprio, University of Helsinki; I am deeply grateful for their collaboration. The research is supported by the National Institute on Alcohol Abuse and Alcoholism (grants AA 00145, AA 08315, AA 09203, and AA 07611) and by the Academy of Finland. I thank Risto Hietala for his skilled assistance in analysis of the peer nomination data of *FinnTwin12* and Jennifer Johnson for her analysis of perceived similarity in *FinnTwin16*.

REFERENCES

Aboud, F. E., and Mendelson, M. J. (1996). Determinants of friendship selection and quality: developmental perspectives. In W. M. Bukowski, A. F.
Newcomb, and W. W. Hartup (eds.), *The company they keep: friendship in
childhood and adolescence*, Cambridge University Press, 87–112.

Bryne, D., and Griffitt, W. (1973). Interpersonal attraction. *Annual Review of
Psychology*, 24, 317–43.

Bukowski, W. M., Newcomb, A. F., and Hartup, W. W. (1996). Friendship and
its significance in childhood and adolescence: introduction and comment. In
Bukowski, W. M., Newcomb, A. F., and Hartup, W. W. (eds.), *The company
they keep: friendship in childhood and adolescence*, Cambridge University Press,
1–15.

Buss, D. M. (1984). Toward a psychology of person-environment correspondence: the role of spouse selection. *Journal of Personality and Social Psychology*,
47, 361–77.

Challman, R. C. (1932). Factors influencing friendships among preschool children. *Child Development*, 3, 146–58.

Cohen, J. M. (1977). Sources of peer group homogeneity. *Sociology of Education*,
50, 227–41.

Ennett, S. T., and Bauman, K. E. (1994). The contribution of influence and selection to adolescent peer group homogeneity: the case of adolescent cigarette
smoking. *Journal of Personality and Social Psychology*, 67, 653–63.

Fisher, L. A., and Bauman, K. E. (1988). Influence and selection in the friend-
adolescent relationship: findings from studies of adolescent smoking and
drinking. *Journal of Applied Social Psychology*, 18, 289–314.

Grant, J. D., Bucholz, K. K., Madden, P. A. F., Slutske, W. S., and Heath,
A. C. (1998). Peer substance use during adolescence: evidence for shared
environmental influences. *Behavior Genetics*, 28, 469 (abstr).

Hartup, W. W., and Stevens, N. (1997). Friendships and adaptation in the life
course. *Psychological Bulletin*, 121, 355–70.

Hartup, W. W., and Stevens, N. (1999). Friendships and adaptation across the
life span. *Current Directions in Psychological Science*, 8, 76–9.

Hodges, V. E., Boivin, M., Vitaro, F., and Bukowski, W. M. (1999). The power
of friendship: protection against an escalating cycle of peer victimization.
Developmental Psychology, 35, 94–101.

Hodges, V. E., Malone, M. J., and Perry, D. G. (1997). Individual risk and
social risk as interacting determinants of victimization in the peer group.
Developmental Psychology, 33, 1032–9.

Kandel, D. B. (1978a). Homophily, selection, and socialization in adolescent
friendships. *American Journal of Sociology*, 84, 427–36.

Kandel, D. B. (1978b). Similarity in real-life adolescent friendship pairs. *Journal
of Personality and Social Psychology*, 36, 306–12.

Kandel, D., Davies, M., and Baydar, N. (1990). The creation of interpersonal
contexts: homophily in dyadic relationships in adolescence and young adulthood. In L. Robins and M. Rutter (eds.), *Straight and devious pathways from
childhood to adulthood*, Cambridge University Press, 221–41.

Kendler, K. S. (1997). Social support: A genetic-epidemiologic analysis.
American Journal of Psychiatry, 154, 1398–404.

Manke, B., McGuire, S., Reiss, D., Hetherington, E. M., and Plomin, R. (1995). Genetic contributions to adolescents' extrafamilial social interactions: teachers, best friends, and peers. *Social Development*, 4, 238–56.

Nance, W. E., Corey, L. A., and Eaves, L. J. (1980). A model for the analysis of mate selection in the marriages of twins. *Acta Geneticae, Medicae et Gemellologiae*, 29, 91–101.

Nance, W. E., Corey, L. A., Rose, R. J., and Eaves, L. J. (1981). Relevance of the marriages of twins to the causal analysis of nonrandom mating. In *Twin Research 3 Part B. Intelligence, Personality, and Development*, Gedda, L., Parisi, P., and Nance, W. E. (eds.), Alan R. Liss, Inc., New York, 61–71.

Price, J. M. (1996). Friendships of maltreated children and adolescents: contexts for expressing and modifying relationship history. In Bukowski, W. M., Newcomb, A. F., and Hartup, W. W. (eds.), *The company they keep: friendship in childhood and adolescence*, Cambridge University Press, 262–85.

Pulkkinen, L. (1987). Offensive and defensive aggression in humans: a longitudinal perspective. *Aggressive Behavior*, 13, 197–212.

Pulkkinen, L., Kaprio, J., and Rose, R. J. (1999). Peers, teachers, and parents as raters of twins' behavioral and emotional problems, and adjustment: the multidimensional peer nomination inventory. *Twin Research*, 2, 274–85.

Rose, R. J. (1998). A developmental behavioral-genetic perspective on alcoholism risk. *Alcohol Health and Research World*, 22, 131–43.

Rose, R. J., Kaprio, J., Winter, T., Koskenvuo, M., and Viken, R. J. (1999). Familial and socioregional environmental effects on abstinence from alcohol at age sixteen. *Journal of Studies on Alcohol, Suppl.* 13, 63–74.

Schooley, M. (1936). Personality resemblances among married couples. *Journal of Abnormal and Social Psychology*, 31, 340–7.

Tolson, J. M., and Urberg, K. A. (1993). Similarity between adolescent best friends. *Journal of Adolescent Research*, 8, 274–88.

Urberg, K. A. (1999). Peer influences in childhood and adolescence, *Merrill-Palmer Quarterly, Journal of Developmental Psychology*, 45, 1–183.

Part III

Continuity in individual life paths

5 Personality types in childhood and adolescence: main effects and person-relationship transactions

Marcel A. G. van Aken, Cornelis F. M. van Lieshout, Ron H. J. Scholte and Gerbert J. T. Haselager

Personality development and its consequences for the functioning of individuals over the life-span has recently received a lot of interest. A full chapter in the new edition of the *Handbook of Child Psychology* (Caspi, 1998) was devoted to the topic, as was a special issue of the *Journal of Personality and Social Psychology* (Diener, 2000). In addition, attempts have been made to broaden the focus of personality research with developmental issues, for example by adapting the Big Five framework to fit the study of childhood and adolescence (Halverson, Kohnstamm, and Martin, 1994), and to connect this paradigm with the well-established tradition of research on children's temperament (Rothbart, Ahadi, and Evans, 2000). In this chapter, we will focus on a recent development in the study of personality in childhood and adolescence, namely the study of personality types. We will present data on the social relationships of these types, and the way type membership and relationships interact in determining psychosocial functioning in childhood and adolescence.

Ego-resiliency and ego-control

As recently noted in several reviews of the literature (Caspi, 1998; Eisenberg, Fabes, Guthrie, and Reiser, 2000; Rothbart and Bates, 1998), there is increasing recognition that the constructs of temperament and personality overlap, and that early temperamental differences are the substrate of personality. This overlap becomes particularly clear when the definition of temperament from the work of Rothbart is followed (see also van Lieshout, 2000). Rothbart defines temperament as individual differences in reactivity and self-regulation, that are assumed to have a constitutional (relatively enduring, biological) basis (Rothbart *et al.*, 2000; Rothbart and Derryberry, 1981).

Reactivity refers to the excitability, responsivity, or arousability of the behavioural and physiological systems of the individual, whereas self-regulation refers to neural and behavioural processes functioning to modulate this underlying reactivity (Rothbart and Derryberry, 1981, p. 40). Formulated in this way, the constructs of reactivity and regulation resemble the constructs of ego-control and ego-resiliency, two personality parameters formulated by J. H. Block and J. Block (elaborated in their article in 1980, although already then the result of "for what ... approaches 30 years", p. 39). Ego-control, globally described as the control of impulse, is defined in terms of overcontrol, "excessive boundary impermeability resulting in the containment of impulse, delay of gratification, inhibition of action and affect, and insulation from environmental distractors" and undercontrol, "excessive boundary permeability and its consequences, insufficient modulation of impulse, the inability to delay gratification, immediate and direct expression of motivations and affects, and vulnerability to environmental distractors" (Block and Block, 1980a, p. 43). Ego-resiliency is defined as the "dynamic capacity of an individual to modulate his/her modal level of ego-control, in either direction, as a function of the demand characteristics of the environmental context." (p. 48). Although Block and Block basically expect ego-control and ego-resiliency to be unrelated, and even define four quadrants that describe four personality types (p. 89), in some publications they more or less seem to describe a curvilinear relation between ego-resiliency and ego-control with persons at a low level of ego-resiliency habitually tending towards overcontrol or towards undercontrol, a relation that is depicted in Figure 5.1, and that has been empirically confirmed (Eisenberg, Fabes, Shepard, Murphy, Guthrie, Jones, *et al.*, 1997).

In later years, the constructs of ego-resiliency and ego-control were conceptually refined by Jack Block and members of his research group (Block and Kremen, 1996; Klohnen, 1996; Kremen and Block, 1998), and were found to be related to a large number of outcome variables, such as identity (Cramer, 2000; Pals, 1999), successful midlife development (Klohnen, van de Water, and Young, 1996), ego-development (Westenberg and Block, 1993), delay of gratification (Funder and Block, 1989), problem behaviour including drug use (Block, Block and Keyes, 1988; Shedler and Block, 1990; Huey and Weisz, 1997; Eisenberg, Fabes, Karbon, Murphy, Wosinksi, Polazzi, *et al.*, 1996), school achievement (van Aken, 1992), and a number of relationship variables, such as parenting behaviours (Kremen and Block, 1998; Roberts, 1999), positive family functioning (Sroufe, 1991), attachment in childhood (Arend, Gove, and Sroufe, 1979) and adolescence (Kobak and Sceery, 1988), and peer relations (van Aken, 1992; Eisenberg *et al.*, 1997).

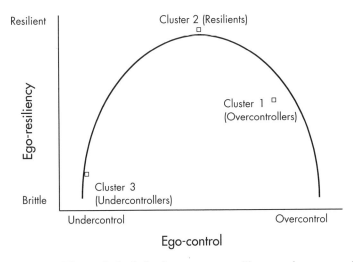

Figure 5.1 Theoretical relation between ego-resiliency and ego-control, and the personality types in childhood presented in the ego-resiliency, ego-control space (adapted from van Lieshout *et al.*, 2000).

Personality types

An often cited definition of personality is the one Allport formulated in 1937: "the dynamic organization within the individual of those psychophysical systems that determine his unique adjustments to his environment" (Allport, 1937, p. 48). Although this definition is often quoted, mostly it is used to introduce the study of personality traits, ignoring the issue of "organisation within the individual", that seems to imply a more holistic, person-centred approach to studying personality.

Lay-psychological concepts, textbook definitions and theoretical reviews of personality often seem to agree with this person-centred view of personality. However, empirical research has approached personality nearly exclusively from a variable-centred trait perspective. Personality is studied in terms of traits, in large groups of persons. The correlational structure of many traits (a property of such a group) has often been labelled "personality structure" (which actually is a property of an individual). Consequently, personality differences within a population have been studied only rarely in terms of interindividual differences in personality structure.

Alternatively, the personality structure of each member of the population can be described by a pattern of multiple variables within that member. Here the units of analysis are persons, not variables. This has been labelled a "person-centred" approach to personality, in which an individual's personality is described by a pattern of trait scores. Subsequently, the personality patterns of many individuals can be compared for similarities. For example, individuals can be classified into personality types that consist of individuals with similar patterns. Each type can be labelled by its prototypical (e.g., average) personality pattern, and each concrete member of a type can be identified based on his or her similarity to this prototypical pattern.

In studies closely following the work of Block and Block, and, more specifically, using their California Q-sort (for adults, or the California Child Q-sort for children), personality types can be identified by the factors in Q-factor analysis. In Q-factor analysis (also called inverse factor analysis), correlations between individuals are factor analysed; each individual is described by a pattern of scores on many variables (e.g., the items of a Q-sort). Q-sort data are particularly suited for a Q-factor analysis because of the large number of items and the forced distribution of the items. Each resulting Q-factor represents a prototypical pattern or a collection of similar patterns. If these patterns describe personality structures, each Q-factor represents a personality type. For each Q-factor, the factor scores of the variables on which the patterns are based (e.g., the Q-sort items) describe the prototypic structure of a personality type. Individuals can be assigned to a type by following certain rules for the similarity between a person's personality profile and the prototype (see Robins, John, Caspi, Moffitt, and Stouthamer-Loeber, 1996; York and John, 1992).

In his seminal work on a person-centred approach to personality development, *Lives through time*, Block (1971) already identified five male and six female personality types. Using the criterion of replicability of factor solutions between random sample halves, York and John (1992) found four replicable Q-factors for the California Adult Q-Set that converged with Block's developmental types (and of which three resembled the factors, or types, found in childhood and adolescence, see also John, Pals, and Westenberg, 1998), and similar personality types in adults were also found by Pulkkinen (1996).

Using the California Child Q-set, Robins *et al.* (1996), Hart, Hofman, Edelstein, and Keller (1997), and Asendorpf and van Aken (1999) found three replicable Q-factors. High to moderate similarity coefficients were reported when Q-factors that were based on expert Q-sorts of seven-year-old Icelandic boys and girls (Hart *et al.*) and teachers' and parents' Q-sorts of four to six and ten-year-old German boys and girls (Asendorpf and van Aken) were compared with the Q-factors found by Robins *et al.*

that were based on parental Q-sorts of ten-year-old US boys. In addition to these Q-sort oriented studies, in childhood and adolescence similar personality types have also been found in studies using other statistical procedures, such as cluster analysis (Caspi and Silva, 1995; Newman, Caspi, Moffitt, and Silva, 1997; van Aken, van Lieshout, and Scholte, 1998; van Lieshout, Haselager, Riksen-Walraven, and van Aken, 1995; Harrington, Chin, Rickey, and Mohr, 1999) or Configural Frequency Analysis (Aksan, Goldsmith, Smider, Essex, Clark, Hyde, *et al.*, 1999, but only for Overcontrollers and Undercontrollers).

Correlates of the three personality types in childhood have been reported by Robins *et al.* (1996), van Lieshout *et al.* (1995), Hart *et al.* (1997), Asendorpf and van Aken (1999), and Caspi (2000). Robins *et al.* (1996) found lower IQ scores and lower teacher ratings of academic performance and school conduct for undercontrolled boys as compared to both resilient and overcontrolled boys. In addition, caregivers and teachers reported more behaviour problems for both undercontrolled and overcontrolled boys than for their resilient agemates, and more externalizing than internalizing problems for undercontrolled boys (e.g., a higher frequency of serious delinquency), and more internalizing than externalizing problems for overcontrolled boys. Van Lieshout *et al.* (1995) showed that the three types in elementary school differed in cognitive competence and in acceptance and rejection by classmates. Resilients scored highest on IQ, school achievement and peer acceptance, and lowest on peer rejection. Undercontrollers showed the reverse pattern, and Overcontrollers scored in between. Hart *et al.* (1997) used individual growth functions to study the development of the three types with regard to academic and social competence up to age 15. Resilients had higher grade point average and lower teacher-rated concentration problems than both Undercontrollers and Overcontrollers. Overcontrollers had higher teacher-rated social withdrawal and lower self-esteem than the other two types. Undercontrollers had higher teacher-rated aggressiveness than Overcontrollers and Resilients. Asendorpf and van Aken (1999) also used individual growth functions to predict various aspects of personality development up to age 12 from Q-types derived from a composite score of personality descriptions at ages four to six. Results show that Undercontrolled children had a consistently lower IQ and school grade than resilient children did; approximately one third of the undercontrollers were late schoolers. Undercontrollers were also judged by their parents as consistently more aggressive with peers. Overcontrolled children were characterized by a high level of observed behavioural inhibition to adult and peer strangers and by high parental judgements of inhibition. Overcontrollers started with a similarly high IQ, school performance, and cognitive self-esteem as Resilients, but subsequently lagged behind them in all three domains. Caspi (2000) summarized findings from the Dunedin study (see also Newman *et al.*, 1997) in which Undercontrollers grew up to be impulsive, unreliable, and antisocial, whereas Overcontrollers were more likely to become unassertive and depressed.

Personality-type main effects and person-relationship transactions

Although dynamic interactionism, in which individuals are assumed to develop in a transactional (i.e., dynamic, continuous, and reciprocal) relation with their environment, has been an important paradigm for research on personality development, empirical research directly addressing the relation between personality and social relationships has been relatively rare. In a study guided by the dynamic interactionist paradigm, Asendorpf and Wilpers (1999) found that during late adolescence, personality traits influenced social relationships but not vice versa. In a re-analysis of these data from a person-centred view, Asendorpf (2000) replicated these findings, and again found that stable personality types show distinct paths of social-relationship development.

From a variable-centred perspective, ego-resiliency has been found to affect (later) relationships, and vice versa. In our own studies, ego-resiliency at age ten was found to be related to peer competence at the same age (measured in terms of sociometric data, van Aken, 1992), which, in turn affected ego-resiliency at age 12. Also, ego-resiliency at age 7 and 10 affected later parental support during a problem-solving task at age 10 and 12 (van Aken and Riksen-Walraven, 1992). On the other hand, an intervention program at nine months, aimed at enhancing parental responsiveness, was found to have an effect on ego-resiliency up to age 12 (but only for girls, see Riksen-Walraven and van Aken, 1997). Relations between ego-resiliency and ego-control ('regulation' and 'emotionality') and social functioning have also been reported by Eisenberg and colleagues (Eisenberg *et al.*, 1996; 1997).

Although most research on personality types in childhood and adolescence has focused on behavioural characteristics of the type members, in some studies data on social relationships were reported. Newman *et al.* (1997, see also Caspi, 2000) found that overcontrolled and undercontrolled children (defined from temperament measures at age three), showed difficulties in interpersonal functioning at age 21. Overcontrolled ('inhibited') children were described as less affiliative, low on social agency, and lacking lively interest and engagement in their worlds, but had relatively unconflicted romantic relationships and good interpersonal adjustment in the workplace. Undercontrollers, on the other hand, showed impaired social relationships across all social contexts. Hart *et al.* (1997) reported that Overcontrolled children showed difficulties in engaging successfully in social interactions in the classroom (as rated by their teacher). Harrington *et al.* (1999) found that Resilients were more often classified as securely attached than Non-Resilients, and Undercontrollers more than Overcontrollers. Asendorpf and van Aken (1999) did not explicitly measure social relationships, but did not find an expected lower social self-esteem for Overcontrollers. All in all, the findings on social relationships for the three personality types suggest that both Over- and Undercontrollers may be at risk for developing inadequate relationships.

In summary, the recent literature on personality types points to clear psychosocial and interpersonal differences between different personality types. The exact processes behind these differences, however, remain largely unclear. Recent studies on the interplay between personality (or temperament), relationships, and developmental outcomes points towards the importance of considering person-environment interactions in studying these processes (following Caspi, 2000, we prefer to use the term 'transactions' because it does not have a statistical connotation). In their review on temperamental research, Rothbart and Bates (1998) conclude that several interesting interaction effects are presented in the literature, but few have been replicated. Notable exceptions here are several studies on parenting, such as Bates, Pettit, Dodge and Ridge (1998), who found that a combination of specific maternal discipline styles and children's (temperamental) resistance to control was most effective in predicting externalizing problems. Another example is the work of Kochanska (1993; Kochanska, Murray, Jacques, Koening, and Vandegeest, 1996), who showed that for fearless children different parental rearing styles lead to the internalization of moral rules than for fearful children.

These person-environment transactions can be placed in a holistic, interactionist perspective on human development (see Magnusson and Stattin, 1998). In such a perspective, not only the person should be regarded as an integrated whole, but the environment should also be considered as part of this whole. Including environmental measures (e.g., on social relationships) in terms of directly related to and/or interacting with personality variables, may lead to a better understanding of the development of personality variables and their association with specific developmental outcomes.

For example, Stattin and Magnusson (1990) found that the frequently reported association between early maturity and deviant behaviour in girls is mediated by environmental measures (e.g., affiliation with older peers). Caspi and Moffitt (1991) also described how this association can be better understood when person-environment transactions are included: they found that this association was only present in coeducational schools (as compared to all-girls schools), suggesting that the presence of boys provides opportunities for deviance. Although processes in which person characteristics and environmental measures interact and jointly determine developmental outcomes are more and more assumed at a theoretical level, there are still relatively few empirical tests of such person-environment transactions.

Therefore, after examining the main effects of personality types in childhood and adolescence on social relationships and psychosocial adjustment, in this chapter we will construct broader 'person-environment' types, by using environmental measures (i.e., measures for sociometric quality of peer relationships) to further divide the three main personality types into subtypes. Our hypotheses are that psychosocial adjustment is the result of the interplay between personality and environment, so that including the environmental variables specifies the effects of personality on psychosocial adjustment. More specifically, we expect that peer relations moderate the effects of personality on psychosocial functioning: Overcontrollers and Undercontrollers with adequate peer relations are expected to function better in a number of psychosocial domains than those with inadequate peer relations. In this chapter, we will try to address these expectations using two samples from childhood and adolescence.

Childhood sample

Participants and procedure

Participants in this study were 79 children (35 boys, 44 girls) who were studied at age 7, 10, and 12. At these ages, children were in elementary school and the great majority of children had the same teacher everyday (see van Aken, 1992 for sample characteristics).

Sociometric data were collected in the classroom of the children. School achievement and intelligence were assessed on separate occasions, in small groups of participants. The Q-sort procedure was explained to the teacher, who completed the procedure at home and mailed the material to the institute. CCQ-descriptions, school achievement tests and intelligence tests were gathered at ages 7, 10, and 12; sociometric data were collected at ages 10 and 12 only.

Measures

Child-descriptions by teachers. A Dutch translation of the California Child Q-set (CCQ, Block and Block, 1980b) was used to acquire a description by the teacher of the child at each age. The CCQ is a Q-sort procedure containing 100 statements about a child's behaviour and personality characteristics. Statements have to be sorted in a forced distribution into nine categories, ranging from (1) 'least characteristic' to (9) 'most characteristic'.

Scores for ego-resiliency and ego-control. Scores for ego-resiliency and ego-control were constructed following the procedure suggested by Block and Block (1980b), correlating the rank ordering of the 100 items given by the teacher with the rank ordering given by experts of a typically ego-resilient or ego-undercontrolled child. These correlation coefficients are then used as indicators of the ego-resiliency and ego-control of the child.

Scores for the Five-Factor Model personality dimensions. The CCQ-descriptions were used to gain scores on equivalents of the Five-Factor Model personality dimensions. Van Lieshout and Haselager (1994) found that factor analyses of a set of 1,836 Q-sorts supported the Five-Factor Model personality. The first five factors closely resembled the five factors assessed in adult studies. A similar factor solution was reported by John, Caspi, Robins, Moffitt, and Stouthamer-Loeber (1994) in their study of the Five-Factor Model in mothers' CCQ-descriptions of boys between 12 and 13 years old.

School achievement and intelligence. At age 7, 10 and 12, children's school achievement and intelligence were assessed using nationally (Dutch) standardized school achievement and intelligence tests, administered in small groups, or individually, during the experimenter's visit to the children's schools. See van Aken (1992) for further details.

Peer acceptance and rejection. At age 10 and 12 a sociometric interview was conducted in the school classes of the adolescents. All children in a class were asked to nominate the three children that they liked most, and the three children they liked least. To correct for unequal class sizes, scores were converted to within classroom probability scores (Newcomb and Bukowski, 1983), for acceptance (liked most) and for rejection (liked least).

olescent sample

cipants and procedure

vere 3,284 students (1,402 girls, 1,882 boys) attending
...ry school. Due to incomplete data because of time restrictions
in some classes, the sample used for this paper consists of 2,176 students. The age of the students ranged from 12 years to 18 years (M =
14.5 years, SD = 9 months). See Scholte, van Aken, and van Lieshout
(1997) for sample characteristics.

Trained research assistants administered all of the measures (self-
reports and peer nominations) in class group testing sessions. Information about the procedures and the instructions were read aloud. Students'
questions were answered whether before, during, or after administration.

Measures

Scores for the Five-Factor Model personality dimensions A self-
report questionnaire consisting of 25 bipolar items was used to assess
the Five-Factor Model personality dimensions. Participants were asked
to rate themselves on a seven-point scale, ranging from (1) *Pole A very true*
to (7) *Pole B very true*, with (4) *Pole A and Pole B a little bit true* in between.
Factor analyses confirmed the Big Five personality factors (Scholte *et al.*,
1997).

Perceived relational support A 27-item self-report questionnaire
was used to measure adolescents' perceived relational support from mothers, fathers, siblings, and best friend. The participants were asked to indicate on a five-point scale how much each of the 27 items held for a
specific person (see Scholte, van Lieshout, and van Aken, 2001, for further details). The items were found to represent five perceived relational
support factors, *parental support* (sample item "my mother/father shows
me that she/he loves me"), *friend support* ("my friend shows me that she/he
loves me"), *sibling support* ("my sister/brother shows me that she/he loves
me"), *convergence of goals* ("this person and I have the same opinions
about the use of drugs, alcohol, or gambling") and *respect for autonomy*
("this person lets me decide what to do as often as possible").

Bullying To assess involvement in bullying, three scales of the
bully/victim self-report questionnaire (Olweus, 1991) were used: *victim
of indirect bullying*, to indicate feelings of isolation from the group, *victim
of direct bullying*, and *bullying others*.

Psychological well-being consisted of five subscales: *self-esteem* (sample item "In most things I am as good as other people"), *loneliness* ("I often feel lonely"), *brooding* ("How often do you brood about your school performances"), *worry about home* ("How often do you feel sad about your parents"), and *somatic complaints* ("How often do you suffer from a headache").

Delinquency consisted of the subscales of overt and covert delinquency, and conflict with authority (cf. Loeber, Wung, Keenan, Giroux, Stouthamer-Loeber, and van Kammen, 1993). *Covert delinquency* concerned such behaviours as running away from home, or staying away without parental permission. *Overt delinquency* concerned violence and getting into fights; *conflict with authority* concerned items like quarrelling with parents or teachers.

Substance use was assessed using three items, i.e., cigarette smoking ("How many cigarettes did you smoke per day over the past month"), alcohol use ("How many glasses of alcohol did you drink over the past month"), and drug use ("How often did you use soft drugs like marihuana over the past 12 months").

Sociometric data: peer preference All classmates were asked to nominate three to five classmates whom they liked most (peer acceptance) and three to five classmates whom they liked least (peer rejection). The like-most and like-least scores for each participant were computed by tallying the number of nominations received and transforming these scores into within classroom probability-scores.

Sociometric data: peer-group functioning Peer-group functioning was based on 20 items concerning attributes of an individual's peer-group functioning. Per item, the students had to nominate three to five classmates. For each participant the raw number of nominations received was transformed into within classroom probability scores. In an earlier study (Scholte *et al.*, 1997), factor analyses on the 20 items revealed five replicable factors: *aggression-unattentiveness* (e.g., being perceived as quarrelsome, lazy, absent-minded, irritable), *achievement-withdrawal* (e.g., being perceived as persistent, hard working, shy, reserved, withdrawn), *self-confidence* (e.g., being perceived as sensible, secure, steady, sincere), *sociability* (e.g., being perceived as enthusiastic, considerate, intelligent), and *emotionality-nervousness* (e.g., being perceived as emotional, anxious, nervous, uncreative).

Results

Cluster analyses of the childhood data

In order to distinguish groups of children with different personality profiles we conducted a cluster analysis using Ward's method on the five personality factor scores of the teachers' CCQ descriptions at each of the ages of 7, 10, and 12 years. All scores on the five personality factors were standardized within measurement wave. A three-cluster solution was found with clearly interpretable clusters, containing a sufficiently large number of children (van Lieshout *et al.*, 1995). A first cluster contained 25 children (15 girls), a second cluster contained 27 children (22 girls), and a third cluster contained 27 children (7 girls).

Qualification of the three main types in childhood

To further qualify the three main clusters (types), we related them to the personality dimensions ego-resiliency and ego-control. On ego-resiliency all clusters differed significantly, with cluster 2 having the highest ego-resiliency score, followed by cluster 1 and cluster 3. On ego-control, again all clusters differed significantly, with cluster 3 having the highest scores (i.e., most in the direction of undercontrol), followed by clusters 2 and 1. The three clusters are plotted in Figure 5.1, along the line representing the assumed theoretical relation between ego-resiliency and ego-control. In line with the research on personality types, our cluster 1 was labelled '*Overcontrollers*', our cluster 2 was labelled '*Resilients*', and our cluster 3 was labelled '*Undercontrollers*'. Within-wave analyses indicated that the differences between the three clusters on ego-resiliency and ego-control were consistently found in each measurement wave.

The three clusters also differed on the Big Five personality factors (Figure 5.2, upper panel). Resilients scored high on all five factors. Overcontrollers scored as high as the resilients on agreeableness, moderate on conscientiousness, but lower on the other three factors, especially extraversion. Undercontrollers scored high on extraversion but low on conscientiousness and agreeableness and moderate on emotional stability and openness. It should be noted that the Big Five profiles of overcontrollers and undercontrollers are mutually complimentary: mean scores of the Big Five dimensions of each of these types are mirrored along an imaginary axis of the mean scores of the two types. This mirroring effect is consistent with the contrast between over- and undercontrol as manifestations of Block and Block's (1980a) ideas about impulse control.

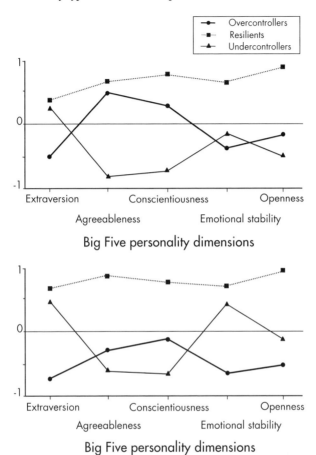

Figure 5.2 Big Five profile of personality types in childhood (upper panel) and adolescence (lower panel; reprinted from van Lieshout *et al.*, 2000).

Cluster analyses of the adolescence data

To investigate whether a similar typology in adolescents' self-descriptions could be distinguished, we conducted a cluster analysis on the five personality dimensions. This cluster analysis was accomplished in two steps. First, the same cluster analyses were performed on a number of randomly selected independent halves of the total sample, yielding three clusters that were similar in terms of the scores on the five personality dimensions. Second, on the basis of these cluster analyses, initial cluster centres, which were obtained by Ward's method, were specified for each variable.

These initial centres were then used to classify each adolescent in the sample to a cluster, using the SPSS-X procedure QUICK CLUSTER. A first cluster contained 41.3 percent of the sample (52 percent girls), a second cluster contained 35.9 percent (41 percent girls), and a third cluster contained 22.8 percent (29 percent girls).

Qualification of the three main types in adolescence

The three clusters (types) of adolescents differed in the configuration of their Big Five scores. These configurations of Big Five scores were very similar to the configurations found in the childhood study. For reasons of comparison we have added our findings in adolescence to those of childhood in Figure 5.2 (lower panel). Because the corresponding profiles of the three types in childhood were related to ego-resilience and ego-control, we consider the findings from the adolescent sample to provide additional support for Block and Block's (1980a) two-dimensional model of personality functioning. To evaluate the importance of this similarity, note that the two samples differed in their age (childhood versus adolescence), in the assessment instrument used for clustering (CCQ versus Big Five ratings) and in the source of personality data (teachers versus self-report, cf. van Lieshout, Haselager, and van Aken, 1998).

Personality types in childhood: differences in school achievement, intelligence, and peer acceptance and rejection

On school achievement, in all three waves the resilient children scored higher than Undercontrollers. Overcontrollers scored in between. On intelligence, in all three waves Resilients and Overcontrollers scored higher than Undercontrollers. In both waves (age 10 and 12) where sociometric data were available, Resilients scored higher on peer acceptance than Undercontrollers, whereas Overcontrollers scored in between, and Undercontrollers scored higher on peer rejection than both Resilients and Overcontrollers.

Personality types in adolescence: differences in adjustment and relationships

Table 5.1 shows the differences between the three adolescent personality types in their psychosocial functioning. As can be seen from this table, Overcontrollers had lowest scores on self-esteem, and highest scores on loneliness, brooding and worrying, and somatic complaints, with almost no differences between the Resilients and the Undercontrollers.

Table 5.1 *Psychosocial functioning of the three personality types in adolescence (standardized scores)*

	Overcontrollers (N = 906)	Resilients (N = 798)	Undercontrollers (N = 472)	F
Well-being				
Self-esteem	−.24[a]	.29[c]	−.01[b]	82.60***
Loneliness	.18[a]	−.16[b]	−.08[b]	35.50***
Brooding	.18[a]	−.15[b]	−.08[b]	35.40***
Worrying about home	.05[a]	−.07[b]	.04[ab]	4.49*
Somatic complaints	.14[a]	−.17[c]	−.01[b]	26.31***
Delinquency				
Overt	−.17[a]	−.02[c]	.29[b]	44.81***
Covert	−.12[a]	−.09[a]	.34[b]	48.84***
Authority conflict	−.07[a]	−.14[a]	.33[b]	47.52***
Substance use				
Cigarettes	−.12[a]	−.05[a]	.27[b]	36.95***
Alcohol	−.19[a]	.01[a]	.33[b]	60.89***
Drugs	−.07[a]	−.06[a]	.24[b]	23.38***

Note: Means that share a superscript are not significantly different from each other
* $p < .05$; ** $p < .01$; *** $p < .001$

For externalizing problems, a complementary pattern was found: Undercontrollers had the highest scores on various forms of substance use, on overt and covert antisocial behaviour, and on authority conflict, with almost no differences between the Resilients and the Overcontrollers.

Table 5.2 gives the comparison of the three personality types on measures of their social relationships. Resilients scored highest on all aspects of perceived support. Overcontrollers and Undercontrollers did not significantly differ, except for convergence of goals, where Undercontrollers scored lowest.

Also in the domain of peer relations, clear differences between the personality types were found. Undercontrollers were most often perpetrators of bullying, while Overcontrollers were most often victims. Overcontrollers were less liked by their classmates, whereas Undercontrollers were most disliked. Overcontrollers showed more internalizing problems according to their classmates (low self-confidence, high emotionality). Undercontrollers showed more externalizing problems (more aggressive, less achievement-oriented). Resilients scored intermediate on aggression and achievement-orientation, but relatively high on self-confidence and relatively low on emotionality.

Table 5.2 *Quality of relationships of three personality types in adolescence (standardized scores)*

	Over-controllers (N = 906)	Resilients (N = 798)	Under-controllers (N = 472)	F
Relational support				
Parental support	−.13[a]	.30[b]	−.19[a]	76.36***
Friend support	−.20[a]	.35[b]	−.15[a]	93.83***
Sibling support	−.16[a]	.28[b]	−.14[a]	59.53***
Convergence of goals	−.04[a]	.24[c]	−.27[b]	62.32***
Respect for autonomy	−.19[a]	.31[b]	−.13[a]	86.85***
Bullying				
Bullying others	−.20[a]	−.11[a]	.49[b]	118.20***
Victim direct bullying	.18[a]	−.21[c]	−.02[b]	42.57***
Victim indirect bullying	.28[a]	−.28[c]	−.09[b]	95.33***
Sociometric data: peer preference				
Peer acceptance	−.10[a]	.15[b]	.06[b]	20.58***
Peer rejection	−.03[a]	−.05[a]	.10[b]	6.14**
Sociometric data: peer group functioning				
Aggression-inattentiveness	−.25[a]	−.03[c]	.44[b]	123.97***
Achievement-withdrawal	.30[a]	−.04[c]	−.42[b]	134.25***
Self-confidence	−.25[a]	.21[b]	.16[b]	80.77***
Sociability	−.16[a]	.16[b]	.09[b]	34.02***
Emotional-nervousness	.17[a]	−.14[b]	−.09[b]	35.92***

Note: Means that share a superscript are not significantly different from each other
* $p < .05$; ** $p < .01$; *** $p < .001$

Personality subtypes based on Big Five profiles combined with peer preference

To construct subtypes based on the combination of personality data and data on the children's peer relations, we first constructed a new variable "peer preference" in both samples, by subtracting the standardized "dislike-score" from the standardized "like-score." "Peer preference" was used to construct liked and disliked subtypes for each of the three personality types. Because of the small sample, for the childhood data this was done using a median-split on peer preference (aggregated over both waves, note that four subjects could not be classified in subtypes because of incomplete sociometric data). For the adolescent data, the sample was large enough the enable somewhat more extreme groups, and we used the upper and lower tertile of the peer preference distribution.

   This procedure resulted in childhood in more liked than disliked Resilients and Overcontrollers (a ratio of approximately 2:1), but clearly more disliked than liked Undercontrollers (a ratio of 5:1). In adolescence, this procedure led to comparable numbers of adolescents in the liked and disliked subtypes within the three types. Person-relationship transactions (i.e., the differences between each pair of subtypes) were tested using a priori contrasts, specified within an ANOVA-procedure.

Differences on the Big Five personality dimensions between the subtypes in childhood and adolescence

Table 5.3 shows the contrasts between the Liked and Disliked subtypes on the Big Five personality dimensions. For the childhood sample, the liked and disliked Overcontrollers differed in their scores on extraversion: Disliked Overcontrollers had even lower scores on extraversion than Liked Overcontrollers. No such differences on extraversion were found for Liked versus Disliked Undercontrollers or Resilients. On Agreeableness, the Liked Resilients scored higher than the Disliked Resilients, whereas no such differences were found among the other subtypes. On conscientiousness and on openness, the Liked Undercontrollers scored

Table 5.3 *Contrasts on personality variables between liked and disliked subtypes of overcontrollers, undercontrollers and resilients in childhood and adolescence (standardized scores)*

Variable	Overcontrollers		Resilients		Undercontrollers	
	Liked (N = 16)	Disliked (N = 9)	Liked (N = 19)	Disliked (N = 7)	Liked (N = 4)	Disliked (N = 20)
Childhood						
Extraversion	**−.29**	**−.93**	.31	.32	.93	.27
Agreeableness	.59	.29	**.71**	**.05**	−.64	−.93
Conscientiousness	.24	.39	.74	.60	**−.34**	**−.97**
Emotional stability	−.25	−.54	.69	.37	.42	−.15
Openness	−.21	−.12	.75	.79	**.16**	**−.58**
Adolescence						
Extraversion	**−.60**	**−.80**	**.60**	**.48**	.43	.38
Agreeableness	**−.17**	**−.42**	**.84**	**.65**	**−.45**	**−.89**
Conscientiousness	−.16	−.11	**.58**	**.80**	**−.91**	**−.75**
Emotional stability	−.67	−.70	**.52**	**.64**	.22	.34
Openness	−.58	−.55	**.67**	**.92**	**−.27**	**−.08**

Note: Significant a priori contrasts ($p < .05$) are underlined and printed in **bold**.

higher than the Disliked Undercontrollers, whereas no such differences were found among the other subtypes.

These differences between Liked and Disliked subtypes in childhood were confirmed in the adolescent sample, although the differences between the Liked and Disliked Undercontrollers on conscientiousness and openness reversed. In addition (and probably because of the larger sample), in adolescence Liked Overcontrollers scored relatively higher on agreeableness than Disliked Overcontrollers, as did liked Undercontrollers compared to Disliked Undercontrollers. Liked Resilients scored higher than Disliked Resilients on extraversion and agreeableness, but lower on conscientiousness, emotional stability and openness. The fact that lower agreeableness was associated with the Disliked subtype in all three main types points to a main effect of agreeableness (or of the Like-Dislike division), rather than a person-relationship transaction.

Differences in adjustment between the subtypes in childhood

Table 5.4 shows the contrasts between the Liked and Disliked subtypes on ego-resiliency, ego-control, school achievement, and intelligence in childhood. Liked resilients were even more resilient than their disliked counterparts. A similar pattern was found for Undercontrollers, where the Liked Undercontrollers were more resilient (or better, less ego-brittle) than their Disliked counterparts. No differences on ego-resiliency were found between Liked and Disliked Overcontrollers, nor were there any differences in ego-control among the pairs of subtypes. Liked Undercontrollers had clearly higher school achievements than Disliked Undercontrollers, a finding that was marginally there for the Resilients ($p = .06$), but clearly not for the Overcontrollers. Finally, no differences among the Liked and Disliked pairs of subtypes were found on intelligence.

Table 5.4 *Contrasts between liked and disliked subtypes of overcontrollers, undercontrollers and resilients in childhood (standardized scores)*

Variable	Overcontrollers		Resilients		Undercontrollers	
	Liked (N = 16)	Disliked (N = 9)	Liked (N = 19)	Disliked (N = 7)	Liked (N = 4)	Disliked (N = 20)
Ego-resiliency	.19	−.13	**.95**	**.53**	**−.01**	**−.83**
Ego-undercontrol	−.58	−.89	−.18	.23	1.01	.80
School achievement	.14	.32	.76	.01	**.62**	**−.46**
Intelligence	.02	.60	.42	.22	.22	−.44

Note: Significant a priori contrasts ($p < .05$) are underlined and printed in **bold**.

*Differences on relationship variables between the subtypes
in adolescence*

Table 5.5 shows the contrasts between the Liked and Disliked subtypes on the relationship variables in adolescence. In this table, it can be seen that person-relationship transactions were found for the support from a best friend, that Disliked Overcontrollers and Resilients perceive as lower, whereas Disliked Undercontrollers see no difference, and for support from a sibling, that only Liked Overcontrollers perceive as higher.

On the sociometric data, mainly major effects of the high-low peer preference distinction were found. In all cases, except achievement-withdrawal for the Liked versus Disliked Undercontrollers, the liked subtypes scored more favourably in the nominations by their peers than their disliked counterparts. Note that is not a necessity by design: the correlations between peer preference and the five peer group reputation factors were only moderate (ranging from $|.08|$ to $|.45|$). On self-report variables related to being a victim of bullying, again only main effects were found: in all comparisons, the Disliked subtypes reported being bullied more. On bullying others, on the other hand, the Disliked Undercontrollers scored higher than the Liked Undercontrollers, whereas there were no differences between Liked and Disliked Overcontrollers or Resilients.

*Differences on adjustment variables between the subtypes
in adolescence*

Table 5.6 shows the contrasts between the Liked and Disliked subtypes on adjustment variables in adolescence. On measures of well being, an effect was found for loneliness: Disliked Overcontrollers reported more loneliness than Liked Overcontrollers, for Resilients and Undercontrollers the subtypes did not differ. On measures of delinquency and substance use, effects were found for covert anti-social behaviour: Disliked Undercontrollers showed more anti-social behaviour than Liked Undercontrollers, whereas no differences were found between Liked and Disliked Resilients or Overcontrollers. On the other hand, Liked Overcontrollers and Liked Resilients reported somewhat more drinking than their Disliked counterparts, whereas no differences in drinking were found between Liked and Disliked Undercontrollers.

Discussion

The aim of this chapter was to replicate findings on the three personality types that recently were reported (see Caspi, 1998) and to extend

Table 5.5 *Contrasts on relationships between subtypes of overcontrollers, undercontrollers and resilients in adolescence (standardized scores)*

Variable	Overcontrollers		Resilients		Undercontrollers	
	Liked (N = 437)	Disliked (N = 469)	Liked (N = 449)	Disliked (N = 349)	Liked (N = 226)	Disliked (N = 246)
Perceived relational support						
Parental support	−.07	−.17	.36	.25	−.19	−.27
Friend support	**−.15**	**−.31**	**.41**	**.24**	−.11	−.28
Sibling support	**−.05**	**−.21**	.35	.23	−.03	−.22
Convergence of goals	−.08	−.05	.23	.23	−.24	−.33
Respect for autonomy	−.21	−.24	.32	.28	−.13	−.15
Sociometric data peer group functioning						
Aggression-inattentiveness	**−.58**	**.11**	**−.38**	**.32**	**−.05**	**.84**
Achievement-withdrawal	**.16**	**.42**	**−.14**	**.02**	**−.47**	−.38
Self-confidence	**.21**	**−.66**	**.59**	**−.28**	**.45**	**−.17**
Sociability	**.37**	**−.68**	**.57**	**−.43**	**.50**	**−.35**
Emotional-nervousness	**−.27**	**.66**	**−.47**	**.17**	**−.45**	**.31**
Bullying						
Bullying others	−.18	−.18	−.15	−.02	**.29**	**.61**
Victim direct bullying	**−.12**	**.66**	**−.40**	**.06**	**−.23**	**.15**
Victim indirect bullying	**−.08**	**.75**	**−.48**	**−.00**	**−.31**	**.15**

Note: Significant a priori contrasts ($p < .05$) are underlined and printed in **bold**.

Table 5.6 *Contrasts on adjustment between subtypes of overcontrollers, undercontrollers and resilients in adolescence (standardized scores)*

	Overcontrollers		Resilients		Undercontrollers	
Variable	Liked (N = 437)	Disliked (N = 469)	Liked (N = 449)	Disliked (N = 349)	Liked (N = 226)	Disliked (N = 246)
Well-being						
Self-esteem (−)	.26	.30	−.23	−.34	.02	.07
Loneliness	**.07**	**.33**	−.17	−.11	−.06	.06
Brooding	.22	.23	−.10	−.19	−.10	−.10
Worrying about home	.09	.05	−.06	−.04	.04	−.03
Somatic	.26	.17	−.17	−.14	.06	.03
Delinquency						
Overt	−.13	−.16	−.05	.06	.25	.41
Covert	−.10	−.11	−.07	−.11	**.20**	**.43**
Authority conflict	−.09	−.07	−.16	−.15	.21	.40
Substance use						
Cigarettes	−.14	−.10	−.03	−.08	.31	.30
Alcohol	**−.13**	**−.29**	**.13**	**−.14**	.27	.33
Drugs	−.07	−.07	−.04	−.08	.22	.25

Note: Significant a priori contrasts ($p < .05$) are underlined and printed in **bold**.

these findings with results on the transaction between personality types and social relationships (i.e., social preference as indicated by peers) in determining psychosocial outcomes.

First, results from earlier studies on personality types were confirmed. Again, three types were found, and these were remarkably similar in childhood and in adolescent samples. One type could be labelled as Resilients, characterized by a high level of resiliency and flexibility in problem-solving, and a moderate level of impulse control (theoretically assumed to modulate in response to particular environmental demands). In terms of their personality profile, they were relatively extraverted, agreeable, conscientious, emotionally stable, and open to experiences. Another type could be labelled as Undercontrollers, characterized by a low level of resiliency and a low level of impulse control (assumed to be fairly rigid). They scored particularly low on agreeableness and conscientiousness. A third type could be labelled as Overcontrollers, again characterized by a relatively low level of resiliency, but with a high level of impulse control (again assumed to be fairly rigid). In terms of their personality profile, they were particularly introverted and low in emotional stability.

Second, earlier findings were confirmed in that these three personality types differed in their psychosocial functioning. The general picture is that of Resilients functioning relatively well in all domains, Overcontrollers tending to show problems in a more internalizing direction (low self-esteem, higher loneliness, more worrying and somatic complaints), and Undercontrollers tending to show problems in a more externalizing direction (higher scores on delinquency and substance use). The results were also clear for the relationships of the three types: the Undercontrollers were more often rejected in their peer group, and, in adolescence, were judged highest on aggression and inattentiveness in their school class. The Overcontrollers were less accepted in their peer group, and judged as achievement oriented, withdrawn and not very sociable. In their own perception of their relational support, Over- and Undercontrollers did not differ, and both scored lower than the Resilients.

Third, the results showed that several instances of person-relationship transactions were found. After combining personality type with a measure for the quality of peer relationships, it was found that disliked Overcontrollers were even more introverted than liked Overcontrollers. They reported even less support from friends and siblings, and were more often the victim of direct and indirect bullying. They also reported more feelings of loneliness than their liked counterparts.

Similarly, the disliked Undercontrollers reported that they were more often bullies, and reported more covert delinquency than Undercontrollers who were liked by their peers. The fact that higher (actually less lower) scores on conscientiousness and openness were related to adequate peer relations for Undercontrollers in childhood, but to less adequate peer relations in adolescence, probably points to a shift in the developmental significance of these variables. In elementary school, school achievements are at stake, and are an important issue for children to get approval, not only from adults but also from their peer mates. Consequently, the children who combine their undercontrol with low conscientiousness and low openness are not well liked in their school class. On the other hand, during adolescence, school achievements are clearly not the way to gain approval from your peers, and might even add to the risk of being disliked. This assumption is confirmed by the fact that also in resilient adolescents, higher conscientiousness and higher openness are associated with lower peer preference.

Differences between liked and disliked Resilients were also found. The liked Resilients were more agreeable, even more resilient, and reported more support from friends. Van Lieshout, Scholte, van Aken, Haselager, and Riksen-Walraven (2000) studied various subtypes of resilient children, and identified small subgroups of 'gifted' individuals, that "... proficiently employ their gifted personality in the social contexts of relationships and groups" (p. 121).

The choice of using peer preference data to further identify subtypes is guided by the assumption that certain personality types are relatively 'risk-free' when they manage to develop adequate relationships (in this case with peers), whereas the same type might be 'at risk' when this is not the case. Of course, other ways of further differentiating the three main types are possible. For example, further subtyping using the Big Five personality dimensions is an option. Using this procedure, Robins, John, and Caspi (1998) found subtypes of Overcontrollers and Resilients. Van Aken *et al.* (1998) found similar subtypes, in addition to subtypes of Undercontrollers. However, using various Big Five factor measures, Asendorpf (1999) did not find replicable subtypes in three samples of young adults.

The choices made for further differentiation in this chapter also reflect assumptions about the nature of person-environment transactions. As mentioned above, our combination reflects the idea that the quality of relationships moderates the effect of personality on psychosocial functioning. Another possibility is that personality moderates the effects of the social environment on psychosocial functioning. Our results did not clearly support this assumption, however. Low peer preference had negative effects for all three personality types, even for the Resilients. However, for Resilients the effects of low peer preference only affected other variables related to peer group functioning. For the other two main personality types the effects of low peer preference were broader, for Overcontrollers 'generalizing' to more internalizing problems (i.e., higher loneliness) and for Undercontrollers to more externalizing problems (i.e., higher covert delinquency).

What are the mechanisms behind these person-relationship transactions leading to adjustment problems? Caspi and Bem (1990) describe mechanisms of contemporary continuity and cumulative continuity. Contemporary continuity refers to the possibility that person characteristics (e.g., personality types) that at earlier ages are related to certain outcomes (e.g., peer rejection), at later ages are related with other outcomes (e.g., delinquency). In this case, the association between personality type and peer preference would be more or less a spurious finding, rather than a mechanism per se. Cumulative continuity refers to the fact that certain person characteristics can have a snowball effect: either rigidly high or very low impulse control might (for some children) lead to problems in their peer relations, and subsequently (because of social rejection and/or deviant peer groups) to problems in psychosocial functioning. Although our results do not allow for a choice between the two mechanisms, we are more inclined to assume cumulative continuity, following, for example, Patterson, DeBaryshe and Ramsey's (1989) model, where aggressive and disruptive behaviour in school classes leads to rejection, and through subsequent truancy and school drop-out into contact with deviant peers and delinquency.

In summary, three personality types in childhood and adolescence that have recently been reported were again found in our studies. One type concerns resilient children, who are flexible in their emotion regulation, and function relatively well. The other two types concern children low in flexibility, who are either over- or undercontrolled. These children are at risk for developing internalizing and externalizing problems respectively, particularly when this personality structure is combined with problematic peer relationships.

ACKNOWLEDGMENTS

The data on the personality types and their main effects were presented earlier at the 61st Biennial Meetings of the Society for Research in Child Development, Indianapolis, USA, 30 March–2 April 1995 (data on childhood) and at the VIIth Biennial Meeting of the Society for Research in Adolescence, San Diego, USA, 26 February–1 March, 1998 (data on adolescence).

REFERENCES

Aksan, N., Goldsmith, H. H., Smider, N. A., Essex, M. J., Clark, R., Hyde, J. S., Klein, M. H., and Vandell, D. L. (1999). Derivation and prediction of temperamental types among preschoolers. *Developmental Psychology*, 35, 958–71.
Allport, G. W. (1937). *Personality: A psychological interpretation*. New York: Holt.
Arend, R., Gove, F. L., and Sroufe, A. L. (1979). Continuity of individual adaptation from infancy to kindergarten: a predictive study of ego-resiliency and curioisity in preschoolers. *Child Development*, 50, 950–9.
Asendorpf, J. B. (1999). *Replicable subtypes of three major prototypes of personality description*. Paper presented at 10th European Conference on Personality, Krakow, Poland, July 2000.
Asendorpf, J. B. (2000). A person-centered approach to personality and social relationships: findings from the Berlin Network Study. In L. Bergman, R. Cairns, L. Nilsson and L. Nystedt (eds.), *Developmental science and the holistic approach*. Mahwah, NJ: Erlbaum, 281–98.
Asendorpf, J. B., and van Aken, M. A. G. (1999). Resilient, overcontrolled and undercontrolled personality prototypes in childhood: replicability, predictive power, and the trait/type issue. *Journal of Personality and Social Psychology*, 77, 815–32.

Asendorpf, J. B., and Wilpers, S. (1998). Personality effects on social relation-ships. *Journal of Personality and Social Psychology*, 74, 1531–44.

Bates, J. E., Pettit, G. S., Dodge, K. A., and Ridge, B. (1998). Interaction of tem-peramental resistance to control and restrictive parenting in the development of externalizing behavior. *Developmental Psychology*, 34, 982–95.

Block, J. (1971). *Lives through time*. Berkeley: Bancroft Books.

Block, J., and Block, J. H. (1980b). Rationale and procedure for developing in-dices for ego-control and ego-resiliency (preliminary draft). Berkely, CA University of California.

Block, J., Block, J. H., and Keyes, S. (1988). Longitudinally foretelling drug usage in adolescence: Early childhood personality and environmental precursors. *Child Development*, 59, 336–55.

Block, J., and Kremen, A. M. (1996). IQ and ego-resiliency: conceptual and empirical connections and separateness. *Journal of Personality and Social Psychology*, 70, 349–61.

Block, J. H., and Block, J. (1980a). The role of ego-control and ego-resiliency in the organization of behavior. In W. A. Collins (ed.), *Minnesota Symposium on Child Psychology*. Hillsdale, NJ: Erlbaum vol. 13, 39–101.

Caspi, A. (1998). Personality development across the life course. In W. Damon (Editor-in-Chief) and N. Eisenberg (Vol. Ed.), *Handbook of child psychology*, (5th edn.), vol. 3: *Social, emotional, and personality development*, 311–88. New York: Wiley.

Caspi, A. (2000). The child is the father of the man: personality continuities from childhood to adulthood. *Journal of Personality and Social Psychology*, 78, 158–72.

Caspi, A., and Bem, D. J. (1990). Personality continuity and change across the life course. In L. A. Pervin (ed.), *Handbook of personality: theory and research*. New York: Guilford Press, 549–75.

Caspi, A., and Moffitt, T. E. (1991). Individual differences are accentuated dur-ing periods of social change: the sample case of girls at puberty. *Journal of Personality and Social Psychology*, 61, 157–68.

Caspi, A., and Silva, P. A. (1995). Temperamental qualities at age three predict personality traits in young adulthood: Longitudinal evidence from a birth cohort. *Child Development*, 66, 486–98.

Cramer, P. (2000). Development of identity: gender makes a difference. *Journal of Research in Personality*, 34, 42–72.

Diener, E. (2000). Introduction to the special section on personality develop-ment. *Journal of Personality and Social Psychology*, 78, 120–1.

Eisenberg, N., Fabes, R. A., Guthrie, I. K., and Reiser, M. (2000). Dis-positional emotionality and regulation: their role in predicting quality of social functioning. *Journal of Personality and Social Psychology*, 78, 136–57.

Eisenberg, N., Fabes, R. A., Karbon, M., Murphy, B. C., Wosinski, M., Polazzi, L., Carlo, G., and Juhnke, C. (1996). The relations of children's dispositional prosocial behavior to emotionality, regulation, and social functioning. *Child Development*, 67, 974–92.

Eisenberg, N., Fabes, R. A., Shepard, S. A., Murphy, B. C., Guthrie, I. K., Jones, S., Friedman, J., Poulin, R., and Maszk, P. (1997). Contemporaneous and longitudinal prediction of children's social functioning from regulation and emotionality. *Child Development*, 68, 642–64.

Funder, D. C., and Block, J. (1989). The role of ego-control, ego-resiliency, and IQ in delay of gratification in adolescence. *Journal of Personality and Social Psychology*, 57, 1041–50.

Halverson, C. F. Jr., Kohnstamm, G. A., and Martin, R. P. (1994). *The developing structutre of temperament and personality from infancy to adulthood.* Hillsdale, NJ: Erlbaum.

Harrington, D. M., Chin, C. S., Rickey, A. D., and Mohr, J. J. (1999). *Relationships between attachment styles and three increasingly replicable personality types.* Paper presented at the Biennial Meetings of the Society for Research in Child Development, 17 April 1999, Albuquerque, NM, USA.

Hart, D., Hofmann, V., Edelstein, W., and Keller, M. (1997). The relation of childhood personality types to adolescent behavior and development: a longitudinal study of Icelandic children. *Developmental Psychology*, 33, 195–205.

Huey, S. J., and Weisz, J. R. (1997). Ego control, ego resiliency, and the five-factor model as predictors of behavioral and emotional problems in clinic-referred children and adolescents. *Journal of Abnormal Psychology*, 106, 404–15.

John, O. P., Caspi, A., Robins, R. W., Moffitt, T. E., and Stouthamer-Loeber, M. (1994). The "Little Five": exploring the nomological network of the five-factor model of personality in adolescent boys. *Child Development*, 65, 160–78.

John, O. P., Pals, J. L., and Westenberg, P. M. (1998). Personality prototypes and ego development: conceptual similarities and relations in adult women. *Journal of Personality and Social Psychology*, 74, 1093–108.

Klohnen, E. C. (1996). Conceptual analysis and measurement of the construct of Ego-resiliency. *Journal of Personality and Social Psychology*, 70, 1067–79.

Klohnen, E. C., Vandewater, E. A., and Young, A. (1996). Negotiating the middle years: ego-resiliency and successful midlife adjustment in women. *Psychology and Aging*, 11, 431–42.

Kobak, R. R., and Sceery, A. (1988). Attachment in late adolescence: working models, affect regulation, and representations of self and others. *Child Development*, 59, 135–46.

Kochanska, G. (1993). Toward a synthesis of parental socialization and child temperament in the early development of conscience. *Child Development*, 64, 325–47.

Kochanska, G., Murray, K., Jacques, T. Y., Koening, A. L., and Vandegeest, K. A. (1996). Inhibitory control in young children and its role in emerging internalization. *Child Development*, 67, 490–509.

Kremen, A. M., and Block, J. (1998). The roots of ego-control in young adulthood: links with parenting in early childhood. *Journal of Personality and Social Psychology*, 75, 1062–75.

Loeber, R., Wung, P., Keenan, K., Giroux, B., Stouthamer-Loeber, M., van Kammen, W. B., and Maughan, B. (1993). Developmental pathways in disruptive child behavior. *Development and Psychopathology*, 5, 103–33.

Magnusson, D., and Stattin, H. (1998). Person-context interaction theories. In W. Damon (Series Editor) and R. M. Lerner (Volume Editor), *Handbook of child psychology, vol. 1. Theoretical models of human development.* New York: Wiley, 685–760.

Newcomb, A. F., and Bukowski, W. M. (1983). Social impact and social preference as determinants of children's peer group status. *Developmental Psychology*, 19, 856–67.

Newman, D. L., Caspi, A., Moffitt, T. E., and Silva, P. A. (1997). Antecedents of adult interpersonal functioning: effects of individual differences in age 3 temperament. *Developmental Psychology*, 33, 206–17.

Olweus, D. (1991). Bully/victim problems among school children: basic facts and effects of a school bases intervention program. In D. J. Pepler and K. H. Rubin (eds.), *The development and treatment of childhood aggression*. Hillsdale, NJ: Erlbaum, 411–48.

Pals, J. (1999). Identity consolidation in early adulthood: relations with ego-resiliency, the context of marriage, and personality change. *Journal of Personality*, 67, 295–329.

Patterson, G. R., DeBaryshe, B. D., and Ramsey, E. (1989). A developmental perspective on antisocial behavior. *American Psychologist*, 44, 329–35.

Pulkkinen, L. (1996). Female and male personality styles: a typological and developmental analysis. *Journal of Personality and Social Psychology*, 70, 1288–306.

Riksen-Walraven J. M. A. and van Aken, M. A. G. (1997). Effects of two mother-infant intervention programs upon children's development at 7, 10, and 12 years. In W. Koops, J. B. Hoeksma, and D. van den Boom (eds.), *Development of interaction and attachment: traditional and non-traditional approaches*. Amsterdam: North Holland, 79–91.

Roberts, W. L. (1999). The socialization of emotion expression: relations with prosocial behaviour and competence in five samples. *Canadian Journal of Behavioural Science*, 31, 72–85.

Robins, R. W., John, O. P., and Caspi, A. (1998). The typological approach to studying personality. In R. B. Cairns, L. R. Bergman, and J. Kagan (eds.), *Methods and models for studying the individual*. Beverly Hills, CA: Sage, 135–60.

Robins, R. W., John, O. P., Caspi, A., Moffitt, T. E., and Stouthamer-Loeber, M. (1996). Resilient, overcontrolled, and undercontrolled boys: three replicable personality types. *Journal of Personality and Social Psychology*, 70, 157–71.

Rothbart, M. K., Ahadi, S. A., and Evans, D. E. (2000). Temperament and personality: origins and outcomes. *Journal of Personality and Social Psychology*, 78, 122–35.

Rothbart, M. K., and Bates, J. E. (1998). Temperament. In W. Damon (Editor-in-Chief) and N. Eisenberg (Vol. Ed.), *Handbook of Child Psychology* (5th edn.), vol. 3: *Social, emotional and personality development*, 105–76. New York: Wiley.

Rothbart, M. K., and Derryberry, D. (1981). Development of individual differences in temperament. In M. E. Lamb and A. L. Brown (eds.), *Advances in developmental psychology*, Hillsdale, NJ: Erlbaum, vol. 1, 37–86.

Scholte, R. H. J., van Aken, M. A. G. and van Lieshout, C. F. M. (1997). Adolescent's personality factors in self-ratings and peer nominations and their prediction of peer acceptance and rejection. *Journal of Personality Assessment*, 69, 534–54.

Scholte, R. H. J., van Lieshout, C. F. M., and van Aken, M. A. G. (2001). Relational support in adolescence: factors, types, and adjustment. *Journal of Research in Adolescence*, 11, 71–94.

Shedler, J., and Block, J. (1990). Adolescent drug use and psychological health: a longitudinal inquiry. *American Psychologist*, 45, 612–30.

Sroufe, J. W. (1991). Assessment of parent-adolescent relationships: implications for adolescent development. *Journal of Family Psychology*, 5, 21–45.

Stattin, H., and Magnusson, D. (1990). *Pubertal Maturation in Female Development*. Hillsdale, NJ: Erlbaum.

van Aken, M. A. G. (1992). The development of general competence and domain-specific competencies. *European Journal of Personality*, 6, 267–82.

van Aken, M. A. G., and Riksen-Walraven, J. M. A. (1992). Parental support and the development of competence in children. *International Journal of Behavioral Development*, 15, 101–23.

van Aken, M. A. G., van Lieshout, C. F. M., and Scholte, R. H. J. (1998). *The social relationships and adjustment of various personality types and subtypes*. VIIth Biennial Conference of the Society for Research in Adolescence, 26 February–1 March, San Diego, USA.

van Lieshout, C. F. M. (2000). Personality development: dimensions, types, and developmental outcomes. *International Journal of Behavioral Development*, 24, 276–88.

van Lieshout, C. F. M., and Haselager, G. J. T. (1994). The big five personality factors in Q-sort descriptions of children and adolescents. In C. F. Halverson, G. A. Kohnstamm, and R. P. Martin (eds), *The developing structure of temperament and personality from infancy to adulthood*. Hillsdale, NJ: Erlbaum, 293–318.

van Lieshout, C. F. M., Haselager, G. J. T., Riksen-Walraven, J. M. A. and van Aken, M. A. G. (1995). *Personality development and formation of identities in middle childhood*. Biennial Meetings of SRCD, 30 March–2 April, 1995.

van Lieshout, C. F. M., Haselager, G. J. T., and van Aken, M. A. G. (1998). *Generalizability of personality types and subtypes across age, gender, and methods of assessment*. Paper presented at the XVth Biennial ISSBD Conference, 1–4 July, 1998, Berne (CH).

van Lieshout, C. F. M., Scholte, R. H. J., van Aken, M. A. G., Haselager, G. J. T., and Riksen-Walraven, J. M. A. (2000). The development of resilient personality, competent relationships, popular group status, and adjustment. In C. F. M. van Lieshout and P. G. Heymans (eds.). *Developing talent across the life-span*, Hove, UK: Psychology Press, 103–23.

Westenberg, P. M., and Block, J. (1993). Ego development and individual differences in personality. *Journal of Personality and Social Psychology*, 65, 792–800.

York, K. L., and John, O. P. (1992). The four faces of eve: a typological analysis of women's personality at midlife. *Journal of Personality and Social Psychology*, 63, 494–508.

6 The influence of early behavior patterns on later life

Glen H. Elder, Jr. and Robert Crosnoe

Introduction

Each stage of life plays a distinctive role in shaping the life-course and its developmental trajectories. This applies in particular to the young adult years, which are typically marked by diversity and flux as young people complete school, enter the labor market, and establish families (Rindfuss, 1991). The recurring wars and economic depressions of the twentieth century have only added to this variability. As a rule, life changes pile up in the 20s and 30s, but a coherent life pattern usually emerges, with intimations of the future. These changes and anticipations involve interrelated domains, from education and work to health and family life. Each domain is best viewed in relation to the others.

The goal of this study is to investigate how young adult behavioral profiles foretell the subsequent life-course of men. Their achievement and emotional health at an early stage of life provide insight regarding their lifetime potential, possibly setting in motion developmental pathways. How might early achievement and emotional health account for the adjustment of men in midlife or late life, their successes and failures? Early advantages and disadvantages might accumulate, widening the gap between success and failure and perhaps strengthening the relation between accomplishment and health (Sampson and Laub, 1997). Alternatively, initial differences among men, or discrepancies between accomplishment and emotional health, might fade over time. Assuming that pressures toward intra-personal coherence increase across the adult years (see Caspi and Roberts, in press), we would expect less evidence of discrepancies between personal achievement and health over time.

Neither the life-course nor developmental trajectories are inalterable or uneventful. A good start in life might be followed by misfortune or greater vulnerability as advantages are squandered in later years through drug use, family dysfunction, or health crises. Conversely, a bad start in life may be turned around by hard work, supportive relationships, or even

157

by chance opportunities (Bandura, 1982). At the heart of these scenarios is the malleability of the life-course.

Evidence on such trajectories is typically obtained by tracking people across their lives on single dimensions of accomplishment, personality, and health. But variable-centered studies of this kind do not capture the reality of human lives, which are better viewed as complex configurations of attributes and behaviors (Magnusson, 1998). For example, achievement and health are important to consider when studying men's lives, but they take on greater meaning as dynamic, interacting aspects of a developmental process. In general, good health promotes achievement, which promotes good health (Adler *et al.*, 1994). The two are intertwined but their relation to each other is not uniform across men.

A person-centered approach, which focuses on the constellation of attributes within men (Caspi and Bem, 1990), is well-suited to taking into account such intra-personal contingencies. In their 20s and 30s, young men are entering the workforce, making important choices about the future, and carving out their own niches at work and in public life. Their emotional health plays a role in this exploration, providing resources for some and obstacles for others. At the same time, the choices they make about work and career are also affecting their emotional health. The interplay between the two can be used to identify certain types, or profiles, of young men.

With these perspectives in mind, we chose to focus on three dimensions of young adulthood:

(1) emotional health, using several barometers of mental adjustment;
(2) career achievement, characterized less by status and income than by consistent upward progression; and
(3) civic involvement, which encompasses service activities (e.g., volunteering for charity) and professional memberships (e.g., membership in the American Medical Association).

Civic involvement may enhance career success, by providing social networks and enhancing visibility in the community, and promote emotional well-being, by providing meaningful and fulfilling activities. Profiles based on these dimensions are likely to offer greater insight into men's lives as they age.

The construction of personal profiles in young adulthood and their comparison across the life course is a demanding task for longitudinal data. Fortunately, we are able to draw upon the unparalleled data archive of the Stanford-Terman study of talented Californians who were born between 1903 and 1920 (Holahan and Sears, 1995). Described at length in the next section, the archive provides information on the life-long development of a sample of exceptionally bright children, following them from 1922 to the mid-1980s. The depth of these data and the advantages of person-centered analyses enable us to address questions about the early behavior patterns of men and their life-course up to the later years.

In the next section, we describe the Stanford-Terman sample at length, explain the measurements and the analytic model, and discuss the process by which we identified and created the behavioral profiles using the 1940 data. The following section turns to the empirical findings of the study, in which the behavioral types are followed across four stages of life: childhood and adolescence, young adulthood, mid-life, and later life.

Sample, measurement, and analysis

The Stanford-Terman study began in 1922, under the direction of Lewis Terman, then professor of psychology at Stanford University. Data were collected on a selected sample of high ability children, 857 males and 671 females, in large public schools across the state of California. The study sought answers to the question of what kind of adults (bright) children tend to become (Terman and Oden, 1959, p. 1). With this objective in mind, Terman selected children for the study who scored in the gifted range on the Stanford-Binet IQ test (the lowest score is 135). By identifying the most able young people through IQ tests, Terman believed that he could enable society to ensure the flow of talent to leadership positions. The sample children generally came from middle-class homes, and they later obtained high levels of education, with half of all men earning professional or graduate degrees. The study members were followed up every five years through 1960, and then again at multiple times in the 1970s and 1980s.

Life-history records were constructed for all respondents by integrating survey data at each time point with qualitative information (e.g., letters, written responses to open-ended questions about family and career) collected during five trips to Stanford University. The methodology for recasting the data to address our questions is reported in Elder, Pavalko, and Clipp (1993). In this chapter, we focus only on men born between 1905 and 1914 in order to minimize age variation. As a result, the men were all between the ages of 26 and 35 when data used to construct the behavioral profiles were collected in 1940.

As mentioned previously, a person-centered approach focuses on the salience and configuration of variables within people, as opposed to the search for variables that distinguish people (Magnusson and Cairns, 1996; Block, 1971). In taking such an approach, we identify behavioral profiles through cluster-analytic techniques that sorted the Terman men into groups based on their configurations of selected characteristics in 1940 (see below). The method employs a two-step procedure (SAS Institute, 1994). First a hierarchical agglomerative technique creates a range of cluster solutions, from a single cluster of all cases to one cluster per case. Study members are grouped with others that are most similar to them, as determined by the squared Euclidean distance between two cases. Ward's hierarchical method enables the investigator to optimize the variance within clusters (Aldenderfer and Blashfield, 1984). The best cluster solution is chosen according to explained variance and other indicators (e.g., cubic clustering criterion).

Once the optimal number of clusters is chosen, study members can be assigned to clusters through an iterative partitioning method that minimizes within-cluster variance and maximizes the variance between clusters. This method calculates the centroid for each of the specified clusters and assigns study members to clusters based on the squared Euclidean distance between the case and the center of the original cluster. The process is repeated until the most homogeneous clusters are identified.

In this study, five standardized measures of emotional health, achievement, and civic involvement from 1940 were included in the cluster analysis. The study men were asked in 1940 to rate themselves on a set of personality characteristics, from 1 (low) to 11 (high). The first measure is *self-confidence* which is based on the sum of self-ratings on confidence and inferiority (reverse-coded); the second is *emotional stability*, indexed by the sum of emotionality, moodiness, and impulsiveness (all reverse coded); and the third is *self direction*, measured by the sum of purposefulness and persistence.

The fourth measure, *worklife achievement*, relies upon evidence of career advancement, 1936-1941. There are two components: worklife progress, indications of upward movement in responsibility, accomplishment, and leadership (yes = 1, no = 0); and the "lack of floundering," the absence of worklife changes with no logical direction (0 = floundering, 1 = none). We summed the two items, unless one was missing, in which case we multiplied the other score by a factor of 2. This measure provides a more comprehensive assessment of early career trajectories than does change in occupational status because it allows for intra-stratum progress, such as an attorney becoming a partner or a professor receiving tenure. *Civic involvement* is measured by the sum of all service activities and the number of memberships in professional organizations, as of 1940. In order to minimize the skew of cases on this index, we used its natural logarithm.

Outliers are especially problematic in cluster analysis. By ranking the cases according to the minimum Euclidean distance, we identified only one case that was unlike all others. By deleting this case, we ended up with 505 study members who had legitimate values on each of the five dimensions. Test statistics from the hierarchical agglomerative procedure indicated that a four to six unit solution would be acceptable. We chose five clusters to ensure sufficient variation. This solution explained 36 percent of the variance in the five variables included in the cluster analysis. Study members were assigned to the five clusters using an iterative partitioning method. We repeated this analysis with another program from Stockholm University which was designed specifically for person-oriented analyses (Bergman and El-Khouri, 1998). The clusters that emerged from this analysis corresponded with those obtained through the SAS program. The mean cluster values on the five dimensions were virtually identical. This comparability across different techniques increases our confidence that the profiles are reliable categories of behavior.

The resulting clusters provide the empirical framework for examining the impact of young adult behavior on behavior, activity, and health in later lives. The study question, whether behavioral profiles of men in young adulthood set in motion different life trajectories, was investigated by a variety of analytic techniques, but especially by one-way ANOVA with Duncan tests for group comparisons. Such analyses compare the behavioral profiles on the mean levels of factors related to work (e.g., income, occupational prestige), family (fatherhood, marital satisfaction), and health (physical health ratings, self-esteem). Appendix 1 provides complete descriptions of all variables. Throughout the chapter, we supplement the empirical findings with life descriptions and quotations from the Terman men themselves. We begin with a description of the behavioral types in 1940, when the Study members were young adults, and then follow the men into their 50s and later years.

Results

Five types of men

The five clusters represent two types of less successful men, "maladjusted" and "adjusted," and three modes of an *achievement-oriented* life style, "maladjusted," "socially disengaged," and "adjusted." Figure 6.1 compares each cluster on the five dimensions, beginning on the left with measures of emotional health and extending on the right to career progress and civic involvement. As might be expected, less successful men in the maladjusted group rank consistently at the bottom on

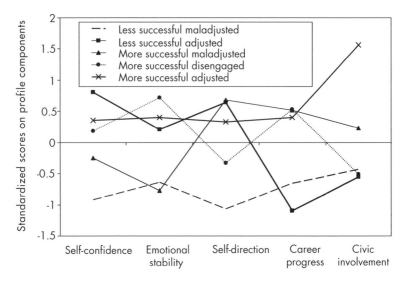

Figure 6.1 Behavioral profiles of Terman men in young adulthood, 1940.

all dimensions. At the other end of the continuum we find men who are both adjusted and more successful. The more successful, disengaged men resemble these men, except for their lower self-direction and relatively weak community ties.

The two remaining profiles are distinguished by a lack of personal consistency or crystallization in young adulthood. The more successful, maladjusted men are prospering in their worklife and possess a well-developed sense of self-direction, but they rank below average on feelings of self-confidence and emotional stability. Objectively, these men are doing well in their careers, but they do not derive emotional rewards from their success. One member of this category was a market researcher for a national corporation in 1939, but he was quite unhappy there because he was "unsuited to the atmosphere" and felt "stifled and hemmed in." This man dreamed of a career in the arts, but he held a series of corporate jobs. How will such men adapt as they advance into the middle years and later life? Will feelings of inadequacy handicap their accomplishments and ambition? Will they be less satisfied with their career than other successful men? Or will career success bolster feelings of confidence, producing a greater sense of competence?

The second "inconsistent" pattern of behavior generates questions of personal integration and change over the life-course. The men in the less successful, well-adjusted group may be characterized by a delayed timetable for worklife advancement, possibly owing to World War II, or by an orientation to life that does not emphasize career success. For example, one young man claimed that his goal in life was "To live the best life I can and to consider so-called 'jobs' as merely a sustaining force necessary to provide food and shelter." His emotional well-being was not predicated on occupational advancement. Will his accomplishments begin to match his emotional health in later life or will a continued lack of worklife progress begin to undermine a sense of well-being?

The backgrounds of men from five behavioral profiles

Men in each of the early adult groups started out their lives with much in common in terms of family background and relationships (Table 6.1). They typically grew up in middle class families. Less successful, maladjusted men are positioned at the bottom of this stratum, with the more successful, well-adjusted men at the top, though no difference is actually statistically reliable. Four out of five of their families were intact and virtually all of the mothers were exclusively engaged as homemakers. Less than a sixth had a paid job, part- or full-time. The men generally reported strong ties to parents, except for those who were not doing well at this time on emotional health and work achievement, the less successful, maladjusted men. Quality family relations bear upon emotional health, and we find that this is the only evidence of their differential

Table 6.1 *Young adult behavior patterns by pre-1940 individual factors and social origins; one-way analysis of variance*

	Less successful 1940		More successful 1940			
	Maladjusted	Adjusted	Maladjusted	Disengaged	Adjusted	F
Social background						
SES	2.51_a	2.37_a	2.36_a	2.41_a	2.29_a	.50
Intact (%)	81_{ab}	78_b	91_a	80_{ab}	87_{ab}	1.94
Maternal emp. (%)	12_a	19_a	15_a	12_a	9_a	1.01
Parent attachment	3.42_b	3.60_{ab}	3.68_a	3.66_{ab}	3.70_a	1.97+
Social competence	1.67_b	1.84_{ab}	1.63_b	1.75_b	1.97_a	3.67**
Individual factors						
Age in 1940	29.96_b	29.65_b	30.16_b	30.12_b	30.91_a	2.93*
Planful competence	36.76_c	39.42_{ab}	39.74_{ab}	38.74_b	40.70_a	4.96***
IQ	149.58_b	150.16_a	151.43_a	150.74_a	146.93_b	2.37+
Education 1940	3.82_c	3.90_c	4.78_a	4.23_b	4.93_a	17.11***
College GPA	2.62_c	2.72_{ab}	2.94_a	2.74_{ab}	2.95_a	3.68**

Notes: All values are means, unless otherwise noted.
Values with the same subscript are not significantly different from each other at $p < .05$ level.
***$p < .001$, **$p < .01$, *$p < .05$, + $p < .10$

influence. However, men who reported friends in childhood and getting along with peers (the social competence index) had fewer emotional health problems in young adulthood, when compared to men who were more isolated.

As might be expected, both individual attributes and education vary between the groups, and mainly between the least and most successful. Planfulness in the adolescent years is generally predictive of early career success (Clausen, 1993), and we find substantial evidence of this in the lives of the Terman men. Planful men were more likely to have successful career beginnings, and their higher educational level and academic success in college are part of this achievement. In view of the extraordinary intellectual ability of the men, as a group, small variations mean very little, though it is interesting that the most accomplished and healthy men in the sample were slightly older and ranked lower on IQ than other men.

Men in young adulthood

Where do men in each cluster stand on family life, career, and health in 1940 (Table 6.2)? Over 90 percent were in the labor force by the end of the 1940 follow-up, and over half were married. Not surprisingly, the less successful and less adjusted men were having the greatest difficulty

Table 6.2 *Young adult attributes and behavior patterns; one-way ANOVA, 1940*

	Less successful 1940		More successful 1940			
	Maladjusted	Adjusted	Maladjusted	Disengaged	Adjusted	F
1940						
Family life						
Married (%)	58$_b$	67$_{ab}$	70$_{ab}$	74$_a$	.73$_a$	1.76
Marital sat.	−.11$_a$	.08$_a$	−.05$_a$	.09$_a$	−.00$_a$	.76
Children (%)	20$_b$	44$_a$	41$_a$	47$_a$	45$_a$	5.55***
Career						
Income	1803.26$_c$	2174.79$_{bc}$	2966.16$_a$	2581.24$_{ab}$	2791.24$_a$	5.64***
Occ. prestige	52.76$_d$	51.97$_d$	64.63$_a$	58.70$_b$	65.38$_a$	17.30***
Work sat.	−.41$_b$	.04$_a$	.24$_a$	.14$_a$	.20$_a$	8.67***
Health						
Gen. health	4.24$_b$	4.42$_{ab}$	4.37$_{ab}$	4.55$_a$	4.48$_a$	2.81*
Low self-esteem	7.07$_a$	4.83$_d$	6.38$_b$	5.37$_c$	5.32$_c$	57.56***
Happiness	6.44$_c$	7.00$_a$	6.58$_{bc}$	6.97$_{ab}$	6.99$_a$	4.39**

Notes: All values are means, unless otherwise noted.
   Values with the same subscript are not significantly different from each other at p < .05 level.
   ***p < .001, **p < .01, *p < .05, + p < .10

in getting started in life. Compared to all other men, they were least likely to have married and started a family; they ranked lowest on income and work satisfaction; and they also ranked lowest on self-ratings of general health, personal happiness, and self-esteem. Compared to all other groups, except the less successful men with good emotional health, these men had entered lower status jobs (such as lower level bureaucrats, sales clerks), consistent with their lower education.

At this stage of the life-course, emotional maladjustment appears to make little difference in the accomplishments of successful men. Compare, for example, the two groups of achievers, one maladjusted and the other well-adjusted. In young adulthood, the two groups resemble each other on yearly income, occupational prestige, and work satisfaction. However, they differ significantly on other measures of well-being. The adjusted men are significantly more healthy on their ratings of self-esteem, happiness, and general health. Will these large differences in emotional health make a difference in men's career patterns as we move to middle age and later life?

Emotional well-being clearly made a difference in how the less successful men viewed their work in the early years of their career. The men with better emotional health were similar in occupational prestige to the men who were more troubled, and they ranked slightly higher on income. But the more healthy men were far less likely to hold negative evaluations. These men were generally happier, according to their self-report, and they claimed to be in good health, when compared to the less adjusted group. The former also held far more positive views of themselves. Lifelong career dissatisfaction may become one of the more costly effects of poor emotional health in young adulthood. And this dissatisfaction could generalize to other aspects of life; to family, for example, or friendships.

One of the most important questions for this early adult stage concerns the impact of World War II. The 1940 follow-up occurred just prior to American entry into the war. The prospects of war were deeply disturbing and unsettling to members of the study since they had so little certainty that they could proceed with their careers, advanced training, and families. Despite an average age of 30 in 1941, 40 percent of the men were called into the armed forces and an additional quarter were recruited into critical war industries. Recruitment into the war effort disrupted men's lives, increased the risk of divorce (Pavalko and Elder, 1990), the likelihood of occupational change, and prospects for an accelerated decline of physical health in the later years (Elder and Chan, 1999). However, we find no evidence in our subgroup of the sample that war experience was concentrated in the lives of men in particular clusters of young adults. As noted earlier, we selected men for this study of early adult patterns in men's lives by minimizing the age range. This design no doubt reduced our chances for identifying historical influences.

Transitions into middle age

A decade or two later, the men were in middle age. They varied in age from the late 30s to the early 50s. Were their different beginnings in young adulthood expressed at middle age in distinct patterns of family life and career, social engagements and health? Two general observations emerge from Table 6.3. First, we observe a general pattern of convergence by midlife. The five differentiated groups in young adulthood have shifted toward a similar behavioral pattern on family life, career, and health. In family life, however, emotional health problems in the young adult years are predictive of a slightly higher divorce rate, regardless of young adulthood career success, although the difference is not statistically reliable. Interestingly, the growing similarity among the groups could result from the decreasing similarity of men within groups. On key variables, such as self-esteem and career advancement, within-group variation increased from young adulthood to later years, but the clusters themselves became less differentiated (results not shown).

Second, the extremes in young adult adaptation – the less successful, maladjusted versus the successful, well-adjusted men – continue to maintain their relative positions. Yet, they are not as far apart at mid-life as they were a decade or two earlier. The successful men in health and careers have remained on a largely stable trajectory, one that reflects their professional prominence, often in the world of college and post-graduate teaching. They continue to score high on civic involvement, career attainment, and personal well-being.

A resilient path, however, is more evident among the most troubled group of young men. The less successful, maladjusted men made significant gains across the years that have helped to close the gap between them and the other groups. Nevertheless, the gap remains substantial in lower achievement, social involvement, and emotional health. These men score highest, among all groups, on low self-esteem and ten years later we find them ranked at the bottom on personal happiness and emotional health. They were also most likely to be engaged in problem drinking. Personal problems of this kind can set in motion a self-defeating dynamic (Sampson and Laub, 1997) in which failure strengthens the expectation of failure, and thus adds fuel to the perpetuation of personal problems in a cumulative process.

In 1960 the Terman men, as a group, were approaching their 50s, a fruitful time for work and a period of transition for their children, who

Table 6.3 *Mid-life status by young adult behavior patterns; one-way ANOVA, 1950–60*

	Less successful 1940		More successful 1940			F
	Maladjusted	Adjusted	Maladjusted	Disengaged	Adjusted	
Family life						
Divorced by 1959 (%)	22_a	24_a	23_a	16_a	16_a	.91
Marital sat. 1951	4.19_a	4.48_a	4.24_a	4.52_a	4.40_a	.44
Civic involve. 1960	1.26_c	1.28_c	1.61_{ab}	1.40_{bc}	1.77_a	7.76***
Career						
Income 1959	13374.94_b	15370.97_{ab}	19186.27_a	19379.47_a	17753.94_{ab}	2.01+
Occ. prestige 1959	58.09_c	62.17_b	66.22_a	63.59_{ab}	66.44_a	8.78***
Health						
Happiness 1950	6.44_a	7.00_a	6.58_a	6.97_a	6.99_a	2.09+
Low self-esteem 1950	6.76_a	5.30_c	6.23_b	5.62_c	5.51_c	17.97***
Physical 1960	3.14_a	3.31_a	3.26_a	3.35_a	3.33_a	1.38
Emotional 1960	4.13_b	4.49_a	4.27_{ab}	4.46_a	4.26_{ab}	2.00+
Alcohol 1960	2.31_a	2.00_b	1.91_b	2.07_{ab}	1.93_b	3.11*

Notes: All values are means, unless otherwise noted.
Values with the same subscript are not significantly different from each other at $p < .05$ level. N (1950, 1960) = 474, 409
*** $p < .001$, ** $p < .01$, * $p < .05$, + $p < .10$

were leaving home, completing an education, marrying, and having children. Unfortunately, the men were not contacted again until 1972, when they were in their 60s, and then for follow-ups every four or so years up to 1986. By their 60s, most men in the sample had done well, though perhaps not reaching the lofty expectations of their childhoods. The men grew up amidst great expectations for their future and their selection for Lewis Terman's study only added to these expectations.

The later years and looking back on life

When contacted in 1972, a large majority of the men were still working. Most had typically moved toward retirement by cutting back on hours. The lowest percentage of full-time workers did not appear among the men who had not done well in career or health, as we had expected. Instead, the "disengaged" men had left work at the highest rate (only 40 percent still working), well above the percentage for any other group or for the sample as a whole (greater than 60 percent still working). Retirement proved unsettling for one successful but socially disengaged man, who referred to the transition from work to retirement as a "traumatic experience" and claimed that it made him feel like a "non-person." Such a statement reflects the greater career-centeredness of men in this group. Once their careers were over, they had little to give them an identity and life purpose.

How did the men view their lives at this time? Life reviews play an important role in defining and redefining the self in the course of aging. Cutting back in work hours and formal retirement mark points at which men are likely to review their past in light of the changes underway. Life satisfaction in the later years is a product of successive life reviews. The same can be said for satisfaction with family life (marital life, relations with children), the intrinsic and extrinsic aspects of worklife accomplishments, relations with friends, associates, and neighbors; and the experiences of leisure and service to others. In 1972, the investigators asked the men about the importance of their goals and their satisfaction with attainment of these goals in five areas: occupational success, family life, cultural life, service to society, and joy in living. Five-point self-rating scales were used to obtain this information, yielding ten measures per area. We averaged goal salience and attainment satisfaction in each area, and then produced a single measure of life satisfaction by summing these five composite scales.

One might expect some accommodation to reality among the less successful men in terms of goals they now deem important, a downward adjustment that would enable some to feel good about their modest accomplishments. By contrast, the achievements of the most successful men should enhance their value, and, in the tradition of perfectionism, make satisfaction with attainment less possible. Whatever the possible scenarios over time, we find a very simple story in the total measure of life satisfaction. Not surprisingly, the more successful men in work and health rank at the top, with the bottom rung occupied by men with a more troubled career and emotional life (mean = 123.6 vs. 103.8, p > .01). The other three groups are positioned between these contrasts and have much in common. The distinction between a goal's importance and its achievement did not produce different results. Men from each young adult cluster gave a similar rating on these measures.

In building upon these results, we asked how much life patterns in young adulthood contributed to the life satisfaction of men, taking other factors into account. To address this question, we viewed the least successful group (on work and health) as the reference category for each of the remaining clusters in a structural equation model, controlling for education, occupational status (1959), and marital happiness. Both education and marital happiness significantly increase men's life satisfaction (see Figure 6.2). The status level of work added little to this picture of positive influences.

Only one of the early adult groups contributed positively to life satisfaction when compared to the less successful, maladjusted group. The

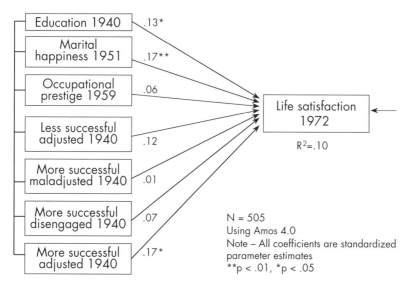

Figure 6.2 Predicting life satisfaction (1972) by young adult behavior types and social factors

more successful men in work and health were far more satisfied with the way that their lives had turned out in 1972. The parameter estimate for the less successful, well-adjusted men was also strongly positive, though it just missed statistical significance (p < .10). By grouping the profiles into two dichotomous categories, we find that the major influence is emotional health and not career success, net of other effects. This finding persists even when occupational prestige is removed from the model. The life of one Terman man illustrates this phenomenon. His adult life was spent moving from one career to another (e.g., sales, contracting, insurance), but he experienced great happiness throughout life, noting the pleasures of family, hobbies, and other activities. In 1972, he observed that "life has been good to me" and that he has "no complaints."

None of the early adult groups contribute positively to life satisfaction when compared to the strong positive influence of career success and emotional health. Both matter, but career success counts for less when it is not coupled with a sense of emotional well-being. Health problems and career problems in the early adult years have diminished life satisfaction for the Terman men.

Our measure of life satisfaction includes multiple domains. Do we find any evidence that satisfaction varies across domains among men who began their adult lives with different behavior patterns? To explore these issues we focused on the separate scales. We assumed that measures of work satisfaction and "joy in life" would vary across the young adult groups. The less successful men would tend to be more critical of their worklife, and men with emotional problems would give a low rating to "joy in life." However, neither of these expectations gain significant support from the data. Only the general index of life satisfaction produced large differences that are consistent with our expectations.

Emotional health and career success interact in their effects on emotional well-being and life satisfaction across the later years. Poor emotional health diminishes the meaning of work and its possibilities as a source of personal gratification. And career troubles can produce lifelong discontents, including less satisfaction in life during the later years.

Discussion

When Lewis Terman launched his panel study of "gifted" Californians in 1922, he selected the study members in terms of exceptional intelligence, an ability that maximized their goodness of fit for positions of high occupational status and leadership. His view of individual qualifications narrowly focused on measured IQ in the gifted range. Left out of the picture were many notable personal qualities, such as ambition and goals, work ethic, leadership skills, and good health, both emotional and physical. The meaning of intellectual ability hinges in part on each of these personal attributes. High intellectual ability is unlikely to predict life accomplishments without ambition and the capacity for disciplined work.

This chapter has focused on the life-course beginnings of the Terman men in the young adult years, and asks whether and how these beginnings influenced their lives and well-being through old age. The young adult years represent a formative life stage, a time when career and family are established. The men were born between 1903 and the 1920s, but we narrowed the age range (from 1905 to 1914) to create a single birth cohort with more social homogeneity and a precise historical location. The men were typically out of high school and in college during the Great Depression and a number served in World War II, from military units abroad to defense industries at home.

Using three key dimensions of young adulthood (emotional health, career progress, and civic involvement), we asked what they tell us as behavioral profiles about men's subsequent life-course and satisfaction in old age. Behavior patterns generally crystallize during young adulthood and persist into the later years, though life-course variations remain substantial, as shown in this study and others. We employed cluster analysis to identify relatively homogeneous groups of men, based on 1940 indicators of self-confidence, emotional stability, self-direction, career progress, and civic engagement. Five groups emerged. The less successful men at this early stage ended up in one of two groups, defined by emotional health or maladjustment. Men who had achieved progress in their career at this early stage included members of three definable groups – the well-adjusted, the less adjusted, and the disengaged who were not involved in community activities.

Not surprisingly, a history of educational achievement distinguished men who were beginning their careers on a successful note. Those who lacked both career success and emotional health were also characterized by weak ties to parents and inadequate social skills. They also tended not to marry at all or at least not until later in life, when compared to other men. Their slower timetable for family events may reflect financial pressures since their initial worklives consisted of low-level sales and clerical jobs, a status far removed from the expectations of Lewis Terman and his research staff. Alternatively, they might have been less desirable candidates for marriage. At the other end of the accomplishment ladder are men who were doubly rewarded, by career success and good health. Most of these men entered the professions, especially teaching at the college level.

The Terman men aged against a backdrop of rapid social change. They came of age in the prosperous 1920s, entering college and the workforce during the late 1920s and Depression decade, only to face the disruptions of World War II in the early 1940s. Two out of five of the men were drawn into the armed forces and another fifth worked in defense industries. However, wartime experiences did not differ among men in the five clusters and we find no evidence in this single cohort that they accounted for their behavioral trajectories across the adult years. In the original sample, however, with birth years ranging from 1903 to 1920, the war years most adversely affected the oldest men, who are not part of this study.

In this privileged cohort of American men, behavioral diversity in young adulthood did not forecast the future with the accuracy we had expected. By the 1950s and the middle years, life had become more rewarding for the men who had relatively unsuccessful careers as young adults. The more and less successful groups of men had converged to some extent. Most notable in upward trajectory are the men who had not done well in their early years, compared to the other men, despite feelings of personal well-being. By the middle years, they had advanced significantly in their careers. Even the least adjusted men had more positive things to say about themselves by mid-life.

This convergence appears across all five groups by the 1950s, though individual trajectories of aging "within" each group had also become more diverse. Consistent with the literature (Dannefer, 1988), we find that individual heterogeneity tended to increase across the adult years (people became more different from each other), a trend that is apparent within groups of men who were relatively similar in behavior during the early years of adulthood. With increasing age, group differences faded as the within-group variation became more pronounced. In this cohort of talented men, then, differential starting points did not play a controlling role in shaping their future life course.

Starting points, however, did play an important role in determining the meaning of men's lives, viewed from the perspective of later life. We asked the men in the 1970s about domains of life satisfaction, from work and family to leisure and service. These individual domains proved to be less important than an overall sense of life satisfaction, an emotional state that had much to do with feelings of well-being in young adulthood. Among the less successful in young adulthood, those who were least positive about themselves as young men had a lower assessment of life satisfaction. Even more compelling is the contrast between the maladjusted achievers in young adulthood and men who were successful and well-adjusted. The former had done better in occupational attainment and earnings than the latter, yet their life satisfaction in old age was appreciably lower.

Negative feelings about self in young adulthood diminished the perceived gratification from life for these men in ways that often contradicted actual accomplishments. Some of these men had reached the pinnacle of their field in medicine, architecture, and engineering, but readily perceived "the things they did not achieve" and resented personal sacrifices along the way. By contrast, an early sense of well-being typically enabled less successful men to feel more fulfilled by their life course. As the Terman men entered their later years, the quality of their life and aging had more to do with early signs of mental health than with past career success and its affirmation.

Appendix 1: *Descriptions of variables included in the study*

Variables	Description
Alcohol problem	Self-reported alcohol use in 1960, 1 (rarely/never drinks) – 6 (severe problem).
Career progress (1936–40)	Mean of two variables: 1) Work progress, 1 (employment record shows evidence of upward movement) – 0 (no movement or downward movement). 2) Reverse coding of floundering, 1 (no evidence in employment record of floundering) – 0 (some floundering).
Civic involvement (1940, 1960)	Natural logarithm of the sum of the number of service activities and the number of memberships in professional organizations.
College GPA	Self-reported grades, 0 (F) – 4 (A).
Education 1940	Education obtained by 1940; 1 (no high school graduation), 2 (high school graduate), 3 (some college), 4 (bachelor's degree), 5 (master's degree), 6 (PhD, MD, JD)
Emotional health 1960	Self-reported emotional health, 1 (poor) – 5 (excellent).
Emotional stability 1940	Sum of self-assessment on an 11-point scale (low to high) on emotionality (reverse-coded), moodiness (reverse-coded), and impulsiveness (reverse-coded).
General health 1940	Self-reported physical health, 1 (very poor) – 5 (very good).
Happiness (1940, 1950)	Self-assessment of happiness of temperament on an 11-point scale (low to high).
Income (1940, 1959)	Self-reported annual income in dollars.
Intact family	1 (two biological parents married in 1922) – 0.
IQ	Binet IQ score.
Life satisfaction 1972	Based on two scales: 1) Sum of self-reported importance of goals, in early adulthood, in occupation, family life, cultural life, service to society, and joy in living (each ranging from 1 to 4, low to high); 2) Sum of self-reported satisfaction with attainment of goals by 1972 in same categories (each ranging from 1 to 5, low to high). The and two scales are combined by the formula: A*B - (A-B).
Low self-esteem (1940, 1950)	Mean of three variables: self-confidence (reverse-coded), sensitivity, and inferiority – an 11-point scale ranging and from low to high.

(*cont.*)

Appendix 1: *(cont.)*

Variables	Description
Marital satisfaction 1951	Self-assessment of happiness in marriage on an 11-point scale (low to high).
Maternal employment	1 (mother works outside home in 1922) – 0.
Occupational prestige (1940, 1959)	Ranking based on Stevens and Hoisington Prestige Ranking (maximum = 80).
Parental attachment	Mean of self-reported attachment to mother and to father, 1 (no attachment) – 5 (very close).
Physical health 1960	Self-reported physical health, 1 (poor) – 4 (very good).
Planful competence	Average of parent and teacher scales. Each scale is the sum of ratings (on a 11-point scale, low to high) on child's perseverance, desire to excel, desire to know, and conscientiousness.
Self-confidence 1940	Sum of self-assessment on an 11-point scale (low to high) on confidence and inferiority (reverse-coded).
Self-direction 1940	Sum of self-assessment on an 11-point scale (low to high) on purposefulness and persistence.
Social competence	Self-rating of social ability in childhood, 1 (difficulty making friends or being accepted), 2 (average), 3 (very adept socially).
Socio-economic status	Rating on Modified Hollingshead Index of SES, which is based on father's professional educational indices and ranges from 1 (high) to 5 (low).
Work satisfaction	Mean of standardized scores on self-reported attitudes towards work and preference for other type of work (low to high).

Appendix 2: *Young adult behavior patterns among the Terman Men; one-way ANOVA, 1940*

	Non-achievers		Achievers			
	Maladjusted	Adjusted	Maladjusted	Disengaged	Adjusted	F
Cluster variables						
Self-confidence	10.13_d	15.66_a	12.25_c	13.80_b	14.38_b	60.22^{***}
Emot. stability	16.63_d	16.70_c	16.13_d	21.92_a	20.66_b	74.18^{***}
Self-direction	11.05_d	15.94_a	16.08_a	13.16_c	15.08_b	96.80^{***}
Career progress	$.85_b$	$.57_c$	1.65_a	1.67_a	1.56_a	95.93^{***}
Civic involve.	$.48_c$	$.39_c$	1.04_b	$.46_c$	1.73_a	133.89^{***}
N	103	86	102	129	85	

Notes: All values are means.
Values with the same subscript are not significantly different from each other at $p < .05$ level. N (1940) = 505
$^{***}p < .001$, $^{**}p < .01$, $^{*}p < .05$, $+ p < .10$

ACKNOWLEDGMENTS

We acknowledge support by the National Institute of Mental Health (MH 00567, MH 57549), and by a grant from the National Institute of Child Health and Human Development to the Carolina Population Center at the University of North Carolina at Chapel Hill (PO1-HD31921A), and a Spencer Foundation Senior Scholar Award to Elder.

REFERENCES

Adler, N., Boyce, T., Chesney, M., Cohen, S., Folkman, S., Kahn, R., and Syme, S. L. (1994). Socioeconomic status and health: the challenge and the gradient. *American Psychologist*, 49, 15–24.

Aldenderfer, M. S. and Blashfield, R. K. (1984). *Cluster analysis*. Beverly Hills: Sage Publications.

Bandura, A. (1982). The psychology of chance encounters and life paths. *American Psychologist*, 37, 747–55.

Bergman, L. and El-Khouri, B. (1998). *Sleipner: A statistical package for pattern-oriented analyses*. Stockholm University.

Block, J. (1971). *Lives through time*. Berkeley, CA: Bancroft.

Caspi, A. and Bem, D. J. (1990). Personality continuity and change across the life course. In L. A. Pervin (ed.), *Handbook of personality: Theory and research*. New York: Guilford Press, 549–75.

Caspi, A. and Roberts, B. (In press). Personality across the life course: the argument for change and continuity. *Psychological Inquiry*.

Clausen, J. A. (1993). *American lives: Looking back at the children of the great depression*. New York: Free Press.

Dannefer, D. (1988). What is a name? An account of the neglect of variability in the study of aging. In J. E. Birren and V. L. Bengston (eds.), *Emergent theories of aging*. New York: Springer, 356–84.

Elder, G. H. and Chan, C. (1999). War's legacy in men's lives. In P. Moen, D. Dempster-McClain, and H. A. Walker (eds.), *A nation divided: Diversity, inequality, and community in american society*. Ithaca, NY: Cornell, 209–27.

Elder, G. H., Pavalko, E. K., and Clipp, E. C. (1993). *Working with archival data: Studying lives*. Newbury Park, CA: Sage.

Holahan, C. K. and Sears, R. R. (1995). *The gifted group in later maturity*. CA: Stanford University Press.

Magnusson, D. (1998). The logic and the implications of a person-oriented approach. In R. B. Cairns, L. R. Bergman, and J. Kagan (eds.), *Methods and models for studying the individual*. Thousand Oaks, CA: Sage, 33–64.

Magnusson, D. and Cairns, R. B. (1996). Developmental science: toward a unified framework. In R. B. Cairns, G. H. Elder, and E. J. Costello (eds.), *Developmental science*. New York: Cambridge University Press, 7–30.

Pavalko, E. K. and Elder, G. H. (1990). World War II and divorce: a life course perspective. *American Journal of Sociology*, 95, 1213–34.

Rindfuss, R. R. (1991). The young adult years: diversity, structural change, and fertility. *Demography*, 28, 493–512.

Sampson, R. and Laub, J. (1997). A life course theory of cumulative disadvantage and the stability of delinquency. In T. P. Thornberry (ed.) *Developmental theories of crime and delinquency: Advances in criminological theory*. New Brunswick, NJ: Transaction Publishers, 7, 133–161.

SAS Institute, (1994). *SAS/STAT user's guide, version 6, fourth edition*. Cary, NC: SAS Institute.

Terman, L. M. and Oden, M. H. (1959). *Genetic studies of genius*, vol. 5: *The gifted group at mid-life: thirty-five years of follow-up of the superior child*. Stanford University Press.

7   Studying processes: some methodological considerations

Lars R. Bergman

The purpose of this chapter is to discuss different approaches for studying processes. Since methods are – or at least should be – intimately related to the theory guiding the research it is natural to start from a meta theoretical perspective. A powerful general theoretical framework for studying personality in a life-course perspective is provided by the holistic-interactionistic research paradigm as incorporated in the new developmental science. Therefore, the chapter starts with a brief introduction of this framework and how it leads to an interest in studying processes. A very thought-provoking and potentially attractive approach to studying processes is given by emerging methods for studying nonlinear dynamical systems (NOLIDS). Some general ideas in NOLIDS are indicated and a few examples given of key concepts that seem relevant in relation to the study of personality. Against this background, the emphasis in current research on what will here be called static statistical methods is questioned and a number of approaches are discussed which stay closer to the process characteristics of the phenomena under study.

The issues treated in this chapter, although methodological and apart from the substantive issues treated elsewhere in this book, may be useful to consider in conjunction with the rest of the book. A careful consideration of the *nature* of the knowledge we have on personality development, and the extent to which that knowledge is confined by the methods used for acquiring it, is important, as is considering new approaches that do not share the limitations of many methods currently in use.

The holistic-interactionistic research paradigm and the person approach

According to a holistic, interactionistic view, the person is regarded in terms of a number of complex systems at different levels, functioning and developing as a totality. The totality is formed by the ongoing interactions among the parts involved with each aspect deriving its meaning from the role it plays in the person's total functioning. Overviews of the holistic interactional paradigm are given in Magnusson (1985, 1996). This research paradigm is considered central in the new developmental science, see Cairns, Elder, and Costello (1996).

The modern *person approach* is a natural outgrowth from a holistic-interactionistic paradigm (Bergman and Magnusson, 1997; Magnusson, 1998; Magnusson and Allen, 1983). In this approach, the focus is on explaining relevant processes of the developmental system under study by taking into account in particular that the various components function together as an "organized whole." Methodologically, this can sometimes be carried out by using various types of variable-oriented methods. However, often it is more straightforward to use methods aiming at capturing structures or configurations relating to essential aspects of the functioning system. An example of this is given by studying profiles of variable values believed to reflect the states of the system under study. This approach is based on the assumption that in many systems there are only a small number of optimal or functional states which are frequently observed and which are characterized by their typical patterns of values in the relevant operating factors. In principle, these typical states would be identifiable by searching for frequent patterns of values in the relevant variables, for instance by means of classification analysis based on similarities between the object's value patterns (Bergman, 1998; Bergman and Magnusson, 1997).

Of course, the basic ideas and many general formulations of the holistic-interactionistic paradigm and the person approach are not new, being discussed and acted on by a number of farsighted scholars starting a long time ago. Pioneers include, for instance, Gordon Allport, Jack Block, Kurt Lewin, and William Stern (see Cairns, 1986; Magnusson,1998, for reviews). Modern work within these areas builds on this earlier work but also contains new elements and more precise formulations. A presentation of these would have to take up considerable space and falls outside the scope of this chapter. The reader is referred to the above mentioned sources for reviews and to Magnusson (1999) for an up-to-date presentation related to the study of personality in the life-course. However, some implications for research methodology should be mentioned which are derived from the general view of reality implied by the theoretical framework presented above:

1. The model for the relationships between different factors may not be the same for every individual studied.
2. Linear relations may not provide useful approximations of relations that hold in reality.

3. Interactions between factors may be the standard rather than the exception. This can imply that variable values characterizing an individual have their most salient meaning not by themselves but as parts in configurations and patterns. This is argued for in the person approach.
4. The findings provided by NOLIDS in the form of principles, concepts, procedures, and mathematical methods seem especially relevant with its emphasis of modeling the process of change.

Taken together, these four propositions have implications for how we could go about studying processes which will be discussed in a later section.

Before ending this brief description of the holistic-interactionistic research paradigm and the person approach it is necessary to comment on one issue that sometimes has led to misunderstandings in relation to personality research. It concerns the concepts of "type" and "typology." Few concepts have caused so much confusion, even resentment and few concepts have been used with such varying meanings in different disciplines and areas, presenting a prime example of Aitken's "jingle fallacy" (Block, 2000). For discussions of types and typologies, see Bailey (1994), Bergman (2000), Blashfield (1980), Cattell (1957) and Waller and Meehl (1998). Here a typology is defined as follows: a set of class descriptions that is of general or theoretical use. If an empirical classification fulfills this condition, the classes taken together become a typology. It is then not the classes and their members per se that constitute the typology but rather the generic properties of these classes. By a type, here it is meant the properties of one such class in a typology, sometimes referred to as a "natural cluster." Often the properties of a type are stated in terms of a value profile in the studied variables (for instance, the variable means for a natural cluster, i.e. its centroid). Waller and Meehl (1998) provide a thoughtful discussion of these issues, preferring the use of the terms "taxon" for, roughly speaking, a meaningful type and "taxometrics" as a generic name for (their) procedures for finding taxa.

Two common goals of a classification analysis, not always clearly recognized, are the following:

1. The identification and description of the emerging classes (often represented by their means in the studied variables).
2. The allocation of subjects to the different classes as a basis for further analysis.

The first aspect directly concerns the typology issue and, fortunately, there are reasons to believe that an empirical classification analysis may do a better job at finding "true" centroids through the mist of sampling error and errors of measurement than it does at allocating the subjects to the "right" cluster. It goes without saying that it is of paramount importance that a purported typology is subjected to a careful validation procedure, see the above mentioned sources and Breckenridge (1989).

It should be noted that a typology, in the sense the term is used here and in contrast to most old typologies, does not represent anything fixed or unchangeable; a connotation sometimes given to the term. Although a certain degree of stability and generality is implied, the changing typologies during development and changing type membership of the individual during his/her development are of primary interest. We are interested in both stability and change and there is nothing fixed or innate in a typology as defined here. For further perspectives and empirical examples concerning typologies, see Block (1971), Pulkkinen (1996) and Robins, John, and Caspi (1998).

A nonlinear dynamical systems view

System here means a) a focus on specific aspects of reality which are assumed meaningful to study in isolation from other possible aspects of reality, and b) that certain general properties are ascribed to the system, sometimes including ideas about its goal or purpose, how included factors are related, etc. This is distinguished from, for instance, a specified causal model assumed to hold for the system and tested on data which is one instance of studying the system. When a temporal dimension is added, the system becomes a process. Time can be viewed as continuous or discrete in its "influence" on the system.

Within the natural sciences, linear dynamical systems have been studied for hundreds of years. The goal is often to arrive at an accurate model for the "motion" of the system in time as described by mathematical formulas for how change occurs (a set of differential or difference equations). Or in other words: we want to understand how the k-dimensional point representing the state of the system at a specific point in time moves in the phase space representing the system's movement in time, depending on the initial conditions and the control parameter values characterizing the system. Thus, the purpose of the quantitative model is not primarily to summarize a set of data relating to the system under study but rather to indicate a recipe for how change comes about in the system. Normally, this presupposes a good understanding of the system under study, including its "function," relevant variables, how to measure them, and the key aspects of the laws governing their mutual dependencies.

It has long been suspected and is now known that many phenomena are best described by dynamic systems which are *nonlinear*. The study of such systems began at the beginning of the twentieth century, first as a branch of mathematics (Poincaré, 1946). However, in NOLIDS the analytical problems in solving the change equations are often insurmountable and with the arrival of modern computers a larger class of NOLIDS problems could be "solved." An especially spectacular property of certain NOLIDS is the emergence of very complex behavior, chaos with its extreme sensitivity to initial conditions. This can occur for certain parameter values in simple, essentially deterministic, systems and raises the hope in some of us of perhaps being able to explain a seemingly complex phenomenon with a powerful simple NOLIDS model. For general overviews the reader is referred to Gleick (1987) and to Jackson (1989).

NOLIDS has made its way into psychology in different forms and in different fields. To give some examples: NOLIDS has been discussed and applied in developmental psychology (Smith and Thelen, 1993), in social psychology (Vallacher and Nowak, 1994), and in personality psychology (see, for instance, van Eenwyk's 1991 discussion of the application of chaos theory to Jungian psychology). Overviews are given by Barton (1994) and by Abraham and Gilgen (1995). However, the payoff so far in the form of useful NOLIDS models seems to be meager and is often more on the metaphoric-conceptual level. Exceptions can be found in some more molecular areas, lending themselves to precise inquiry and controlled experiments. A good example is here given by Kelso and his co-workers in their work on the dynamics of motor coordination (Kelso, 1995).

Several central concepts in NOLIDS are potentially attractive for the researcher interested in the study of personality in the life-course. For example, concepts like "self-organization," "attractor," "basin of attraction," "hysteresis," "multi-stability," "bifurcation," and "agent dynamics" are sometimes referred to and used by researchers in personality. Of special significance for this presentation are the following aspects of NOLIDS:

1. The frequent existence of sudden changes in the behavior of a system, which could be described as *qualitative* change in *quantitative* systems, and the importance of studying these phenomena in order to understand the system (Kelso, 2000). This is the antithesis of linear modeling.

2. The importance of obtaining a global, qualitative understanding of the character of the systems dynamics. This was pointed out already by Poincaré, the "father of NOLIDS," almost a hundred years ago.

3. The difficulties in identifying/choosing relevant system properties for carrying out NOLIDS modeling (including defining time scales, relevant collective variables, and the level of analysis).

Problems with a static statistical approach for studying processes

It is probably fair to say that many experienced researchers are sometimes uneasy about the lack of correspondence between, on the one hand, their theoretical thinking and the problems they are studying and, on the other hand, their use of standard statistical methods to investigate these problems. The degree of sophistication in their thinking (often including an interactionistic perspective) and problem formulation may not be matched by the statistical methods used for analysis. Or to be a bit more precise: although the statistical methods per se often are highly sophisticated that does not help if they are not suitable (isomorphic) to the problem under investigation. This point has been made many times, see for instance, Magnusson (1992) and Magnusson *et al* (1991).

Ongoing criticism against statistical practices in psychology has concerned many different aspects, including the following three:

1. There is no strong reason to assume that the real world we are interested in is a linear world with additive effects and no interactions, even approximately. Of course, whether or not this creates a problem depends on the choice of statistical method and the specific problem setting. An extreme example is given by some applications of structural equation modeling (SEM) where linearity is assumed, the same model for every member in the sample is assumed, independence between errors and true scores is assumed, and the fit of the resulting model building on all these assumptions (and more) is tested, not on the "real data set" but on a linear representation of it in the form of a correlation matrix (Bergman, 1988a). Along similar lines Brown (1995, p. 6) argues that

   > Anyone familiar with modeling from a probabilistic perspective will state that the worst error that can be made with any model is specification error. In the presence of misspecification, no estimate is reliable. Yet it is precisely because of the convenience of linear models (because of their mathematical simplicity and the ease with which probabilistic assumptions may be inserted in them) that researchers often seriously depart from isomorphic parallels between social theory and nonlinear algebraic formalisms, leading them into the most dangerous of terrains.

2. The procedure of hypothesis testing using significance tests can be highly useful and informative in situations when the conditions for

the tests are fulfilled, especially in controlled experiments. However, in many situations the procedure degrades to a ritual of little scientific value. This is argued convincingly by Meehl (1990) and by Richters (1997). To give just one example, Richters (op. cit.) points to the frequent use of a significance test of a correlation coefficient, with the null hypothesis being that the coefficient is zero and a result proclaimed as significant and indicating support for one's theory when the observed correlation deviates so much from zero that it is unlikely to occur if the null hypothesis is true. However, as he points out, many, if not most, variables measured in psychology are correlated, at least a little (the so called "crud factor," see Lykken, 1991 and Meehl, 1990). Hence, the result can be fairly uninteresting even if the formal assumptions are fulfilled (which they usually are not, for instance random samples are the exception rather than the rule).

3. Usually the institutionalized statistical methods do not emphasize replication to anything close to its true scientific value (Lindsay and Ehrenberg, 1993). It is common in psychology to pay lip service to replication but uncommon to carry it out. For instance, when discussing this issue, Rutter and Pickles (1990, p. 48) say:

> The unpleasant, but inevitable, conclusion is that sample size must be taken rather more seriously than it is and that the task of replication, dull though it may be, is crucial. We do not doubt that we shall join the others who have made these points in being ignored.

Let us now come back to our interest in the study of processes. Here the above mentioned mismatch between theory-problem and method can become especially obvious. Frequently processes are not studied by methods which stay close to these phenomena: the methods/models used simply lack process characteristics. The same mismatch has been noticed within sociology and Aage Sorensen (1998, pp. 14–15), a leading sociologist, says the following:

> The failure to consider mechanisms of change and to try to formulate them in models of the processes we investigate, however primitive the result may be, has important consequences for the state of sociological research. The almost universal use of statistical models and specifications have two sets of important implications. First, we are constrained by the statistical models to not consider whether or not we actually obtain, from our research, a greater understanding of the processes we investigate. In other words, the statistical models give us theoretical blinders. ... Second, we may actually produce results that on closer consideration seem theoretically unfounded and very likely misleading.

Consider in this context the following example, contrasting a dynamic and a static approach. It is taken from Bergman (2001). Zenon, a classic Greek philosopher, states a paradox claiming to show that the

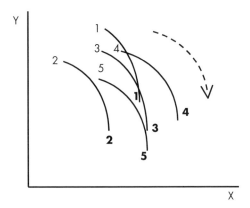

Figure 7.1 Fictitious data for five persons illustrating the difference between static and dynamic change. The unbroken curves indicate data
in continuous time.The dotted curve indicates the direction of time.
Ordinary numbers refer to data from Time 1 and numbers in bold to
data from Time 2 (figure modified from Bergman, 2001).

movement of a spear is impossible. It goes as follows: in every instance
the spear is at a specific place so how does it move between these places?
Although this paradox is easily solved nowadays using calculus it points
to an issue that is modern. How can we understand a continuous process
using information of a snap-shot character collected at just a few points
in time? The problem is illustrated by the example based on fictitious
data given in Figure 7.1.

In Figure 7.1, five persons are traced in continuous time in two variables, X and Y. The direction of time is indicated by the dotted line.
From a *dynamical* perspective there is a complete lawfulness in how
X and Y evolve. Given interindividual differences in the starting positions (initial states), all individuals follow the same law of change and
for each person, X completely "determines" Y and vice versa. However,
assume that information from only two time points was available, indicated by ordinary numbers at Time 1 and bold numbers at Time 2.
The Pearson correlations between X and Y would then be zero at both
points in time and the two stability coefficients would be 1.0. Thus, from
this *static* perspective, the interpretation would be that there is no relation between X and Y and no change, if the ordinary interindividual perspective is applied. Of course, mean changes would show a different picture than that given by the correlations and the application
of p-technique, based on intensive data, would be more informative.
Nevertheless, the example illustrates the possibility of missing even a

strong dynamical lawfulness in a studied process by an insensitive use of static standard statistical methods. Attention should also be given to the importance of the scaling of the variables for the interpretation of the results and the contrasting interindividual and intraindividual perspectives.

What does this example say about the study of personality development? It shows that a conventional correlational study based on cross-sectional and longitudinal correlations of, for instance, personality dimensions could completely miss important dynamic relationships. The results obtained may be severely confined by the method used.

Wanting to understand a process, and starting from the theoretical framework presented in the first section, the prime interest is in making inferences about the mechanism that produces the change we observe and we would expect this mechanism to include strong interactions and nonlinearities among the operating factors. Ideally, we would like to construct a valid model that "explains" how the system changes depending on time, initial conditions, and (changing) configurations of relevant contextual factors. NOLIDS, if successfully applied, comes close to offering a mathematical model that does this with the control parameters corresponding to the contextual factors. The discrepancy between a dynamical model like this and a conventional static statistical model should be noticed. The latter type of model is essentially not a model of the change process but rather a model of the (longitudinal) data at hand. It may not easily lend itself to be used for understanding the effects of contextual changes and normally cannot *generate* model-based data outside the time range studied. To some extent this gap in what a model can do is being bridged by modern formulations of standard statistical methods, for instance, in the latent growth curve modeling tradition. However, their capacity for handling complex interactions seems limited.

Against this background one might wonder why it is so rare to use the NOLIDS approach for studying processes. Although there are undoubtedly bad reasons for sticking to conventional methods, as convincingly argued by Richters (1997), there are also sound reasons for this conservatism. Two reasons that carry weight are the following:

1. An ingenious researcher can often even from a sophisticated process-oriented theory devise predictions which can be tested by the statistical methods she is familiar with.
2. The obstacles in the valid application of a full-fledged NOLIDS modeling are formidable in most areas of psychology. The studied systems tend to be so complex that a realistic NOLIDS model is difficult to

construct. Examples can be given of such model applications which are more mathematical toys than really useful and examples can be given of uninformed bandying of NOLIDS concepts at the level of loose metaphors, only contributing to the "jingle and jangle" of psychology (Block, 2000).

Notwithstanding what has just been said, it is still argued here that we should move in the direction of a more direct study of the processes. This can be done in many different ways, a selection of which is discussed in the next section.

Some approaches to studying processes

In this section, some approaches to studying processes are presented which naturally emerge from the theoretical and methodological considerations given above. It is by no means an exhaustive list and does not include the applications of newer formulations of a number of statistical methods like latent growth curve modeling, time-series analysis, event history analysis, and latent transition analysis. They are highly useful in certain situations but seem to the present author less promising for the purposes discussed here, although reformulations of them might make them suitable (see, for instance, Schmitz's, 1990, work on time-series analysis and McArdle's, 1995, vector field analysis). We will instead focus on other approaches, less extensively treated in the literature, but which may allow the researcher to come closer to studying processes.

The application of standard person-oriented methods

In certain situations, the appropriate application of standard person-oriented methods can achieve the purpose of coming close to studying the process (see Bergman, 1998, for an overview of such methods). For instance, longitudinal classification analysis of value patterns could be undertaken, based on Lienert's configurational frequency approach (Krauth and Lienert, 1982; von Eye, 1990) or on a cluster analysis approach, for instance the LICUR-rationale. There are mainly two reasons, briefly mentioned before, for believing such methods can be useful in the study of processes:

1. It seems reasonable to assume that the essential aspects of a system sometimes can be captured by considering the *patterning* of the values in the variables describing the system.

2. Dynamical systems appropriately described by relevant variables, i.e. order parameters, often exhibit only a small number of optimal states which will become attractors and they may emerge in the equilibrium which is assumed to dominate at the time scale of the measurements used. If this is true, typical value patterns tend to capture essential aspects of the dynamics of the system.

See Bergman and Magnusson (1997), Block (1971), Gangestad and Snyder (1985) and Kelso, Ding and Schöner (1993) for discussions of issues relating to the categorical approach and to the study of dynamical systems.

We find in both Elder's and van Aken's *et al.* chapters (in this volume) examples of the application of a person-oriented approach. In both chapters, cluster analysis is used to identify typical patterns within the domain of study. Elder then uses the cluster analysis results as the basis for carrying out a variant of Cairns'prodigal analysis (Cairns and Rodkin, 1998) to study developmental outcomes for the different types found. It should be noted that in both instances a hierarchical method is used and only very few clusters are extracted. This is certainly defensible as a way of finding a structure on a meta level. However, it is interesting to consider how their approach relates to the above discussion about typical value patterns. It seems to the present author unlikely that (almost) all typical patterns can be represented by a few more "global" clusters. The chances are that some of these patterns are not so frequent and will be made fuzzy by being forced together with other patterns in large clusters of subjects. For this reason it would be interesting to go further in the analyses and clarify the homogeneity of the clusters obtained and also to move to a more detailed level in the hierarchical classification tree to find out if a different picture emerges.

The application of concepts and ideas taken from the study of nonlinear dynamical systems

Concepts and ideas taken from the study of NOLIDS can be applied to the study of processes without carrying out an actual mathematical modeling of the phenomena under investigation. This is often a more realistic alternative to a complete modeling process. Different forms are possible and include the theoretical and/or the methodological levels:

Predictions are tested which have been obtained in a NOLIDS framework. Standard statistical methods can be used for testing the theories but the predictions are arrived at using concepts and ideas taken from NOLIDS. For instance, the property of hysteresis ($\sim$multistability depending on the systems "memory" of the control parameter values) can sometimes be relevant and studied by examining time-related mean changes in important variables describing the system as a function of the history of context change. The use of NOLIDS at the theoretical stage can also be more formal but this topic lies outside the scope of this chapter.

Reformulations of ordinary statistical methods. Ordinary methods can be reformulated to fit better into depicting processes, as was hinted at in the introduction to this section. They could then either concern optimization, assuming equilibrium, like in certain models of rational choice behavior, or, more naturally, include the time dimension. It is then essential that they directly concern the multivariate growth of the key time-dependent aspects of the system. Some work along these lines has begun at our laboratory and two methods are currently under development (I-states as objects analysis, ISOA; Bergman and El-Khouri, 1999) and I-states sequence analysis (ISSA; Bergman, in prep.). Cf. here also the use of methods for sequence analysis (Abbott, 1995).

The modeling of phenomena using methods for studying nonlinear dynamical systems

It was stated above that it is often extremely difficult to model complex phenomena in psychology using the NOLIDS approach. Kelso (2000, p. 13), who has considerable experience of NOLIDS modeling, paints a fairly gloomy picture, saying that:

Development has been depicted as a landscape of collective variables against time (Thelen, 1995). Thus far, this metaphor and the difficult task of actually identifying collective variables, the control parameters that act upon them and the collective variable dynamics has yet to be accomplished in the developing organism for even a single task context. ... So far, only in the case of acquiring perceptual-motor coordination has it been possible to identify an individual's initial "attractor landscape" (collective variable dynamics) prior to learning and to track how it changes during learning. Importantly, this turns out to be unique to each learner.

Difficulties that tend to arise when implementing a NOLIDS model in psychology include the following:

1. Frequently extremely complex systems are under investigation and the understanding of them is often very incomplete both with regard to identification of the crucial operating factors, the mechanism that

generates the dynamics of the system, and the delineation and interfaces of the system under study to other possibly interacting systems.
2. The choices of an appropriate time scale and level of analysis are often very difficult.
3. The development of a well-functioning NOLIDS model is greatly aided if careful experiments can be made where the behavior of the system is systematically studied under varying conditions, exploring the effects of changing the values of the control parameters. This is not possible in most developmental areas.
4. The generalization from the single individual to a population of individuals is not self-evident, a problem somewhat similar to the one encountered when using p-technique.

Considering the difficulties mentioned above, what are then the rewards that could motivate the ambitious researcher to try this difficult path anyway? They include the following highly desirable goals or outcomes of a successful NOLIDS modeling:

1. A mathematical model of the process is obtained which can be very close to the theory the researcher has developed. It gives information about how change and stability come about and how they depend on contextual factors.
2. The model can be used for exploring a wide variety of possible consequences of parameter changes and changes in initial conditions, at best giving a (preliminary) understanding of many phenomena that have not yet even been observed. One aspect of this is that the model actually can generate "data" to be explored.
3. Sometimes even seemingly very complex system behavior can be explained by a simple, essentially deterministic, model which can exhibit chaos properties (Ott, 1993). The relation between chaos and statistical randomness can also sometimes be used to explain phenomena we have avoided explaining by using the simple strategy of calling them "random" (Berliner, 1992).
4. By the application of a NOLIDS approach we gain access to powerful mathematical results about general properties of classes of dynamical systems, and also to a broad variety of empirical results concerning these different classes. They can be useful for construction and validation of one's model.
5. It is true that parameter estimation can be extremely difficult in NOLIDS. However, the interest of statistical science now shown in this branch of applied nonlinear mathematics gives hope that methods for this purpose will be developed that diminish the burden of the researcher of an exact *a priori* specification.

The search for process-related measurements

It has been pointed out many times that many of the variables used in longitudinal, developmental studies are not ideal for that purpose, originally having been constructed for cross-sectional studies (Bereiter, 1963; Bergman, 1993). Bereiter (op. cit.) pointed out what he called "the unreliability-invalidity dilemma" implying that a high reliability in a static variable and a high correlation between measurements from two points in time would often lead to a low reliability of a change score for such a variable. For this reliability to be high, the correlation over time would have to be low, indicating the possibility that not "the same thing" is measured at the two time points. A "solution" to this dilemma is that the dimension of change can be of interest in itself without necessarily being identical to the static dimensions and the possibility of applying this different, more process-related perspective should be considered (see also Rogosa and Willett, 1985, for a more modern discussion). Coming closer to the study of processes, Kliegl and Baltes (1987) have argued within the context of micro-genetic studies that measurements should be constructed which are especially designed for indicating what is going on in the process. A somewhat similar argument within the context of carrying out a person-oriented approach, taking into account an intra-individual perspective, is given by Nesselroade and Ghisletta (2000). Finally, within the context of NOLIDS it is emphasized that, in principle, the number of possible variables for describing the system is almost infinite. The selection and construction of relevant variables capturing the essentials of the system (the so called "order parameters") is a prerequisite for successful modeling (Nowak and Lewenstein, 1994).

From this starting point at least four types of measurements for studying processes can be discerned:

1. In certain situations, the conventional static measurements are quite adequate, especially when one is interested in the equilibrium properties of the system under study.
2. Sometimes it is essential that the variables are very sensitive to changes in a short time perspective and should be constructed with that in mind (cf. the measurement of state as contrasted to the measurement of trait).
3. Relating to what was discussed above, a good theoretical understanding of a dynamical system will often help in finding/constructing variables expressing it. Since the theoretical origin of such variables is different from the usual variables used in developmental studies it is to be expected that the variables depicting the dynamical system often will be different from the usual ones. It might be guessed that often they

will involve relational properties. Examples of innovative measurement procedures within the personality field are James' (1998) use of conditional reasoning for measuring personality and Gustafson's approach to measuring ASP's (Gustafson and Ritzer, 1995). It may be possible to revise such procedures in order to incorporate dynamic components.

4. An interesting approach that can be used in some situations, especially when self-reports are at focus, is the following. Instead of asking the subjects to report on "how it is" right now (or averaged over a period) they are instead directly asked for their estimation of change (or even of change in the rate of change). Indeed, this approach might be natural within the personality field since many of the variables studied are salient to the person investigated and he/she might experience almost continuous feedback from interpersonal contexts relating to the concepts under study. At a superficial level, this approach lends support from the well-known property of our perception system for being especially good at detecting changes. Wikman (1991) reported a series of results referring to longer time periods which illustrates the issue. They concerned Swedish workers' reports of exposure to certain health risks on the job. Comparing the results based on these reports between different time periods, about a decade broad, indicated a deterioration of the workers' environment during the 1970s; a result known to be untrue. However, if they were asked to report the *change* during the last five-year period, the majority reported improvements in their working environment in this regard. The reports of change can, of course, refer to different lengths of time periods and be carried out with both an intra-individual and/or an inter-individual focus. Such information might be useful for a variety of purposes.

In a NOLIDS situation, reports of change could aid in constructing the equations of movement (the differential or different equations describing the dynamical system). Obviously, item construction is here difficult and of another kind than is usually undertaken. Different possibilities need to be explored in a number of areas of self-report, both with regard to the formulation of questions and response format and the length of the reference time periods. Such a study is now being planned at our laboratory. Possibilities for constructing individual-level measurements based on a nonlinear framework should also not be overlooked (Bartholomew, 1996).

Conclusions

Many experienced researchers within the developmental field would agree that a stronger emphasis should be given to empirical studies aimed at understanding *mechanisms* of development at different levels at the expense of conventional correlational studies (cf. Brown, 1995; Giele and Elder, 1998; Richters, 1997; Rutter, 1996). This is, in fact, a plea for a more process-oriented approach and it is consistent with what has been proposed in this chapter. The main difference being that here this line of reasoning has been driven in a more extreme form than is usual and "new" methodological alternatives have been suggested as possible means for gaining insights into the processes of interest. This "hard line" is almost inevitable if a holistic-interactionistic perspective is taken seriously for the study of personality in a life-course perspective (Magnusson, 1999; Pervin, 1989). Within this general area it would be useful if an epistemologically-oriented work were to be carried out where aspects of theory, mathematical/statistical modeling and methods for estimation are considered simultaneously, as exemplified by the work of Casti (1989). What are the general requirements for a useful mathematical/statistical model within the theoretical framework presented here?

The problems of handling interactions and nonlinearities using standard variable-oriented methods have been pointed out. Cronbach (1975) even made the metaphor of entering a hall of mirrors when pursuing such an approach. These problems tend to be aggravated when processes are at focus. It was pointed out that a highly useful property of a statistical/mathematical model is if it is isomorphic to the theory the researcher has constructed. Otherwise it is difficult to use a model to advance the knowledge basis in a meaningful way or even to evaluate its basic quality. It was further argued that standard statistical models often may not have this isomorphic property when processes are at focus and various ways of studying dynamical systems were suggested.

The problems of carrying out NOLIDS modeling within many areas of psychology, including personality in the life-course, were briefly discussed. However, in agreement with Sorensen (1998) the potential usefulness of even a primitive NOLIDS modeling as a complement to the ordinary approach must be emphasized. Properly carried out, it at least provides a method for sharpening one's thinking and forces the researcher to formulate more precisely a number of dynamical concepts which are relevant in the study of processes. On the other hand, there are formidable obstacles to the construction of well-functioning dynamical models. These obstacles are rooted in the extreme difficulty in obtaining sufficient knowledge about the complex system under study and its delineation to other possibly interacting systems. Without this knowledge, the modeling may prove impossible. This is sometimes pointed out as a defense against applying a standard static statistical modeling approach. However, the criticism is double-edged: what credibility does *any* model maker have who claims he/she can model a process without understanding it?

It is natural if the reader at this point feels a little confused. Current approaches have been criticized from a process perspective and alternatives have been discussed only in broad terms not providing a concrete example from our own research. The reason for this is that a useful example would have to be detailed to explain procedures which are new to most readers. It would demand considerable space, bringing the chapter out of format. On the other hand, the importance of making a strong theoretical argument for the process perspective should be obvious and motivates a chapter in itself.

As an example of a dynamic approach the reader could consult Boker and Graham (1998) who carried out a dynamic systems analysis of adolescent drug use. Dynamic systems models were fitted to intra-individual variability in adolescent self-reported cigarette and alcohol use. The analysis was focused on a model with two independent dampened oscillators and the parameters of the model indicated a self-regulation mechanism in which small changes in substance use grew over time. A procedure for using structural equation modeling as an aid in representing the dynamic models was used (Boker and Nesselroade, 1998). In this way, the "change parameters" of the dynamic model could be approximately estimated using the panel data at hand. Boker and Graham (1998) point out limitations in their preliminary trial and they say as follows:

The area of differential structural equation modeling is only beginning to be explored, and like other modeling techniques will no doubt offer its share of insights as well as frustrations. The promise of dynamical systems techniques is that it encourages theoretical thinking about human behavior as a changing, adapting and self-organizing system: influenced by the environment, influencing the environment, and with its own intrinsic dynamics that result from a wide variety self-regulation mechanisms. (p. 505).

The person approach could be useful for studying processes. This applies both to theoretical formulations and to the pattern methods developed within this framework. To mention just one aspect: the search for typical developmental patterns could give information about how the process under study is organized within individuals. For example, Bergman and Magnusson (1991) have shown that strong types occur with regard to externalizing adjustment problems; types which exhibit structural and individual stability over time and which give alternative explanations to results from correlational studies where these types may "explain" correlations found in such studies.

An issue dealt with within the person approach relates to the concepts of "white spots" (Bergman and Magnusson, 1997) and "residue" (Bergman, 1988b; Edelbrock, 1979). An important aspect of understanding development is finding its limits or boundaries, i.e. the delineation to what cannot occur or at least occurs very rarely. Confined by what theoretically could be observed, the patterns that occur often and those that occur hardly at all describe a large part of the empirical world. Such a mapping of the boundaries for non-occurring developmental patterns is seldom made despite the obvious relevancy for theory testing. This approach has been discussed by, for instance Lewin (1935) who analyzed boundary conditions in terms of "region of freedom of movement". Valsiner (1984) pointed out that the observed behavioral variability of a person is only a fraction of what is possible. Cairns and Rodkin (1998) present a "prodigal analysis" for highlighting pathways for persons who do not follow a normative developmental pathway. It is clear that the concept of white spots suggests additional ways of testing theories in terms of predicting what should *not* happen in development. This is in line with modern work in studying NOLIDS where empty regions of the phase-space that are never traveled are part of the mapping of the system under study.

Taking a bird's eye view of the findings presented in this book, one is struck by two things:

1. The wealth of interesting results and theories presented.
2. The dearth of method applications along the lines suggested in this chapter and the comparative absence of a discussion of a possible mismatch between the sophisticated theories presented and the statistical methods used to carry out the analyses.

What has just been said should not be seen as a critique of the presented findings but rather as an encouragement to go one step further in future analyses and consider possibilities for adding new methodological approaches in the different areas.

Methodological presentations, like the one given here, can and should only convince somebody to try new approaches along the lines suggested here. There is a good chance that there are areas where this can be done reasonably well. And I hope that the criticism to such attempts will not be overtly harsh, bearing in mind that it is better to attempt to answer a difficult but important question than produce a good answer to a less meaningful question. A stronger process perspective is much needed in the study of personality in the life-course.

ACKNOWLEDGMENTS

This study has been supported by a grant from the Swedish Council for Research in the Humanities and Social Sciences and by the Swedish STINT Foundation. The author is grateful to Bassam M. El-Khouri, David Magnusson, and Margit Wångby for useful comments.

REFERENCES

Abbott, A. (1995). Sequence analysis: new methods for old ideas. *Annual Review of Sociology*, 21, 93–113.

Abraham, F. D., and Gilgen, A. R. (eds.) (1995). *Chaos theory in psychology*. London: Praeger.

Allport, G. (1937). *Personality: A psychological interpretation*. New York: Rinehart and Winston.

Bailey, K. D. (1994). *Typologies and taxonomies*. New York, NY: Sage.

Bartholomew, D. J. (1996). *The statistical approach to social measurement*. San Diego, CA: Academic Press.

Barton, S. (1994). Chaos, self-organization, and psychology. *American Psychologist*, 49, 5–15.

Bereiter, C. (1963). Some persistent dilemmas in the measurement of change. In C. Harris (ed.), *Problems in measuring change*. Madison, WI: University of Wisconsin Press, 3–20.

Bergman, L. R. (1988a). Modeling reality: some comments. In M. Rutter (ed.), *Studies of psychosocial risk. The power of longitudinal data*. Cambridge University Press, 354–66.

Bergman, L. R. (1988b). You can't classify all of the people all of the time. *Multivariate Behavioral Research*, 23, 425–41.

Bergman, L. R. (1993). Some methodological issues in longitudinal research: looking ahead. In D. Magnusson and P. Casaer (eds.), *Longitudinal research on individual development: Present status and future perspectives*. Cambridge University Press, 217–41.

Bergman, L. R. (1995). Describing individual development using i-state sequence analysis (ISSA). Reports from the Department of Psychology, Stockholm University, no. 805.

Bergman, L. R. (1998). A pattern-oriented approach to studying individual development: snapshots and processes. In R. B. Cairns, L. R. Bergman, and J. Kagan (eds.), *Methods and models for studying the individual* Thousand Oaks, CA: Sage, 83–121.

Bergman, L. R. (2000). The application of a person-oriented approach: types and clusters. In L. R. Bergman, R. Cairns, L-G Nilsson, and L. Nystedt (eds.), *Developmental science and the holistic approach*. Mahwah, NJ: Erlbaum, 137–54.

Bergman, L. R. (2001). A person approach in research on adolescence: some methodological challenges. *Journal of Adolescent Research*, 16, 28–53.

Bergman, L. R., and El-Khouri, B. M. (1999). Studying individual patterns of development using I-states as objects analysis (ISOA). *Biometrical Journal*, 41, 753–70.

Bergman, L. R., and Magnusson, D. (1991). Stability and change in patterns of extrinsic adjustment problems. In D. Magnusson, L. R. Bergman, G. Rudinger, and B. Törestad, (eds.) *Problems and methods in longitudinal research.* Cambridge University Press, 323–45.

Bergman, L. R., and Magnusson, D. (1997). A person-oriented approach in research on developmental psychopathology. *Development and Psychopathology,* 9, 291–319.

Berliner, L. M. (1992). Statistics, probability and chaos. *Statistical Science,* 7, 69–90.

Blashfield, R. K. (1980). The growth of cluster analysis: Tryon, Ward and Johnson. *Multivariate Behavioral Research,* 15, 439–58.

Block, J. (1971). *Lives through time.* Berkeley, CA: Bancroft Books.

Block, J. (2000). Three tasks for personality psychology. In L. R. Bergman, R. Cairns, L-G Nilsson, and L. Nystedt (eds.), *Developmental science and the holistic approach.* Mahwah, NJ: Erlbaum, 155–64.

Boker, S. M., and Graham, J. (1998). A dynamic systems analysis of adolescent substance use. *Multivariate Behavioral Research,* 33, 479–507.

Boker, S. M., and Nesselroade, J. (1998). *A method for modeling the intrinsic dynamics of intraindividual variability: Recovering the parameters of simulated oscillators in multi-wave panel data.* Unpublished manuscript.

Breckenridge, J. N. (1989). Replicating cluster analysis: method, consistency and validity. *Multivariate Behavioral Research,* 24, 147–61.

Brown, C. (1995). Chaos and catastrophe theories. *Quantitative Applications in the Social Sciences,* 107. Thousand Oaks, CA: Sage.

Cairns, R. B. (1986). Phenomena lost: issues in the study of development. In J. Valsiner (ed.), *The individual subject and scientific psychology.* New York: Plenum, 79–112.

Cairns, R. B., Elder, G. H. Jr, and Costello, E. J. (eds.) (1996). *Developmental science.* Cambridge University Press.

Cairns, R. B., and Rodkin, P. C. (1998). Phenomena regained: from configurations to pathways. In R. B. Cairns, L. R. Bergman, and J. Kagan (eds.), *Methods and models for studying the individual.* Thousand Oaks, CA: Sage, 245–64.

Casti, J. L. (1989). *Alternate realities. Mathematical models of nature and man.* New York, NY: Wiley.

Cattell, R. B. (1957). *Personality and motivation structure and measurement.* New York, NY: World Books.

Cronbach, L. J. (1975). Beyond the two disciplines of scientific psychology. *American Psychologist,* 30, 116–27.

Edelbrock, C. (1979). Mixture model tests of hierarchical clustering algorithms. The problem of classifying everybody. *Multivariate Behavioral Research,* 14, 367–84.

Gangestad, S., and Snyder, M. (1985). To carve nature at its joints: on the existence of discrete classes in personality. *Psychological Review,* 92, 317–49.

Giele, J. Z., and Elder, G. H. Jr, (eds.). (1998). *Methods of life course research.* Thousand Oaks, CA: Sage.

Gleick, J. (1987). *Chaos. Making a new science.* New York, NY: Viking Press.

Gustafson, S. B., and Ritzer, D. R. (1995). The dark side of normal: a psychopathy-linked pattern called aberrant self-promotion. *European Journal of Personality*, 9, 147–83.

Jackson, A. E. (1989). *Perspectives on nonlinear dynamics*, Cambridge University Press, vol. 1.

James, L. R. (1998). Measurement of personality via conditional reasoning. *Organizational Research Methods*, 1 (2), 131–63.

Kelso, J. A. S. (1995). *Dynamic patterns: the self-organization of brain and behavior*. Cambridge, MA: The MIT Press.

Kelso, J. A. S. (2000). Principles of dynamic pattern formation and changes in human behavior. In L. R. Bergman, R. Cairns, L-G Nilsson, and L. Nystedt (eds.), *Developmental science and the holistic approach*. Mahwah, NJ: Erlbaum, 63–83.

Kelso, J. A. S., Ding, M., and Schöner, G. (1993). Dynamic pattern formation: a primer. In L. B. Smith and E. Thelen (eds.), *A dynamic systems approach to development*. Cambridge, MA: The MIT Press.

Kliegl, R., and Baltes, P. B. (1987). Theory-guided analysis of development and aging mechanisms through testing-the-limits and research on expertise. In C. Schooler and K. W. Schaie (eds.), *Cognitive functioning and social structure over the life course*. Norwoord, NJ: Ablex, 95–119.

Krauth, J., and Lienert, G. A. (1982). Fundamentals and modifications of configural frequency analysis (CFA). *Interdisciplinaria*, 3, (1).

Lewin, K. (1935). *A dynamic theory of personality*. New York, NY: McGraw-Hill.

Lindsay, R. M., and Ehrenberg, A. S. C. (1993). The design of replicated studies. *American Statistician*, 43, 217–28.

Lykken, D. T. (1991). What's wrong with psychology anyway? In D. Cicchetti and W. M. Grove (eds.), *Thinking clearly about psychology* (vol. 1). Minneapolis, MN: University of Minnesota Press.

Magnusson, D. (1985). Implications of an interactional paradigm for research on human development. *International Journal of Behavioral Development*, 8, 115–37.

Magnusson, D. (1992). Back to the phenomena: theory, methods and statistics in psychological research. *European Journal of Personality*, 6, 1–14.

Magnusson, D. (ed.) (1996). *The life-span development of individuals: Behavioral, neurobiological and psychosocial perspectives. A synthesis*. Cambridge University Press.

Magnusson, D. (1998). The logic and implications of a person approach. In R. B. Cairns, L. R. Bergman, and J. Kagan (eds.), *Methods and models for studying the individual*. Thousand Oaks, CA: Sage, 33–63.

Magnusson, D. (1999). Holistic interactionism: a theoretical framework. In L. A. Pervin and O. P. John (eds.), *Handbook of personality: Theory and research* (2nd edn.). New York, NY: Guilford Press, 219–47.

Magnusson, D., and Allen, V. L. (1983). Implications and applications of an interactional perspective for human development. In D. Magnusson and V. L. Allen (eds.), *Human development: An interactional perspective*. New York: Academic Press, 369–87.

Magnusson, D., Bergman, L. R., Rudinger, G., and Törestad, B. (eds.) (1991). *Problems and methods in longitudinal research: Stability and change*. Cambridge University Press.

McArdle, J. J. (1995). A statistical vector field analysis of longitudinal aging data, *Experimental Aging Research*, 21, 77–93.

Meehl, P. E. (1990). Appraising and amending theories: the strategy of Lakatosian defense and two principles that warrant it. *Psychological Inquiry*, 1, 108–41.

Nesselroade, J. R., and Ghisletta, P. (2000). Beyond static concepts in modeling behavior. In L. R. Bergman, R. Cairns, L-G Nilsson, and L. Nystedt (eds.), *Developmental science and the holistic approach*. Mahwah, NJ: Erlbaum, 121–35.

Nowak, A., and Lewenstein, M. (1994). Dynamical systems: a tool for social psychology? In R. R. Vallacher and A. Nowak (eds.), *Dynamical systems in social psychology*. San Diego, CA: Academic Press.

Ott, E. (1993). *Chaos in dynamical systems*. Cambridge University Press.

Pervin, L. A. (1989). Psychodynamic-systems reflections on a social intelligence model of personality. *Advances in Social Cognition*, 2, 153–61.

Poincaré, H. (1946). *The foundations of science*. Lancaster, UK: The Science Press.

Pulkkinen, L. (1996). Female and male personality styles: a typological and developmental analysis. *Journal of Personality and Social Psychology*, 70, 1288–306.

Richters, J. E. (1997). The Hubble hypothesis and the developmentalist's dilemma. *Development and Psychopathology*, 9, 193–229.

Robins, R. W., John, O. P., and Caspi, A. (1998). The typological approach to studying personality. In R. B. Cairns, L. R. Bergman, and J. Kagan (eds.), *Methods and models for studying the individual*. Thousand Oaks, CA: Sage, 135–8.

Rogosa, D., and Willett, J. B. (1985). Understanding correlates of change by modeling individual differences in growth. *Psychometrika*, 50, 203–28.

Rutter, M. (1996). Developmental psychopathology as an organizing research concept. In D. Magnusson (ed.), *The life-span development of individuals: Behavioral, neurobiological, and psychosocial perspectives. A synthesis.* Cambridge University Press, 394–413.

Rutter, M., and Pickles, A. (1990). Improving the quality of psychiatric data: classification, cause, and course. In D. Magnusson and L. R. Bergman (eds.), *Data quality in longitudinal research*. Cambridge University Press, 32–57.

Schmitz, B. (1990). Univariate and multivariate time-series models: the analysis of intraindividual variability and intraindividual relationships. In A. von Eye (ed.), *Statistical methods in longitudinal research*. vol. II: *Time series and categorical longitudinal data*. San Diego, CA: Academic Press, 351–86.

Smith, L. B., and Thelen, E. (1993). *A dynamic systems approach to development. Applications*. Cambridge, MA: The MIT Press.

Sorensen, A. B. (1998). *Statistical models and mechanisms of social processes*. Paper prepared for presentation at the conference on "Statistical issues in the social sciences", Swedish Academy of Sciences, Stockholm, Sweden, 1-3 October, 1998.

Stern, W. (1911). *Die Differentielle Psychologie in ihren metodischen Grundlagen* (Methodological foundations of differential psychology). Leipzig, Germany: Barth.

Thelen, E. (1995). Motor development: a new synthesis. *American Psychologist*, 50, 79–95.

Vallacher, R. B., and Nowak, A. (1994). *Dynamical systems in social psychology.* San Diego, CA: Academic Press.

Valsiner, J. (1984). Two alternative epistemological frameworks in psychology: the typological and variational modes of thinking. *Journal of Mind and Behavior,* 5, 449–70.

Van Eenwyk, J. R. (1991). Archetypes: The strange attractors of the psyche. *Journal of Analytical Psychology,* 36, 1–25.

von Eye, A. (1990). Configural frequency analysis of longitudinal multivariate responses. In A. von Eye (ed.), *Statistical methods in longitudinal research,* vol. 2. New York, NY: Academic Press.

Waller, N. G., and Meehl, P. E. (1998). *Multivariate taxometric procedures. Distinguishing types from continua.* Thousand Oaks, CA: Sage.

Wikman, A. (1991). Att utveckla sociala indikatorer. (To develop social indicators.) *Urval, No. 21.* Stockholm Statistiska Centralbyrån.

Part IV

Environmental contributions to personality development

8 The role of ethnic identity in personality development

Brett Laursen and Vickie Williams

Environmental contributions to personality development are often overlooked, perhaps because of a tendency to focus on internal dispositions. Departing from this position, Kurt Lewin (1939) asserted that context permeates all aspects of development, including personality. His work was instrumental to the realization that race and ethnicity shape and define many psychological environments, and that ethnic identity is contextually constructed. The degree to which ethnicity influences personality development depends upon the degree to which ethnic groups are a salient feature of the environment: the more prominent ethnicity is in the environment, the more central ethnic identity will be to self-concepts.

In this chapter, we present the argument that ethnic identity is an important component of personality, with developmental trajectories and sequellae that vary according to context. This thesis will be developed across four sections. First, we present a conceptual model that specifies mechanisms whereby group membership contributes to personality development. Lewin's (1939) field theory will serve as the framework for our discussion of group membership and ethnic identity. Second, we review the literature on ethnic identity development, paying particular attention to environmental factors that contribute to variations in developmental trajectories. Third, we discuss research that describes associations between ethnic identity and individual adjustment. There is evidence that ethnic identity promotes self-esteem, academic achievement, and psychosocial adjustment, especially among minority culture youth. Finally, we will summarize new findings that describe the correlates of adolescent ethnic identity. Links from parenting practices to ethnic identity, and from ethnic identity to individual adjustment evince context and domain specific patterns of association.

Conceptual models of group membership and ethnic identity

Natural language descriptions of personality often extend beyond traits to encompass mental schema and self-conceptions (Allport and Odbert,

1936). Consistent with this tradition, we define personality as a phenomenological process in which cognitions and perceptions mediate links between the individual and the environment (Lewin, 1935). Seen in this light, ethnic identity may be viewed as a central personality construct that helps to define the self in ways that shape both subjective reality and objective behavior.

The person and the psychological environment

Field theory (Lewin, 1939) contains a compelling account of why group membership is an important component of identity for some individuals but not others. It starts from the premise that behavior and development are a function of the person and the environment. Figure 8.1 depicts a life space, which contains the person and his or her psychological environment. The psychological environment is broad and diverse, encompassing the people, places, and things that influence the person. More than a categorization of physical surroundings, it describes the individual's subjective perceptions of the environment. Prominent features of the psychological environment shape different inner regions or facets of the self. Ethnic identity is an example of one such inner region, and the characteristic of the psychological environment that affects it most directly is ethnic group membership.

These precepts are further elaborated in social identity theory (Tajfel, 1981), which describes the interplay between ethnic group membership, ethnic identity, and self-concept. According to this model, the social

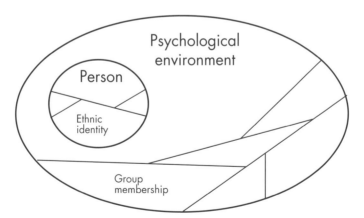

Figure 8.1 The Life Space (adapted from Lewin, 1935).

world is categorized into units representing similar and dissimilar others. A positive self-concept derives, in part, from favorable evaluations of the in-group relative to an out-group. Ethnic identity bolsters self-worth by conferring the perceived benefits of in-group membership on participants.

Ethnic groups in the psychological environment

Ethnicity refers to broad categorizations made on the basis of race and culture of origin. An ethnic group comprises persons who share racial and cultural attributes. Ethnic groups are quite heterogeneous, yet distinctions based on ethnicity are prevalent in most cultural contexts (Zuckerman, 1990). Individuals who belong to the same ethnic group may differ on most sociodemographic indices yet still share attributes related to ethnicity, including cultural values, attitudes and behaviors, a subjective sense of group belongingness, and experiences related to group membership (Phinney, 1996).

Ethnic group labels are problematic because they carry different meanings for individuals inside and outside the group. Nevertheless they are widespread and important insofar as they signify distinctions that are meaningful in a particular place and time. In keeping with current practice, we will refer to the three largest ethnic groups in the United States as African Americans (Blacks), Anglo Americans (non-Hispanic Whites), and Hispanic Americans (Latinos), although whenever possible a subgroup label (e.g., Mexican American, Puerto Rican, or Cuban American) will be substituted for the latter.

Developmental changes in the salience of ethnic group membership

The life space, to use Lewin's terminology, becomes more differentiated with development. The psychological environment of children grows more complex as they age, encompassing an increasingly broad array of settings and interaction partners. Greater complexity in the psychological environment prompts diversification of inner regions. Thus, self-definitions grow more sophisticated with experience and development.

For these reasons, ethnic group membership becomes an increasingly important component of the psychological environment as children grow older. Young children tend to be reared in homogeneous environments: diversity within settings is minimal because family and friends usually belong to the same ethnic group as the child (Katz and Kofkin, 1997). Development is usually accompanied by greater exposure to social distinctions based on ethnic group membership. By early childhood, racial similarity emerges as an important factor in the composition of peer groups (Boulton and Smith, 1993). By adolescence, ethnic group membership dominates the selection of recreational activities and friends (Schofield, 1982). Thus, as the salience of ethnic group membership in the psychological environment increases, ethnic identity assumes a more prominent place in self-definitions.

Ethnic identity and self-definitions

At the most basic level, ethnic identity describes a perception of the self as a member of an ethnic group, possessing attributes common to those in the group (Aboud, 1987). Most scholars in the area, however, prefer a more expansive definition that also encompasses the attitudes and values that are attached to membership in the ethnic group (Tajfel, 1981). Phinney (1992) defines ethnic identity in terms of self-identification, involvement, belonging, and exploration. Self-identification describes the ethnic label applied to the individual. Involvement encompasses participation in cultural traditions and social activities with members of that ethnic group. A sense of belonging refers to positive feelings toward membership in the ethnic group. Exploration describes inquiries designed to enhance appreciation for the ethnic group. Bernal and colleagues (Bernal, Knight, Ocampo, Garza, and Cota, 1993) add constancy to the list of traits that define ethnic identity. Constancy refers to the awareness that ethnic group characteristics and membership are unalterable.

Because psychological environments differ in the significance of ethnic group membership and in the characteristics of ethnicity emphasized, there is considerable variability across environments in the form and content of ethnic identity and in its contribution to self-definitions. Exposure to different cultures enhances awareness of one's own culture; the more heterogeneous the psychological environment, the more salient ethnicity is to self-classificatory schema (McGuire, McGuire, Child, and Fujioka, 1978). It follows that individuals embedded in an environment rich in cultural diversity are more apt than those in homogeneous contexts to emphasize ethnic identity in their definition of self.

To summarize, the psychological environment is divided into different portions, some defined by group membership. In all but the most uniform settings, group membership distinctions are made on the basis of ethnicity which, in turn, shapes ethnic identity. The importance of ethnic identity varies from one person to the next, depending upon the salience of ethnicity in the psychological environment. Thus, ethnic group membership influences definitions of self only insofar as environmental manifestations of ethnicity prompt the development of a coherent ethnic identity.

The development of ethnic identity

Research suggests that most individuals achieve an ethnic identity some-time during late adolescence or early adulthood (Phinney and Chavira, 1992). The developmental process begins much earlier, however, when children first grapple with racial and ethnic group classifications. Context influences even the most basic appreciation of group membership categories and accumulating evidence suggests that pathways to the development of an ethnic identity vary as a function of the psychological environment.

The perceptual and cognitive origins of ethnic identity

Racial and ethnic constancy are prerequisites to ethnic identity. The developmental process begins with awareness and proceeds through self-identification to constancy (Ocampo, Bernal, and Knight, 1993). First, children recognize differences between groups, then they categorize themselves into groups, and finally they understand that group membership is fixed. Awareness and self-identification of race emerge before ethnicity, perhaps because the latter, based on attributes such as religion and cultural practices, contain fewer perceptual cues than the former. In contrast, racial and ethnic constancy emerge simultaneously, suggesting that constancy is a manifestation of an underlying cognitive ability. Longitudinal evidence suggests that a nonverbal awareness of racial categories emerges by six months of age (Katz and Kofkin, 1997), with a verbal articulation of racial distinctions by three years of age (Goodman, 1952). A typical preschool child can correctly identify his or her own racial group (Fox and Jordan, 1973). Ethnic group awareness is not evident until at least age five, and reliable ethnic group self-identification emerges two years later (Aboud, 1987). Some evidence indicates that awareness and self-identification develop earlier in children from minority cultures than in those from majority cultures, perhaps because race and ethnicity are more frequently discussed by ethnic minority parents (Aboud and Amato, in press). Racial and ethnic constancy develop between the ages of 7 and 12, with no apparent differences between groups in this developmental milestone (Clark, Hocevar, and Dembo, 1980). Thus, by the time children are on the cusp of adolescence, they have a clear understanding of their own ethnic group; they know its traditions and practices, and they are aware of the images and stereotypes assigned to it by others (Aboud, 1987). This knowledge provides a foundation for subsequent ethnic identity development.

Two divergent theories address these developmental trends. One school of thought holds that classification and constancy reflect stages of cognitive development. Preoperational children are purportedly egocentric and unaware of natural groups; categorization requires concrete operations (Piaget and Weil, 1951). Global processes of early concept formation are applied to the development of concepts about people, which means that perceptual distinctions on the basis of race and ethnicity precede categorization (Katz, 1983). Once formed, categories are elaborated through the acquisition of knowledge about social groups. An alternative school of thought describes classification and constancy in terms of information processing abilities. In one such model, categorization precedes perceptual distinctions, which means that racial concepts give rise to an appreciation of group differences (Hirschfeld, 1996). Evidence that racial awareness does not undergo marked developmental shifts after accounting for improved memory is interpreted as support for the premise that what develops during early childhood is the ability to calibrate and combine the perceptually oriented and domain oriented categories that define ethnic groups.

Stages of ethnic identity

Ethnic identity development has also been described in terms that correspond with Marcia's (1980) well-known stages of ego identity development (Phinney and Kohatsu, 1997). During the first stage, ethnic identity consists of conformity or indifference, and is analogous to the foreclosure (commitment without exploration) or diffusion (failure to explore or commit) stage of ego identity development. During the intermediate stage, ethnic identity is characterized by exploration, which is akin to the moratorium (exploration without commitment) stage of ego identity development. During the final stage, ethnic identity is marked by awareness, which is comparable to the achievement stage of ego identity development. We consider each in turn.

The conformity or indifference stage is characterized by failure to consider the meaning of ethnic group membership. Some adolescents adopt a fixed ethnic identity from an external source. "I don't go looking for my culture. I just go by what my parents say and do, and what they tell me to do" (Phinney, 1989, p. 44). Others assume the ethnic identity prescribed by the dominant culture, which may include denigrating the subordinate group to which one belongs. "If I could have chosen, I would choose to be American White, because it's America and I would then be in my country" (Phinney, 1989, p. 44). There are still others who simply do not care about ethnic group membership and have given little thought to ethnic identity. "My parents tell me about where they lived, but what do I care? I never lived there" (Phinney, 1989, p. 44).

The exploration stage is noteworthy for reflection about issues concerning ethnicity and immersion in ethnic group activities. "I want to know what we do and how our culture is different from others. Going to festivals and other cultural events helps me learn more about my own culture and about myself" (Phinney, 1989, p. 44). Some scholars argue that among ethnic minority youth, exploration is preceded by a period of critical questioning triggered by experiences with racism (Cross, 1991; Helms, 1990), but clear evidence to support this encounter or dissonance stage is lacking (Phinney and Kohatsu, 1997). Regardless of whether it is precipitated by a period of dissonance, exploration by ethnic minority youth involves a heightened sensitivity to discrimination, often accompanied by a desire for distance from the dominant culture. Little is known about exploration by ethnic majority youth, but it is logical to assume that it includes a heightened interest in cultural heritage and traditions.

The achievement stage is marked by a committed ethnic identity that involves positive feelings about one's own ethnic group and tolerance toward other ethnic groups. Among ethnic minority youth, competing cultural demands may be reconciled through biculturalism and selective participation in important elements of the majority culture (LaFromboise, Coleman, and Gerton, 1993). "I'm here in America and people of many different cultures are here too. So I don't consider myself only Filipino, but also American" (Phinney, 1989, p. 44). That majority culture youth achieve a committed ethnic identity is presumed but undocumented.

The stage theory model of ethnic identity development awaits empirical confirmation. A single longitudinal study (Phinney and Chavira, 1992) reported that from mid-adolescence to late adolescence there was a greater tendency to progress to higher levels of ethnic identity than regress to lower ones, but these findings were qualified by a small sample size and a high attrition rate. Otherwise, firm evidence to support the proposed ontogenetic model of ethnic identity development is lacking. Future scholars would do well to reconsider the presupposition that ethnic identity proceeds through orderly, linear stages in light of strong evidence indicating that ego identity does not (Stephen, Fraser, and Marcia, 1992).

Group differences in ethnic identity

Consistent with the premise that context affects personality development, research indicates that minority culture youth have, on average, higher levels of ethnic identity than majority culture youth (see Phinney, 1990, for review). The paradox that members of the majority culture are often less cognizant of their own ethnic heritage than members of a minority culture can be explained by the fact that the dominant culture is so pervasive that it goes unnoticed. "'It would hardly be fish who discovered the existence of water,' as Clyde Kluckhorn (1949) so aptly stated. Like the fish that is unaware of water until it has left the water, humans often take their own community's ways of doing things for granted" (Rogoff, in press). Ethnic majority youth are probably as familiar with their own culture as ethnic minority youth, but cultural practices and behaviors may not be attributed to group membership because of the mistaken assumption that they represent cultural standards or universals. In contrast, minority culture youth are keenly aware of the ways in which ethnic group membership sets them apart: "Ignorance of the 'other' is a luxury that minority group members cannot afford" (Katz and Kofkin, 1997, p. 7).

That majority groups differ from minority groups on ethnic identity seems obvious, but less clear are variations among minority groups. Different groups hold different attitudes toward the majority, and these attitudes may make markedly different contributions to ethnic identity development. This point is best illustrated by the different cultural frames of reference adopted by voluntary minorities and involuntary minorities (Ogbu, 1993). Voluntary minorities include those who moved to a new society of their own accord because they believed migration would improve their economic well-being and provide greater political or religious freedom. Their primary cultural reference groups are peers in the homeland and immigrant neighborhoods, and they usually fare well in such comparisons. Voluntary minorities tend to attribute low status to a lack of familiarity with the new culture, so they make every effort to adapt in the belief that this will improve their chances of success. The majority culture is not a threat to their cultural identity because they make a clear distinction between public behaviors that foster success in the dominant culture and private behaviors that serve to maintain and cultivate the minority culture. Thus, most voluntary minorities hold positive views of their own ethnic group and of the majority. Voluntary minority status may shape ethnic identity development. For instance, because they tend to overlook discrimination by the dominant culture, voluntary minority youth may have little difficulty adopting a bicultural perspective.

In contrast, involuntary minorities include those who were brought into a dominant culture and placed in inferior positions against their will. Members of the dominant culture serve as the primary reference group for involuntary minorities, against whom they often compare unfavorably. Because they tend to attribute their low status to racism, involuntary minorities view the majority culture as a threat. Rather than participate in an oppressive system, involuntary minorities cultivate an oppositional perspective that preserves cultural distinctiveness and group cohesiveness by rejecting the majority culture. Thus, positive views of the dominant group are considered antithetical to positive views of the subordinate group. Ethnic identity development should reflect unique features of an involuntary minority status. For instance, a focus on systemic racism may prompt a period of dissonance that raises obstacles to a bicultural ethnic identity.

Attitudes toward the dominant culture vary across immigrant cohorts. Ethnic identity is positively related to age at immigration and negatively related to years since immigration (Phinney, 1990). Descendents of immigrants report declines in ethnic identity with each successive generation. To complicate matters, immigration is often confounded with the type of minority group membership status. For instance, recent North American immigrants are almost exclusively voluntary minorities or refugees (who are neither voluntary nor involuntary minorities). Some settle in communities with cultural traditions established by voluntary minorities but others reside in communities that reflect the mores of involuntary minorities. Research has yet to address the interplay between immigration and cultural frame of reference, so it is not clear how these influence ethnic identity development.

The socialization of ethnic identity

Enculturation describes the ethnic socialization provided by the psychological environment. Three important enculturation settings will be considered: (1) parents and family; (2) neighborhood and peers; and (3) school and the media. Because context and domain specific influences reflect the psychological environment (Laursen and Bukowski, 1997), each of these settings uniquely affects ethnic identity development.

As a primary agent of socialization, parents make critical contributions to ethnic identity, especially among minority culture youth. The ethnic heritage of parents serves as the basis for self-identification and parents provide opportunities for participation in cultural practices. Typically, parents engage in direct instruction. Minority culture parents provide more information on race and ethnicity than majority culture parents, starting from the time when children are about five years old (Katz and Kofkin, 1997), on topics ranging from ethnic traditions and history to strategies for self-development and coping with racial barriers (Bowman and Howard, 1985).

Intergenerational transmission of ethnic identity among minority culture youth also is accomplished indirectly, primarily through the psychological environment that parents create. Three examples illustrate the process. First, mothers comfortable with their Mexican American background have children with higher levels of ethnic identity than those ambivalent about their cultural heritage (Knight, Bernal, Garza, Cota, and Ocampo, 1993). Second, opportunities for interracial contact and the quality of relationships with parents and friends make independent contributions to ethnic identity among African American children (Demo and Hughes, 1990). Third, warmth, control, and autonomy granting in parent-child relationships have been linked to ethnic identity among ethnic Chinese adolescents in Australia and in the USA (Rosenthal and Feldman, 1992).

Parent and peer influences interact in a complex fashion that is moderated by ethnic group membership. Parents shape peer and neighborhood influences on their children through the selection of a residence, but minority culture parents often have less control in this regard than majority culture parents. Financial resources may circumscribe neighborhood options, and choices may be constrained by the desire or need to live in an ethnic enclave. Unlike majority culture parents, minority culture parents often have difficulty selecting an environment that supports traditions and values consistent with their own. Strong family ties may compensate by restricting contact with the outside world, but peers are powerful countervailing forces who exert greater control than parents over the day to day behavior of adolescents. It is often the case that ethnic minority children must choose socialization partners from among a limited number of same-race peers (Steinberg, Dornbusch, and Brown, 1992), so, contrary to the wishes of parents, children of voluntary immigrants often select friends who encourage enculturation and children of involuntary minorities may pick friends who promote an oppositional identity.

Schools and the media consistently advocate enculturation. Schools tend to reinforce the socialization messages of families in the dominant culture, but in so doing they may foster cultural discontinuities among ethnic minorities (Bernal, Saenz, and Knight, 1991). Not only is the curriculum geared toward the dominant culture, but children are taught to work and interact in a manner consistent with what is required for success in that culture. These messages are reinforced by the media, where ethnic minorities are frequently overlooked or portrayed in a stereotyped fashion, and where contemporary youth culture is glorified at the expense of traditional values and practices (Huston *et al.*, 1992).

To summarize, an understanding of race and ethnicity emerges during childhood that presages the development of a committed ethnic identity during adolescence. The role of context is apparent as developmental trajectories differ across ethnic groups, and interact with family, peer, and societal influences in complex ways that are not fully understood.

Ethnic identity and individual adjustment

There is good reason to suspect that ethnic identity contributes to the well-being of ethnic minority youth. Positive self-perceptions are an important asset when coping with environments containing discrepant and conflicting cultural expectations. Ethnic identity is less central to the self-concept of ethnic majority youth and, correspondingly, it plays less of a role in shaping their attitudes and behaviors. In this section, we will review evidence that describes the influence of ethnic identity on adjustment, with particular emphasis on self-esteem, school achievement, and psychosocial functioning during the adolescent years.

The role of ethnic identity in self-esteem

The self-concept is a multifaceted entity that consists of several different identities, each constructed within a specific social context (Oyserman, Gant, and Ager, 1995). Ethnic identity is one such construct, forged by experiences as a member of a dominant or subordinate group. Lewin (1939) argued that identification with a group was essential to maintaining a positive self-concept, because the group was both a point of reference and a source of pride. But the fit between the group and the psychological environment is much better for majority culture youth than minority culture youth (Harrison, Wilson, Pine, Chan, and Buriel, 1990). Exposed to environments in which ethnicity is a source of conflict with the dominant group, ethnic minorities must navigate settings where values are dictated by the majority culture (e.g., school and work) and settings where values are defined by the minority culture (e.g., home and neighborhood). "The Marginal Man is a person who stands on the boundary between two groups. He does not belong to either of them, or at least he is not certain about his belongingness. Not infrequently this situation occurs for members of an underprivileged minority group... If the person is partly successful in establishing relationships with the privileged group without being fully accepted, he becomes a Marginal

Man, belonging to both groups but not fully to either of them" (Lewin, 1939). Under these circumstances, ethnic identity may serve to organize definitions of self and to provide a buffer against environmental assaults on self-worth.

Considerable evidence supports the assertion that ethnic identity promotes self-esteem. A recent unpublished meta-analysis, summarizing results from 93 research reports, identified moderate associations between self-esteem and ethnic identity (Steen and Bat-Chava, 1996). There were differences between ethnic groups in the magnitude of the association: effects were strongest for Asians and weakest for Hispanics, with blacks and whites falling in between. Unfortunately, the findings did not distinguish minority groups from majority groups so ethnicity was confounded with group status (e.g., Whites were not members of the dominant culture in every study). Developmental differences emerged such that effects declined from mid-adolescence to adulthood, suggesting that ethnic identity is of greatest importance to self-esteem during the adolescent years.

The role of ethnic identity in school achievement

Ethnic group differences in school performance have been the subject of considerable debate. Relative to their counterparts from majority groups, ethnic minority children tend to underperform in school. There are also differences in school achievement between immigrant and indigenous minority groups, such that the latter underperform relative to the former and these differences persist after taking language and socioeconomic status into account (Bernal *et al.*, 1991).

Although most ethnic minority children strive to do well in school, some adopt an oppositional identity that embraces school failure as a means of repudiating the dominant culture (Ogbu, 1993). This raises the question: are oppositional identity and ethnic identity separate or overlapping constructs? Perhaps minority culture youth are confronted with two types of ethnic identity: one put forward by peers that embraces oppositionalism and rejects schooling, and another put forward by parents that rejects oppositionalism and embraces schooling. Alternatively, ethnic minority youth may possess two distinct social identities: an oppositional identity oriented towards peers that holds sway over schooling, and an ethnic identity oriented towards parents that dominates other behavioral domains.

Research has yet to disentangle ethnic identity and oppositional identity. Most assessments confound the type of identity with the level of identity achieved: high levels of ethnic identity presume a positive ethnic identity and the absence of an oppositional identity. Studies based on such indices indicate that ethnic identity is associated with school grades, but only for minority culture youth (Taylor, Casten, Flickinger, Roberts, and Fulmore, 1994). The one study to examine ethnic identity in conjunction with other forms of identity found that self-constructs combine to influence academic outcomes in a manner that varied across ethnic groups (Oyserman *et al.*, 1995). The greater the priority African American youth place on ethnic identity, the better they perform in school, but only if they also endorse an identity consonant with an orientation to succeed in school. In contrast, school performance among Anglo Americans is unrelated to ethnic identity and is instead tied to achievement-related identity.

The role of ethnic identity in psychosocial functioning

There is also reason to expect ethnic identity to be related to psychosocial functioning, especially among minority culture youth. Those with high levels of ethnic identity should be better equipped to cope with competing social pressures than those with low levels of ethnic identity, insofar as ethnic identity assists in the avoidance of cultural conflicts and provides a buffer against discrimination when conflicts do arise. But the evidence is sparse.

A review of the literature suggests links between ethnic identity and internalizing disorders among minority culture youth (Phinney and Kohatsu, 1997). Two studies indicate that among African American college students, low levels of racial identity are associated with heightened anxiety, substance abuse, and hostility (Carter, 1991; Parham and Helms, 1985). The links between ethnic identity and adolescent adjustment appear to be strongest for this particular ethnic group. Racelessness (i.e., the absence of a clear ethnic identity) has been found to be weakly correlated with anxiety and depression among African Americans, but not Anglo Americans (Arroyo and Zigler, 1995), and this latter finding is consistent with two reports that ethnic identity is unrelated to global functioning among Mexican Americans and majority culture youth (Grossman, Wirt, and Davids, 1985; Rosenthal and Cichello, 1986). There is longitudinal evidence that ethnic identity predicts less alcohol and tobacco use among African Americans and Hispanic Americans (Scheier, Botvin, Diaz, and Ifill-Williams, 1997). Other findings indicate that African Americans and Anglo Americans with a strong ethnic group orientation have fewer behavior problems than those who are either mainstream or bicultural; in contrast, ethnic group identification is associated with more behavior problems among Hispanic Americans and is unrelated to behavior

problems among Asian Americans (Rotherham-Borus, 1990). Taken together, there is consistent support for the assertion that a strong ethnic
identity protects African American youth from adjustment difficulties,
but the data are inconclusive with respect to the link between ethnic
identity and adjustment among other ethnic groups.

Sequellae of adolescent ethnic identity

Having discussed the theoretical and empirical literature on the development of ethnic identity, we turn to results of a new program of research
that explores the sequallae of ethnic identity. Our research framework may
be succinctly summarized. The investigation started from the premise
that group membership features more prominently in the identities of
minority culture youth than majority culture youth (Lewin, 1939). It incorporated the suggestion that different minority groups hold different
attitudes toward the majority group and that these attitudes differentially
shape adolescent outcomes (Ogbu, 1993). It assumed that relationships
exert context and domain specific influences over developmental outcomes (Laursen and Bukowski, 1997). The purpose of the study was
to identify the impact of parenting practices on adolescent ethnic identity, and to determine the extent to which ethnic identity and parenting
practices shape adolescent psychosocial and academic outcomes.

The investigation was conducted in the greater Miami metropolitan
area, which includes three large, distinct ethnic groups: African Americans
(involuntary minorities), Anglo Americans (the majority culture), and
Cuban Americans (voluntary minorities). Miami is unique among major US cities in several respects. As the youngest metropolis, its settle-
ment and development occurred primarily during the second half of the
twentieth century. Miami was originally settled by Anglo Americans and
African Americans. Just prior to and following the revolution in Cuba,
immigrants poured into Miami, and many Anglo Americans moved to
the surrounding suburbs. Today, Miami is the only major US city where
more than half of the population speaks Spanish and where Hispanics
hold political power. Although the suburban communities are quite affluent, Miami itself is the third poorest US city in per capita income.
Cuban Americans, the third largest Hispanic group in the USA are the
largest ethnic group in Miami. On average they are older, more affluent, better educated, and more apt to be employed than other Hispanic
Americans. Unlike Mexican Americans and Puerto Ricans, who were
originally involuntary minorities, most of the first Cuban immigrants
were voluntary minorities and their attitudes persisted as the community
absorbed subsequent waves of refugees and involuntary immigrants.

Research hypotheses

We derived four hypotheses from our research framework. The first concerned group differences in ethnic identity. Consistent with previous research (see Phinney, 1990, for review), we expected minority culture youth to report higher levels of ethnic identity than majority culture youth because ethnicity is more salient for those who must cross cultural boundaries than for those who participate exclusively in the dominant culture. No differences between voluntary and involuntary minorities were anticipated.

The second hypothesis concerned group differences in the influence of parenting practices on ethnic identity. As others have suggested (Knight, Bernal, Cota, Garza, and Ocampo, 1993), we expected parenting practices to play a more prominent role in shaping the ethnic identity of minority culture youth than majority culture youth because the values and practices of the majority are pervasive and communicated through many mediums, but minority culture is transmitted primarily at home and in the neighborhood. No differences between voluntary and involuntary minorities were anticipated.

The third hypothesis concerned group differences in the influence of ethnic identity on psychosocial adjustment and school achievement. We agree with those (Bernal *et al.*, 1991) who argue that a secure ethnic identity may help to mitigate cultural conflicts over ethnicity. It follows that ethnic identity should be more strongly linked to behavioral and academic outcomes for minority culture youth than majority culture youth, because conflicts over ethnicity are more common among the former than the latter. Involuntary minorities were expected to provide evidence of stronger linkages between ethnic identity and adjustment than voluntary minorities because involuntary minorities interpret difficulties as evidence of discrimination by the majority culture whereas voluntary minorities attribute similar difficulties to sources unrelated to ethnic group membership.

The fourth hypothesis concerned group differences in the influence of parenting practices on adolescent psychosocial adjustment and school achievement. Previous studies indicated that parents influence behavior problems in much the same manner across ethnic groups (Lamborn, Dornbusch, and Steinberg, 1996; Greenberger and Chen, 1996), but that they may differentially affect academic grades (Steinberg *et al.*, 1992). Consistent with these findings, we predicted that the relation of variation in parenting practices to that in psychosocial adjustment would be similar for minority and majority culture youth, but that parents would influence the academic achievement of majority culture adolescents more than minority culture adolescents.

Research participants and procedures

Participants included a total of 469 adolescents enrolled in public schools. Each of the three ethnic groups included an approximately equal number ($n = 25$ to 30) of males and females in early adolescence (11- to 12-year-olds), mid-adolescence (14- to 15-year-olds), and late adolescence (17- to 18-year-olds). All adolescents were born in the USA. African American and Anglo American adolescents spoke English at home. Cuban American adolescents were fluent in English but spoke Spanish at home. Most participants came from the middle of the socioeconomic spectrum, although the full range of social classes was represented in each ethnic group. Sampling procedures minimized ethnic group differences in socioeconomic status, but Anglo American participants were nevertheless slightly more affluent than African American and Cuban American participants. Household structure differences emerged, with African Americans reporting the highest rates of single parent households and the lowest rates of two-parent intact households, but household structure was unrelated to parenting practices, ethnic identity, or adolescent outcomes.

Adolescents completed three instruments during one-hour class sessions, yielding assessments of ethnic identity, parenting practices, and psychosocial and academic adjustment. *Ethnic identity* was measured with the Multigroup Ethnic Identity Measure (Phinney, 1992), a composite index encompassing affirmation and belonging, ethnic behaviors, and ethnic identity achievement. Parent influences were assayed with the Parenting Practices Scale (Steinberg, Mounts, Lamborn, and Dornbusch, 1991), which describes perceptions of parental *involvement* (affection and affiliation), *psychological autonomy granting* (encouragement of individuality), and *supervision* (monitoring and discipline). Psychosocial functioning was measured with the Youth Self-Report (Achenbach, 1991), which measures *total problems* across eight areas of functioning. Cumulative grade point average (GPA), the mean of all school grades received during the past academic year, was obtained from school records.

Research findings

Consistent with our first hypothesis, minority culture adolescents reported higher levels of ethnic identity than majority culture adolescents, but there were no differences between voluntary and involuntary minority adolescents. These findings reinforce the view that ethnic identity is more important to minority culture youth than to majority culture youth.

To test the remaining hypotheses, separate sets of regressions were conducted for the full sample and for each ethnic group separately (see

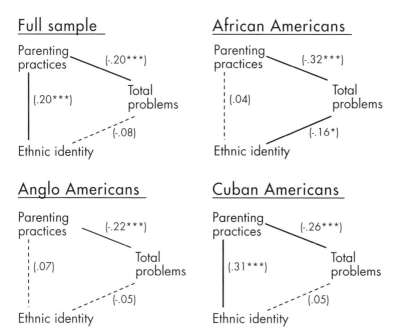

Figure 8.2 Summary of regressions predicting ethnic identity and be-havior problems.
Notes: $^*p < .05$, $^{**}p < .01$, $^{***}p < .001$. Values in parentheses represent average beta weights.

Figures 8.2 and 8.3). The first analyses examined the influence of parent-ing practices (involvement, psychological autonomy granting, and super-vision) on ethnic identity. The second analyses examined the influence of parenting practices on total problems and GPA. The third analyses examined the influence of ethnic identity on total problems and GPA. Age, gender, and SES were entered into each regression on the first step, to statistically remove the contributions of these demographic variables.

Parenting practices were associated with ethnic identity for the sample as a whole. However, analyses of group differences provided only mixed support for our second hypothesis. As anticipated, associations emerged between parenting practices and ethnic identity among voluntary mi-norities but not among majority culture youth. Contrary to expectations, parenting practices were unrelated to ethnic identity among involuntary minorities.

Ethnic identity was unrelated to total problems and cumulative GPA for the full sample. In this case, group differences were generally in accord with our third hypothesis. As predicted, ethnic identity was unrelated

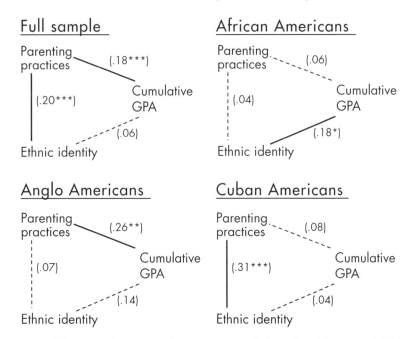

Figure 8.3 Summary of regressions predicting ethnic identity and GPA. *Notes:* $^*p < .05$, $^{**}p < .01$, $^{***}p < .001$. GPA = Grade Point Average. Values in parentheses represent average beta weights.

to adolescent adjustment among majority culture youth, and linkages from ethnic identity to school grades and psychosocial functioning were stronger for involuntary minorities than for voluntary minorities.

Parenting practices were associated with adolescents' total problems and cumulative GPA for the sample as a whole. The group differences that emerged were consistent with our fourth hypothesis. Parenting practices were associated with psychosocial functioning in all ethnic groups, but parenting practices were linked to school achievement only among youth from the majority culture and not for those from minority cultures.

Research conclusions

The foregoing analyses revealed that correlates of ethnic identity differ across ethnic groups. Among Cuban Americans, parenting practices are associated with ethnic identity, but ethnic identity is unrelated to behavior problems and school functioning. These findings are not easily interpreted because so little research has been conducted on Cuban

Americans and because their voluntary minority status sets them apart from other Hispanic Americans. The fact that most of the parents in this group were born in Cuba reinforces the view that recent immigrants play an active role in shaping the ethnic identities of their children. Yet despite the importance of ethnic identity to their self-concept, Cuban American adolescents apparently do not to use ethnic identity as a shield against the dominant culture, perhaps because voluntary minorities attribute their successes and failures to factors other than ethnic group membership (Ogbu, 1993). As a consequence, ethnic identity has little bearing on adjustment where standards are determined by the majority.

In contrast, although parenting practices are unrelated to ethnic identity among African Americans, ethnic identity is associated with adolescent psychosocial functioning and school grades. The first finding was unexpected and requires replication. It may reflect the fact that African American parents have less influence on adolescent children, both relative to peers and relative to parents in other ethnic groups (Steinberg *et al.*, 1992). It also may reflect the fact that parenting practices operate in circumscribed socialization domains (Darling and Steinberg, 1993) distinct from explicit forms of African American racial socialization. Regardless of how it develops, ethnic identity clearly plays a role in psychosocial adjustment and school achievement, helping to protect involuntary minorities against the debilitating effects of real and perceived racism. These findings add to the growing list of studies (Rotherham-Borus, 1990; Taylor *et al.*, 1994) suggesting that ethnic identity helps African American adolescents navigate environments in which standards of behavior are dictated by the dominant culture.

Among Anglo Americans, parenting practices are unrelated to ethnic identity, and ethnic identity is associated with neither behavior problems nor school performance. Little is known about parent influences on the ethnic identities of majority culture youth in North America, so these results must be interpreted with caution. But there is general agreement that ethnic identity has little to do with Anglo American outcomes (Arroyo and Zigler, 1995; Taylor *et al.*, 1994). Taken together, the findings suggest that ethnic identity does not resound in the lives of adolescents from the dominant culture. This is not to say that issues of ethnicity and identity are unimportant to majority culture youth, but rather that ethnic identity is not specifically tied to socialization and adjustment.

The findings suggested that parenting practices are linked to behavior problems in all ethnic groups but to school achievement only among Anglo Americans. This is not the first study to find parent influences to be more uniform in the dominant culture than in minority cultures (Lamborn *et al.*, 1996). Parents in all ethnic groups place a high priority on education, but many ethnic minority youth live in poor neighborhoods where less value is attached to school achievement than in the middle-class communities where most majority culture youth reside. Because adolescents congregate in racially defined crowds, minority culture youth may have difficulty identifying peers who share their parents' attitudes about school (Steinberg *et al.*, 1992). As a consequence, there is an increased likelihood in ethnic minority cultures that parental influences on achievement will be diluted by contradictory pressures from peers.

Summary and conclusions

Ethnic identity is an important facet of personality whenever ethnicity is an important feature of the environment. Many ethnic minority youth rely on ethnic identity to help them balance the demands of the dominant culture against the norms of the subordinate culture. In contrast, most majority culture youth find that ethnic identity offers no practical assistance in navigating the psychological environment. Parents, peers, schools, and the media have all been invoked to explain the development of ethnic identity; the evidence presented here suggests that pathways of influence vary as a function of group, domain, and context.

Although most aspects of this topic could profit from additional inquiry, the need for further research appears greatest in three areas. First, the construct of ethnic identity requires articulation. Minimally, tools to assess ethnic identity must be empirically validated so as to specify its developmental sequence and its distinctiveness from other self-constructs. Second, mechanisms of influence involving ethnic identity require elaboration. Studies are needed that identify how different environmental factors combine to affect ethnic identity development and how different components of ethnic identity affect specific areas of individual adjustment. Third, contextual variations require consideration. We cannot claim to understand ethnic identity until we know what it means to identify with a particular minority culture and how that differs from identifying with a particular majority culture. By the same token, we cannot claim to understand mechanisms of influence until we know how the origins and correlates of ethnic identity interact with the circumstances of individual environments.

As research reveals the increasing complexity of the topic, it may seem that the more we learn about ethnic identity the less we know, but surely this is a function of the fact that the domain of inquiry is large, the enterprise is new, and the laborers are few. We know enough to say with some certainty that ethnic identity can be an important determinant of individual functioning in areas as critical and diverse as academic achievement and psychosocial adjustment. In time we will be able to explain how and why this is the case for some individuals but not for others.

ACKNOWLEDGMENTS

This chapter was written while the first author was a visiting scholar at the Center of Excellence for Human Development and Its Risk Factors, Department of Psychology, University of Jyväskylä, Finland. Additional support for the preparation of this chapter and for the research described herein was provided by a grant to the first author from the US National Institute of Child Health and Human Development (R29 HD33006). Portions of this chapter include results from the second author's doctoral dissertation submitted to the Department of Psychology at Florida Atlantic University. Dissertation research support also was provided by a grant from the Division of Sponsored Research at Florida Atlantic University. Thanks are extended to Lea Pulkkinen for the support provided by the Center for Excellence and to Erika Hoff for insightful comments on an earlier draft of the manuscript.

REFERENCES

Aboud, F. (1987). The development of ethnic self-identification and attitudes. In J. Phinney and M. Rotheram (eds.), *Children's ethnic socialization: Pluralism and development* Newbury Park, CA: Sage, 32–55.

Aboud, F., and Amato, M. (in press). Developmental and socialization influences on intergroup bias. In R. S. Brown and S. Gaertner (eds.), *Handbook of Social Psychology*. vol. 4: *Intergroup Processes*. New York: Blackwell.

Achenbach, T. M. (1991). *Manual for the Youth Self-Report and 1991 profile*. Burlington: University of Vermont.

Allport, G. W., and Odbert, H. S. (1936). Trait-names: a psycho-lexical study. *Psychological Monographs*, 47 (whole no. 211).

Arroyo, C. G., and Zigler, E. (1995). Racial identity, academic achievement, and the psychological well-being of economically disadvantaged adolescents. *Journal of Personality and Social Psychology*, 69, 903–14.

Bernal, M. E., Knight, G. P., Ocampo, K. A., Garza, C. A., and Cota, M. K. (1993). Development of Mexican American identity. In M. E. Bernal and G. P. Knight (eds.), *Ethnic identity: Formation and transmission among Hispanics and other minorities*. Albany, NY: SUNY Press, 31–46.

Bernal, M. E., Saenz, D. S., and Knight, G. P. (1991). Ethnic identity and adaptation of Mexican American youths in school settings. *Hispanic Journal of Behavioral Sciences*, 13, 135–54.

Boulton, M. J., and Smith, P. K. (1993). Ethnic, gender partner, and activity preferences in mixed-race schools in the UK: playground observations. In C. H. Hart (ed.), *Children on playgrounds: Research perspectives and applications*. Albany, NY: SUNY Press, 210–37.

Bowman, P. J., and Howard, C. (1985). Race-related socialization, motivation, and academic achievement: a study of Black youths in three-generation families. *Journal of the American Academy of Child Psychiatry*, 24, 134–41.

Carter, R. (1991). Racial attitudes and psychological functioning. *Journal of Multicultural Counseling and Development*, 19, 105–14.

Clark, A., Hocevar, D., and Dembo, M. (1980). The role of cognitive development in children's explanations and preferences for skin color. *Developmental Psychology*, 16, 332–9.

Cross, W. (1991). *Shades of black: Diversity in African-American identity*. Philadelphia: Temple University Press.

Darling, N., and Steinberg, L. (1993). Parenting style as context: an integrative model. *Psychological Bulletin*, 113, 487–96.

Demo, D. H., and Hughes, M. (1990). Socialization and racial identity among Black Americans. *Social Psychology Quarterly*, 53, 364–74.

Fox, D. J., and Jordan, V. D. (1973). Racial preference and identification of Black, American Chinese, and White children. *Genetic Psychology Monographs*, 88, 229–96.

Goodman, M. (1952). *Race awareness in young children*. Cambridge, MA: Addison-Wesley.

Greenberger, E., and Chen, C. (1996). Perceived family relationships and depressed mood in early and late adolescence: a comparison of European and Asian Americans. *Developmental Psychology*, 32, 707–16.

Grossman, B., Wirt, R., and Davids, A. (1985). Self-esteem, ethnic identity, and behavioral adjustment among Anglo and Chicano adolescents in West Texas. *Journal of Adolescence*, 8, 57–68.

Harrison, A. O., Wilson, M. N., Pine, C. J., Chan, S. Q., and Buriel, R. (1990). Family ecologies of ethnic minority children. *Child Development*, 61, 347–63.

Helms, J. (1990). *Black and white racial identity: Theory, research, and practice*. New York: Greenwood.

Hirschfeld, L. A. (1996). *Race in the making: Cognition, culture, and the child's construction of human kinds*. Cambridge, MA: The MIT Press.

Huston, A. C., Donnerstein, E., Fairchild, H., Feshbach, N. D., Katz, P. A., Murray, J. P., Rubinstein, E. A., Wilcox, B. L., and Zuckerman, D. (1992). *Big world, small screen: The role of television in American society*. Lincoln, NE: University of Nebraska Press.

Katz, P. (1983). Developmental foundations of gender and racial attitudes. In R. L. Leahy (ed.), *The child's construction of social inequality*. New York: Academic Press, 41–78.

Katz, P. A., and Kofkin, J. A. (1997). Race, gender, and young children. In S. S. Luthar and J. A. Burack (eds.), *Developmental psychopathology: Perspectives on adjustment, risk, and disorder*. New York: Cambridge University Press, 51–74.

Kluckhorn, C. (1949). *Mirror for man*. New York: McGraw-Hill.

Knight, G. P., Bernal, M. E., Cota, M. K., Garza, C. A., and Ocampo, K. A. (1993). Family socialization and Mexican American identity and behavior. In

M. E. Bernal and G. P. Knight (eds.), *Ethnic identity: Formation and transmission among Hispanics and other minorities*. Albany, NY: SUNY Press, 105–29.

Knight, G. P., Bernal, M. E., Garza, C. A., Cota, M. K., and Ocampo, K. A. (1993). Family socialization and the ethnic identity of Mexican-American children. *Journal of Cross-Cultural Psychology*, 24, 99–114.

LaFromboise, T., Coleman, H., and Gerton, J. (1993). Psychological impact of biculturalism: evidence and theory. *Psychological Bulletin*, 114, 395–412.

Lamborn, S. D., Dornbusch, S. M., and Steinberg, L. (1996). Ethnicity and community context as moderators of the relations between family decision making and adolescent adjustment. *Child Development*, 67, 283–301.

Laursen, B., and Bukowski, W. M. (1997). A developmental guide to the organisation of close relationships. *International Journal of Behavioral Development*, 21, 747–70.

Lewin, K. (1935). *A dynamic theory of personality*. New York: McGraw-Hill.

Lewin, K. (1939). Field theory and experiment in social psychology: concepts and methods. *American Journal of Sociology*, 44, 868–97.

Marcia, J. (1980). Identity in adolescence. In J. Adelson (ed.), *Handbook of adolescent psychology*. New York: Wiley, 159–87.

McGuire, W. J., McGuire, C. V., Child, P., and Fujioka, T. (1978). Salience of ethnicity in the spontaneous self-concept as a function of one's ethnic distinctiveness in the social environment. *Journal of Social and Personality Psychology*, 36, 511–20.

Ocampo, K. A., Bernal, M. E., and Knight, G. P. (1993). Gender, race, and ethnicity: the sequencing of social constancies. In M. E. Bernal and G. P. Knight (eds.), *Ethnic identity: Formation and transmission among Hispanics and other minorities*. Albany, NY: SUNY Press, 11–30.

Ogbu, J. U. (1993). Differences in cultural frame of reference. *International Journal of Behavioral Development*, 16, 483–506.

Oyserman, D., Gant, L., and Ager, J. (1995). A socially contextualized model of African American identity: possible selves and school persistence. *Journal of Personality and Social Psychology*, 69, 1216–32.

Parham, T. A., and Helms, J. E. (1985). Relation of racial identity attitudes to self-actualization and affective states of black students. *Journal of Counseling Psychology*, 28, 250–7.

Phinney, J. S. (1989). Stages of ethnic identity in minority group adolescents. *Journal of Early Adolescence*, 9, 34–49.

Phinney, J. S. (1990). Ethnic identity in adolescents and adults: review of research. *Psychological Bulletin*, 108, 499–514.

Phinney, J. S. (1992). The Multigroup Ethnic Identity Measure: a new scale for use with diverse groups. *Journal of Adolescent Research*, 7, 156–76.

Phinney, J. S. (1996). When we talk about American ethnic groups, what do we mean? *American Psychologist*, 51, 918–27.

Phinney, J. S., and Chavira, V. (1992). Ethnic identity and self-esteem: an exploratory longitudinal study. *Journal of Adolescence*, 15, 271–81.

Phinney, J. S., and Kohatsu, E. L. (1997). Ethnic and racial identity development and mental health. In J. Schulenberg, J. L. Maggs, and K. Hurrelmann (eds.), *Health risks and developmental transitions during adolescence*. New York: Cambridge University Press, 420–43.

Piaget, J., and Weil, A. M. (1951). The development in children of the idea of the homeland and of relations to other countries. *International Social Science Journal*, 3, 561–78.

Rogoff, B. (in press). *The cultural nature of human development*. Oxford University Press.

Rosenthal, D. A., and Cichello, A. M. (1986). The meeting of two cultures: ethnic identity and psychosocial adjustment of Italian-Australian adolescents. *International Journal of Psychology*, 21, 487–501.

Rosenthal, D. A., and Feldman, S. S. (1992). The relationship between parenting behaviour and ethnic identity in Chinese-American and Chinese-Australian adolescents. *International Journal of Psychology*, 27, 19–31.

Rotherham-Borus, M. J. (1990). Adolescents' reference-group choices, self-esteem, and adjustment. *Journal of Personality and Social Psychology*, 59, 1075–81.

Scheier, L. M., Botvin, G. J., Diaz, T., and Ifill-Williams, M. (1997). Ethnic identity as a moderator of psychosocial risk and adolescent alcohol and marijuana use: concurrent and longitudinal analyses. *Journal of Child and Adolescent Substance Abuse*, 6, 21–47.

Schofield, J. W. (1982). *Black and White in school: Trust, tension, or tolerance?* New York: Praeger.

Steen, E. M., and Bat-Chava, Y. (1996, March). How is ethnic identity measured in studies on ethnic identity and self-esteem? In J. S. Phinney (Chair), *Ethnic identity: Current perspectives on conceptualization and measurement*. Paper presented at the meetings of the Society for Research on Adolescence, Boston, MA.

Steinberg, L., Dornbusch, S. M., and Brown, B. B. (1992). Ethnic differences in adolescent achievement: an ecological perspective. *American Psychologist*, 47, 723–9.

Steinberg, L., Mounts, N., Lamborn, S., and Dornbusch, S. (1991). Authoritative parenting and adolescent adjustment across various ecological niches. *Journal of Research on Adolescence*, 1, 19–36.

Stephen, J., Fraser, E., and Marcia, J. E. (1992). Moratorium-achievement (Mama) cycles in lifespan identity development: value orientations and reasoning system correlates. *Journal of Adolescence*, 15, 283–300.

Tajfel, H. (1981). *Human groups and social categories*. New York: Cambridge University Press.

Taylor, R. D., Casten, R., Flickinger, S. M., Roberts, D., and Fulmore, C. D. (1994). Explaining the school performance of African-American adolescents. *Journal of Research on Adolescence*, 4, 21–44.

Zuckerman, M. (1990). Some dubious premises in research and theory on racial differences. *American Psychologist*, 45, 1297–303.

9 Time and change: psychosocial transitions in German young adults 1991 and 1996

Rainer K. Silbereisen, Matthias Reitzle and Linda Juang

Seen from a historical perspective, German unification will be perceived as a major social change which represented gross interruptions in the routines of the lives of many, and yet with surprisingly small and circum-scribed effects, at least in the short run. In contrast to widely held ex-pectations, soon after unification, East-West differences in adolescents' development appeared quite minimal or even non-existent, in spite of the remarkable differences in the political fabric of the two Germanys. Looking more closely, however, it was quite clear that life was much more similar to begin with, and that the changes concerned primarily those dimensions of development directly affected by social institutions (Silbereisen and Zinnecker, 1999).

Unification was engineered by the transfer of basic social institutions, namely, parliamentary democracy, the legal system, and the capitalist economy, from the West to the East. By providing such institutions ac-cording to the Western model, the lack of differentiated social structures in the East – together with the reliance on central planning presumed to be the main cause of the East's failure in face of new technological and political changes – was expected to be resolved. Given the existence of a civic society in spite of all the havoc, many scientists believed that people would feel encouraged to develop these structures further by their own agency (Zapf, 1996).

This particular German model of social change actually worked well in the East as indicated by increases in real income, tremendous im-provements in the infrastructure, growing efficiency in production, and people's positive evaluation of their own standing. Nevertheless, negative attitudes towards the West, particularly rooted in the total restructuring of entire industries, with tremendous job losses, revealed that people were not well enough prepared to utilize the mold of the new social institutions and to shape the organization of public life through their own activities (Zapf and Habich, 1999).

As is true for social change in general (see Elder, 1998), the mismatch between new requirements and established ways of life gives rise to new adaptations only insofar as individuals perceive situational imperatives to act in a particular way. The unprecedented decline in the birth rate in former East Germany is a case in point (Eberstadt, 1994). The implementation of Western social institutions did not overtly set obstacles against parenthood. Nonetheless, people found enough reason to postpone family formation, in part as a reaction to their insecure economic outlook (Adler, 1997), in part because other activities for self-improvement were high on the agenda, such as occupational retraining. As the recent recovery of birth rates illuminates, the scale of the decline was probably an over-reaction.

The transfer of institutions did not only concern the basic fabric of a democratic society, but also entailed many more specific arrangements for adolescent development. The replacement of the comprehensive school system of former East Germany is a case in point. It was changed in 1991 in favor of the three-track system common in West Germany, which as early as age ten branches out into tracks leading to professional as opposed to academic training and careers (Schimpl-Neimanns, 2000).

Over the last few years, we have investigated commonalities and differences between the formerly divided political regions in a particular aspect of adolescent "competence" (Masten et al., 1995). Adolescence and young adulthood can be characterized by a series of biographical transitions or developmental tasks (Havighurst, 1972). Such tasks reflect the intersection of social and historical factors with psychological development and biological growth, and thus show considerable variation across time and space (Marini, 1986). Typically they are composed of a number of new behaviors, centered around a focal achievement (Dekovic, Noom, and Meeus 1997). Some, like the transition from school to work, mirror the influence of normative expectations, implemented by social institutions, more than other influences which are more personal in nature, such as the experience of a first romantic involvement.

In a formal sense, then, German unification can be described with regard to the life-course as a series of events which altered the social constraints for the accomplishment of certain developmental tasks. The already mentioned three-track school system will not have a salient influence on the biological, psychological, and social processes related to the development of romantic involvement. It may, however, exert quite a substantial influence concerning the development of first occupational orientations.

Various aspects can be distinguished with regard to the accomplishment of a developmental task, such as the actual outcome in substantive terms (e.g., the occupation chosen or the quality of romantic involvement achieved). A much more basic feature, on which our investigations focused, refers to the timing in which particular developmental tasks were resolved. Individuals (or groups) may differ in the age at which they found self-sufficient employment or left home for the first time.

Such "developmental timetables" (Feldman and Rosenthal, 1994) are known to show some plasticity under changed social constraints. The paradigmatic case is acculturation in an immigration context. Adaptation to the timing structure of developmental tasks in the host country happens faster, when the influence of the "social clocks" exerted by the cultural values and social institutions is more proximal. The pragmatics of life in the new context can dictate a rather quick adaptation in domains which are not central to the beliefs in the culture of origin (Schmitt-Rodermund and Silbereisen, 1999).

We took such research and results as a model for the potential change of developmental timetables in the former East Germany after unification. The linkage between the change in social institutions and individual development represents a case of "loose coupling," a principle Elder and O'Rand (1995) used in characterizing the mechanisms of social change. Certainly, there is no direct translation of new constraints (and opportunities) into the timing of a particular aspect of competence. Rather, various aspects may be affected in different degrees. Furthermore, as many factors within the family and individuals' personality are involved in the processing of new situational imperatives, substantial individual differences will evolve.

Utilizing this framework, we began a research program on the change in the timing of important developmental tasks in Germany soon after unification, in 1990. In terms of methodology, a cohort approach was chosen, thereby comparing large quota samples from the East and West, gathered in 1991, in the age range between 13 and 29 years (see Fischer, 1992, for details of the sample) and, as equivalent as possible, again in 1996 (see Wiesner and Pickel, 1996). Such a cohort design certainly has its limitations; however, lacking an alternative it gave a handle on a particularly interesting period during the unification process. In the East, in 1991, the peak of experiences of control loss, such as unemployment, was not yet achieved. Moreover, depending on the specific age, our Eastern participants had lived a substantial portion of their adolescence (and even young adulthood) under the old rule. Five years later, the younger age groups had attended elementary school after the school system was changed to the Western mold. Many other social institutions related to major developmental tasks had changed, particularly in the domain of work and related fields (e.g., housing subsidies for young families were reduced, day care was no longer offered at nominal costs, see Adler, 1997). Furthermore, people felt threatened by growing crime rates and, in general, saw a lack of social justice in the East, particularly with regard to important life-course opportunities (Bulmahn, 2000; Noll and Weick, 2000).

Utilizing this design, the timing of the achievement of developmental tasks was investigated through two types of approaches well known in the tradition of life-course research (George, 1993). First, mean trends in the transition ages were compared between regions across cohorts. Second, in order to better understand potential regional and cohort differences in the mechanisms that connect the timing of transitions with past experiences, a select number of socialization variables was used to predict within sample-variation in the timing.

In a series of previous publications (for an overview see Silbereisen and Zinnecker, 1999; Crockett and Silbereisen, 2000; Bynner and Silbereisen, 1999) that mark the departure point for the present analyses, we have studied the timing of a number of important transitions in adolescence. Basically, we distinguished between two domains. One referred to the personal nature of age-typical autonomy in behavior and social relationships. Among the 13- to 19-year-olds, for instance, the timing was analyzed concerning steps into romantic involvement (e.g., the first steady friendship) and to individual freedom (e.g., the age at which one stays out overnight without parental consent). The 20- to 29-year-olds were investigated concerning the age at which they formed a partnership and became a parent the first time.

The second domain concerned the timing of the transition to age-typical work roles, thus exemplifying socio-institutional tasks. Among the 13- to 19-year-olds, the question was the age at which the participants formed their first occupational plans. The 20- to 29-year-olds gave information on the age at which they began to work. It is obvious that this domain is more influenced by social institutions such as school and training. These institutions in particular underwent a profound change in the years after 1990, requiring more exploration and considerate action by the individual, as exemplified by the school-to-work transition (Kornadt, 1996). Consequently, we expected a difference in the median timing in favor of an earlier timing in the East in 1991 as compared to the West, and no (or a smaller) difference between the regions in 1996. Concerning predictors of individual differences within samples, we expected a more exclusive role of status variables (like age) at the expense of individual experiences and decisions (like participation in peer groups) for Easterners compared to Westerners in 1991, and no (or a smaller) difference in this regard in 1996.

Our results basically confirmed this expectation. For instance, with regard to first occupational plans where changes in the school system and vocational guidance had begun in 1991, an earlier timing was observed in the East in 1991, but less so in 1996. Furthermore, we found indications that individual experiences during childhood and adolescence played a greater role in the West in 1991 and in both regions in 1996 (Vondracek, Reitzle, and Silbereisen, 1999). Recently, Silbereisen and Wiesner (2000) conducted analyses concerning the comparison between first romantic involvement and first vocational preferences. For the latter, timing differences between the East and West were expected (in 1991 only). We also predicted that a family's "vulnerability" to unification consequences would play a role in the timing of transitions, however, only concerning the latter aspect of work-related development. More specifically, the following vulnerability variables were introduced: the number of children was included because support for families in general was reduced or became more expensive. Also, due to its roots in structural changes in the industries after unification, unemployment of parents and adolescents should convey the need to adapt to the new challenges. Additional variables were negative attitudes towards unification and descriptions of the housing situation (often tenants had to expect to lose their house or apartment because Western owners reclaimed their property). We acknowledge that all these indicators represent crude proxies for the actual experiences, but believe that they tap into the situational imperatives perceived vis-à-vis the changed opportunities.

The results were other than expected. Concerning romantic involvement, no effect of the vulnerability indicators was expected and in fact none was found. In contrast to our predictions, however, the same applied to the timing of first vocational preferences. Thus, the difference between the regions in 1991 (and, on a smaller scale, in 1996) was confirmed, but it did not make a difference whether people had experienced family vulnerabilities or not.

This result was disappointing, but at closer scrutiny two alternative explanations for the negative outcome turned up (see Silbereisen and Wiesner, 2000, for a discussion). One is that the vulnerability measures we used were too unspecific and remote. Certainly this seems to be true if compared with the highly differentiated pattern of linking experiences in research concerning the reduction of expenditures and consequences of economic hardship (see Conger, Ge, Elder, Lorenz, and Simons, 1994). The other, more radical explanation is that the mode of adaptation is less individual to begin with. Rather, people may adapt because "collective molds" are provided whether they are personally affected or not. Examples for such molds would be commonly shared, propagated views as to what people do (or should do), such as be more cautious with life-course decisions. In more general terms, the question here is whether features of the meso-context (like unemployment rates) or individual experiences are more important (Zelle, 1998). The current study, then, builds on our previous research and takes it a step further by examining how more proximal influences to our two developmental transitions of interest predict their timing.

The remainder of this chapter is organized into three parts. We first give an overview of the aims and methods of the current analyses. Next, results are reported concerning the timing of two developmental transitions. Finally, the chapter concludes with a summary and discussion which emphasizes what we learned about the linkages between social change and developmental timetables.

Aims

In this chapter, our aim is to compare two exemplary transitions in early adulthood, the timing of financial self-support and the timing of leaving home. Both represent important way-stations to adulthood, and both were certainly influenced by the social changes induced by German unification, although this was probably more profound for financial autonomy. We have previously published on these issues (e.g., Juang, Silbereisen, and Wiesner, 1999; Juang, Reitzle, and Silbereisen, in press; Reitzle and Silbereisen, 1999), but the current paper adds a new conceptual and analytical aspect which allows us to better understand the proximal processes which result in the cohort changes observed in our previous research.

Hypotheses

We expect that, in general, the Eastern participants should show more adaptation of the new context in 1996 compared to 1991. As far as the mean trends are concerned, the hypothesis with regard to the age at achieving financial self-support was that this was achieved earlier in the East than in the West in 1991 and, to a lesser degree, in 1996. Further, we hypothesized that the differences between the regions can be "explained away" in part by taking into consideration the level in 1996 of specific delaying experiences (e.g., unemployment and retraining), which often are a precipitation of unification and reflect attempts to cope with the situation. Inter-individual differences in personal and family experiences, however, were expected to have a small effect at best.

With regard to the timing of leaving home, generally speaking we expected a less pronounced effect. The decision to leave one's parents' home probably involves more personal-level experiences, and the changed social institutions (like school or work) certainly are less relevant in setting social clocks. Basically, the same applies to the role of the vulnerability indicators, which should be less relevant here in explaining away regional differences (unfortunately the survey data entail no indicators which would be specific for leaving home). Nevertheless, it should be clear that the changed opportunity structure for education and occupational training may have some influence on the timing of leaving home as well. It is well known, for instance, that extended education delays the taking on of adult roles (Marini, 1986), and this effect may be caught indirectly by the chosen indicators. In sum, what we expect to be more relevant to the decision of leaving home are individual differences in personal and family factors such as peer group involvement or experiencing a parental divorce. Given the greater emphasis on individual autonomy in the East after unification, in 1996 such effects should be stronger than in 1991.

Method

Sample

The two studies concerning the transitions of leaving home and the achievement of financial self-support were each based on two surveys independently conducted in 1991 and 1996 in newly unified Germany. In this cross-sectional approach, 13- to 19-year-old adolescents and 20- to 29-year-old young adults, all of them German nationals, were interviewed. Non-random stratified samples were used that were representative of the respective populations in terms of community size, schooling, and gender. Data were gathered by trained interviewers from reputable commercial survey companies who selected suitable persons according to profiles they were given based on the stratification variables. The present study includes only the older sample of young adults.

In 1991, 1,470 young adults were interviewed in the West and 703 in the East. The studies of the present chapter were based on a sub-sample comprising young adults from vocationally-oriented and academically-oriented school tracks. The former had graduated from "Realschule," an intermediate secondary school in the West, or from "Politechnikum," the unitary technical secondary school in the former East. The latter had graduated from an academically-oriented school track, and had achieved some kind of baccalaureate degree in either system. Graduates from "Hauptschule," the lowest track of the three-tier Western school system, were omitted for the sake of comparability between East and West because there was no equivalent to this school track in former East Germany. For the comparison of the two political regions, it was crucial to also exclude cases who had migrated from the East to the West, and vice versa.

The final 1991 sample comprised 997 Westerners and 665 Easterners. In the West, 479 young adults had graduated from vocationally-oriented school tracks (195 males and 284 females; mean age = 24.4 years, SD = 2.8), whereas 518 had achieved a baccalaureate degree (273 males and 245 females; mean age = 24.2 years, SD = 2.7). The corresponding figures in the East were 454 young adults from vocationally-oriented school tracks (231 males, 223 females; mean age = 24.2 years, SD = 2.7), and 211 from academically-oriented school tracks (110 males and 101 females; mean age = 23.9 years, SD = 2.5).

The original sample of the 1996 survey consisted of 959 young adults interviewed in the West and 850 interviewed in the East. Again, we included only graduates from the above mentioned school tracks, and only young adults who had been living in either part of Germany since birth. The final 1996 sample was comprised of 651 Westerners and 675 Easterners. Among the Western young adults, there were 288 from vocationally-oriented tracks (121 males and 167 females; mean age = 25.1 years, SD = 2.8), and 363 from academically-oriented tracks (177 males and 186 females; mean age = 24.1 years, SD = 2.8). The Eastern sub-sample consisted of 506 vocationals (230 males and 276 females; mean age = 25.1 years, SD = 2.9) and 169 academics (86 males and 83 females; mean age = 24.5 years; SD = 2.9).

Transition variables

A set of questions concerning transitional events were introduced in the following way: "In the course of our lives, some events occur that change us and our lives... If you have already experienced it (a specific event), how old were you at the time?" The specific events in question for our analyses were stated as follows: "Earning enough money to be self-supporting" (Timing of Financial Self-support), and "Leaving the parental home, living separately from parents" (Timing of Leaving Home). Retrospectively reported transitions in the 1991 survey largely fell into the times before unification and thus reflected the peculiarities of the different systems in the East and the West. In contrast, in 1996 when we studied the same age groups of 20- to 29-year-olds, a high share of their retrospectively reported transitions occurred after unification.

Social change-related variables

Participants were asked if and when they had experienced the following three vulnerability events: unemployment as an adolescent, the unemployment of their parents, and termination of a training program or apprenticeship. From these questions we formed dichotomous indicators using the following rationale. A score was given if the event in question happened within the last six years and before the transition of interest. We felt it necessary to impose a time-constraint on the proximity of the event to their current age to ensure that the variables indicated an event happening within the scope of unification. Furthermore, because we are using these events to predict a transition, logically, it should occur before the transition happened. In addition, we used a dummy variable indicating whether young adults were engaged in retraining at the time of assessment.

Individual and family background variables

As a measure of adjustment during adolescence, deviant behaviors were assessed by averaging eight items asking participants to report how frequently (1 = never to 3 = often) they engaged in certain illegal or nonnormative behaviors such as shoplifting These items were based on the work of Lösel (1975). Cronbach's alphas were .82 in 1991 and .79 in 1996. These adolescent experiences were based on retrospective reports by the participant.

In addition, deviant peer affiliation measured the attitudes of the adolescent's peers regarding deviant behaviors. First, it was assessed whether participants belonged to a clique at this age. If not, they were assigned a score of 0. If so, they were then asked to rate how strongly their peers approved if one "gets really smashed" or "skips school" on a scale from 1 (they are strictly against it) to 4 (they don't care about it). These two items were based on the work of Kaplan (1980) and were averaged. A higher score indicated that the peers the adolescent associated with were more problematic. Pearson's correlation of the two items was .58 ($p < .001$) in 1991 and .81 ($p < .001$) in 1996.

Family background was represented by four indicators. First, the level of parental involvement in school activities was retrospectively measured by averaging four items. A sample item was "My parents asked me regularly how I did in school." Cronbach's alpha for parental involvement concerning school activities was .71 in 1991 and .79 in 1996. Second, the degree to which respondents had informed their parents over their whereabouts and activities when they were adolescents was measured with two items, "How often did you tell your mother (father) where you spend your time after school or work?" and "How often did you tell your mother (father) what is going on in your life?" Participants rated these questions from 1 = always to 4 = never. Responses were inverted so that a higher score indicated a higher level of informing. Mothers' and fathers' responses were combined (the mean score was calculated) to create an "informing parent" measure. According to Kerr and Stattin (1998) such a measure is a good proxy to parental monitoring. Cronbach's alphas were .78 in both 1991 and 1996.

Third, respondents were also asked whether and when their parents had divorced, and whether and when they had experienced the death of a parent. From this information, dummy variables were formed on which young adults scored if they had experienced a parental divorce, or death of a parent before age 18. We coded these events only if they had occurred before age 18 because they were deemed particularly influential during the formative years of adolescence. Finally, the number of siblings was recorded.

Data analysis

The analyses concerning the timing of leaving home and the age of financial self-support focus on two different aspects. In the first part of each analysis, we tried to "explain away" differences in the mean ages of transitions between 1991 and 1996 at the aggregate level with the help of predictors reflecting the impact of institutional and economic change in the course of unification. In this first step, we only included Eastern graduates from vocationally oriented tracks because preliminary analyses showed that there were no substantial timing differences among academics and Westerners, in general, neither for leaving home, nor for self-support. In the second part of each analysis, we turned to the prediction of inter-individual differences in the timing of transitions based on the entire cohorts of 1991 and 1996. Timing differences which, of course, exist between academics and non-academics (particularly regarding self-support) were partialed out. Additionally, we always used gender, community size, and federal state as control variables in order to level out minor deviations in the composition of the sub-samples.

As predictors of inter-individual differences, we used the social change-related vulnerability indicators, such as unemployment or retraining, plus the set of variables representing individual adjustment and family resources, and ran the models within each of the different contexts of East and West in 1991 and 1996, respectively. The timing of the two transitions in question was predicted with the help of Cox regressions (Cox, 1972) which belong to the family of methods called survival analysis (see Willett and Singer, 1991; Yamaguchi, 1991). A common problem in the analysis of timing data is that there are usually cases for which the event of interest has not yet occurred, and hence the corresponding age has a missing value ("right censored" cases). Omitting these cases and employing ordinary multiple regressions would lead to downward biased estimates of the timing of the event. Taking into account the ages given for the event as well as the actual ages of the "not yet" cases, the so-called baseline hazard function in Cox regression represents the ratio of the probability of having the event at time (age) t, divided by the probability of not having the event prior to time t for the average person in the sample (Yamaguchi, 1991). In Cox regression, the effects of categorical or continuous predictors on this hazard function are expressed in the form of "risk ratios" or hazard ratios, indicating by which factor the hazard rate is increased (or decreased) as a result of a one-unit change in the predictor at any given time. Hazard ratios above one indicate a higher "risk" of having the event (corresponding to being earlier), whereas ratios below one indicate lower "risk" (corresponding to being later).

For the explanation of mean differences in the timing of transitions between 1991 and 1996 within the Eastern and Western part of Germany, we also used Cox regressions, but in a different way. After the control variables, a dummy representing the year of the survey ($1991 = 0$, $1996 = 1$) was entered as a predictor. The effect of this dummy represented the average difference in the hazard functions of the transitions between 1991 and 1996. In the next step, the social change-related predictors such as unemployment and retraining were included. We were not interested in their effects per se. Instead, the central question was whether the inclusion of these indicators would substantially reduce the former effect of the Year dummy, thus explaining part of the cohort difference. Note that only the vocationally-oriented subsamples were analyzed this way.

Timing of financial self-support

Unification changed the developmental context for young Easterners, specifically with regard to work and personal economic circumstances. In the former Eastern system, highly standardized and sponsored pathways into work preformed by a national plan, employment guarantees at the first threshold (transition from school to occupational training) and the second threshold (transition from training into full-time employment), allowed the vast majority of young people from vocationally-oriented school tracks to achieve their financial independence within a narrow age range, and at the earliest time possible, at age 18 or 19 (Reitzle and Silbereisen, 1998). In other words, there were few individual options, concerning occupational choice (Autsch, 1995; Burkhardt, 1992), and extended education or retraining. It was also true, however, that careful career planning and adjustments to the labor market were not needed, because the application for a training position determined one's career pathway for many years or even the entire working life (Bertram, 1994). With unification, young Easterners were confronted with the entirely changed requirements of a highly competitive labor market that did not value many of the traditional qualifications. Employment in sectors such as agriculture, mining, energy, and manufacturing dropped between 50 and 80 percent (Baethge and Wolf, 1995). With the introduction of the Western school system and the Vocational Education Act, a greater variety of options emerged. In order to profit from the new opportunities, however, young people had to show explorative behaviors, initiative and planfulness, including adjustments to the market to a formerly unknown extent.

Explaining cohort differences

Against this backdrop, we expected, on average, a later transition into financial independence in 1996 as compared to 1991, due to factors which are closely related to the institutional and economic changes characteristic of the East. The results of two hierarchical Cox regressions are summarized in Table 9.1. Besides the control variables, the first regression only included the Year dummy. In the following analysis, the block of social change-related factors was tested for an attenuating effect on the coefficient of the Year dummy.

The initial risk coefficient of the Year dummy, which represents the average timing difference regarding the achievement of self-support, was .65, indicating delayed self-support in 1996. In order to get an impression

Table 9.1 *Explaining away cohort differences between 1991 and 1996 in the timing of financial self-support: Easterners from vocational school tracks*

Variable	Exp (B)	Exp (B)
Measurement year	.65***	.74***
Adolescent unemployment		.41***
Terminated training		.55*
Retraining		.74
Parental unemployment		.69*
Overall chi-square (df)	53.37(13)	107.50(17)***
% censored cases	8.7	8.7

Note: Controlled for gender, community size, and federal state
$^*p < .05$, $^{***}p < .001$

of the effect size, it is more illustrative to invert the coefficient ($1/.65 =$ 1.52), and express the effect in terms of "being earlier" in 1991. To put it this way, the same-aged cohorts assessed in 1991 had a 52 percent higher hazard of becoming self-supportive as compared to their 1996 successors. When the additional predictors were entered, the coefficient actually moved closer to one (.74), i.e., became weaker. In terms of the inverted coefficient (1.34), the 1991 cohorts had only a 34 percent higher hazard when the proxies for social change were taken into account. In other words, roughly a third of the 1996 young Eastern adults' "delay" in self-support could be attributed to unemployment and extended education as represented by our four predictors.

Inter-individual differences in timing

For the prediction of inter-individual differences in the timing of financial self-support within each region and year, individual and family background factors were added to the indicators of social change. For young Easterners in 1991, we did not expect the individual and family variables to account for much timing variability because most of the transitions into self-support had occurred before unification when pathways into employment were highly standardized. This should have changed among the 1996 cohorts with a considerable number of transitions occurring after unification, thereby requiring more individual competence and resources. This, of course, holds true for the Western situation, irrespective of the year. The results of Cox Regressions separated for West and East and 1991 and 1996 are reported in Table 9.2.

Throughout the four sub-samples studied, the control variable school track had a substantial effect on the timing of financial self-support, indicating that graduates from academic tracks achieved financial self-support later than their peers from vocationally-oriented tracks. This came as no surprise, of course, because students from academically-oriented tracks spend two or even three years longer in school before starting vocational training or even college studies.

Altogether, the individual and family background factors do not substantially contribute to the prediction of interindividual timing differences. There are, however, a couple of exceptions. Western young adults in 1991 who reported higher levels of deviant behavior during their adolescent years achieved financial self-support earlier. In addition, Easterners assessed in 1996 achieved self-support earlier the more siblings they had. A plausible interpretation would be that children from big families are pushed to early autonomy instead of prolonged education for economic reasons. Although the size of the effect was not big, this finding

Table 9.2 *Hierarchical Cox Regressions predicting timing of financial self-support by region and year: Exp (B), final step*

Variable	West		East	
	1991	1996	1991	1996
School track	.26***	.30***	.30***	.52***
Gender	1.12	1.19	1.02	1.15
Number of siblings	1.01	1.08	1.02	1.10*
Parent death before age 18	1.05	.86	1.25	1.26
Parent divorce before age 18	1.03	1.19	1.02	1.06
Informing parents	1.00	1.01	.91	.96
Parental school involvement	1.04	.94	.89	.86
Adolescent deviant behavior	1.50**	1.12	1.15	1.08
Deviant peer affiliation	.95	1.05	.97	1.04
Retraining	.93	1.00	.75	.76
Adolescents' unemployment	.70*	.43**	.30**	.50***
Parents' unemployment	.74	1.25	.21***	.58***
Terminated training	.86	.67	.83	.49*
Overall chi-square (df)	321.94(29)***	174.46(29)***	197.61(24)***	136.63(24)***
% censored cases	32.1	35.7	18.4	18.6

Note: Controlled for community size and federal state by entering it as the first step in all analyses
*p < .05, **p < .01, ***p < .001

showed that family background started to matter among the later Eastern cohorts.

A consistently delaying factor for young adults' self-support was the experience of own unemployment during the school-to-work transition, irrespective of region and year. This also applied to Easterners assessed in 1991. Some of them probably have become unemployed shortly after unification and had never achieved financial independence until the time of the survey. Independent of adolescents' unemployment, in the East but not the West, parents' unemployment also delayed financial self-support.

Besides these single findings, the bigger picture for the East is one of unification-related events predominantly accounting for the variability in the timing of self-support in 1991, even more so in 1996, when termination of training also became a substantial predictor. Note also that the proportion of those who were already financially self-supportive was much higher in the East.

Timing of leaving home

In these analyses we focus on when one leaves the parental home for the first time. Some of the social changes mentioned earlier with regard to the transition to financial self-support may have an influence on home leaving as well. For instance, in the East, the growing availability of options to enter into further training may delay the timing of leaving home, as there is a well-established positive correlation between higher levels of education with the age of making adult-oriented transitions (Marini, 1986). Participating in further training may delay an accumulation of the financial resources necessary to move out and establish a household of one's own. However, it may also be the case that the growing availability of options may occur in a region that is beyond a commutable distance, thus encouraging the young adult to leave home in order to take advantage of new training options. Therefore, we do expect to see some difference between 1991 and 1996 with regard to a change in the timing of home leaving in the East. However, this more "private" developmental transition involves more personal-level experiences than the timing of financial self-support. In other words, there is not a particular social institution which would dictate that young adults at a certain age must leave the parental home. Thus, this transition is not so tightly bound, as in becoming self-supportive, to the macro-level structural changes during unification (e.g., in the school and training systems). Consequently, more proximal micro-system level variables, such as the quality of relationship with parents or experiencing a parental divorce (Mitchell, 1994) may be more influential on the timing of home leaving. These indicators of "social capital" (Coleman, 1988) available in the family can either delay (as with having parents who are more involved in their children's schooling), or accelerate (as with the child experiencing a parental divorce) the timing of when the young adult leaves home. In sum, because of the more personal nature of the timing of home leaving relying more heavily on familial factors, we do not expect this transition to be as profoundly affected by unification changes concerning school and training as those reported earlier.

Table 9.3 *Explaining away cohort differences between 1991 and 1996 in the timing of leaving home: Easterners from vocational school tracks*

Variable	Exp (B)	Exp (B)
Measurement year	1.35	1.34
Retraining		1.18
Overall chi-square (df)	95.89 (13)***	96.88 (14)***
% censored cases	29.2	29.2

Note: Controlled for gender, community size, and federal state
***$p < .001$

Explaining cohort differences

Analyses concerning home leaving were conducted in a similar way as with financial self-support. In the East, there was a significant difference in the hazard functions between 1991 and 1996. As indicated in Table 9.3, Easterners assessed in 1996 had a 35 percent greater hazard of leaving the parental home as compared to their 1991 predecessors. Thus, regarding the personal decision of when one chooses to leave the parental home, we see a slight change in this biographical transition under the unification process for vocationally-oriented people. Unlike the results with financial self-support, there was not a delay, but a speeding up, of this transition to leave home.

In order to "explain away" the cohort differences, it would have been straightforward to enter the same predictors as in the case of self-support. A closer look into the data, however, revealed that three of the four social change-related variables, namely, young adults' and parents' unemployment and termination of training, were entirely confounded with the fact of still living in the parental home. Technically speaking, these events only occurred among censored cases, thereby unduly inflating coefficients as well as their standard errors. But still, this coincidence bears valid information. For instance, concerning experiencing unemployment, no young adult who experienced unemployment in the last six years left home, which is not too surprising. Unemployment may indicate a lack of self-sufficient financial resources, which may then render one more likely to be dependent on parents. Subsequently, this will prevent, or delay, the young adult from leaving home.

Thus, only the "retraining" variable could be included in the present analyses. As the coefficients in Table 9.3 show, retraining did not significantly predict the timing of leaving home and did not account for the average cohort difference. Perhaps other reasons not related to the change in educational systems, such as availability of housing, could better explain the cohort differences.

Interindividual difference in timing

In the last set of analyses we shifted the focus from predicting cohort differences to predicting interindividual differences in the timing of leaving home. As with the financial self-support analyses, the predictors included individual and family background factors in addition to the social change-related predictors. For the above mentioned reasons, again only the retraining indicator could be used. Table 9.4 shows the final step of the analyses, separately for region and year.

In all four analyses, school track did not predict timing differences with respect to leaving home. Gender, however, proved to be a substantial predictor irrespective of region and year. Females were always more likely to leave home earlier than males. In the West, several individual and family

Table 9.4 *Hierarchical Cox Regressions predicting timing of leaving the parental home by region and year: Exp (B), final step*

Variable	West		East	
	1991	1996	1991	1996
School track	.97	.97	1.10	1.12
Gender	1.70***	1.67***	1.53***	1.84***
Number of siblings	1.09*	1.00	1.01	1.18***
Parent death before age 18	.73	1.03	1.03	1.12
Parent divorce before age 18	1.11	1.40*	.95	1.07
Informing parents	.86*	.82*	.86	.90
Parental school involvement	.84*	.91	1.11	.87
Adolescent deviant behavior	1.52**	1.59**	1.14	1.34*
Deviant peer affiliation	.90**	1.03	1.08	1.07
Retraining	1.00	.94	1.11	.77
Overall chi-square (df)	141.82(26)***	92.79(26)***	55.48(21)***	117.53(21)***
% censored cases	36.6	29.2	36.3	24.0

Note: Controlled for community size and federal state by entering it as the first step in all analyses

*p < .05, **p < .01, ***p < .001

predictors showed significant effects on timing. Factors such as engaging in higher levels of deviant behavior as an adolescent contributed to an earlier timing of leaving home. In contrast, factors such as informing parents of whereabouts and activities as an adolescent tended to delay the timing of leaving home, indicating that adolescents who enjoy more social capital resources in the home tend to stay longer.

The family background variables did not significantly predict the timing of home leaving in the East in 1991. However, five years later, individual and family factors do significantly predict interindividual differences in the timing of leaving home, tentatively suggesting social change at work. For Eastern young adults in pre-unification Germany the timing of home leaving may have been determined primarily by structural and not individual and family factors (Silbereisen, Meschke, and Schwarz, 1996). By 1996 however, Easterners look more similar to their Western counterparts with individual and family factors coming into play. Finally, retraining did not significantly predict the timing of leaving home for young adults regardless of region or year.

A comparison with the results concerning financial self-support revealed that with the East sample, the social-change variables (e.g., retraining) had an impact on the timing of becoming self-supportive and not the family background variables. However, this trend was reversed for the more personal, private transition of leaving the parental home – the family background variables had a strong impact while the social change-related variable did not.

Discussion

The achievement of particular developmental tasks and related way-stations is a prime marker of competence in adolescence and young adulthood. Of particular interest is the timing of such transitions. From our previous research on acculturation among immigrants, we know that timetables in domains such as behavioral autonomy and social relationships undergo a gradual change once the ecological transition has taken place. Admittedly, in the case of German unification it was not the population that moved but the social institutions, and yet we were safe to predict an adaptation of the timing in the achievement of those developmental tasks on which the change of social institutions had an impact. A case in point is the transformation of the systems concerning education and work, from the macro level of the legal regulations to the proximal level of everyday organization and advice.

The timing of financial self-support and the timing of leaving home were the focus of the present paper. The first aim was to demonstrate that differences in the mean trends in the East between 1991 and 1996 would disappear in part when considering individuals' unification-related experiences. Concerning the age at the achievement of financial self-support, the prediction was confirmed. While there was no difference between the cohorts in the West, in the East the transition age in 1996 was higher than in 1991 as reported previously (Reitzle and Silbereisen, 1999). Moreover, once we considered adolescent and parental unemployment in the previous years and whether one had terminated an occupational training program (independently of each other), the difference was reduced remarkably. In other words, these particular events are candidates for experiences which link the changed social constraints and individual timetables. Tentatively, the same applied for the attendance of retraining programs.

Concerning the age at which the young left home, parallel analyses again revealed a cohort difference in that the timing in the East was earlier in 1996 compared to the timing in 1991. As expected, unemployment and the other vulnerability variables did not play a role in explaining this cohort difference. Consequently, the reasons behind the earlier timetable for leaving home in the East in 1996 are probably not due to the time spent out of gainful employment.

Thus, the good news is that we were able to identify some of the likely proximal processes which bring about the change in the timing of financial self-support between 1991 and 1996 in the East. As the same variables did not play an equivalent role in the timing of first vocational preferences among the adolescents investigated by Silbereisen and Wiesner 2000, the linkage presumably is a rather specific one. Given the fact that own unemployment and self-initiated termination of a training contract were important, the upward shift in the mean timing may be rooted in the extra time spent without an income from own work (unemployment benefits and other substitute payments would not count as financial self-support), thus delaying this transition. At closer scrutiny, however, the effect observed cannot rely solely on this phenomenon. As the independent effect of parental unemployment shows, other linkages are implied as well.

Although we have no specific indication in the present data, the groups' further occupational formation may have been delayed due to the stressed financial family resources which did not allow one to finish training in due time. Or, the delay may have been due to the necessity to take up a job which did not return enough to become financially independent. Alternatively, confronted with parental unemployment the young may have concluded that a re-orientation of their occupational plans and training is required, for instance in favor of a higher and better qualification, which then leads to a longer period of financial dependency.

At any rate, it is obvious that these arguments would not also apply to the timing of first vocational preferences as studied previously, or the age at which the young left the parental home. Parental unemployment certainly could be informative for one's own plans, particularly if it is rooted in an inadequate match between qualification and demand on the labor market, but the first steps in the formation of an occupational perspective are probably fueled more by relatively broad interests, and their timing would thus not be affected. This is not to say, however, that the content of the occupational plans would not show unification-related cohort differences. Quite the contrary, previous analyses showed that in the East in 1996 (but not 1991) there was a larger discordance between parents' occupation and adolescents' plans than was common in the West (thus indicating an interruption in the generational transmission as is typical of times of social change), and substantively the choices of occupations reflected the new priorities after German unification (Vondracek, Silbereisen, Reitzle, and Wiesner, 1999). As reported, the adolescents in 1996 preferred occupations in financing, trades, and the public sector much more than their agemates five years earlier. Moreover, those in 1996, were less likely to prefer occupations related to the traditional industries (which were particularly hit by the structural changes following unification).

As far as the leaving home age is concerned, again one could have expected unemployment and the other vulnerability variables to play a role, but obviously the linkage is not proximal and specific enough. For those in pre-unification East Germany, scarcity of apartments was a reality (Nauck, 1993). In 1996 these structural restrictions were no longer in place. Thus, perhaps it was this increased availability of housing that acted as an incentive to leave home earlier in 1996 compared to 1991 for Easterners. Unfortunately, we did not have data measuring these types of structural changes that may have been more relevant to home leaving.

The second approach pursued in this chapter concerned the prediction of interindividual differences in the timing of the transitions by markers of socialization experiences. Before we turn to a discussion of the results, some remarks are in place concerning the selection of predictors. Obviously, this did not represent a comprehensive list of events and predictors known to play a role in the timing of the respective transitions. In earlier papers on particular transitions we were able to cover more of the known risk factors (within the limits of the survey data available), but in the current comparative analyses we confined ourselves to variables which are likely to be relevant for both domains. Take the number of siblings as an example. If high, this indicator of the family structure reflects a possible shortage of resources available to the family and thus, benefits a child could gain from remaining dependent on the family (Mitchell, 1994). In other words, other things being equal, one could assume that youth from larger families leave the parental home earlier and also attain financial self-support earlier in life – both are probably related to a stronger move to become independent. Similar arguments would apply to the loss of a parent due to death or divorce.

Compared to the analyses on leaving home, it is clear that interindividual differences in the timing of financial self-support were not affected by parental investments and peer affiliations, in neither the regions nor time periods. Certainly this is not to say that these micro-contexts do not play a role – the effects reported were net of (large) school track effects which of course catch some socialization differences. The main action with regard to financial self-support, however, involved the vulnerability indicators, and here an interesting difference between the regions turned up. Whereas in the West unemployment of the young delayed economic independence, in the East it was parents' unemployment as well, plus in 1996 whether the young had precociously finished a training contract (e.g., given up an apprenticeship). In other words, one's own fate with regard to financial self-support in the East was tied to the employment and thus the economic situation (and certainly related issues concerning psychological well-being) of the entire family. This makes a difference concerning the role of co-development within families between the regions.

Similar to the financial self-support transition, there was a regional difference in leaving home, namely, that the role of socialization variables was more pronounced in the West. Nevertheless, in 1996 there was a hint as to a possible change in the East towards the Western mold (e.g., affiliation with deviant peers became as important in the East as in the West).[1] Further, whereas the transition to financial self-support was strongly influenced by school track, in the case of leaving home it was gender.

A few caveats need to be noted. Admittedly, the cohort design realized in the youth surveys conducted in 1991 and 1996 was far from being the perfect vehicle to study the role of social change, and the research protocol was not especially suited for our purpose. Prominent among the weaknesses are the reliance on retrospective self-report, but in line with the literature we see this as permissible (Brewin, Andrews, and Gotlib, 1993). Further, the lack of variables which would tap directly into the linkage between the new challenges and individual action is important. Nevertheless, in our view the present study was especially informative on the What and, to a certain degree, the How of the unification-related changes in the timetabling of transitions.

Seen in the greater perspective of research on the linkages between social change and individual development – what did we learn from the current analyses? Certainly, there was support for our notion that in order to change developmental timetables a change in social constraints which have a rather direct relationship to the particular competence is required. Thus, as expected, the timing of financial self-support revealed adjustments in the East when observed five years into unification, whereas this was not the case with leaving home. This view was further supported by the fact that experiences like unemployment which (certainly in the East) are a precipitation of unification-related structural difficulties, played a role in explaining the shift in the timetabling between 1991 and 1996. Again, in line with our predictors this was a specific linkage to the timing of financial self-support and had no effect on leaving home.

According to other results of our research program the current transitions were not the only ones which were affected by unification. Juang and Silbereisen (in press) recently reported that family-related transitions (marriage, giving birth to a child) took place considerably later in the East in 1996 compared to 1991. Traditionally, the timing of these events was earlier in the East than in the West. The adaptation to the new challenges and insecurities, however, again revealed the specificity of the linkage between the particular life circumstances and the changed social constraints. On looking closer, the trend towards later transitions was confined to women, whereas men reported pretty much the same pattern as in 1991 (and were not too much different from their Western counterparts anyway). More importantly, among the females it was those with a vocational track background in particular who shifted. It is clear, indeed, that this group was hit the most by unification-related changes in the opportunity structures (Heinz, 1996).

Thus, the adaptations we found (for more examples see the series of books edited by Zinnecker and Silbereisen, 1996; Silbereisen, Vaskovics, and Zinnecker, 1996; Silbereisen and Zinnecker, 1999) not only seem to take more time than expected, probably due to the multi-level linkages from institutions through families to the individuals ("loose coupling"; Elder and O'Rand, 1995), but also seem to be rather specific to the particular constraints and life circumstances. In our view this specificity indirectly illuminates the nature of the processes involved. Thus, when elsewhere (Silbereisen and Wiesner, 2000) we considered the possibility that it is not so much individuals' experiences with the unification-related events which trigger change in vocational interests, but rather collective experiences (e.g., views propagated through the media or attitudes based on the perception of aggregate trends), we are now more assured that the experiences investigated were too unspecific for the development of vocational interests.

Based on the current research, a much more comprehensive search for the particular new challenges and the particular situational imperatives with regard to major developmental tasks should rank high on the agenda. Now we have illuminated some general links (like job-related insecurities), but the relevant linkages need to be more finely tuned for the respective task. Unfortunately, the present survey data will not be of much help due to the lack of relevant information (see Silbereisen and Zinnecker, 1999).

An often asked question in Germany is whether all regional differences in developmental timetables will disappear once the societal structures are identical across the country. In our view the answer is a qualified No – some of the differences, for instance, concerning the high rate of single parents in the East as compared to the West, were not confined to post-war societies but date back much further, based on a traditional North-South divide. Consequently, it is unlikely that the change in the supports for such families alone would change the pattern. Some societal innovations in the former East, like the "Jugendweihe," a non-religious transitional ceremony to adolescence, probably will be maintained, in spite of the change in the ideological background, because the event became "functionally autonomous" due to its role as a family ritual (including gifts for the young, which often mark the transition to new freedoms, like a motor bike).

NOTE

1 A reviewer expressed concerns that potential predictors of interindividual differences in the timing of transitions were overlooked due to multicollinearity of predictors in our Cox Regressions. Following his suggestions, we additionally examined the bivariate relationships between each of our predictors and the timing of transitions in question. With financial self-support the results did not change considerably. With leaving home we find that the participants from the East in 1996 look even more similar to those from the West in that each of the parenting and peer variables are now significant predictors of leaving home. These results emphasize the difference reported between the financial self-support and leaving home transitions – the financial self-support transition is more "institutionalized" as demonstrated by few individual/family factors predicting this transition before and after unification. Concerning leaving home, however, we do see a difference in the East after unification. Individual/family factors were not linked to leaving home for Easterners in 1991. However, by 1996, many of these factors did predict leaving home as was the case with the Westerners. The emerging salience of individual/family factors as opposed to social change factors in the East suggests that leaving home is a more private, less institutionalized transition. Hence, it is less susceptible to unification-related changes as may be the case with financial self-support.

ACKNOWLEDGMENTS

The research reported in this chapter was conducted with the support of the German Research Council (Si 296/14-4,5; Principal Investigator R. K. Silbereisen). We want to thank the other principal investigators of our interdisciplinary research consortium (J. Zinnecker, L. Vaskovics) and all the participants of the studies.

REFERENCES

Adler, M. A. (1997). Social change and declines in marriage and fertility in Eastern Germany. *Journal of Marriage and the Family*, 59, 31–49.

Autsch, B. (1995). Ausgangsbedingungen bei der Umstellung des DDR-Berufsbildungssystems aus der Sicht rechtlicher und organisatorischer Rahmenbedingungen [The initial conditions in the transformation of the occupational training system of the former GDR from a legal and organizational perspective]. In Bundesinstitut für Berufsbildung (eds.), *Berufsausbildung in den neuen Bundesländern: Daten, Analysen, Perspektiven*. Bielefeld: Bertelsmann, 15–29.

Baethge, M., and Wolf, H. (1995). Continuity and change in the "German model" of industrial relations. In R. Locke, T. Kochan, and M. Priore (eds.), *Employment relations in a changing world economy*, Cambridge, MA: The MIT Press, 231–262.

Bertram, B. (1994). Berufswahl in der Planwirtschaft – Auswirkungen in der Marktwirtschaft [Occupational choices in the plan economy – consequences in the market economy]. In B. Bertram, W. Bien, T. Gericke, M. Höckner, L. Lappe, and H. Schröpfer (eds.), *Gelungener Start – unsichere Zukunft? Der Übergang von der Schule in die Berufsbildung* [*Happy beginning – insecure future? The transition from school to occupational training*], München: Verlag Deutsches Jugendinstitut, 53–90.

Brewin, C. R., Andrews, B., and Gotlib, I. H. (1993). Psychopathology and early experience: a reappraisal of retrospective reports. *Psychological Bulletin*, 113, 82–98.

Bulmahn, T. (2000). Freiheit, Sicherheit und Gerechtigkeit. [Freedom, security, and justice]. *Informationsdienst Soziale Indikatoren*, 23, 5–8.

Burkhardt, D. (1992). Strukturen der Berufsbildung in der DDR [Structures of vocational training in the GDR]. In Bundesinstitut für Berufsbildung (ed.), *Neue Länder – Neue Berufsausbildung? Prozesse, Probleme und Perspektiven des Übergangs der Berufsausbildung in den neuen Bundesländern* [New Laender – new occupational training? Processes, problems, and perspectives concerning the transition into occupational training in the new Laender]. Berlin: Bundesinstitut für Berufsbildung, 31–49.

Bynner, J., and Silbereisen, R. K. (eds.) (1999). *Adversity and challenge in life in the New Germany and England*. Hampshire, London: Macmillan.

Coleman, J. (1988). Social capital in the creation of human capital. *American Journal of Sociology*, 94, 95–120.

Conger, R. D., Ge, X., Elder, G. H., Lorenz, F. O., and Simons, R. L. (1994). Economic stress, coercive family process, and developmental problems of adolescents. *Child Development*, 65, 541–61.

Cox, D. R. (1972). Regression models and life tables. *Journal of the Royal Statistical Society*, 34, 187–202.

Crockett, L. A., and Silbereisen, R. K. (eds.) (2000). *Negotiating adolescence in times of social change*. Cambridge: Cambridge University Press.

Dekovic, M., Noom, M. J., and Meeus, W. (1997). Expectations regarding development during adolescence: parental and adolescent perceptions. *Journal of Youth and Adolescence*, 26, 253–72.

Eberstadt, N. (1994). Demographic shocks after Communism: Eastern Germany, 1989–1993. *Population and Development Review*, 20, 137–52.

Elder, G. H. (1998). The life course and human development. In R. M. Lerner and W. Damon (eds.) *Handbook of child psychology*. vol. 1: *Theoretical models of human development*, New York: Wiley, 939–99.

Elder, G. H., and O'Rand, A. M. (1995). Adult lives in a changing society. In K. S. Cook, G. A. Fine, and J. S. House (eds.) *Sociological perspectives on social psychology*. Needham Heights, MA: Allyn and Bacon, 452–75.

Feldman, S. S., and Rosenthal, D. A. (1994). Culture makes a difference or does it? A comparison of adolescents in Hong Kong, Australia, and the United States. In R. K. Silbereisen and E. Todt (eds.), *Adolescence in context*. New York: Springer, 99–120.

Fischer, A. (1992). Zur Stichprobe [Sample Description]. In Jugendwerk der Deutschen Shell (ed.), *Jugend 92*, Vol. 4. Opladen, Germany: Leske and Budrich.

George, L. K. (1993). Sociological perspectives on life transitions. *Annual Review of Sociology*, 19, 353–73.

Havighurst, R. J. (1972). Developmental tasks and education (3rd ed.). New York: Longmans, Green.

Heinz, W. R. (1996). Berufsverläufe im Transformationsprozess [Career trajectories during the social and political transformation]. In S. E. Hormuth, W. R. Heinz, H. J. Kornadt, H. Sydow, and G. Trommsdorff (eds.), *Individuelle Entwicklung, Bildung und Berufsverläufe* [Individual development, education, and occupational career]. Opladen, Germany: Leske and Budrich, 273–329.

Juang, L. P., and Silbereisen, R. K. (in press). Übergänge zum Erwachsenenalter – Wie hängen sie zusammen? [Transitions to adulthood: What goes with what?]. In R. Pekrun and S. Walper (eds.). *Familie und Entwicklung – Perspektiven der Familienpsychologie* [Family and development – Perspectives of family psychology]. Goettingen: Hogrefe.

Juang, L., Silbereisen, R. K., and Wiesner (1999). Predictors for leaving the parental home in young adults raised in former East and West Germany in 1996: a replication and extension of a 1991 study. *Journal of Marriage and the Family*, 61, 505–15.

Juang, L., Reitzle, M., and Silbereisen, R. K. (2000). The adaptability of transitions to adulthood under social change: the case of German unification. *European Review of Applied Psychology*, 50, 275–82.

Kaplan, H. (1980). Deviant behavior and self enhancement. *Journal of Youth and Adolescence*, 7, 253–77.

Kerr, M., and Stattin, H. (1998, June). *How general is the relation between monitoring and good adjustment?* Paper presented at the biennial conference of the European Association for Research on Adolescence, Budapest.

Kornadt, H. J. (1996). Erziehung und Bildung im Transformationsprozeß [Development and education in the process of transformation]. In S. E. Hormuth, W. R. Heinz, H.-J. Kornadt, H. Sydow, and G. Trommsdorff (eds.). *Individuelle Entwicklung, Bildung und Berufsverläufe* [Individual development, education, and occupational career]. Opladen: Leske and Budrich, 273–329.

Lösel, F. (1975). *Handlungskontrolle und Jugenddelinquenz: Persönlichkeitspsychologische Erklärungsansätze delinquenten Verhaltens – theoretische Integration und empirische Überprüfung* [Behavior control and juvenile delinquency: personality psychological framework for delinquent behaviors – theoretical integration and empirical testing.] In University of Erlangen-Nürnberg: SFB22 (ed.), *Sozialisation und Kommunikation*, 4, 1–279. Stuttgart, Germany: Enke Verlag.

Marini, M. M. (1986). Initiation of the process of adult role entry. *Population and Environment*, 8, 240–74.

Marvin, G. M. (1995). Two steps back and one step forward: East German women since the fall of the wall. *Humanity and Society*, 19, 37–52.

Mitchell, B. A. (1994). Family structure and leaving the nest: a social resource perspective. *Sociological Perspectives*, 37, 651–71.

Masten, A. S., Coatsworth, J. D., Neemann, J., Gest, S. D., Tellegen, A., and Garmezy, N. (1995). The structure and coherence of competence from childhood through adolescence. *Child Development*, 66, 1635–59.

Nauck, B. (1993). Sozialstrukturelle Differenzierung der Lebensbedingungen von Kindern in West-und Ostdeutschland [Social structural differences of living conditions of children in West and East Germany]. In M. Markefka and B. Nauck (eds.), *Handbuch der Kindheitsforschung* [Handbook of studies in childhood]. Neuwied, Germany: Luchterhand, 143–63.

Noll, H.-H., and Weick, S. (2000). Bürger empfinden weniger Furcht vor Kriminalität [Citizens less sensitive to fears of criminality]. *Informationsdienst Soziale Indikatoren*, 23, 1–5.

Reitzle, M., and Silbereisen, R. K. (1998, July). *The role of individual variability and institutional structure in the timing of the school-to-work transition.* Paper presented at the XVth Biennal ISSBD Meetings, Berne, Switzerland.

Reitzle, M., and Silbereisen, R. K. (1999). Der Zeitpunkt materieller Unabhängigkeit und seine Folgen für das Erwachsenwerden. [Timing of financial self-support and its consequences for becoming adult] *Entwicklung im sozialen Wandel*. [Development under social change]. Weinheim: Psychologie Verlags Union, 131–52.

Schimpl-Neimanns, B. (2000). Hat die Bildungsexpansion zum Abbau der sozialen Ungleichheit in der Bildungsbeteiligung geführt? [Has the expansion of education led to the increase in social disparity of educational participation?]. Mannheim: Zentrum für Umfragen, Methoden und Analysen: ZUMA-Arbeitsbericht, 02/2000.

Schmitt-Rodermund, E., and Silbereisen, R. K. (1999). Determinants of differential acculturation of developmental timetables among adolescent immigrants to Germany. *International Journal of Psychology*, 34, 219–33.

Silbereisen, R. K. (1999). Einleitung [Introduction]. In R. K. Silbereisen and J. Zinnecker (eds.), *Entwicklung im sozialen Wandel* [Development under social change]. Weinheim: Psychologie Verlags Union, 13–38.

Silbereisen, R. K., Meschke, L. L., and Schwarz, B. (1996). Leaving the parental home: predictors for young adults raised in former East and West Germany. In J. A. Graber and J. S. Dubas (eds.), *Leaving home: Understanding the transition to adulthood.* San Francisco: Jossey-Bass, 71-81.

Silbereisen, R. K., Vaskovics, L. A., and Zinnecker, J. (eds.) (1996). *Jungsein in Deutschland.* [*Being young in Germany*] Opladen: Leske and Budrich.

Silbereisen, R. K., and Wiesner, M. (2000). Cohort change in adolescent developmental timetables after German unification: trends and possible reasons. In J. Heckhausen (ed.), *Motivational psychology of human development: Developing motivation and motivating development,* Amsterdam: Elsevier, 271–84.

Silbereisen, R. K., and Zinnecker, J. (1999). *Entwicklung im sozialen Wandel.* [Development under social change] Weinheim: Psychologie Verlags Union.

Vondracek, F. W., Reitzle, M., and Silbereisen, R. K. (1999). The influence of changing contexts and historical time on the timing of initial vocational choices. In R. K. Silbereisen and A. von Eye (eds.), *Growing up in times of social change.* New York: DeGruyter, 151–69.

Vondracek, F. W., Silbereisen, R. K., Reitzle, M., and Wiesner, M. (1999). Vocational preferences of early adolescents: their development in social context. *Journal of Adolescent Research*, 14, 267–88.

Wiesner, M., and Pickel, G. (1996). Stichprobe und Methoden [Sampling and methods]. In R. K. Silbereisen, L. A. Vaskovics, and J. Zinnecker (eds.) *Jungsein in Deutschland* [Being young in Germany]. Opladen: Leske and Budrich, 369–80.

Willett, J. B., and Singer, J. D. (1991). How long did it take? Using survival analysis in educational and psychological research. In L. Collins and J. L. Horn (eds.), *Best methods for analysis of change: Recent advances, unanswered questions, future directions.* Washington, DC: American Psychological Association, 263–304.

Yamaguchi, K. (1991). *Event history analysis. Applied Social Research Methods Series.* vol. 28. Newbury Park: Sage.

Zapf, W. (1996). Zwei Geschwindigkeiten in Ost- und Westdeutschland [Two speeds in East and West Germany]. In M. Diewald and K. U. Mayer (eds.), *Zwischenbilanz der Wiedervereinigung. Strukturwandel und Mobilität im Transformationsprozeß* [An interim assessment of reunification. Structural change and mobility in the process of transformation]. Opladen: Leske and Budrich, 317–28.

Zapf, W., and Habich, R. (1999). *Die Wohlfahrtsentwicklung in der Bundesrepublik Deutschland 1949 bis 1999* [Welfare trends in the Federal Republic of

Germany 1949 to 1999]. Wissenschaftszentrum Berlin Jahrbuch. Berlin, Germany: Wissenschaftszentrum.

Zelle, C. (1998). Soziale und liberale Wertorientierungen: Versuch einer situativen Erklaerung der Unterschiede zwichen Ost- und Westdeutschen [Social and liberal value orientations: An approach toward situative explanations of differences between East and West Germans]. *Aus Politik und Zeitgeschichte*, 41/42, 24–36.

Zinnecker, J., and Silbereisen, R. K. (eds.) (1996, 2nd ed. 1998). *Kindheit in Deutschland. Aktueller Survey über Kinder und ihre Eltern* [*Childhood in Germany: a survey of children and their parents*]. Weinheim, München: Juventa.

Part V

Life transitions

10   Developmental regulation of life-course transitions: a control theory approach

Jutta Heckhausen

A control theory approach

In this chapter a control-theoretical approach to developmental regulation in adulthood is proposed (Heckhausen, 1999). The first section addresses the fundamental challenges posed for the individual's developmental regulation across the life-span, as they result from the general shift in the developmental ecology towards greater risks for decline and fewer chances for growth at increasing age levels during adulthood. In this section, I also discuss a repertoire of control strategies based on the life-span theory of control (Heckhausen and Schulz, 1995; Schulz and Heckhausen, 1996) and their orchestration by the individual's attempts to optimize development in terms of maximizing age appropriateness, manage inter-domain trade-offs, and maintain diversity. After this wide-angle view of life-span development and its regulation, the chapter's perspective zooms to the pursuit of major developmental goals. For each developmental goal there is an age-based trajectory of opportunities and constraints, which reflects first increasing, then peaking, and finally decreasing potential to realize the respective developmental goal (Heckhausen, 2000a). Based on this analysis, an action-theoretical model of developmental regulation around developmental deadlines is introduced. Exemplar empirical evidence for age-graded action cycles of engagement and disengagement with developmental goals in the domain of childbearing and of partnership is discussed.

Fundamental challenges for developmental regulation

The life-span theory of control, developed by Heckhausen and Schulz (1995; Schulz and Heckhausen, 1996) focuses on the individual as the agent in development (see also Lerner and Busch-Rossnagel, 1981; Brandtstädter, 1998). It starts from the assumption that any human behavior in order to be effective needs to fulfill two basic requirements: the management of selectivity and the compensation of failure experiences. Both these requirements result from the extensive variability and flexibility of human behavior (see more extensive review of this issue in Heckhausen, 1999). Because of the great flexibility and thus immense scope in human behavior, the individual needs to select out specific behavioral options and needs to protect this selection against competing action tendencies. This requires a powerful system of motivational and volitional regulation, which guides the *choice* of action goals, and also safeguards and enhances *focused* commitment to a chosen action goal. The regulatory mechanisms of selectivity are jointly scaffolded by evolved behavioral modules (see detailed review in Heckhausen, 2000b) and socio-structural constraints (Heckhausen and Schulz, 2000a). In lifespan developmental context, the selectivity requirement becomes even more essential and amplified in its implications. (For the concept of selectivity see also Baltes and Baltes, 1990; Carstensen, Isaacowitz, and Charles, 1999.)

Human functioning and its development rely on experiences of failure. Precisely *because* human behavior is flexible, failure is a likely event throughout processes of skill acquisition and problem solving. Moreover, failure is the prominent source of feedback for adjusting action means and improving performance. However, failure experiences entail two types of costs: the negative affect that accompanies frustrations of goal intentions, and the detrimental impact of failure experiences on perceptions of the self. These two types of costs of failure are intertwined in that conceptions of the self provide a powerful buffer against frustration (Heckhausen, 1999). Anticipatory self reinforcement enables the individual to maintain persistence in spite of failure. It relies on the ability to reflect upon the self, and thus relate action outcomes back to characteristics of the self, such as strength, ability, and skills.

However, this powerful resource is also a major peril, because repeated failure experience may in fact deflate a positive self image and lead to perceptions of low personal control, pessimism, embarrassment, and even helplessness. These are, of course, major threats to the individual's motivational resources for future action. Therefore, individuals need to protect their perceived self by compensatory means. Again the context of the life span enhances the implications of failure experiences (Havighurst, 1952). Developmental goals typically span extensive periods of life time and therefore present ample opportunity for frustration. They also carry extensive risks in case of wrong decisions, because life time may have been invested irretrievably. Moreover, towards the end of the life span, processes of aging confront the individual with experiences of loss and decline. All these negative experiences have to be compensated for in order to maintain the individual's capacity to actively influence her environment.

Control striving and developmental regulation across the life span

In this section, the conceptual foundations of the life span theory of control are first introduced and then examined in terms of empirical support for major shifts in control behavior across the life span. In addition, a conception of adaptive control strategies for developmental regulation is discussed as the model of Optimization in Primary and Secondary Control (OPS Model) and as the foundation of a multi-scale measurement instrument for control behavior (OPS Scales; Heckhausen, Schulz, and Wrosch, 1998).

Key propositions of the life-span theory of control

In their life-span theory of control, Heckhausen and Schulz apply the distinction between primary and secondary control to life-span development. This distinction was first introduced by Rothbaum, Weisz, and Snyder (1982) and has received ever increasing attention in recent years (Azuma, 1984; Band and Weisz, 1990; Gould, 1999; Heckhausen, 1997; Heckhausen and Schulz, 1995, 1999; Schulz and Heckhausen, 1996; Seginer, Trommsdorff, and Essau, 1993; Skinner, 1996; Thompson *et al.*, 1998; Weisz, Rothbaum, and Blackburn, 1984; Wrosch and Heckhausen, 1999). Primary control refers to behaviors directed at the external world and involves attempts to change the world to fit the needs and desires of the individual. Secondary control is targeted at internal processes and serves to focus and protect motivational resources needed for primary control.

We conceive of primary control as the driving force in the control system (see debate about this claim in *Psychological Review*, articles by Gould, 1999 and by Heckhausen and Schulz, 1999b). Primary control holds functional primacy. Because primary control is directed outward, it enables individuals to shape their environment to fit their particular needs and developmental potential. This does not mean that secondary control is inferior or dysfunctional in any way. In contrast, secondary control is used to promote both the *current* and the *long-term* potential of primary control. It is employed in view of the necessities of maintaining the primary control potential.

Across the human life-span, the availability of primary control undergoes major changes. Figure 10.1 illustrates hypothetical trajectories for primary control striving, primary control capacity, and use of secondary control processes. In accordance with the notion that primary control striving holds functional primacy, Figure 10.1 depicts a stable striving

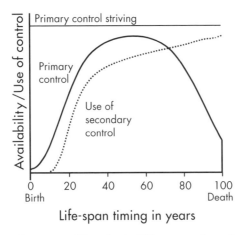

Life-span timing in years

Figure 10.1 Hypothetical life-span trajectories of primary control striving, primary control capacity, and use of secondary control process (adapted from Heckhausen, 1999).

for primary control striving across the life span. However, the capacity for primary control undergoes major life span changes in that it increases rapidly during childhood, plateaus in midlife, and declines in old age. The use of secondary control strategies depends on their developmental availability and their functional necessity. Children between the ages of three and four develop the ability to perceive failure as an indicator of lacking competence, and thus first experience failure-related threats to self esteem. Most likely this threat triggers the need for compensatory mechanisms. Moreover, during mid childhood the cognitive capacities of children increase dramatically, enabling them, for instance, to use complex schemes of causal attribution. Accordingly, it is in mid childhood and throughout adolescence that secondary control strategies have been shown to flourish. Primary and secondary control capacities develop further in early adulthood up into early midlife, when most people reach the peak of their career, and have founded a family. During late midlife and in old age, primary control becomes increasingly constrained as social roles become restricted and biological declines take their toll. This is when secondary control becomes more and more needed, and is therefore increasingly activated.

Empirical evidence for control theory propositions

In the previous section, I have discussed the general predictions of the life span theory of control. But is this actually reflected in adults' conceptions

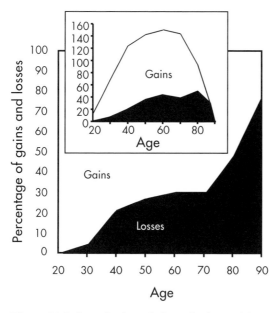

Figure 10.2 Quantitative relation of gains and losses across the adult life span. Insert: percentages and absolute numbers. Gains and losses in development throughout adulthood as perceived by different adult age groups (adapted from Heckhausen, Dixon, & Baltes, 1989).

of development, and what is more, is it shown in their attempts to influence their own development? The first question relates to the degree of awareness adults at various ages have about the age-based changes in developmental chances and risks. In an earlier study, Heckhausen, Dixon, and Baltes (1989) asked adults at various age levels about the expected increases for a great variety of psychological characteristics (e.g., forgetful, friendly, intelligent, knowledgeable, calm, responsible, etc.) across the span of adulthood. Figure 10.2 informs about the pattern of findings obtained from the adults' conceptions about normal developmental change during adulthood (the insert informs about the absolute frequencies of expected gains and losses). As can be seen in Figure 10.2, higher age groups were increasingly associated with risks for decline, while chances for developmental growth were viewed as decreasing steadily across later midlife and old age.

The study by Heckhausen *et al.* (1989) had shown that laypersons at various adult age levels concurred with the view that primary control potential was increasingly at stake in later midlife and particularly in old age. However, the key question is, of course, would such normative conceptions also lead to complementary attempts to regulate development? A

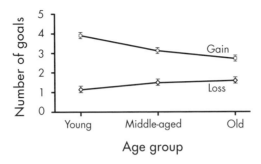

Figure 10.3 Gain- and loss-related developmental goals in young, middle-aged, and old subjects (adapted from Heckhausen, 1997).

complementary pattern of developmental regulation would mean striving for developmental gains more during young adulthood, when the potential for growth was higher, and striving to avoid developmental losses during later midlife and old age, when greater risks for losses were pending. In a separate study, adults at various age levels were requested to nominate five developmental goals (i.e., goals, hopes and plans you are currently pursuing) for the next five to ten years (Heckhausen, 1997). These self-nominated goals were then coded in terms of content area, and in terms of whether they reflected striving for a developmental gain or avoiding a developmental loss. Figure 10.3 presents the findings regarding the distribution of goal-oriented and loss-oriented goals in the three adult subject groups. In accordance with the perceived challenges at the different age periods, younger adults reported a greater number of gain-oriented goals, while older adults were more focused on loss-oriented goals.

The next questions following from Figure 10.1 about the expected age-trajectories of primary and secondary control address the striving for primary control and the use of secondary control processes. The study by Heckhausen (1997) also speaks to these questions, since it has used a questionnaire by Brandtstädter and Renner (1990), which addresses key components of primary control striving (i.e., tenaciousness of goal pursuit) and secondary control behavior (i.e., flexibility of goal adjustment). Figure 10.4 shows the age group differences in these two indicators of primary and secondary control behavior. As is clear from the age group pattern, primary control striving remains stable across adult age groups into old age, whereas secondary control in terms of the readiness to disengage from a goal increases steadily across adulthood.

In sum, the findings about laypersons' conceptions of developmental change, their nominations for developmental goals, and their self-reports about tenacious goal striving and flexible goal adjustment support the

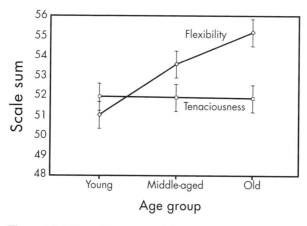

Figure 10.4 Tenaciousness and flexibility in young, middle-aged, and old subjects (adapted form Heckhausen, 1997).

propositions of the life-span theory of control. Primary control striving is stable across the adult life-span and addresses goals of developmental growth in earlier adulthood, while shifting to goals of maintenance and loss-avoidance during later midlife and old age. Secondary control in terms of goal disengagement becomes ever more prominent in the developmental regulation of older adults.

Adaptive control strategies for optimizing development

Having identified in the first section of this chapter the two basic requirements of human functioning, selectivity and failure compensation, and two fundamental types of control, primary and secondary, we can integrate these two dimensions into a joint model of developmental regulation. The model of Optimization in Primary and Secondary Control, or OPS model, is illustrated in Table 10.1 (Heckhausen, 1999; Heckhausen and Schulz, 1993; Heckhausen *et al.*, 1998). It should be noted at this point, that with regard to the major role of selectivity and failure compensation, our model converges with the Baltes and Baltes model of Selective Optimization with Compensation. However, we integrate the concepts of selectivity and compensation with the life-span theory of primary and secondary control, and we conceptualize optimization as a higher order regulatory process. I will return to the role of optimization a bit later in this presentation.

As you can see in Table 10.1, the OPS model is constructed by two conceptually orthogonal types of strategies: primary and secondary control on the one hand, and selection and compensation on the other hand. The

Table 10.1 *OPS-Model: optimization in primary and secondary control*

	Optimization
	- adaptive goal selection: long term
	  and age-appropriate goals
	- management of positive and negative
	  trade-offs for other life domains
	- and future life course
	- maintain diversity, avoid dead ends

Selective primary control - invest effort, abilities - invest time - learn new skills - fight difficulties	*Selective secondary control* - enhance goal value - devalue competing goals - enhance perception of control - anticipate positive consequences of goal attainment
Compensatory primary control - recruit others' help - get others' advice - use of technical aids - employ unusual means	*Compensatory secondary control* - goal disengagement (sour grapes) - self-protective attributions - self-protective social comparisons - self-protective intra-individual comparisons

Source: Adapted from J. Heckhausen and Schulz 1993

integration of these two fundamental dimensions comprise a set of four strategies in developmental regulation: selective primary and compensatory primary control, selective secondary and compensatory secondary control.

Selective primary control refers to the focused investment of resources such as effort, time, abilities, and skills into the pursuit of a chosen goal. Selective primary control may also include the development of skills by processes of acquisition and practice. Thus, selective primary control is action that directly aims at attaining goals.

Compensatory primary control is necessary when the given internal resources of the individual prove insufficient to attain the chosen goal. This is the case, for instance, in young children or frail elderly people. Compensatory primary control typically involves other people's help or assistance, the utilization of technical aids such as glasses or a wheelchair, or the employment of activity-external skills. The latter type of compensations involve new or unusual action means to substitute lost or otherwise unavailable skills inherent to the activity. An example is lip-reading, which enables people with hearing impairments to understand speech.

Selective secondary control serves to enhance the *selectivity* of resource investment in *ongoing* pursuits of primary control goals. In motivational psychology terms, these selective secondary control strategies can be likened to volitional strategies. They keep the actors' attention, effort, and skill activation focused on the current action goal and prevent distractions by alternative action paths or goals.

Compensatory secondary control buffers the potential negative effects of failure on the motivational resources of the individual, and thus promotes the *long-term* potential for primary control. Failure experiences can undermine an individual's perceived control, self efficacy, and even self esteem and therefore may endanger her future willingness to pursue challenging goals of primary control. Secondary control strategies such as disengagement from unobtainable goals, downward social comparisons, and egotistic causal attributions are important instruments to buffer such negative consequences of inevitable failure experiences throughout the life-span.

The employment of each of these strategies and combinations thereof have to be orchestrated in accordance with the structure of opportunities and constraints encountered in a given developmental ecology. Neither of these four strategies is functional in and of itself. Instead, they might become dysfunctional under unfavorable situational conditions. Selective primary control, for instance, can become very ineffective and even harmful for future primary control, when invested in inappropriate goals. And compensatory primary and secondary control may become dysfunctional when the individual prematurely seeks assistance or gives up the goal altogether, although the goal could have been attained on the bases of available own resources.

Therefore, the regulation of the four strategies requires a higher order process, which we refer to as optimization. Developmental optimization is also required for the maintenance of a balance between the four types of strategies so as to promote long-term outcomes. What are the desirable long-term outcomes of developmental regulation? What is the criterion of adaptive functioning across the life-span?

Based on our basic position that primary control holds functional primacy, Rich Schulz and I have defined the criterion of successful developmental optimization as follows: human functioning is adaptive if and insofar as it promotes and maintains the potential for primary control across the life-span (Heckhausen and Schulz, 1995, in press b; Schulz and Heckhausen, 1996). It is important to stress the life-span *encompassing* nature of this criterion, because short- and long-term primary control may be incompatible in certain cases. The time and effort required in childhood and adolescence to become a world class athlete, for instance, may well seriously restrain education and occupational training and thereby damage the individual's long-term primary control potential. Moreover, we take a relativist stance with regard to the life-span *timing* of control striving. What is functional control striving at a certain point in the life span may be dysfunctional at another. It is the totality of realized primary control across domains of functioning and across the life span that makes up a successful life. How does the individual regulate control striving across the life span such as to satisfy this general and ambitious criterion? We propose three general principles of optimization in developmental regulation: first, selectivity of resource investment; second, maintenance of diversity of functioning; and third, management of trade-offs between domains and life-span phases.

First, control resources have to be invested selectively. While selectivity in general is a basic requirement of human functioning, *selection* of appropriate goals in particular is the key to optimization in developmental regulation. Appropriate goals are those that make the best use of developmental ecologies, and have a long-range potential extending beyond the currently present opportunities and constraints. For the typical life-course, such goals correspond to age-normative developmental tasks. At higher ages, when the resources for primary control decrease, the selection of fewer goals becomes more important. This principle of age-appropriate resource investment will be addressed again and in more detail in the second section of this chapter when the action cycles for specific developmental goals are addressed.

Second, it is essential that the individual maintains some *diversity* (or variability) in primary control potential. Diversity is important in ontogenetic development for similar reasons as in evolution. Diversity avoids the vulnerability of too narrow specialization, and most importantly, diversity provides the "raw material" for selection to work on. Without variability there is no opportunity for adaptive choice.

Third, developmental regulation across the life span involves the *management of positive and negative trade-offs* across domains and life-span phases. Investments in one domain restrain simultaneous investments in other domains. This may have positive or negative implications for the non-chosen domain. In the case of superathletes, the selective investment required for developing the athletic ability usually prevents a broad education and therefore endangers the individual's functioning after the athletic career is over. In contrast, developing general purpose abilities, such as intellectual skills typically has positive transfer to various domains of functioning.

Based on our model of Optimization in Primary and Secondary Control, a set of measurement instruments was developed, which addresses the control strategies and optimization in a domain-general version as well as domain-specific versions (OPS-Health: Schulz and Heckhausen, 1999; OPS-Partnership: Wrosch and Heckhausen, 1999; OPS-Childbearing:

Heckhausen, Wrosch, and Fleeson, in press). The domain-general OPS-Scales are designed to assess strategies of developmental regulation irrespective of domain of functioning (Heckhausen *et al.*, 1998). Like the OPS model itself the OPS-Scales comprise four strategies of developmental regulation, and a higher-order process of optimization.

This section on the optimization and the specific control strategies concludes the first part of this chapter, which addresses the global life-span changes in challenges and general control strategies in developmental regulation. Being a section on specific control strategies and especially on the optimized employment of control strategies in view of age-graded opportunities and constraints, this section also leads over to the second part of this chapter, which takes a more detailed look at control strategies activated in the context of action cycles in pursuing specific developmental goals.

Control striving in action cycles of engagement and disengagement with developmental goals

The second part of this chapter applies a zoom to developmental regulation, and narrows the angle of vision from an overall life-span view to a more detailed investigation of action cycles of engagement and disengagement with developmental goals. First, the action-phase model of developmental regulation and its foundation in modern action theory and the Rubicon model of action phases is introduced. Subsequently, empirical evidence from three domains of developmental regulation, childbearing, partnership, and health is considered.

An action-phase model of developmental regulation around developmental deadlines

The concept of developmental deadlines integrates the life-span theory of control with a motivational model of action phases (e.g., Rubicon model, H. Heckhausen, 1991). This integration is summarized in a new model that assumes different processes of developmental regulation when individuals approach a deadline, pass it successfully, and cross the deadline without attaining the goal. The model itself will be described below as the "Action-Phase Model of Developmental Regulation" (Heckhausen, 1997, 1999; Wrosch and Heckhausen, 1999). Moreover, the concept of adaptive regulation processes around deadlines is not exclusively related to developmental phenomena. It could also be used as a theoretical framework to study human action regulation in a broader, more general context (Heckhausen, 1999).

Developmental deadlines are defined as final reference points to realize a certain goal (Heckhausen, 1999; Heckhausen *et al.*, 1999). A typical example is the biologically based developmental deadline for childbearing (biological clock). Beyond age forty, fertility in women greatly decreases while risk pregnancies increase in likelihood. Similar shifts from facilitative to inhibitory conditions can be found for various developmental tasks. Implicit and explicit age-graded norms and deadlines (Settersten and Hagestad, 1996a, 1996b) provide guidelines for individual life planning.

Deadlines for different developmental tasks may vary in age-timing and in terms of abruptness of the shift from conducive to inhibitory conditions. For example, some work-related deadlines like entering vocational training characterize young adulthood, whereas deadlines for the postponement of childbearing should influence individual developmental regulation especially in middle adulthood. In late midlife and old age, for example, separated or divorced individuals confront deadlines for realizing new partnerships (Wrosch, 1999). In addition, developmental deadlines vary in terms of their modifiability (malleability). Biologically based deadlines (e.g., for childbearing after menopause) are less subject to individuals' attempts to surmount them. For biological deadlines, constraints cannot be overcome by especially intense investment and psychological commitment. Age-normative conceptions, by contrast, can be ignored, although often at a substantial cost. The individual can choose to take a non-normative path. Despite this variability in life-course timing and intensity of change in opportunity structures, deadline phenomena are related to a substantial shift from a favorable developmental ecology (more opportunities, less constraints) to an unfavorable developmental ecology (more constraints, less opportunities) with respect to specific goal attainment.

Developmental regulation around transition points like intention formation or deactivation requires a shift in motivational mindsets. In the context of the Rubicon model of action phases (H. Heckhausen, 1991) such mindsets with contrasting functions during different phases of action were first identified and characterized in terms of differential modes of information processing. The Rubicon-model of action phases was developed in a non-developmental context to capture the essence of motivational processes in general (H. Heckhausen, 1991; H. Heckhausen and Gollwitzer, 1987). According to the Rubicon-model of action phases, four distinct phases of action motivation can be distinguished. A predecisional phase preceding the Rubicon of deciding for an action goal, the preactional phase after crossing the Rubicon and before initiating the action, the actional phase, and the postactional phase. The four

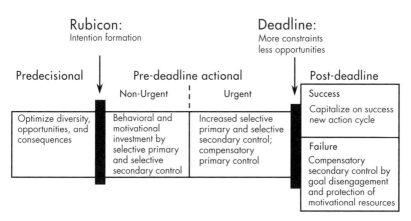

Figure 10.5 Action-phase model of developmental regulation (adapted from Heckhausen, 1999).

phases differ critically in their function and corresponding mind-sets. The predecisional and the postactional phase serve to make a choice and evaluate the action outcome, respectively. These motivational functions require relatively balanced, objective, and open mind-sets of deliberation. In contrast, the preactional and actional phases require volitional commitment in terms of more biased and focused mind-sets of implementation. Heckhausen, Gollwitzer and their colleagues have shown that the transition from pre-Rubicon deliberative to post-Rubicon implemental mind-set is marked by a shift in cognitive processing as indicated by various cognitive-motivational indicators (Beckmann and Gollwitzer, 1987; Gollwitzer, 1990; H. Heckhausen and Gollwitzer, 1986). For example, both intentional and incidental memory was more biased towards the chosen action during the post-Rubicon phases than during the pre-Rubicon phases (Gollwitzer, H. Heckhausen, and Steller, 1990; H. Heckhausen and Gollwitzer, 1987).

The action phase model of developmental regulation (J. Heckhausen, 1999; see Figure 10.5) extends the Rubicon model by including another critical transition, the deadline. The deadline for action represents a point in time when opportunities for action change from rich and favorable to poor and unfavorable. In developmental terms this means that opportunity structures related to chronological age provide good opportunites to attain a developmental goal at certain phases of the life-span during which the goal represents a developmental task (Havighurst, 1952), while at a later phase goal attainment is impossible or severely constrained. The developmental deadline marks the age transition from favorable to unfavorable opportunities. This shift in age-graded opportunities can be anticipated by the individual, and thus sets up phases of urgent goal striving just before the deadline is reached, and of disengagement after the deadline has been passed.

Figure 10.5 identifies on three levels (from top to bottom) the following aspects of the extended model of action phases: critical transition points, functions and challenges of the sequential action phases (pre-decisional, non-urgent and urgent pre-deadline, and post-deadline), and control strategies adaptive to meet these phase-specific challenges. First, the two critical transitions are the "Rubicon" when intentions are formed and the "Deadline," when the action ecology shifts to more constraints and less opportunities (see also J. Heckhausen, 1997, 1999; Wrosch and J. Heckhausen, 1999). The deadline marks a point in time,[1] after which action opportunities are no longer available or radically reduced.

Second, the extended model of action phases further differentiates the pre-deadline actional phase into a non-urgent and an urgent phase of goal-oriented primary control striving. Thus, if action is delayed for whatever reason, goal attainment has to come up against ever narrowing time constraints. In order to still attain the goal, the individual needs to invest enhanced effort and volitional commitment in this urgent pre-deadline phase. On the level of control processes (see third level from top of Figure 10.5) the urgency phase created by the deadline calls for increased and focused behavioral (i.e., "selective primary control") and motivational (i.e., "selective secondary control") investment in goal striving. After passing the deadline, goal intentions have either been realized or failed. Those who failed the deadline (see post-deadline "failure" condition in model, Figure 10.5) need to shift radically from intense goal engagement to compensatory secondary control in terms of goal disengagement and self-protective interpretations. This way, deadline-failers may protect their motivational resources for future primary control striving. In contrast, those who were successful (see post-deadline "success" condition in model, Figure 10.5) can invest in further primary control striving and capitalize on the action resources strengthened by their success, either in the same domain or in a different domain that might have been neglected during the deadline-related phase of life.

Pre-versus post-deadline control behavior: evidence from three domains

The Project "Motivational Psychology of Ontogenesis" based at the Berlin Max Planck Institute for Human Development has conducted a research program on developmental regulation around developmental deadlines (Heckhausen, 1999, Wrosch and Heckhausen, 1999). The deadlines studied in this research program are located in the core of midlife (Heckhausen, 2001). The two developmental deadlines studied in the Berlin Project were the "biological clock" deadline for childbearing (Heckhausen *et al.*, 1999), and the deadline associated with rapidly waning chances of finding a new intimate partner during midlife (Wrosch, 1999; Wrosch and Heckhausen, 1999).

The childbearing deadline was addressed in a quasi-experimental study conducted by Heckhausen *et al.* (1999). The developmental regulation of women in different age groups before versus after a presumed developmental deadline for childbearing at age 40 was examined. We contrasted control processes associated with being engaged with the goal of having a child in younger (less than 40 years of age) childless women with control processes in older childless women, who were being disengaged from the goal of childbearing. In addition, we investigated the developmental regulation in pregnant women and in women with children.

In the first childbearing-deadline study we compared women without children at age 27 to 33 (urgency group), at age 40 to 46 (passed deadline group), and women who had a young child and varied in age between 19 and 44 years. The study participants were requested to nominate the five most important goals for the next five to ten years. In order to assess non-intentional biases in information processing we conducted an incidental memory task. This way we hoped to find out whether these women showed selective recall of sentences which reflect goal engagement versus goal disengagement in accordance with their position in the life-course and their parental status. In accordance with our expectations it was found that pre-deadline women and those with a child nominated more child and family-related goals than women in the passed deadline group. Women in the pre-deadline urgency group in particular expressed the most goals about childbearing. In contrast, older women, who had passed the deadline without bearing a child, expressed a greater engagement with self-development, promoting their health, and improving their social network and relations to friends. The assessment of potentially biased information processing yielded findings in support of our predictions of deadline-dependent functioning. The incidental memory task showed that women in the urgency condition just before passing the deadline recalled more sentences about children; whether these sentences implied good or bad evaluations about children did not make a difference. Older women, who had passed the deadline without bearing a child exhibited particularly good recall of sentences about causal attributions which avoid self-blame (e.g., "Having children is largely a matter of luck."). Finally, it was found that action-phase congruent compared to incongruent recall of information was beneficial in terms of psychological well-being. Negative affect was particularly high in those older childless women, who exhibited good recall of sentences about children, parental goals, and blaming the self for childlessness. Positive affect was enhanced in those older childless women, who recalled more sentences about substitute goals for childbearing (e.g., being a good aunt) and recalled fewer sentences about the benefits of having children.

In the second study on the childbearing deadline (Heckhausen *et al.*, 1999) we added two further groups to our design by including pregnant women and women who had passed the deadline by a few years, thus having a five-group design: group with child (18 to 41 years), pregnant group (21 to 39 years in third trimester of pregnancy), urgency group, just passed deadline group (39 to 46 years), long passed deadline group (49 to 56 years). In addition to investigating the developmental goals, we used the OPS-Scales for assessing control strategies (*O*ptimization in *P*rimary and *S*econdary Control-Scales, OPS-Scales; Heckhausen *et al.*, 1998). In order to capture the potential adaptation of control strategies to the particular domain at stake, we used a version of the OPS-Scales, which was specifically adapted to the childbearing domain (Heckhausen *et al.*, 1999). Similarly to the first study, we found that both pre-deadline women and women with a child nominated more goals related to childbearing, childrearing, and family. In contrast, women in the two passed deadline groups (just passed deadline and long passed deadline) expressed other non-family goals regarding friends, leisure, and self more frequently. The control strategies assessed by the OPS-Scales yielded a pattern across the groups, which supported our predictions with regard to each of the four types of control strategies. In the pre-deadline groups (i.e., no child before deadline group and pregnant group) and the group with a child, higher ratings for selective primary control, selective secondary control, and compensatory primary control reflected a greater goal engagement with childbearing. In contrast, in the post-deadline groups higher ratings in compensatory secondary control indicated a disengagement from childbearing goals and a tendency for self-protective cognitions (self-serving social comparisons and causal attributions).

Again, as in the first study, the congruency of control strategies with pre- versus post-deadline developmental status was investigated in terms of its association with adaptive outcomes of psychological well-being. We found that selective primary control had inverse predictive relations with depressive symptoms in pre- versus post-deadline women. Women in the urgency group (just before passing the deadline), who rated selective primary control strategies for childbearing, reported fewer depressive symptoms. In contrast, women in both passed deadline groups, who expressed a high endorsement of selective primary control for childbearing, significantly increased their risk of experiencing depressive symptoms. Thus, in both studies the pattern of findings about control strategies used by women in different life-course status, before and after the childbearing deadline, and in terms of the adaptiveness of these strategies for important outcomes of psychological development, supports our model of adaptive control strategies in different action phases before and after passing a developmental deadline.

Another domain of adult development we studied in our Berlin project, using the research paradigm of developmental deadline, is the partnership domain. National German statistics show that opportunities to remarry decline sharply from 80 percent for 30-year-olds to 20 percent at age 60 (Braun and Proebsting, 1986). This decline creates a radical shift in opportunities to realize goals for an intimate partnership from favorable during early adulthood to close-to-impossible during late midlife and old age. In a study combining cross-sectional comparisons and longitudinal follow-up, Wrosch (1999; Wrosch and Heckhausen, 1999) investigated control striving in four groups of adults: Young (20 to 34 years) and recently committed to a new partner; young and recently separated, late midlife (49 to 59) and recently commited; late midlife and recently separated. In a similar way to the childbearing studies, Wrosch investigated developmental goals, domain-specific control strategies, and biases in information processing (i.e., phase-congruent selection in incidental recall of adjectives describing partnerships in positive or negative ways). With regard to developmental goals, this study focused on gain-oriented versus loss-oriented partnership goals. The findings show that the partnership-related goals nominated by younger and older committed or separated adults reflected their developmental status with regard to partnership. Figure 10.6 informs about the number of goals oriented towards achieving gains (e.g., finding a new partner, improving the partnership) and towards avoiding losses (e.g., separating, not getting on). As can be seen in Figure 10.6, younger adults irrespective of whether they were committed to a partner or separated focused on gains in the partnership domain. Late midlife adults, in contrast, were less gain-oriented, and focused in particular on avoiding loss of the partner when they had recently found a new partnership. It is as if these late midlife adults wanted to protect this uncommon and thus precious luck of a late love.

Domain-specific control strategies were also investigated in the deadline study on partnership. The findings support the predictions of the action-phase model of developmental regulation. Young adults, irrespective of their partnership status, endorse higher ratings of selective

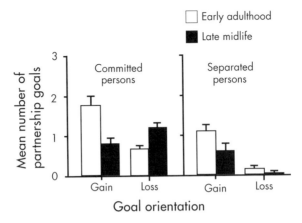

Figure 10.6 Number of gain-oriented and loss-avoiding partnership goals in recently committed and separated adults in early adulthood and late midlife.
Note: The error bars reflect the respective standard error (adapted from Wrosch & Heckhausen, 1999).

primary and selective secondary control, thus expressing enhanced goal engagement. For the older mid-lifers goal engagement control strategies (i.e., selective primary and selective secondary control) were high only in the group who was recently committed. In contrast to this pattern of control strategies, the post-deadline group of late mid-lifers who were recently separated, expressed higher compensatory secondary control and lower selective primary and selective secondary control. Finally, the incidental recall task yielded model-congruent findings too. Younger separated adults recalled relatively more positive compared to negative words about partnerships, whereas older adults recalled relatively more negative words. Most interesting are the findings of the longitudinal follow-up, which Wrosch conducted 15 months after the initial data collection. Figure 10.7 illustrates that compensatory secondary control, that is disengagement from partnership goals and self-protection about a failing partnership, had contrasting long-term effects for separated adults in young adulthood and late midlife. Improved positive affect was attained over the 15 month period by adults using relatively more compensatory secondary control only when they were in late midlife. In contrast, positive affect deteriorated for those users of compensatory secondary control who were in young adulthood.

A third area of investigation with regard to developmental deadlines is a collaborative effort with the research group around Richard Schulz at the

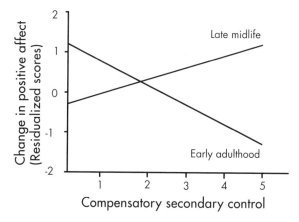

Figure 10.7 Compensatory secondary control as predictor of adjustment of positive affect in separated individuals in early adulthood and late midlife (adapted from Wrosch & Heckhausen, 1999).

University of Pittsburgh. In this research, the maintenance of health is investigated as an important developmental goal. Health maintenance plays a prime role in primary control striving throughout the life-span (Schulz and Heckhausen, 1996; Schulz, Heckhausen, and O'Brien, 1993). However, the aging-related losses in physical health at advanced ages place an increased salience on this goal in later adulthood, and at the same time render tenacious goal striving in this regard a fruitless enterprise. By comparing older adults with acute health stress and chronic disease, Schulz and colleagues (Schulz, Wrosch, Yee, Heckhausen, and Whitmer, 1998) aimed at contrasting potentially controllable health-related threats with uncontrollable health-related losses. This contrast between potentially controllable acute health problems and uncontrollable disease can be viewed as emulating pre- versus post-deadline challenges for developmental regulation. For assessing control strategies Schulz et al. (1998) used a version of the OPS-Scales adapted to the domain of health and illness (Health OPS-Scales; Schulz and Heckhausen, 1997). The predictive relations of using goal engagement control strategies (selective primary, selective secondary, and compensatory primary control) and goal disengagement strategies (compensatory secondary control) with depressive symptoms were investigated for adults with acute and with chronic health problems. In accordance with the action-phase model of developmental regulation, it was found that control strategies were differentially effective in preventing depressive symptoms after health-compromising events for those who suffered acute versus chronic problems. Acute and thus more controllable problems were more adaptively dealt with when using goal engagement control strategies. Subjects with acute health stress managed to prevent depressive symptoms when they used goal engagement control strategies. For these subjects with controllable health problems, using compensatory secondary control did not help. In contrast, initial findings suggest that subjects with chronic disease were able to avoid depressive symptoms by using compensatory secondary control. For them, coping with a mostly uncontrollable disease was not facilitated by any of the three goal disengagement control strategies.

To summarize, the studies about developmental regulation around deadlines for important life goals show the adaptive value of anticipated age changes in opportunities for goal attainment. The age-structured opportunities and constraints associated with developmental deadlines help the individual to set up an agenda for using life time effectively. Developmental goals and the associated action cycles can thus be scheduled and sequenced, so that overlap, excess burdening and conflict may be avoided and the opportunities provided by the biology and societal structuring of the life-course used to its best. With the time-schedule in mind adults can put off for a while, and then intensely pursue, important goals and developmental tasks for which time runs out. The developmental deadlines also provide prompts when to disengage from a goal. This way, futile investments and frustrations are avoided, and at the same time a focus on self-protection is facilitated, so as to minimize negative affect and depressive symptoms. This way, individuals can cherish their motivational resources for future primary control pursuits for goals which are still attainable.

Summary

A life-span theory of control and its implications for a model of developmental regulation have been discussed. According to this theory, primary control striving holds functional primacy in the regulation of behavior throughout the life-span. Secondary control strategies serve to focus and optimize the motivational resources for primary control. When applied to the regulation of developmental change and the attainment of developmental goals, a control-theory approach can much profit from an integration with recent advances in motivational action theory. Following this perspective, an action-phase model of developmental regulation is proposed, which allows the control processes involved in engagement with and disengagement from developmental goals to be conceptualized. This action-phase model particularly emphasizes the role of developmental deadline, which marks the radical transition from favorable to unfavorable conditions for reaching certain developmental goals. Such deadline-related models of developmental regulation also furnish specific predictions about adaptive and maladaptive control processes in individuals at contrasting developmental status before versus after passing the deadline. A set of studies in three domains of functioning (childbearing, partnership, and health) was reported which illustrates the usefulness of the model and leads the way for advances in the study of mature developmental regulation in adulthood. Currently ongoing work is extending the paradigm of developmental deadline to the longitudinal study of adolescents' transition from school to work.

NOTE

1 One could also extend the concept of developmental deadlines beyond the time dimension to situational action opportunities in general. Such a general concept might be conceived as a "transition to a condition of lost opportunities" and would include situations when, in the process of goal striving, the external or internal prerequisites for goal attainment are lost. Examples would be a teacher, who in his early career is confronted with radically vanishing job opportunities in the school system, or an athlete who in the process of training for peak performance suffers an incapacitating and irreversible injury.

REFERENCES

Azuma, H. (1984). Secondary control as a heterogeneous category. *American Psychologist*, 39, 970–1.

Baltes, P. B., and Baltes, M. M. (1990). Psychological perspectives on successful aging: the model of selective optimization with compensation. In P. B. Baltes and M. M. Baltes (eds.), *Successful aging: Perspectives from the behavioral sciences*. New York: Cambridge University Press, 1–34.

Band, E. B., and Weisz, J. R. (1990). Developmental differences in primary and secondary control coping and adjustment to juvenile diabetes. *Journal of Clinical Child Psychology*, 19, 150–8.

Beckmann, J., and Gollwitzer, P. M. (1987). Deliberative and implemental states of mind: the issue of impartiality in predecisional and postdecisional information processing. *Social Cognition (Special Issue: Cognition and Action)*, 5, 259–79.

Brandtstädter, J. (1998). Action perspectives on human development. In W. Damon (Editor-in-Chief) and R. M. Lerner (Vol. Ed.), *Handbook of child psychology* (5th edn.), vol. 1: *Theoretical models of human development*, 807–63. New York: Wiley.

Brandtstädter, J., and Renner, G. (1990). Tenacious goal pursuit and flexible goal adjustment: explication and age-related analysis of assimilative and accommodative strategies of coping. *Psychology and Aging*, 5, 58–67.

Braun, W., and Proebsting, H. (1986). Heiratstafeln verwitweter Deutscher 1979/82 und geschiedener Deutscher 1980/83 [Marriage tables of widowed, 1979/82, and divorced, 1980/83, Germans]. *Wirtschaft und Statistik*, 107–12.

Carstensen, L. L., Isaacowitz, D. M., and Charles, S. T. (1999). Taking time seriously: a theory of socioemotional selectivity. *American Psychologist*, 54, 165–81.

Gollwitzer, P. M. (1990). Action phases and mind-sets. In E. T. Higgins and R. M. Sorrentino (eds.), *Handbook of motivation and cognition: Foundations of social behavior*, New York: Guilford Press, 2, 53–92.

Gollwitzer, P. M., Heckhausen, H., and Steller, B. (1990). Deliberative and implemental mind-sets: cognitive tuning toward congruous thoughts and information. *Journal of Personality and Social Psychology*, 59, 1119–27.

Gould, S. J. (1999). A critique of Heckhausen and Schulz' life-span theory of control from a cross-cultural perspective. *Psychological Review*, 106, 597–604.

Havighurst, R. J. (1952). *Developmental tasks and education*. New York: McKay Company.

Heckhausen, H. (1991). *Motivation and action*. New York: Springer.

Heckhausen, H., and Gollwitzer, P. M. (1986). Information processing before and after the formation of an intent. In F. Klix and H. Hagendorf (eds.), *In memoriam Hermann Ebbinghaus: Symposium on the structure and function of human memory*. Amsterdam: Elsevier, 1071–82.

Heckhausen, H., and Gollwitzer, P. M. (1987). Thought contents and cognitive functioning in motivational and volitional states of mind. *Motivation and Emotion*, 11, 101–20.

Heckhausen, J. (1997). Developmental regulation across adulthood: primary and secondary control of age-related challenges. *Developmental Psychology*, 33, 176–87.

Heckhausen, J. (1999). *Developmental regulation in adulthood: Age-normative and sociostructural constraints as adaptive challenges*. New York, NY: Cambridge University Press.

Heckhausen, J. (2000a). Developmental regulation across the life span: age-graded sequencing of developmental goal-related action cycles. In J. Heckhausen (ed.), *Motivational psychology of human development: Developing motivation and motivating development*. Amsterdan, Netherlands: Elsevier.

Heckhausen, J. (2000b). Evolutionary perspectives on human motivation. In J. Heckhausen and P. Boyer (eds.), Evolutionary psychology: potential and limits of a Darwinian framework for the behavioral sciences [Special Issue]. *American Behavioral Scientist*, 43, 1015–29.

Heckhausen, J. (2001). Adaptation and resilience in midlife. In M. E. Lachman (ed.), *Handbook of midlife development*. New York: Wiley.

Heckhausen, J., Dixon, R. A., and Baltes, P. B. (1989). Gains and losses in development throughout adulthood as perceived by different adult age groups. *Developmental Psychology*, 25, 109–21.

Heckhausen, J., and Schulz, R. (1993). Optimisation by selection and compensation: balancing primary and secondary control in life-span development. *International Journal of Behavioral Development*, 16, 287–303.

Heckhausen, J., and Schulz, R. (1995). A life-span theory of control. *Psychological Review*, 102, 284–304.

Heckhausen, J., and Schulz, R. (1999). The primacy of primary control is a human universal: a reply to Gould's critique of the life-span theory of control. *Psychological Review*, 106, 605–09.

Heckhausen, J., and Schulz, R. (in press). Biological and societal canalizations as adaptive constraints in individuals' developmental regulation: optimization of developmental selectivity by sequential pursuit of age-graded developmental goals. In R. Lerner and J. Brandtstädter (eds.), *Development and action: Origins and functions of intentional self-development*. London: Sage.

Heckhausen, J., Schulz, R., and Wrosch, C. (1998). *Developmental regulation in adulthood: Optimization in primary and secondary control*. Unpublished manuscript, Max Planck Institute for Human Development, Berlin.

Heckhausen, J., Wrosch, C., and Fleeson, W. (in press). Developmental regulation before and after a developmental deadline: The sample case of "biological clock" for childbearing. *Psychology and Aging*.

Lerner, R. M., and Busch-Rossnagel, N. A. (eds.). (1981). *Individuals as producers of their development: A life-span perspective*. New York: Academic Press.

Rothbaum, F., Weisz, J. R., and Snyder, S. S. (1982). Changing the world and changing the self: a two-process model of perceived control. *Journal of Personality and Social Psychology*, 42, 5–37.

Schulz, R., and Heckhausen, J. (1996). A life-span model of successful aging. *American Psychologist*, 51, 702–14.

Schulz, R., and Heckhausen, J. (1997). *The Optimization in Primary and Secondary (OPS) Control-Scale for the health domain*. Unpublished questionnaire, University of Pittsburgh, USA.

Schulz, R., and Heckhausen, J. (1999). Aging, culture and control: setting a new research agenda. *Journal of Gerontology: Psychological Sciences*, 54(3), pp. 139–45.

Schulz, R., Heckhausen, J., and O'Brien, A. T. (1993). *A conceptual model for subsyndromal depression*. 46th Annual Scientific Meeting of the Gerontological Society of America.

Schulz, R., Wrosch, C., Yee, J. L., Heckhausen, J., and Whitmer, R. (1998, June). *Avoiding depression in late life. Using selective and compensatory control processes to manage physical illness and disability*. Paper presented at the XVth Biennial Meeting of ISSBD, Berne, Switzerland.

Seginer, R., Trommsdorff, G., and Essau, C. (1993). Adolescent control beliefs: cross-cultural variations of primary and secondary orientations. *International Journal of Behavioral Development*, 16, 243–60.

Settersten, R. A., and Hagestad, G. O. (1996a). What's the latest? Cultural age deadlines for family transitions. *The Gerontologist*, 36, 178–88.

Settersten, R. A., and Hagestadt, G. O. (1996b). What's the latest? Cultural age deadlines for educational and work transitions. *The Gerontologist*, 36, 602–13.

Skinner, E. A. (1996). A guide to constructs of control. *Journal of Personality and Social Psychology*, 71, 549–70.

Thompson, S. C., Thomas, C., Ricakbaugh, C. A., Tanatamjarik, P., Otsuki, T., Pan, D., Garcia, B. F., and Sinar, E. (1998). Primary and secondary control over age-related changes in physical appearance. *Journal of Personality and Social Psychology*, 66, 583–605.

Weisz, J. R., Rothbaum, F. M., and Blackburn, T. C. (1984). Standing out and standing in: the psychology of control in America and Japan. *American Psychologist*, 39, 955–69.

Wrosch, C. (1999). *Entwicklungsfristen im Partnerschaftsbereich: Bezugsrahmen für Prozesse der Aktivierung und Deaktivierung von Entwicklungszielen* [Developmental deadlines in the partnership domain: reference frame for activating and deactivating developmental goals]. Münster: Waxmann.

Wrosch, C., and Heckhausen, J. (1999). Control processes before and after passing a developmental deadline: activation and deactivation of intimate relationship goals. *Journal of Personality and Social Psychology*, 77, 415–27.

11 Social selection, social causation, and developmental pathways: empirical strategies for better understanding how individuals and environments are linked across the life-course

Avshalom Caspi

At a time when psychiatric research has become molecular biology and the study of personality has turned into a gene hunt, in this chapter I pose an old-fashioned question: does social structure matter for psychological functioning? Specifically, this chapter addresses three questions. First, do psychological differences create social inequalities? Here I deal with research in the *social-selection tradition* and ask: how do people end up where they do in the social structure of society? Second, do social inequalities generate psychological problems? Here I deal with research in the *social-causation tradition* and ask: does it make a difference in people's well-being where they end up in the social structure of society? Third, can social engineering improve life chances? Here I deal with how social conditions can modify the expression of psychological characteristics and thereby shape paths to successful development. This chapter is divided into three sections, each addressing one of the above questions. This chapter does not pretend to have the answers to all these questions. My aim is more modest; to communicate the scientific logic of a research program and to share with readers some of the theoretical and policy implications that arise from this work.

Do psychological differences create social inequalities?

To address this question we have been studying how youth make the transition from adolescence to adulthood. This developmental period, roughly between ages 15–30, is the most critical time in the life-course for generating life chances and opportunities. Whether one adopts the psychodynamic language of stage resolution or the demographic language of state transitions, this is the most turbulent period in the life-course. It is the peak age period of residential mobility, of school leaving, of marriage, of fertility, and of unemployment. Some demographers have called the transition to adulthood a period of *demographic density* because it is characterized by many and closely spaced life changes (Rindfuss, 1991).

Our work on the transition to adulthood has made use of the Dunedin Study, a longitudinal investigation of a representative birth cohort of all the babies born in 1972–73 in the city of Dunedin, New Zealand's fourth largest city. Members of this cohort have been assessed on a regular basis at ages 3, 5, 7, 9, 11, 13, 15, 18, and 21. At each assessment age, the study members have participated in a day long program that involves medical, psychological, and sociological assessments. Retention has been excellent; over 95 percent of the original study members continued to participate in the study as adults. This assures that none of the findings about social inequalities and health are compromised by selective attrition, in which poor or mentally ill people drop out of a study.

In the context of the Dunedin study we have focused special attention on transition into the labor force and asked who is at risk for unemployment. Why unemployment? Because youth unemployment is not just a transient problem. It reduces the probability of later employment, depresses future wage earnings, and inhibits socioeconomic mobility. Most importantly, low socioeconomic status is linked to physical and mental illness (Petersen and Mortimer, 1994).

During the time period under study, members of the Dunedin study encountered one of the worst economic downturns in New Zealand's history. Figure 11.1 shows two interesting features. First, the figure shows that New Zealand's unemployment rate surpassed the unemployment

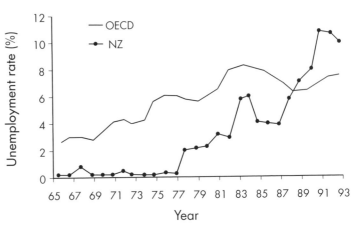

Figure 11.1 New Zealand and OECD unemployment rates 1966–1993.

rate in most other OECD countries (Prime Ministerial Task Force on Employment, 1994). In the early 1990s, New Zealand had one of the highest unemployment rates in the Western world. Second, the figure highlights a natural experiment. When the Dunedin study members were children, there was virtually no unemployment in New Zealand. But by 1994, when most study members had entered the labor force, the unemployment rate among adolescents and young adults was 18 percent. This tells us that unemployment is unlikely to be directly transmitted across generations. That is, simple modeling of parental behavior could not have taken place, and mechanistic models of intergenerational transmission are unlikely to be theoretically fruitful for understanding paths to successful development. Rather, the Dunedin study offers an historically unique opportunity to test if the familial transmission of vulnerability factors can increase the risk of, or propensity to, unemployment in adulthood.

In the Dunedin study we have examined which factors place youth at risk for unemployment. For heuristic purposes we have grouped these factors into three types of capital: human, social, and personal. *Human capital* refers to the resources, qualifications, skills, and knowledge that are available to and acquired by individuals to maximize their own employability. Here we include such variables as economic resources in one's family of origin, educational achievement, and IQ. *Social capital* refers to those social relationships that provide access and control over various types of resources. Here we include such variables as the presence and strength of relationships between parents and children, and ties to social institutions such as schools. *Personal capital* refers to those behavioral characteristics and resources that affect both the motivation and capacity to work. Here we include such variables as antisocial behavior, symptoms of mental illness, and chronic health problems. We use the term capital to emphasize that people possess different amounts of goods whether expressed in terms of resources, skills, connections, or personal styles that can be used to secure other goods. The distinctions between different forms of capital are elastic (e.g., IQ is both human capital and personal capital) and heuristic. The purpose of our tripartite designation is primarily to draw attention to the fact that variables historically favored by different disciplines (economics, sociology, psychology) may all matter and all thus require measurement.

To make a long story short, the results from our longitudinal analyses show that a constellation of characteristics, assessed during the first decade of life, predicts unemployment in young adulthood (Caspi, Wright, Moffitt, and Silva, 1998). Table 11.1 illustrates the results from a series of Tobit regressions which show that it is possible to predict,

Table 11.1 *Preschool predictors of months of unemployment during the transition to adulthood (ages 15-21)*

	Probability of unemployment	Increase # mths unemployment	Significant multi-variate predictor
Human capital			
Low occupational status	20.1%	3.0	√
Low intelligence	20.0%	3.0	√
Social capital			
Single-parent family	11.5%	1.8	√
Deviant mother-child interaction			
Personal capital			
Difficult temperament	22.9%	3.5	√

already at age three and with some degree of precision, the probability of who will become unemployed as well as the increase in the duration of unemployment that is associated with various development risk factors measured in the first few years of life. As the table shows, some of the most important risk factors for unemployment are early emerging psychological characteristics, such as difficult temperament. The fact that psychological characteristics, observed during the toddler years, can predict unemployment and labor-market difficulties in young adulthood suggests that these characteristics set in motion processes of cumulative social disadvantage already found at an early age.

Another way to think about the problem of unemployment is to ask: is unemployment disproportionately accounted for by some people in the population? Figure 11.2 shows that the answer is yes. The 1,000 Dunedin study members were unemployed for a total of 4,500 months during the six year period from age 15 to age 21. But what the figure also shows is that about 5 percent of the Dunedin study members accounted for over 50 percent of this total. Moreover, our results show that this minority can be accurately classified on the basis of numerous early characteristics, most notably a history of undercontrolled behaviour and neurocognitive deficits.

But these various findings tell us nothing about the mechanisms by which risk factors make a difference; that is, what are the pathways and mechanisms that mediate the influence of early developmental risk factors on later unemployment? Figure 11.3 summarizes the strategy for answering this question. We begin our inquiry with the childhood predictors identified in our risk analyses and then we systematically test hypotheses about the mechanisms that mediate the influence of these early

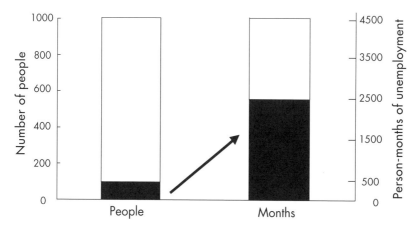

Figure 11.2 Unemployment is concentrated among a small number of young adults

risk factors on later economic difficulties. For example, is the influence of early developmental characteristics (such as antisocial behaviour) on unemployment mediated by educational differentials? Or is it perhaps that antisocial youth do not engage in productive job-search behaviour? Or perhaps the reason that antisocial youth experience difficulties getting a job and holding onto it is because of a matching process in which they

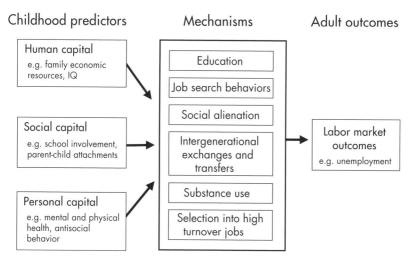

Figure 11.3 Disentangling mechanisms that link childhood characteristics to adult outcomes

are selected into high-turnover jobs. Each mechanism needs to be tested and, importantly, it may be that *different developmental risk factors affect unemployment through different pathways*. By identifying and testing the multiple mechanisms that mediate the influence of different developmental characteristics on later labor-market outcomes we hope to inform policy makers about the behaviors, skills, resources, and attitudes that need to be targeted to increase at-risk youths' ability to acquire and keep a job.

The answers that are emerging from the early stages of our research are by no means obvious. For example, our results revealed that adolescent conduct disorder is associated with a six-month increase in unemployment between ages 18 to 21; compared to males without a history of conduct disorder those with conduct disorder were unemployed for an average of 11 months during this 36-month period. But educational differentials accounted for only about 15 percent of this difference. This finding is important because it suggests that keeping youth in school is not going to eliminate their continued difficulties when they join the labor force. Our empirical tests do reveal that substance dependence is a very important contributing factor to why conduct-disordered youth go on to have difficulties in the labor market; this mediating variable accounted for over 20 percent of the association between conduct disorder history and unemployment.

In practical terms, these results suggest a need to reconsider institutional practices that separate research into and services for drug and alcohol abuse from economic research about and services for unemployment. It makes no sense for these highly related domains to be the purview of separate agencies and services. But in terms of research on risk factors and risk processes, this analysis is but a first step. It is not sufficient to know that substance dependence is an important mediating variable because it is still not known how its mediating influence is expressed. For example, are antisocial youth who become ensnared in drug and alcohol abuse unable to hold down a job or is it that antisocial youth who become involved in the drug economy learn that dealing in drugs can offer an alternative to legitimate employment? I have described but the first steps that we are taking to address these questions but, more generally, this type of research illustrates two points. First, it underscores the need to move from prediction analyses to process analyses in order to understand how psychological characteristics create social inequalities. Second, it reminds us that in order to design effective policies it is necessary to know not only which are the risk factors but also what are the mechanisms by which these factors influence outcomes of interest. This dual message contains a still more subtle, but important point. Even the presence of strong and early-emerging selection effects does not negate the importance of environmental experiences, whose mediating role must be unpacked and analysed to understand how early characteristics can have such long-term effects on the nature of developmental pathways.

Do social inequalities generate psychological problems?

In the section above I have shown how psychological differences can create social inequalities and illustrated the type of empirical strategies that are needed to explore these issues further, especially in terms of demarcating the processes through which risk factors operate. In this section I turn the question on its head and ask if social inequalities generate psychological problems.

It is known that mental illness is overrepresented in the lower classes. What is less clear is whether lower social status serves as *cause or consequence* of mental illness. Research in the "causation" tradition argues that social conditions in the lower strata of society cause mental illness. Research in the "selection" tradition argues that the mentally ill "select" themselves into the lower class as a consequence of impaired social mobility. This tension has vexed social scientists for over 50 years, and its resolution bears implications for the delivery of public health services: to whom should we target services and when?

Historically, these two alternatives have been difficult to sort out because random assignment of people to social class is hardly a possibility and social scientists have, for the most part, been stuck with cross-sectional social surveys. But it is possible to try to estimate causation effects using correlational data. One approach has been to develop statistical models to control for selection effects (e.g., Manski, 1995). These models control for unobserved population heterogeneity. But these models require strong assumptions, and controlling for unmeasured factors often fails to reveal what those factors might be. Another approach has been to use ethnic group designs or migration studies to try to tease apart causation from selection processes (e.g., Dohrenwend *et al.* 1990), and these studies have shed light on causal mechanisms. In our work we have been using two additional strategies. Specifically, we use longitudinal studies of intra-individual change as well as behavioral genetic studies to try to identify whether social inequalities generate mental health problems.

Using longitudinal studies of intra-individual change to isolate the health effects of social inequalities

To illustrate this strategy, I rely again on the Dunedin study to show how one can attempt to untangle social-selection effects from social-causation effects in the complex association between psychiatric disorders and educational attainment (Miech, Caspi, Moffitt, Wright, and Silva, 1999). In terms of life-course development, our research focuses on the transition to young adulthood, because the downward slide in the class structure begins at the time that adolescents leave school. Our measure of social inequality focuses on differences in educational attainment in young adulthood because this is a key component of subsequent social class. Our measure of mental health focuses on psychiatric disorders measured at multiple time periods, at age 15 and again at age 21.

We used three empirical tests to examine the influences of selection and causation. First, we examined the association between mental disorders at age 15 and family SES background. Second, we examined the extent to which these mental disorders impaired social mobility by evaluating their influence on subsequent educational attainment, using models that contained traditional status attainment controls such as IQ, family SES background, and gender. Third, we examined the extent to which increases in mental disorder between ages 15 and 21 were associated with early adulthood SES, as indexed by educational attainment at age 21. No test by itself provides enough information to discriminate between the three interpretations of selection, causation, and joint effects, but, taken together, they lead to discerning patterns of expected results, as outlined in Table 11.2.

A selection effect would suggest that psychiatric disorders are related to educational attainment because vulnerable persons select themselves out of education. Evidence for exclusive selection effects would be indicated

Table 11.2 *Expected patterns of evidence for selection and causation processes*

Type of evidence	Association between parental SES and disorder at age 15	Effect of disorder at 15 on subsequent educational attainment	Effects of truncated education on increased disorder between 15 and 21
Evidence for selection	no	yes	no
Evidence for causation	yes	no	yes
Evidence for joint effects	yes	yes	yes
Evidence for no effects in early adulthood	no	no	no

by a pattern in which mental disorder at age 15 impaired educational attainment, but in which mental disorder in adolescence and in adulthood was uninfluenced by socioeconomic conditions. Evidence for exclusive causation effects would be indicated by a pattern in which mental disorder in adolescence and in adulthood was influenced by socioeconomic conditions but in which mental disorder did not impair subsequent educational attainment. Of course, it is also possible that there are joint, or mutually reinforcing effects. This would be indicated by a pattern of three significant findings: mental disorders in adolescence were influenced by SES of origin; mental disorders impaired status attainment; and mental disorders in adulthood were additionally influenced by SES of early adulthood.

The results show that different disorders are related to educational attainment for different reasons. Table 11.3 shows clear evidence for social causation effects with regard to anxiety disorders. Adolescents who grew up in deprived SES families were more anxious. However, anxiety disorders in adolescence did not affect their subsequent educational attainment. But losing out in formal education did increase the risk of anxiety disorders in adulthood, even after controlling for initial levels of anxiety in adolescence. Apparently, then, the association between anxiety disorders and social class does not arise because anxious adolescents select themselves into the lower strata; rather, there must be something about the conditions of life in the lower strata, whether in adolescence or in young adulthood, that makes people anxious.

The picture is complicated with regard to antisocial disorders (see Table 11.4). First, the results show that parental social class is correlated with conduct disorder. Second, the results show that antisocial disorders impair educational attainment. We broke educational attainment down into three separate transitions. The first transition asks whether psychiatric disorders predicted failure to earn a school certificate degree,

Table 11.3 *Social class and anxiety: selection and causation processes*

| Association between low parental SES and disorder at age 15 | Effect of disorder at 15 on truncated education attainment[a] | | | Effect of truncated education on increased disorder between 15 and 21[a] |
	Transition 1: School Cert.	Transition 2: Bursary	Transition 3: University entry	
2.1*	.86	1.2	1.3	2.2*

Notes: Entries in table are odds ratios
[a]controlling for parental SES, sex, comorbidity

Table 11.4 *Social class and antisocial disorders: selection and causation processes*

| Association between low parental SES and disorder at age 15 | Effect of disorder at 15 on truncated education attainment[a] | | | Effect of truncated education on increased disorder between 15 and 21[a] |
	Transition 1: School Cert.	Transition 2: Bursary	Transition 3: University entry	
CD 2.8*	4.5*	2.5*	2.3	2.8*

Notes: Entries in table are odds ratios
[a]controlling for parental SES, sex, comorbidity

which are taken by New Zealand youth by age 16 and which determine promotion in secondary school. The results show that conduct disorder predicted failure at this transition. The second transition asks whether psychiatric disorders predicted failure to earn a sixth form certificate, the equivalent of an American high school degree or O-levels in England. The results show that conduct disorder predicted failure at this transition as well. The third transition asks whether psychiatric disorders predicted failure to enter university. Conduct disorder did not significantly predict failure at this transition. This is because the selection effects were so strong at earlier transitions that there were few severely disturbed adolescents left to even make this transition. Despite strong selection effects, the results reveal that, even after controlling for earlier psychiatric morbidity, losing out in formal education increased the risk of further antisocial behaviour. Indeed, with regard to antisocial disorders, selection and causation are mutually supportive dynamics. Adolescents with conduct disorder are selectively likely to experience downward drift, and once they lose out on educational opportunities they are increasingly likely to continue engaging in antisocial behavior.

With regard to depression, the results are different yet again (see Table 11.5). Our analysis provides support for neither causation nor selection, suggesting that SES and depression have little influence on each other before age 21. These results suggest that the SES/depression association found in some studies of adults (Kessler *et al.*, 1995, but not all, see Weissman *et al.*, 1991) may be specific to adulthood, reflecting the consequences of adult-specific processes, such as divorce or becoming trapped in lower-status jobs, that place lower-SES adults at increased risk of depression. Clearly, with regard to the association between SES and depression, a more detailed treatment may benefit from a life-course

Table 11.5 *Social class and depression: selection and causation processes*

Association between low parental SES and disorder at age 15	Effect of disorder at 15 on truncated education attainment[a]			Effect of truncated education on increased disorder between 15 and 21[a]
	Transition 1: School Cert.	Transition 2: Bursary	Transition 3: University entry	
1.2	1.3	.96	.53	1.1

Notes: Entries in table are odds ratios
[a]controlling for parental SES, sex, comorbidity

analysis that examines age-specific mechanisms linking social conditions and mental disorders (Elder, George, and Shanahan, 1996; Miech and Shanahan, 2000).

In terms of theory, this set of findings highlights the need for disorder-specific explanations of the relations between social status and mental illness. Simply put: one can no longer speak about psychiatric disorders and social class. Rather, one must speak more specifically about anxiety and social class, conduct disorder and social class, and so forth, because different psychiatric disorders are related to social status for different reasons and through different mechanisms.

In terms of methodology, these findings suggest that research on social status and mental health has much to gain by incorporating measures of specific mental illness into study designs rather than relying on omnibus measures of psychological distress. Many researchers continue to use such omnibus measures because these are quick and easy to use in large samples, but it looks like the very omnibus nature of these measures is likely to generate mis-specifications in models of the relation between social status and mental illness because measures of psychological distress alone cannot discriminate between different disorders (see Krueger *et al.*, 1998). Moreover, with a few notable exceptions, most previous studies of the relation between social status and psychiatric disorders have relied on measures of distress that contain a mixture of physical and psychological symptoms rather than any specific clinical syndrome. The problem with such lack of specificity is that (a) it stymies efforts to advance social-psychological theory and (b) it stymies efforts to derive recommendations for intervention and treatment. Let me argue by analogy: a neuropathologist concerned with localization will not perform MRIs on a patient who scores highly on a measure of psychological distress. Likewise, social psychiatrists and medical sociologists are unlikely to make much progress in understanding how low socioeconomic status affects mental health until they adopt well-conceived measurement practices. But the more general point from this research is that it is possible to understand how environmental experiences influence developmental pathways by focusing on intra-individual change and by studying people during those developmental periods when they make critical social selections (e.g., during the transition to adulthood).

Using behavioral genetic studies to isolate the health effects of social inequalities

Thus far, I have shown how longitudinal studies of intra-individual change can shed light on whether social inequalities generate psychological problems. Perhaps the biggest challenge to this proposition, however, has come from behavioral genetics research. This research suggests that dual inheritance (genetic and social) complicates the interpretation of research findings about the effects of social inequalities on mental health. For example, the child who inherits genes that predispose to behavioral problems may be exposed also to economic hardships because the tendency of his parents to become poor is influenced by the same genes that increase his own behavior problems.

The responsible way to tackle this possibility is head-on, by using genetically-sensitive designs that can provide leverage in identifying environmental risks (Plomin, 1994). Consider twin studies. The twin method is a natural experiment that relies on the different level of genetic relatedness between monozygotic (MZ) and dizygotic (DZ) twin pairs to estimate the contribution of genetic and environmental factors to individual differences in a phenotype of interest. Similarity between siblings in a family may be produced by genetic similarity and by shared or family-wide environmental experiences that impinge equally on children in the same family and so serves to make them alike (e.g., growing up in the same neighborhood). Differences between children in a family are produced by nonshared or child-specific environmental experiences that impinge exclusively on a child and so serve to make that child different from siblings.

Most twin studies show that family-wide environmental conditions are less important than child-specific environmental experiences (e.g., Rutter *et al.*, 1998). That is, siblings resemble each other because of their genetic similarity and they differ from each other because of their unique experiences, but sharing the same environmental experiences does not make them similar to each other above and beyond their genetic similarity. There are two problems with this conclusion, however. First, traditionally, most twin studies have treated environmental factors as an unmeasured black box; the environment in most twin studies is a variance component, not a true variable. Second, most twin studies do not adequately represent the full socio-economic variation in the population, and restricted range may render many twin studies unable to reveal the influence of seriously deprived environments on children's development. But these are not inherent limitations in twin analysis. It is possible to measure and incorporate specific environmental risk factors into representative twin studies to determine the contribution of these risk factors to creating similarities between children growing up in the same family above and beyond genetic similarity (Kendler, 1993).

We adopted this strategy in order to explore whether growing up in deprived neighborhoods makes a difference to children's development (Caspi, Taylor, Moffitt, and Plomin, 2000). The sample for this study was drawn from the Twins Early Development Study, a register of twins born in England and Wales in 1994, administered by the Office of National Statistics. This analysis is based on a sample of two-year-old same-sex twins: 1,081 MZ pairs and 1,061 DZ pairs. Neighborhood conditions were assessed using A Classification of Residential Neighborhoods (Acorn), a geodemographic discriminator developed by CACI Limited (1997) for use in commercial and policy studies conducted in Great Britain (Budd, 1999). Acorn is built entirely using 1991 Census data at the Enumeration District (ED) level, the smallest area at which Census data are made available by the Office of National Statistics (ONS). Great Britain is composed of some 150,000 EDs, each containing approximately 150 households.

After analysis of data items produced by ONS, 79 different items that registered reliable differences (e.g., age, educational qualifications, unemployment, single parent status, housing tenure and dwelling type, and car availability) were combined to give a comprehensive picture of socio-economic differences between different areas. Hierarchical cluster analysis was used to group EDs that shared similar characteristics across the Census variables into 54 distinct and homogeneous neighborhood types. The 54 neighborhood types aggregate into 17 groups and thence into six ordinal categories. The broad categories range from the most affluent neighborhoods in Britain, which have high incomes, large single-family houses, and access to many amenities (Category 1) to the most deprived neighborhoods in Britain, which are dominated by government-subsidized housing estates, low incomes, high unemployment, and single parents (Category 6).

At the phenotypic level, children growing up in deprived neighborhoods were characterized by significantly more behavioral and emotional problems than children growing up in well-to-do areas. But the truly interesting

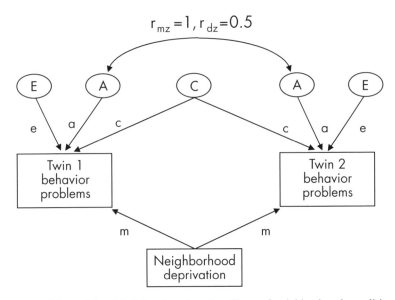

Figure 11.4 Model estimating the effects of neighborhood conditions on children's behavior problems in a genetic design

question is whether neighborhood deprivation affects children's behavioral and emotional problems above and beyond a genetic liability to these problems. The basic model for this analysis is shown in Figure 11.4, where we used structural equation modeling to test different hypotheses about how individual differences in children's mental health problems are affected by three classes of latent factors – additive genetic effects (A), family-wide environment effects (C), and child-specific environment effects (E, which also includes measurement error) – as well as to examine the contribution of a measured environmental risk, neighborhood deprivation, to children's early maldevelopment. The results revealed that the proportion of variance accounted for by additive genetic effects was 55 percent, by family-wide environmental effects 20 percent, and by child-specific environmental conditions 24 percent. Adding neighborhood conditions to the model improved its fit, and the results showed that neighborhood deprivation accounted for approximately 5 percent of the family-wide environmental effect on children's behavioural and emotional problems. The remainder of the family-wide effect was attributable to other, unmeasured family-wide environmental factors.

This analysis demonstrates that growing up in deprived neighborhoods may make a difference in children's lives above and beyond genetic risks.

Neighborhood deprivation is thus a significant family-wide factor, but only one among potentially many other such factors that contribute to problem behaviors. However, it is still not clear even from this analysis whether this is a true environmental effect because it is possible that where families live is influenced by heritable parental traits (e.g., selective migration of vulnerable families into poor neighborhoods), and if so the neighborhood effect may be an environmental mediator of a genetic effect. In order to answer this and related questions, the design we used in this study must be expanded to include information about the parents in a more complete twin-family study so that one may determine whether family-wide environmental risks are true environmental effects or environmental mediators of genetic risk. Such designs are difficult to execute and analyze, yet do-able. But my point in reviewing this work is more general: genetic designs are environmentally informative and can be used to identify modifiable environmental risk factors in the service of promoting more successful development.

Do socio-environmental conditions alter or modify the effects of psychological characteristics on behaviour?

Thus far I have provided illustrations of research strategies for sorting out social-selection from social-causation effects. These empirical strategies are primarily concerned with teasing apart person-environment correlations; that is, with addressing why certain psychological characteristics covary with some environmental features. It remains to be seen, however, if social conditions can modify the expression of psychological characteristics. Our work on the social contexts of adolescent development suggests that the environment can have a profound effect on how attributes of the developing child are channeled in different directions in different settings.

As part of the Pittsburgh Youth Study (Loeber *et al.*, 1998), we sought to test whether the effects of impulsivity on crime varied depending on where children grow up. We focused on a group of approximately 500 fourth grade boys who were enrolled in Pittsburgh's public schools in 1988. One half the sample was white and the other half African American. When the children were 13 years old, we brought them to our laboratory to participate in an extensive testing session that included a multi-method assessment of impulsivity. Not surprisingly, individual differences in impulsivity were linked to delinquency, and impulsive boys committed more of virtually every type of crime (e.g., White, Moffitt, Caspi, Needles, Jeglum-Bartusch, and Stouthamer-Loeber, 1994). But are these effects conditioned by where adolescents live?

To test this hypothesis we first sought to capture important variations in children's neighborhoods. Using census data about various poverty-related conditions (e.g., median household income, percentage of families with children headed by a single parent, percentage of households on public assistance), the children were classified as living in one of three neighborhood types, ranging from well-off neighborhoods (i.e., those that were in the highest 25 percent percent of the distribution of an aggregate-level SES factor) to badly-off neighborhoods (those in the bottom 25 percent of the distribution). This bottom group was further subdivided into high-poverty neighborhoods with concentrations of publicly-assisted housing versus other high poverty areas, on grounds that public housing in Pittsburgh afforded extreme density and homogeneity of criminogenic influences.

The results shown in Figure 11.5 reveal that the effects of impulsivity on delinquency are stronger in worse neighborhoods. The effect of impulsivity on delinquency was nonsignificant in the better neighborhoods and very large in the worst neighborhoods (Lynam, Caspi, Moffitt, Wikstrom, and Loeber, 2000). Why are the effects of impulsivity potentiated in poorer neighborhoods? Part of the answer may be that socioeconomically disadvantaged neighborhoods are characterized by lower levels of informal social control (Sampson *et al.*, 1997). Given lower levels of informal social controls, there are two possible accounts of the potentiation of impulsivity in poorer neighborhoods. The first account suggests that the absence of capable public guardians increases dramatically the opportunities for crime, where opportunity is defined as the coming together in time and space of a potential perpetrator with a potential victim in the

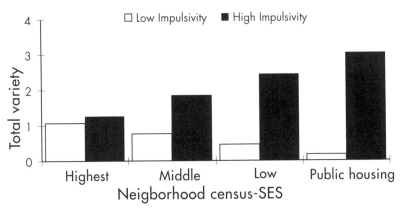

Figure 11.5 The effects of impulsivity on delinquency are stronger in worse neighborhoods

absence of capable public guardians (Cohen and Felson, 1979). According to this account, impulsive persons in poor neighborhoods may encounter and take advantage of more opportunities to commit crime than impulsive persons in better-off neighborhoods. A second account relies on the idea that individuals who lack adequate internal controls must depend more heavily on the environment for structure and restraint to develop adequate self-regulatory capacities (Henry, Caspi, Moffitt, and Silva, 1996). Poorer neighborhoods fail to provide the necessary external structure and restraints because they contain fewer capable and willing public guardians. Thus, youth lacking internal controls in poor neighborhoods fail to develop adequate self-regulatory abilities and are even more dysregulated than their counterparts in better-off neighborhoods (see Eisenberg, this volume). We do not yet know what accounts for this interaction effect, but, whatever the mechanism, here is a clear case in which the expression of a psychological vulnerability is clearly shaped by the ecology of development.

In a different part of the world, we have discovered a similar, but less obvious effect: it concerns how ecological settings shape the expression of biological variables. One of the most striking features of adolescent development is that teens of the same chronological age vary widely in their biological growth. For example, in the aforementioned Dunedin study, the range of age at menarche is from eight years of age to 16 years of age. Some girls begin menstruating in late childhood whereas others only in later adolescence. Importantly, variations in the onset of puberty are also linked to a variety of behavior problems, and there is now converging cross-national evidence that the early onset of puberty is associated with adjustment difficulties (e.g., Ge et al., 1996; Magnusson, 1988; Simmons and Blyth, 1987). This is summarized in Figure 11.6, with data from approximately 500 girls in the Dunedin study. Early-puberty girls were characterized by the most behavior problems at age 13, and this effect persisted when we studied the girls again at age 15. But are these effects of early biological maturation inevitable?

The answer emerging from our research is no. The effects of puberty are conditioned by the social world that teenagers occupy and, in particular, by features of school settings. One of the important ways in which schools vary from one another is in terms of their gender composition, and in our work we have looked at whether it makes a difference whether a girl attends a single-sex school (with only other girls as her peers) or a coed school (with both girls *and* boys as her peers). Gender composition may be important for girls' delinquency because the prevalence of antisocial behaviour is much higher in boys. As a result, the normative rate of delinquency is higher in coed schools than in girls' schools. This suggests

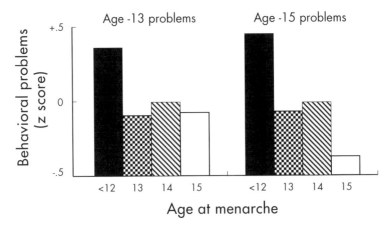

Figure 11.6 Age at menarche and behavioral problems among girls in the Dunedin study.

that girls in coed schools will be more likely to engage in delinquency than girls in same-sex schools because opportunities for delinquent peer affiliations as well as social reinforcements for delinquency are differentially distributed across the two contexts. The Dunedin study also offers a nice natural experiment. About half of the girls attend single-sex schools and the other half attend coed schools, and there are no important social class or family selection effects into who goes where (Caspi, 1995).

Using this natural experiment we discovered that the effect of early puberty on delinquency was restricted to girls attending coed schools. These results are illustrated in the two panels of Figure 11.7, which show girls' delinquent activity at ages 13 and 15. At age 13, early-maturing girls in coed schools were more delinquent than their peers in single-sex schools. But there were no school differences among the on-time maturing girls or among the late-maturing girls. Two years later, at age 15, there was a distinct catch-up effect, in that the girls who had physically matured during the two-year period resembled the early-maturing girls in their delinquency, but this catch-up effect was especially pronounced among girls attending coed schools. This pattern of results leads us to suggest that at least two factors may be necessary for the initiation of female delinquency: puberty and boys (Caspi, Lynam, Moffitt, and Silva, 1993). The onset of puberty appears to operate like a releasor or sign stimulus to others in the social environment; it creates a press for new ways of behaving. But apparently this press is only expressed in some settings, not others. There are many conclusions that one can draw from this research. In New Zealand, the media asked, Is coed bad for girls?

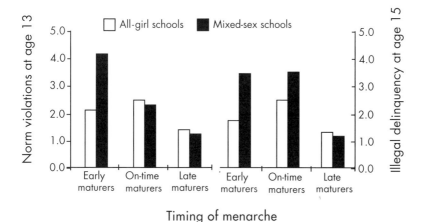

Figure 11.7 Norm violations in early adolescence (*panel A*), and illegal delinquency in middle adolescence (*panel B*), as a function of age at menarche and school type

The message I draw is more subtle, but no less powerful: the impact of universal-biological events on behavioral development is controlled by the social context of development.

Summary

There is much hand-wringing in the social and behavioral sciences about how to study environmental influences on behavioral development, partly as a result of research demonstrating that many putative environmental influences do not matter as much as previously thought (Rowe, 1994). The appropriate reaction to this should be neither despair nor defensiveness, but the adoption of self-critical empirical strategies that can more effectively and responsibly answer questions about how individuals and environments are linked across the life-course. Where random assignment and experimentation are not possible, behavioral scientists can capitalize on natural or quasi-experiments to get a handle on these issues. The goal of this chapter has been to summarize and illustrate research strategies that can be used to better tease apart issues of social-selection and social-influence in life-course development. The research examples have focused on development during the first two decades of life, but I hope the strategies and self-critical attitude toward disentangling person-environment effects can generalize to research across the life-span.

ACKNOWLEDGMENTS

The research described in this chapter was supported by grants from the National Institute of Mental Health (MH-49414, MH-45070, MH-56344) and the Medical Research Council.

REFERENCES

Budd, T. (1999). *Burglary of domestic dwellings: Findings from the British Crime Survey. Home Office Statistical Bulletin 4/99*. London: Home Office.

CACI Information Services. (1997). *Acorn user guide*. London: CACI Limited.

Caspi, A. (1995). Puberty and the gender organization of schools: how biology and social context shape the adolescent experience. In L. Crockett and A. Crouter (eds.), *Pathways through adolescence: Individual development in relation to social context*. Hillsdale, NJ: Erlbaum, 57–74.

Caspi, A., Lynam, D., Moffitt, T. E., and Silva, P. A. (1993). Unraveling girls' delinquency: biological, dispositional, and contextual contributions to adolescent misbehavior. *Developmental Psychology*, 29, 19–30.

Caspi, A., Taylor, A., Moffitt, T. E., and Plomin, R. (2000). Neighborhood deprivation affects children's mental health: environmental risks identified in a genetic design. *Psychological Science*, 11, 338–42.

Caspi, A., Wright, B. R., Moffitt, T. E., and Silva, P. A. (1998). Early failure in the labor market: childhood and adolescent predictors of unemployment in the transition to adulthood. *American Sociological Review*, 63, 424–51.

Cohen, L., and Felson, M. (1979). Social change and crime rate trends: a routine activity approach. *American Sociological Review*, 44, 588–608.

Dohrenwend, B. P., Levav, I., Shrout, P. E., Schwartz, S., Naveh, G., Link, B. G., Skodol, A. E., and Stueve, A. (1992). Socioeconomic status and psychiatric disorders: the causation-selection issue. *Science*, 255, 946–52.

Elder, G. H., Jr., George, L. K., and Shanahan, M. J. (1996). Psychosocial stress over the life course. In H. B. Kaplan (ed.), *Psychosocial stress: Perspectives on structure, theory, life-course, and methods*. San Diego, CA: Academic Press, Inc, 247–92.

Ge, X., Conger, R. D., and Elder, G. H., Jr. (1996). Coming of age too early: pubertal influences on girls' vulnerability to psychological distress. *Child Development*, 67, 3386–400.

Henry, B., Caspi, A., Moffitt, T. E., and Silva, P. A. (1996). Temperamental and familial predictors of violent and non-violent criminal convictions: from age 3 to age 18. *Developmental Psychology*, 32, 614–23.

Kendler, K. S. (1993). Twin studies of psychiatric illness: current status and future directions. *Archives of General Psychiatry*, 50, 905–15.

Kessler, R. C., Foster, C. L., Saunders, W. B., and Stang, P. E. (1995). Consequences of psychiatric disorders, I: Educational attainment. *American Journal of Psychiatry*, 152, 1026–32.

Krueger, R. F., Caspi, A., Moffitt, T. E., and Silva, P. A. (1998). The structure and stability of common mental disorders (DSM-III-R): a longitudinal-epidemiological study. *Journal of Abnormal Psychology*, 107, 216–77.

Loeber, R., Farrington, D. P., Stouthamer-Loeber, M., Moffitt, T. E., and Caspi, A. (1998). The development of male offending: key findings from the first decade of the Pittsburgh Youth Study. *Studies on Crime and Crime Prevention*, 7, 1–31.

Lynam, D. R., Caspi, A., Moffitt, T. E., Wikstrom, P. H., and Loeber, R. (2000). The effects of impulsivity on delinquency are stronger in poor neighborhoods. *Journal of Abnormal Psychology*, 109, 563–74.

Magnusson, D. (1988). *Individual development from an interactional perspective*. Hillsdale, NJ: Erlbaum.

Manski, C. F. (1995). *Identification problems in the social sciences*. Cambridge, MA: Harvard University Press.

Miech, R. A., Caspi, A., Moffitt, T. E., Wright, B. R. E., and Silva, P. A. (1999). Low socioeconomic status and mental disorders: a longitudinal study of selection and causation during young adulthood. *American Journal of Sociology*, 104, 1096–131.

Miech, R. A., and Shanahan, M. J. (2000). Socioeconomic status and depression over the life course. *Journal of Health and Social Behavior*, 41, 162–76.

Petersen, A. C., and Mortimer, J. T. (1994). *Youth unemployment and society*. New York: Cambridge University Press.

Plomin, R. (1994). *Genetics and experience: The interplay between nature and nurture*. Thousand Oaks, CA: Sage.

Prime Ministerial Task Force on Employment. (1994). *Employment outlook, July 1994*. Paris: Organisation for Economic Co-operation and Development.

Rindfuss, R. R. (1991). The young adult years: diversity, structural change, and fertility. *Demography*, 28, 493–512.

Rowe, D. C. (1994). *The limits of family influence*. New York: Guilford Press.

Rutter, M., Silberg, J., O'Connor, T., and Simonoff, E. (1999). Genetics and child psychiatry. vol. II: Empirical research findings. *Journal of Child Psychology and Psychiatry*, 40, 19–55.

Sampson, R. J., Raudenbush, S. W., and Earls, F. (1997). Neighborhoods and violent crime: a multilevel study of collective efficacy. *Science*, 277, 918–24.

Simmons, R. G., and Blyth, D. A. (1987). *Moving into adolescence: The impact of pubertal change and school context*. New York: Aldine De Gruyter.

Weissman, M. M., Bruce, M. L., Leaf, P. J., Florio, L. P., and Holzer, C. E. (1991). Affective disorders. In L. N. Robins and D. A. Regier (eds.), *Psychiatric disorders in America: The Epidemiologic Catchment Area Study*. New York: Free Press, 53–80.

White, J., Moffitt, T. E., Caspi, A., Jeglum-Bartusch, D., Needles, D., and Stouthamer-Loeber, M. (1994). Measuring impulsivity and examining its relationship to delinquency. *Journal of Abnormal Psychology*, 103, 192–205.

12 Pathways through challenge: implications for well-being and health

Carol D. Ryff, Burton H. Singer and
Marsha Mailick Seltzer

Introduction

In this chapter we explore how various life challenges influence psychological well-being and health. Our conception of life challenge encompasses both normative (typical, anticipated, planned) life transitions as well as nonnormative (atypical, unexpected, sometimes traumatic) life experiences. The individual difference variable we link to these challenges is psychological well-being. Drawn from depictions of positive functioning in developmental, clinical, and mental health literatures, well-being encompasses numerous dimensions of positive functioning (e.g., self-acceptance, quality of ties to others, mastery, purpose). The question thus is how these various aspects of well-being are affected by, or themselves affect, the experiential challenges that comprise an individual's life history.

Our chapter is organized into three sections, which in themselves, represent an evolving research program that began largely with questions in domains of life-course development and personality, and in recent years, has moved progressively in the direction of connecting life challenge and well-being to health. The first section is focused on single normative and nonnormative experiences of adulthood and aging, where we highlight findings from three categories of studies, which deal, respectively, with the parental experience in midlife, community relocation and caregiving in old age, and health challenges of later life. Across each of these, the focus is on how such experiences have impact on psychological well-being. The second section addresses cumulative profiles of life experience that combine both normative and nonnormative challenges. Here again, the focus is on the imprint of such long-term profiles of experience on positive psychological functioning. In the final section, we describe an unfolding program of studies that explores the implications of well-being for health. Framed as inquiries in "positive health," we examine the physiological substrates of flourishing, with emphasis on whether psychosocial strengths and successful negotiation of life challenges afford protection against morbidity and early mortality. The construct of resilience emerges as a conceptual theme across these latter studies. The central scientific task therein is explication of how resilience comes about, i.e. identifying the processes that make it possible.

Normative and nonnormative challenges: implications for well-being

A mainstay of life-course research is the idea of age-graded roles and life tasks (Baltes, 1987; Brim and Ryff, 1980; Caspi, 1987). These refer to socially sanctioned, frequently prescribed (hence, the term "normative") transitions that individuals expect to encounter as they journey across life. Such challenges are thus anticipated, they are frequently shared with others going through the same transition, and oftentimes, they are preceded by socialization processes that help individuals successfully negotiate the life change. Underscoring their age-graded features, there is also implicit understanding as to "when" such experiences should occur, which then creates perceptions at the individual level that one is "on-time" or "off-time" with regard to these normative experiences (Fallo-Mitchell and Ryff, 1981; Neugarten, Moore, and Lowe, 1965).

Juxtaposed with normative experiences are challenges and events that come unexpectedly and for which there may be little socialization. These nonnormative experiences include the voluminous literatures on stressful life events, but also encompass normative events that are experienced in atypical ways (e.g., giving birth to a child with a disability; having a spouse die in early adulthood). Nonnormative experiences are generally construed as having adverse influences on health and well-being, although there is growing interest in how some are able to thrive in the face of adversity and even benefit from it (Ickovics and Park, 1998; Krauss and Seltzer, 1999; Ryff, Singer, Love, and Essex, 1998).

Normative experiences, in contrast, are viewed as generally positive. Not only are they socially sanctioned (if not, prescribed) movement through these expected challenges of life can enhance well-being, such as perceptions of personal growth, mastery, purpose, and positive self-regard. That is, the usual "hurdles of life" (e.g., getting an education, finding a good job, marrying, having a family) provide the *experiential basis* for seeing growth and development in oneself through time, and in the process, acquiring new knowledge, skills, insight, and purpose.

We acknowledge that psychological strengths are not only consequences of successfully negotiated life challenges, but may also be significant contributors to how transitions are negotiated. Most of our investigations below examine the former question, but we also consider the latter to underscore the reciprocities between life challenges and psychological well-being.

These initial studies focus on single experiences, three categories of which are discussed in this chapter. The first pertains to the parental experience in midlife; the second to community relocation and caregiving in later life; and the third to the experience of increased health problems with aging. Some of these (e.g., relocation, later life health problems) pose particularly interesting questions for well-being, because, although they are somewhat age-graded and typical, they may not be desired experiences. Hence, how they are negotiated adds further insight to the successful negotiation of life challenges that are normative, in the sense of frequently occurring and anticipated, but not necessarily sought after (e.g., retirement, widowhood). In addition to examining the import of these diverse experiences for well-being, we also describe various intervening mechanisms (e.g., social comparison processes, causal attributions, coping strategies) that help clarify individual differences among those who show high profiles of well-being following, or during, these experiences from those who do not.

The parental experience in midlife

Extensive research has been conducted on the topic of parenthood (see Bornstein, 1995), which for many is a central challenge of adult life. Many have studied the effects of parents on the development of their children, while others have examined how the experience of becoming a parent affects the development and well-being of parents themselves (Ryff and Seltzer, 1996). Most of this latter work has emphasized the transition into parenting – the early years of this experience when children are young and parents tend to be in early adulthood. Alternatively, gerontological researchers have focused on the later years of being a parent when adult children may assume caregiving roles (Hagestad, 1987; Rossi and Rossi, 1990). A neglected period of the parental experience is midlife, particularly when children are emerging as adults in their own right and parents are establishing adult-to-adult relationships with them.

Ryff and Seltzer (1996) brought together numerous investigators to examine the developmental challenges and issues of this midlife period in parenting. Within this forum, Ryff, Schmutte, and Lee (1996) targeted a particular question believed to have consequence for parents' well-being: namely, how their adult children "turn out." An earlier investigation (Ryff, Lee, Essex, and Schmutte, 1994) had begun this query by investigating in a community sample of midlife adults how their adult children (27 years of age on average) were doing, both in terms of their educational and occupational accomplishments and their personal and social adjustment. The prediction was that parents whose grown children were doing well would be those with high levels of self-acceptance, purpose in life, environmental mastery, and autonomy (see Ryff, 1989, 1995 for summary of these key dimensions of well-being). Moreover, we brought social comparison processes into the evaluation, predicting that parents who saw their adult children as doing well as, or better than, themselves, would also have higher levels of well-being than parents who perceived their children had done more poorly than themselves.

Findings showed that parents' well-being (both mothers and fathers) was significantly predicted by how children had turned out, particularly in terms of their personal and social adjustment. Specifically, parents' ratings of self-acceptance, purpose in life, environmental mastery, personal growth, and positive relations with others were predicted by the perception that they had raised children who were self-confident, happy, and well-liked by others. To address the problem of source overlap (does parents' well-being bias how they view their children?), we also obtained data from spouses to validate that ratings of children's success or failure are not driven by parents' well-being (see Ryff, Lee, Essex, and Schmutte, 1994). Children's educational and occupational attainment also significantly predicted parents' self-acceptance, purpose in life, personal growth, and positive relations with others, but the effects were not as strong as for children's adjustment.

The social comparison influences added further intrigue to these findings. Parents' comparisons with their children were, in fact, significant predictors of their own well-being (above and beyond the effects described above), but these outcomes were in the *opposite* direction to what we had predicted. That is, parents who perceived that their children had done better than themselves had *lower* rather than higher well-being. Such effects pertained primarily to comparisons about personal and social adjustment, although for mothers, effects were also evident for comparisons about attainment (education, occupation). Such outcomes varied, however, as a function of mothers' level of education (i.e., there were significant interactions between mothers' education and their children's attainment in predicting their own well-being). Specifically, mothers with greater education had higher self-acceptance and purpose in life *if* their children's attainment was better than their own. However, for mothers with lower levels of education, having children with attainment profiles better than their own was associated with lower levels of self-acceptance and life purpose. Presumably, mothers who had experienced their own educational opportunities were more likely to "bask" in having children who exceeded their own achievement.

Ryff, Schmutte, and Lee (1996) added attributional perspectives by asking about the extent to which parents viewed themselves as *responsible* for how their grown children had turned out. Parents reported whether they took credit or responsibility for how well their children had done and indicated to what extent they viewed themselves as role models for their children as well as what their level of involvement had been across multiple domains of children's lives. The prediction was that parents would report differing levels of responsibility depending on how well children had turned out: those with successful children were hypothesized to report higher levels of responsibility than those with children who had not done so well. In addition, following attribution theory, we predicted that among parents of less successful children, their levels of well-being would be "protected" by their perception that they were not responsible for such outcomes.

The findings were again surprising. As predicted, parents who viewed their children as less successful in adjustment and attainment did, in fact, report lower levels of responsibility for these children. This attribution did not, however, protect parental well-being (by avoiding self-blame for negative outcomes). Rather, parents with the lowest levels of life purpose and mastery as well as the highest levels of depressive symptoms were those whose children had not turned out well *and* who reported low levels of responsibility and involvement with these children. We did not include questions about other external influences (e.g., peers, school); thus it was impossible to address whether parents of unsuccessful children might attribute these outcomes to external factors. What we did learn, however, was that attribution theory, when applied to the parental realm, seems to require modification. That is, parenting may invoke strong normative expectations in which parents believe they *should be* actively involved in and responsible for their children's lives. Thus, well-being can be undermined not only by having a child turn out poorly, but also by perceiving that one fell short of being a responsible and involved parent.

Schmutte and Ryff (1994) elaborated gender effects (mothers and fathers, sons and daughters) in the above analyses. Their findings showed that although parents did not report different levels of success for sons and daughters, parental well-being was more closely tied to success of sons. With regard to social comparisons, however, it was comparisons with daughters that were more strongly linked to parental well-being. Responsibility assessments showed cross-sex patterns: mothers' well-being was more strongly predicted by their ratings of responsibility for sons, while fathers' well-being was aligned with their ratings of responsibility for daughters. These findings were interpreted within contexts of gender-role socialization as well as changing opportunity climates for women (see Ryff, Schmutte, and Lee, 1996).

A final perspective on the parental experience and well-being invokes more explicit developmental paradigms – specifically, the Eriksonian construct of generativity (Erikson, 1959; McAdams and de St Aubin, 1998). Generativity poses that a central challenge or task of the middle years of adulthood is to guide and direct the next generation. This can occur in the context of parenting, but may also apply to mentoring activities in one's workplace, or leadership roles in one's community. Generativity is now a flourishing arena of inquiry (see McAdams and de St Aubin, 1998; Ryff, Kwan, and Singer, 2001) in which life-course developmentalists are detailing its diverse forms and relating it to other aspects of personality as well as social structural influences. Keyes and Ryff (1998), for example, showed that the expression of generativity is contoured by social structural factors. That is, midlife and older adults with higher levels of education show more generative behavior and commitment, likely underscoring the role of differential access to resources and opportunity required to be a generative person. These authors further documented links between generativity and psychological and social well-being. High profiles of generativity were strongly linked with individuals' feeling good about themselves and judging their lives to be worthwhile and meaningful.

Community relocation and caregiving in old age

Relocation In contrast to parenthood, which is a continuous, ongoing normative experience, community relocation in later life is a discrete event that for many is an increasingly common transition. In the typical case, community relocation involves an aging woman or couple who are moving from the home they may have lived in for many years to an apartment or a retirement community. Not included in this research are moves signaling decline – i.e., relocation to nursing homes. While a typical later life transition, relocation at any period in the life-course is stressful. In old age, it is also a change that is sometimes "resisted." Thus, relocation provides a useful example of a later life challenge that occurs with high frequency, but may be accompanied by ambivalent or negative expectations.

We have followed an aging sample of women (N = 301) through four waves of data collection punctuated by the relocation transition. Baseline data were obtained prior to their moves and on three occasions post-move (four-six weeks later, seven-eight months later, about 15 months later). This design has enabled tracking of actual changes in reported levels of psychological well-being as well as other processes (e.g., social comparisons, coping strategies) thought to influence adaptation to this later life challenge. Importantly, these data have documented the dynamics of well-being, showing significant gains and losses in positive psychological functioning, even though the measures themselves are highly reliable (test-retest, internal consistency) (Ryff, 1989; Ryff and Keyes, 1995). Such variation, in contrast to more trait-like dimensions of personality (McCrae and Costa, 1990), renders well-being particularly informative for evaluating the impact of normative and nonnormative life challenges.

Ryff and Essex (1992) drew on Rosenberg's self-concept theory to specify the interpretive, or meaning-making activities, through which life experiences, like community relocation, might influence well-being. These include how individuals see themselves doing in multiple life domains relative to others (social comparisons), how they perceive that they are viewed by others across multiple life domains (reflected appraisals), and what they define as central to their own identities (psychological centrality). Kling, Ryff, and Essex (1997) used these differing assessments to investigate whether cross-time well-being is maximized by increasing the psychological centrality of domains in which one is doing well (measured by social comparisons and reflected appraisals) and decreasing the centrality of life domains in which one is doing poorly. Such changes in centrality would demonstrate flexibility in the self-concept, which may be needed to successfully negotiate life transitions. These predicted patterns were found in domains of health and friendships: women who enhanced the importance of these aspects of their self-definition in which they saw themselves doing well post-relocation, were those who showed *gains* in multiple aspects of well-being following relocation.

Psychological well-being is not only an outcome of life challenge, but also a contributing factor to how challenge is negotiated. To explore this possibility, Smider, Essex, and Ryff (1996) employed the longitudinal relocation data to investigate short-term emotional reactions to relocation based on pre-move psychological resources (i.e., well-being) as well as contextual factors surrounding the move itself (e.g., difficulty of the move, pressure to move, unexpected gains in moving). As predicted, pre-move levels of environmental mastery and autonomy buffered the effects of a difficult move and thereby reduced negative emotional reactions (sadness, aggravation) shortly after relocation. On the other hand, women with lower levels of autonomy and personal growth prior to the move experienced more of an emotional uplift (more optimism, less sadness) post-move when relocation involved high levels of unexpected gains. These findings underscore the diverse ways in which psychological strengths and vulnerabilities influence how one enters particular life events and is subsequently affected by them.

Caregiving Another perspective on parenting and individual differences in well-being derives from a longitudinal program of research on aging parents who are caregivers for their adult son or daughter with developmental disabilities (Krauss and Seltzer, 1999; Seltzer and Ryff, 1994). Seltzer and Ryff (1994) clarified that while parenting is, in itself, largely a normative age-graded task, it can be and frequently is experienced nonnormatively. For example, one can give birth to a child with mental retardation, autism, or other forms of developmental disability, which may greatly transform the parental experience. It is not, however, just the transition to parenthood that likely differs in these cases, but also the middle and later years of the parental experience. And, it is not, as may be expected, inevitably the case that parental well-being is undermined by parenting in the nonnormative case (Seltzer, Krauss, Choi, and Hong, 1996; Von Riper, Ryff, and Pridham, 1992). Older mothers of adult children with mental retardation, for example, frequently appear more similar to than different from their peers with regard to multiple indicators of health and well-being.

Seltzer, Greenberg, Floyd, Pettee and Hong (2001), using data from the Wisconsin Longitudinal Study, found that whereas midlife parents of individuals with severe mental health problems had poorer physical and psychological well-being than comparison group parents (whose child was not affected by health problems or disabilities), parents whose child had mental retardation had a profile similar to the comparison group in physical health, depressive symptoms, and alcohol symptoms. They also had similar profiles of marital stability, signifying that stress in one domain (i.e, parenting) does not necessarily spill over into other spheres of life. In related research, parents of adults with mental retardation were found to be above the population mean in positive psychological well-being, life satisfaction, and health (Krauss and Seltzer, 1999).

How long-term caregiving for a child with mental retardation can be positive implicates the coping strategies of the parents facing this challenge (Seltzer, Greenberg, and Krauss, 1995; Essex, Seltzer, and Krauss, 1999) and the different aspects of the context, such as the availability of support (formal and informal) for dealing with the nonnormative challenge (Greenberg, Seltzer, Krauss, and Kim, 1997). We have found that aging mothers of adults with mental retardation are very effective at using problem-focused coping strategies to regulate their psychological distress and well-being, a likely explanation for why nonnormative, chronically stressful demands tend not to result in compromised levels of psychological well-being. For example, aging mothers of adults with mental retardation who plan ahead and who are able to positively reinterpret stressful circumstances have lower levels of depressive symptoms even when they are faced with high demand for hands-on caregiving (Seltzer *et al.*, 1995). However, this positive effect of problem-focused coping strategies was not found when such strategies were used by aging mothers of adults with severe mental illness. This set of findings signifies that the resources that buffer the stresses of caregiving (e.g., problem-focused coping) are differentially effective, depending on the nature of the caregiving challenge (mental retardation versus mental illness, in this example).

Another buffer to the stresses of caring for an adult child with a disability such as mental retardation is social support (Greenberg *et al.*, 1997). As in the general population, aging mothers of adults with mental retardation tend to have lower levels of depressive symptoms if they have a large network of friends and family who provide them with support. In contrast, for aging mothers of adults with severe mental health problems, the size of the informal support network of friends and families was found to be immaterial to their psychological well-being. By way of explanation, the diagnosis of severe mental illness tends to be made in the son's or daughter's early adulthood, and thus the older mothers in the Greenberg *et al.* (1997) study had much less time to adapt to their caregiving challenge, the stigma of the disability, and to develop a network of supportive friends and family than their age peers whose adult child had mental retardation.

These studies suggest that midlife and aging mothers who experience nonnormative parenting such as having a child with mental retardation may succeed in maintaining healthy levels of psychological well-being by using selective coping strategies (such as planning ahead and positive reinterpretation and growth) and by having sustained relationships with friends and family members who can provide support to them. However, not all nonnormative challenges are alike, as having a son or daughter with mental illness poses stresses more difficult to overcome than parenting an adult child with mental retardation. This difference is largely because mothers of adults with mental retardation benefit from moderating and mediating processes such as using adaptive coping strategies and amassing social support, factors which tend to be less effective in maintaining the psychological well-being of aging mothers caring for adult children with mental illness.

Overall, parenting grown children with severe disabilities is an atypical version of family caregiving. It differs from caregiving for elderly relatives in its duration (lasting five or six decades as contrasted with a period generally one-tenth as long), progression (marked by a gain rather than loss of skills and competencies in the care recipient over time), and outcome (the care recipient outlives the caregiver rather than the reverse). Yet it is similar to more conventional forms of caregiving in that caregivers can flourish in the context of high levels of stress depending on individual differences in intervening mechanisms (such as coping and social support).

For example, using structural equation modeling, Li, Seltzer, and Greenberg (1999) showed that daughters providing care to elderly parents were more effective in using problem-focused coping to maintain and improve their well-being over the course of their caregiving "career" if they had high initial levels of mastery. In another analysis from this study, social support was found to be more important to sustaining the psychological well-being of wife caregivers than daugher caregivers (Li, Seltzer, and Greenberg, 1997), underscoring the significance of the kinship relationship between caregiver and care recipient in conditioning the course of caregiving and its outcomes.

Thus, the effects of the increasingly common challenge of family caregiving are not uniform, and reflect individual differences in factors such as psychological and social resources, the type of disability for which care is provided, the life-course location of the caregiver, and the kinship relationship between the caregiver and the care recipient.

Relocation and caregiving Although life challenges are frequently studied individually, as illustrated by the above summaries, it is informative to contrast their effects on well-being as well as to examine whether intervening processes vary depending on the nature of the challenge encountered. Addressing such questions, Kling, Seltzer, and Ryff (1997) contrasted the experience of relocation, a typical and discrete later life event, with later life caregiving for an adult child with mental retardation, an atypical, long-term challenge. Data from the separate longitudinal studies described above were used to test the hypothesis that women experiencing community relocation (the more normative, expected, and short-term event), would report more positive cross-time change in psychological well-being than women with long-term caregiving responsibilities. In addition, relocation women were predicted to use more problem-focused coping strategies than caregiving mothers. Both predictions were supported. Women in the caregiving sample, however, showed stronger relationships between coping and well-being, underscoring possible gains in coping expertise that accompany challenges of lengthy duration.

Health challenges in later life

Later life, for many, brings increased incidence of health problems (chronic conditions, symptoms, functional impairment). That is, physical challenges of aging are quite common, typical, and even expected. For example, in the 60–69 age range, about 45 percent of women and 35 percent of men report two or more chronic conditions; these figures rise to 61 percent of women and 47 percent of men aged 70–79, and 70 percent of women and 53 percent of men aged 80–89 (Jaur and Stoddard, 1999). Do such changes undermine psychological well-being? What factors influence links between physical health and mental health as individuals grow old? These questions have been explored in several studies by Heidrich and Ryff (1993a, b; 1996; Heidrich, 1999). Social comparison processes were again emphasized as intervening mechanisms in the link between physical health and psychological well-being. A first finding was that older women who are in poor physical health engage more frequently in comparison with others, not just about their health, but also about their activity levels, physical appearance, and how they cope with aging. Moreover, such comparisons moderate the influence of their physical health on psychological well-being. That is, those in poor health who saw themselves comparing favorably with others had higher well-being (i.e., scores on personal growth, positive relations with others) and lower depressive symptoms than women in poor health who perceived more negative comparisons (Heidrich and Ryff, 1993a).

A further investigation (Heidrich and Ryff, 1993b) examined multiple aspects of the "self-system" as mediators of relationships between physical (chronic conditions, symptoms, functional limitations, subjective health) and mental health (depression, anxiety, life satisfaction, affect balance, well-being) in later life. In addition to social comparison processes, Heidrich and Ryff (1993b) assessed the extent to which older persons see themselves as having meaningful roles, reference groups, and normative guidelines. These ideas, drawn from Kuypers and Bengtson's (1973) "social breakdown syndrome," implicate the social feedback processes and socialization guidelines, or lack thereof, that contribute to negative self-perceptions in the elderly. Also examined was the degree to which the respondents' ideals about themselves fell short of their actual self-perceptions – ideas drawn from Higgins' (1987) self-discrepancy theory. Structural equation modeling provided empirical support for social comparisons and social integration (i.e., ratings of roles, reference groups, and normative guidelines) as mediators of the link between physical and mental health, but not for self-discrepancies.

Additional work on the latter, with a sample of young, middle-aged, and older adults, clarified that self-discrepancy varies with age (Heidrich,

1996). Ideal self-ratings converged with actual self-ratings for older adults, but were significantly different among young and middle-aged adults. Self-discrepancies were also found to mediate the effects of health problems on numerous indicators of psychological well-being and distress.

Summary

The preceding studies elaborate how normative and nonnormative experiences are linked with various aspects of psychological well-being in adulthood and later life. Well-being has also been examined as an *a priori* factor that influences how transitions are negotiated. Across all of these investigations, considerable emphasis has been given to mediating and moderating factors, such as social comparisons, reflected appraisals, attributions, coping strategies, and self-discrepancies. These have clarified the interpretive processes through which various life challenges are linked with a strong sense of purpose, mastery, growth, quality ties to others, and positive self-regard.

The above investigations have emphasized largely single life challenges– that is, they have tracked changes in well-being following a particular event (relocation) or an enduring experience (parenthood, caregiving, increased health problems). Such a *one-at-a-time* approach is not, however, consistent with how life is experienced for most individuals. That is, most people, at most periods in their lives, are dealing simultaneously with numerous life challenges. This fact was richly illustrated with members of the relocation sample, who over the course of the study reported, on average, that nine other events had co-occurred along with the move. Included were such experiences as death of significant others, health events, having someone move in or out of their home, changing jobs, and multiple events in the lives of children (marriage, parenthood, divorce, relocation, job change). In light of these observations, our next section examines cumulative profiles of experience and how they are linked with psychological well-being.

Putting normative and nonnormative experience together: cumulative profiles of challenge and psychological well-being

In this section, we will illustrate the integration of normative and nonnormative experience to create "whole lives" via two different studies, one cross-sectional, and the other longitudinal. In both the focus was on relating profiles of prior life challenge to psychological well-being. Ryff and Heidrich (1997) interviewed a sample of over 300 young, middle and old-aged adults, each of whom completed past life event inventories and rated their psychological well-being. Normative experiences across these age groups were divided into three broad domains: educational and occupational events; family life events and friendships; and community and leisure involvements. Underscoring the age-graded nature of these experiences, respondents indicated how many of the events had occurred in their lives and how satisfying they found the experience to be. Nonnormative stresses were assessed with a modified version of the Life Experiences Survey (Sarason, Johnson, and Siegel, 1978), which measures the number and impact of a variety of unexpected life challenges (e.g., divorce, unemployment, financial problems) over a designated period of prior time.

The general prediction was that the completion of normative (expected, planned, positively sanctioned) events would contribute to perceptions of personal growth and development as well as a sense of mastery, purpose, and positive self-regard. Nonnormative experiences are typically construed as having adverse effects on health and well-being, although the literatures on resilience and growth through trauma (noted earlier) suggest that, under some circumstances, negative life stresses can ultimately have positive consequences. For both realms of experience, the objective was to quantify the accumulation of events through time and use them to predict variation in multiple dimensions of psychological well-being.

Regression analyses revealed that normative events were, in fact, significant predictors of well-being, but there were marked age differences in which domains of life were key influences. For young adults, it was participation in extracurricular and social activities that was strongly predictive of self-acceptance, mastery, and life purpose. For midlife adults, it was experiences in the relationship domain (family, friends) that strongly produced self-acceptance, mastery, and positive relations with others. For older adults, it was prior work and educational experiences that were strong predictors of personal growth, purpose in life, and environmental mastery. Nonnormative stresses had generally weaker linkages to psychological well-being, although for young adults, such adverse experiences were, as prior literature would suggest, significant positive predictors of personal growth.

The above investigation, while emphasizing the accumulation of normative and nonnormative events through time, analyzed these as separate realms of experience and did so with a largely nomothetic, group-differences approach. In a separate investigation (Singer, Ryff, Carr, and Magee, 1998) based on findings from the Wisconsin Longitudinal Study, we combined experiences across all these realms to create profiles of cumulative adversity and cumulative advantage over approximately 35 years (from senior year in high school to midlife). Life events and conditions included in these profiles included extensive information about family background, adolescent aspirations and resources, education and training, job characteristics, marriage and parenting experiences, social participation, and acute events. The general prediction was that adversity and its accumulation over time would have negative mental health consequences, whereas advantage and its accumulation over time would have positive mental health consequences.

With regard to mental health outcomes, we cross-classified positive and negative aspects of mental health (i.e., psychological well-being, clinical depression) to identify various "types." Of particular interest was the group described as "resilient," which consisted of individuals who at some prior period in their lives had experienced major depression, but who in midlife reported high psychological well-being. Such individuals embody a *recovery* conception of resilience, in which they had gone through a difficult period, or periods, but subsequently, regained a strong sense of positive functioning. We used *person-centered* data analytic strategies to identify the primary life history pathways to such resilience among a sample of 168 resilient women. The analytic steps began with the writing of narratives for individual lives that summarized, in chronological order, the information evident in over 250 variables. Subsequent steps pared these variables down into frequently co-occurring conditions/events across particular subgroups and culminated in tests of distinguishability across subgroups (see Singer and Ryff, in press for a condensed summary of the analytic progression).

Four primary pathways to midlife resilience were identified. These differed in the timing and nature of the life adversities experienced as well as the timing and nature of offsetting advantage factors. A first pathway consisted of those with generally positive beginnings (e.g., high starting abilities, no alcoholism in childhood home) who subsequently experienced upward job mobility and related positive social comparisons. Despite these advantages, all of these women had experienced the death of one parent, most had had caregiving responsibilities for an ill person, and more than half had chronic health conditions. These were lives of chronic and acute adversities that were offset by positive work experiences, good beginnings, and favorable evaluations of self compared to others.

A second pathway consisted of women for whom the primary early adversity was growing up with an alcoholic parent. In addition, many of these women had experienced three or more acute events (i.e., death of parent, spouse, child; divorce; job loss). However, these women had important advantages involving social relationships and social participation as well as early employment with stable or upward occupational status.

These latter "plusses" may have contributed to their capacity to overcome notable early life difficulties combined with subsequent loss events.

A third pathway consisted of women who showed, primarily, advantage in early life: all had parents who were high school graduates, there were no alcohol problems in the childhood home, and the women had strong starting resources (high school grades, IQ). Later, however, they confronted various forms of adversity (e.g., poor social relationships, downward occupational mobility, job loss, divorce, single parenthood, caregiving). Their lives were thus characterized largely by adversity in adulthood, but they began their life journeys with important early strengths that likely facilitated recovery from the adverse experiences.

The final pathway consisted of women with more mixed profiles of advantage (e.g., intact families) and disadvantage (e.g., low parental education). As life unfolded, they confronted an array of adversities (e.g., single parenthood, downward mobility, living with alcohol problems in the home, acute events). As such, the resilience of the final pathway was more difficult to explain and underscored the need for additional information, pertaining perhaps to the women's reactions to their life challenges as well as the quality of their significant social relationships.

Overall, these findings underscore the diverse ways in which life challenges can accumulate across time and be offset by countervailing accumulation of positive experience. A central message is that there are *multiple pathways through life challenges* to generally positive outcomes, but that this variation can nonetheless be organized into groups of whole lives. Person-centered methods are valuable for organizing such cross-time, cross-domain data, illustrating as they do, complex but discernable patterns, in how challenge accumulates in individuals' lives and is successfully negotiated.

Linking life experience and well-being to health

Existing research connecting life experience to health is predominantly negative: life stresses and/or psychological disorders related to them are used to predict physical illness, disease, and death. Such inquiries do not advance understanding of what it means to thrive, flourish, and be well, sometimes in the face of adversity (Ickovics and Park, 1998; Ryff and Singer, 1998a, b). Construed positively, human health encompasses the above-described aspects of positive functioning, such as leading a meaningful, purposeful life and having quality ties to others. What is largely unknown, however, are the consequences of such well-being for biology. Full understanding of positive health thus requires mapping how positive psychological or relational experience is instantiated in neural circuitry, and downstream endocrinological and immunological systems. The key question is whether these aspects of well-being, through various neurophysiological processes, culminate in physical health, vitality, and longevity.

In this section we will first briefly review concepts and empirical findings on the physiological signature of well-being. Second, focusing on one specific aspect of well-being – namely, good quality social relations with others – we will examine the extent to which cumulative relational experience is related to cumulative physiological burden (or its absence). Underscoring the theme of resilience, we will also describe an empirical investigation of whether the adverse consequences (physiologically-speaking) of cumulative economic disadvantage can be offset or protected against by enduring, high quality relationships with significant others.

The physiological signature of well-being

The most extensive work on physiological substrates of flourishing is found in animal models focused on positive affiliation (Carter, 1998; Panksepp, 1998). In particular, Carter (1998) provides a neuroendocrine perspective on attachment and love, noting that in animals attachment can be operationalized as selective social bonds, thereby facilitating observation and experimentation that connects such bonds to physiological substrates. A review of caregiver-infant and adult-heterosexual pair bonds reveals recurrent associations between levels of activity in the HPA (hypothalamic-pituitary-adrenal) axis and subsequent expression of social behaviors and attachments. Positive social behaviors (e.g., social bonds) appear to reduce HPA axis activity, whereas negative interactions sometimes have the opposite effect. Central neuropeptides, especially oxytocin and vasopressin, are implicated in social bonding and central control of the HPA axis. In prairie voles, for example, where there is clear evidence of pair bonds, oxytocin has been shown to increase social behavior, and both oxytocin and social interaction appear to reduce activity of the HPA axis. These processes, Carter suggests, may be relevant for understanding the health benefits that underlie loving relationships. In humans, positive patterns of interpersonal interaction have been found to predict lower levels of physiological arousal, particularly in the neuroendocrine and cardiovascular systems (Seeman and McEwen, 1996; Uchino, Cacioppo, and Kiecolt-Glaser, 1996).

Uvnas-Moberg (1997, 1998; Petersson, Alster, Lundeberg, and Uvnas-Moberg, 1996) further elaborates how oxytocin may mediate the benefits of positive social interaction and emotions. Oxytocin levels are raised by somatosensory stimulation (e.g., breast feeding or suckling) as well as touch and warm temperatures. In both male and female rats, oxytocin exerts potent anti-stress effects, such as decreasing blood pressure, heart rate and cortisol levels, with effects lasting from one to several weeks. Rates of wound healing and weight gain are also promoted by oxytocin treatment. Extrapolating over the long term, salubrious social bonds can lead to repeated exposure to positive social stimuli, and thereby repeated release of oxytocin. More importantly, in humans such positive social experiences can be stored in memories, which may, in themselves reactivate these physiological processes.

Further avenues for linking positive human experience, particularly of the relational variety, to health, pertain to nerve growth factors and the anabolic growth promoting hormones that embody thriving (Epel, McEwen, and Ickovics, 1998) and help maintain and repair the body. A major task for future inquiry is to identify the naturally occurring interactions and activities (e.g., zestful group play in children; loving and supportive relationships in adulthood) that activate these growth-promoting processes.

Shifting attention to negative aspects of relational well-being, there is a substantial literature demonstrating associations between social ill-being and risk for morbidity and mortality. Using data from the Alameda County Study, a community-based prospective investigation, Berkman and Syme (1979) showed that those who lacked ties to others were nine years later two to three times more likely to have died than those who were socially connected. Subsequent inquiries have extended the documentation of health risks associated with social isolation, or lack of social support, to include risk of various diseases as well as reduced longevity (Berkman, 1995; Seeman, 1996; House, Landis, and Umberson, 1988).

The health effects of the social environment have been examined across the life-span. Taylor, Repetti, and Seeman (1997) explored the nature of "unhealthy environments" in childhood and pointed to three characteristics that undermine the health of children and adolescents: (a) a social climate that is conflictual and angry, or even violent and abusive; (b) parent-child relationships that are unresponsive and lacking in cohesiveness, warmth and emotional support; and (c) parenting style that is either overly controlling and dominating, or uninvolved with little imposition of rules and structure. Such characteristics were linked to depression and maladaptive ways of coping in children as well as health-threatening behaviors in adolescence.

With respect to older ages, studies have linked negative aspects of social interaction to increased cardiovascular and/or neuroendocrine activity (Seeman and McEwen, 1996; Uchino, Cacioppo, and Kiecolt-Glaser, 1996). Marital conflict has been linked to high blood pressure (Ewart,

Taylor *et al.*, 1991), elevated pituitary and adrenal hormones (Malarkey, Kiecolt-Glaser *et al.*, 1994), and physiological arousal (Levenson, Carstenson, and Gottman, 1994).

Three features of the human studies mentioned above deserve special attention. One is the general focus on individual biological parameters. Examination of single biomarkers neglects the possibility of co-occurring physiological risks, which may accumulate over time, and in turn, significantly impact health outcomes. The concept of allostatic load, introduced by McEwen and Stellar (1993), reflects this cumulative view of physiological risk, proposing that wear and tear across multiple physiological systems is a significant contributor to overall health risk. This wear and tear is hypothesized to ensue, at least in part, from repeated exposure to life challenges, such as social relational conflict and adversity. Further conceptual elaboration of allostatic load has been provided by McEwen (1998) and McEwen and Seeman (1999), and an initial operationalization of this concept has been put forth by Seeman *et al.*, (1997; 2000). Higher allostatic load – using measures of HPA axis, sympathetic nervous system, and cardiovascular activity, metabolism and adipose tissue deposition, glucose metabolism – has been shown in longitudinal studies to predict later life incident cardiovascular disease, decline in physical and cognitive functioning, and mortality. These diverse outcomes underscore the need for an early warning system of biomarkers that signal pending malfunction across a multiplicity of physiological systems. Allostatic load provides an initial candidate for such an early warning system.

A second significant feature of the extant social relationship/physiology literature is that most studies focus on single point-in-time assessments of relationships (e.g., in childhood, or adulthood, or later life). While useful, such queries do not provide insight into long-term profiles across multiple significant relationships. The potential health effects of cumulative relational adversity or advantage cannot be ascertained from such investigations. For example, some who experience conflictual relationships in adulthood, may have also experienced relational problems with parents in childhood. On the positive side, there may be continuity between nurturing and supportive relationships in childhood and emotional intimacy with a spouse or partner in adulthood. Thus, relational experience, positive or negative, may cumulate over time. Differences in the valence of such cumulative experience should have a physiological signature reflected in differing levels of allostatic load which, as indicated above, predicts a multiplicity of later-life health outcomes.

Finally, underscoring the theme of positive health, comparatively little prior research, especially in humans, has probed the links between "interpersonal flourishing" (i.e., loving, nurturing, enjoyable social relationships) and intervening biological processes or health outcomes. That is, the science that connects the relational realm to neuroendocrine factors or immune function is heavily weighted on the side of documenting the adverse physiological sequelae of interpersonal conflict, or linking social isolation to morbidity and mortality. Missing from the literature are studies explicitly focused on relational strengths as possible contributors to positive health promotion (Ryff and Singer, 2000a). The physiological signature of well-being will also require incorporating additional neuroendocrine factors, such as oxytocin, which track the physiological substrates of interpersonal well-being.

Relationship pathways and allostatic load

The linkage of social well-being with biology is illustrated in a study in which we assessed cumulative relational experience and cumulative physiological burden (i.e., allostatic load) on the same respondents. The general prediction was that negative relational experience, in both childhood and adulthood, would contribute to increased allostatic load, while positive relational experience across time would mitigate against wear and tear on the organism. We explored this prediction with a biological sub-sample (N = 106) of participants from the Wisconsin Longitudinal Study (WLS), which is a large random sample of men and women who graduated from Wisconsin high schools in 1957 and were subsequently re-interviewed in 1975 and 1992/93. This biological subsample matched the income distribution of the full WLS population on family household income in 1957 and adult household income in 1992/93. In 1997, these respondents participated in a new wave of data collection that included, among other things, a detailed social relationship questionnaire, a physical health examination, and blood and urine samples. Laboratory assays and measurements taken during the physical examination were used to operationalize allostatic load.

The specific biomarkers included were: systolic and diastolic blood pressure (indices of cardiovascular activity); waist-hip ratio (an index of mesolism and adipose tissue deposition, thought to be influenced by increased glucocorticoid activity); serum HDL and total cholesterol (markers whose levels are known to influence the development of atherosclerosis – increased risk being associated with higher levels in the case of total cholesterol and lower levels in the case of HDL); blood plasma levels of glycosilated hemoglobin (an integrated measure of glucose metabolism over several days); serum dihydroepiandrosterone sulfate (DHEA-S; a functional HPA antagonist); 12-hour urinary cortisol excretion (an integrated measure of HPA axis activity); 12-hour urinary norepinephrine and epinephrine excretion levels (integrated indices of SNS activity).

For each of the ten biological parameters, subjects were classified into quartiles based on the distribution of scores in the MacArthur Study of Successful Aging (Seeman *et al.*, 1997), the data set that was initially used to calibrate risk zones for allostatic load. The allostatic load score for an individual was calculated by counting the number of parameters for which the person fell into the "highest" risk quartile (i.e., top quartile for all parameters except HDL cholesterol and DHEA-S for which membership in the lowest quartile corresponds to highest risk). Based on previous studies (Seeman *et al.*, 1997; 2000) persons with allostatic load scores of three or more are at elevated risk of incident cardiovascular disease, cognitive impairment, functional decline, and mortality. The same scoring procedures were used in the WLS biological subsample.

With regard to relational well-being, respondents were asked to report about their relationship with their mother and father (separately) when they were growing up. The items, derived from a parental bonding scale (Parker, Tupling, and Brown, 1979), probed the emotional, affective, and caring features of these relationships. In addition, multiple aspects of current connection to a spouse or significant other were assessed using four sub-scales from the PAIR (Personal Assessment of Intimacy Relationships) inventory (Schaefer and Olson, 1981). The emotional and sexual sub-scales were included because of their focus on the most intimate forms of connection between people. The intellectual and recreational sub-scales emphasize mutually enjoyed experience, companionship, and the scope of shared communication. A combined emotional/sexual scale (E + S) and a combined intellectual/recreational scale (I + R) were created as part of the specification of relationship pathways.

Putting together ratings of the parental ties and adult spousal connections, we defined an individual to be on the *negative pathway* if s/he experienced negative relationships with *both* parents and/or negative interaction with a spouse on both combined aspects of intimacy (E + S and I + R). We defined an individual to be on a *positive pathway* if s/he had a positive relationship with at least one parent and positive interaction with a spouse on at least one of E + S and I + R. Technical details about pathway construction are available elsewhere (Singer and Ryff, 1999). The positive pathway underscores the cumulative nature of positive emotional experiences with significant others in childhood and adulthood.

Both men and women on the negative pathway were significantly more likely to have higher allostatic load than their counterparts on the positive pathway. Stated negatively, persistent relational difficulty from childhood to adulthood was linked with greater wear and tear across multiple physiological systems. On the positive side, the findings suggested that having good quality social connections, with parents in childhood and spouse/significant other in adulthood, was associated with keeping allostatic load low. This, in turn, implies substantially lower risk of negative downstream health consequences. The findings also portray allostatic load as a physiological signature of the cumulative social relational well-being or adversity.

The health import of cumulative life challenge can also be applied to economic well-being. At the level of income dynamics and its connection to health over the life-course, there is evidence showing that elevated permanent income, rather than contemporary cross-sectional income, has a strong protective effect on mortality (Deaton, 1999). The cumulative negative impact of persistent poverty on health has also received considerable attention (Korenman and Miller, 1997; Starfield et al., 1991). Using 1957 household income of parents of WLS respondents (i.e. the economic environment when they were growing up) and their own household income in 1992/93 (i.e., their economic circumstances at age 52–53), we classified persons as being on one of four economic trajectories. These were labeled $(-, -)$, $(-, +)$, $(+, -)$, and $(+, +)$, where the first symbol (i.e., $-$ or $+$) identifies negative $(-)$ or positive $(+)$ economic circumstances in childhood and the second symbol identifies negative $(-)$ or positive $(+)$ economic circumstances in adulthood. For persons on the persistently negative economic trajectory $(-, -)$, 50 percent had high allostatic load, assessed in 1997. For persons on the persistently positive economic trajectory $(+, +)$, only 36 percent had high allostatic load. The mixed trajectories had intermediate percentages at high allostatic load: 43 percent of those on $(+, -)$ [i.e. downward mobility] had high allostatic load and 37 percent of those on $(-, +)$ [i.e. upward mobility] had high allostatic load. Technical details about these economic categories are available in Singer and Ryff (1999).

Linking these economic trajectories with the relationship pathways, we found that cumulative positive relationships can have a protective, or compensating effect – reflected physiologically in allostatic load – against persistently negative economic circumstances. In particular, 69 percent of persons on the $(-, -)$ economic trajectory who were also on the negative relationship pathway had high allostatic load at age 59. Alternatively, only 22 percent of persons on the $(-, -)$ economic trajectory who are also on the positive relationship pathway had high allostatic load at the same age. Thus, cumulative relational well-being appeared as a possible basis for resistence to the physiological wear and tear of persistent negative economic circumstances. Further details about the interrelationships between cumulative economic, relational, and physiological pathways are available in Singer and Ryff (1999).

These findings are clearly preliminary, given the small sample size and retrospective features of the relational assessments. In addition, our emphasis on positive pathways needs to be linked with physiological markers that capture, not only the absence of risk, but also the presence of protective factors, of which oxytocin may be a promising candidate. Nonetheless, we include the work as an example of scientific agendas that can incorporate diverse aspects of experiential histories and relate them to biology and health. The work also illustrates the ways in which psychosocial strengths can be studied as factors implicated in resistance to illness and disease (Ryff and Singer, 2000b).

Summary and conclusions

We have covered extensive territory in this chapter. Several realms of study, using both cross-sectional and longitudinal investigations, have documented links between psychological well-being, broadly defined, and normative and nonnormative life challenges. The point of these investigations is to show that life events and transitions both affect, and are affected by, individual differences in levels of positive self-regard, life purpose, sense of mastery, continued growth, autonomy, and quality of ties to others. Intervening mechanisms (e.g., social comparison processes, coping strategies, social support) were part of understanding who does well in such transitions and who does not. Augmenting the focus on single life challenges (e.g., parenthood, relocation, caregiving) was an emphasis on multiple co-occurring and cumulative life challenges. These latter studies combined assessments of normative and nonnormative life experiences, emphasizing the import of accumulation in both realms for well-being. The theme of resilience was invoked by targeting those individuals who are able to maintain high well-being in the face of challenges confronting them one at a time, or cumulatively.

Our final section sketched possible implications for health of cumulative life experience and persistent well-being (or ill-being). We reviewed emerging research on the physiological signature of well-being, giving particular emphasis to positive functioning in the social relational realm. Although considerable work has linked interpersonal conflict, strain, or loneliness to morbidity and mortality, as well as to intervening neuroendocrine and immunological processes, we called for greater emphasis on the positive side. Drawing on our recent work, we demonstrated connections between persistent relational strengths (the positive relationship pathway) and low physiological wear and tear (allostatic load). Resilience was again illustrated by showing that, in the face of cumulative economic adversity, good quality social relations appear to provide protection against high allostatic load.

Future research situated at the interface of unfolding life challenges, psychological well-being, and health is usefully organized via this pathway approach. Pathways are familiar territory to life-course developmentalists;

what may be novel, however, is the integration of age-graded (normative) and nonnormative experience on these pathways. Extending disciplinary boundaries beyond developmental psychology, the emphasis on positive psychological functioning in the face of cumulative challenge provides promising venues for understanding individual differences in health, vitality, and length of life.

ACKNOWLEDGMENTS

This research was supported by the John D. and Catherine T. MacArthur Foundation Research Networks on Successful MidLife Development and Socioeconomic Status and Health as well as National Institute on Aging grants (R01-AG13613, R01-AG08768), a National Institute of Mental Health grant (P50-MH61083), and a grant to the General Clinical Research Center of the University of Wisconsin-Madison (M01-RR03186).

REFERENCES

Baltes, P. B. (1987). Theoretical properties of life-span developmental psychology: on the dynamics between growth and decline. *Developmental Psychology*, 23, 611–26.

Berkman, L. F. (1995). The role of social relations in health promotion. *Psychosomatic Medicine*, 57, 245–54.

Berkman, L. F., and Syme, S. L. (1979). Social networks, host resistance, and mortality: a nine year follow-up study of Alameda County residents. *American Journal of Epidemiology*, 100, 186–204.

Brim, O. G., Jr., and Ryff, C. D. (1980). On the properties of life events. In P. B. Baltes and O. G. Brim, Jr. (eds.), *Life-span development and behavior*. New York: Academic Press, 3, 268–88.

Carter, C. S. (1998). Neuroendocrine perspectives on social attachment and love. *Psychoneuroendocrinology*, 23, 779–818.

Caspi, A. (1987). Personality in the life course. *Journal of Personality and Social Psychology*, 53, 1203–13.

Deaton, A. (1999). Inequalities in income and inequalities in health. NBER Working Paper 7141. National Bureau of Economic Research, Cambridge, MA.

Epel, E. S., McEwen, B. S., and Ickovics, J. R. (1998). Embodying psychological thriving: physical thriving in response to stress. *Journal of Social Issues*, 54, 301–22.

Erikson, E. (1959). Identity and the life cycle. *Psychological Issues*, 1, 18–164.

Essex, E. L., Seltzer, M. M., and Krauss, M. W. (1999). Differences in coping effectiveness and well-being among aging mothers and fathers of adults with mental retardation. *American Journal on Mental Retardation*, 104, 545–63.

Ewart, C. K., Taylor, C. B., Kraemer, H. C., and Agras, W. S. (1991). High blood pressure and marital discord: not being nasty matters more than being nice. *Health Psychology*, 10, 155–63.

Fallo-Mitchell, L., and Ryff, C. D. (1981). Cohort differences in preferred timing of female life events. *Journal of Research on Aging*, 4, 249–67.

Greenberg, J. S., Seltzer, M. M., Krauss, M. W., and Kim, H. (1997). The differential effects of social support on the psychological well-being of aging mothers of adults with mental illness or mental retardation. *Family Relations*, 46, 383–94.

Hagestad, G. O. (1987). Parent-child relations in later life: trends and gaps in past research. In J. B. Lancaster, J. Altman, A. S. Rossi, and L. R. Sherrod (eds.), *Parenting across the life span: Biosocial dimensions*. New York: Aldine de Gruyter, 405–34.

Heidrich, S. M. (1999). Self-discrepancy across the life span. *Journal of Adult Development*, 6, 119–30.

Heidrich, S. M., and Ryff, C. D. (1993a). The role of social comparisons in the psychological adaptation of elderly adults. *Journal of Gerontology*, 48, P127–P136.

Heidrich, S. M., and Ryff, C. D. (1993b). Physical and mental health in later life: the self-system as mediator. *Psychology and Aging*, 8, 327–38.

Heidrich, S. M., and Ryff, C. D. (1995). Health, social comparisons, and psychological well-being: their cross-time relationships. *Journal of Adult Development*, 2, 173–86.

Heidrich, S. M., and Ryff, C. D. (1996). The self in later years of life: changing perspectives on psychological well-being. In L. Sperry and H. Prosen (eds.), *Aging in the twenty-first century: A developmental perspective*. New York: Garland, 73–102.

Higgins, E. T. (1987). Self-discrepancy: a theory relating self and affect. *Psychological Review*, 94, 319–40.

House, J. S., Landis, K. R., and Umberson, D. (1988). Social relationships and health. *Science*, 241, 540–5.

Ickovics, J. R., and Park, C. L. (1998). Paradigm shift: why a focus on health is important. *Journal of Social Issues*, 54, 237–44.

Keyes, C. L. M., and Ryff, C. D. (1998). Generativity in adult lives: social structural contours and quality of life consequences. In D. P. McAdams and E. de St Aubin (ed.), *Generativity and adult development: How and why we care for the next generation*. Washington, DC: American Psychological Association, 226–63.

Kling, K. C., Ryff, C. D., and Essex, M. J. (1997). Adaptive changes in the self-concept during a life transition. *Personality and Social Psychology Bulletin*, 23, 989–98.

Kling, K. C., Seltzer, M. M., and Ryff, C. D. (1997). Distinctive life challenges: implications for coping and well-being. *Psychology and Aging*, 12, 288–95.

Korenman, S., and Miller, J. E. (1997). Effects of long-term poverty on physical health of children in the National Longitudinal Survey of Youth. In G. J. Duncan and J. Brooks-Gunn (eds.), *Consequences of growing up poor*. New York: Russell Sage Foundation, 70–99.

Krauss, M. W., and Seltzer, M. M. (1999). An unanticipated life: the impact of lifelong caregiving. In H. Bersani (ed.), *Responding to the challenge: International trends and current issues in developmental disabilities*. Brookline, MA: Brookline Books.

Kuypers, J. A., and Bengtson, V. L. (1973). Social breakdown and competence. *Human Development*, 16, 181–201.

Levenson, R. W., Carstensen, L. L., and Gottman, J. M. (1994). The influence of age and gender on affect, physiology, and their inter-relations: a study of long-term marriage. *Journal of Personality and Social Psychology*, 67, 56–68.

Li, L. W., Seltzer, M. M., and Greenberg, J. S. (1997). Social support and depressive symptoms: differential patterns in wife and daughter caregivers. *Journal of Gerontology: Social Sciences*, 52B, S200:S211.

Li, LW., Seltzer, M. M., and Greenberg, J. S. (1999). Change in depressive symptoms among daughter caregivers: an 18-month longitudinal study. *Psychology and Aging*, 14, 206–19.

Malarkey, W., Kiecolt-Glaser, J. K., Pearl, D., and Glaser, R. (1994). Hostile behavior during marital conflict alters pituitary and adrenal hormones. *Psychosomatic Medicine*, 56, 41–51.

McAdams, D. P., and de St Aubin, E. (eds.) (1998). *Generativity and adult development: How and why we care for the next generation*. Washington, DC: American Psychological Association, 227–63.

McEwen, B. S. (1998). Protective and damaging effects of stress mediators. *New England Journal of Medicine*, 338, 171–9.

McEwen, B. S., and Stellar, E. (1993). Stress and the individual: mechanisms leading to disease. *Archives of Internal Medicine*, 153, 2093–101.

Neugarten, B. L., Moore, J. W., and Lowe, J. C. (1965). Age norms, age constraints, and adult socialization. *American Journal of Sociology*, 70, 710–17.

Panksepp, J. (1998). *Affective neuroscience: The foundations of human and animal emotions*. New York: Oxford University Press.

Parker, G., Tupling, H., and Brown, L. B. (1979). A parental bonding instrument. *British Journal of Medical Psychology*, 52, 1–10.

Petersson, M., Alster, P., Lundeberg, T., and Uvnas-Moberg, K. (1996). Oxytocin causes long-term decrease of blood pressure in female and male rats. *Physiology and Behavior*, 60, 1311–15.

Rossi, A. S., and Rossi, P. H. (1990). *Of human bonding: Parent-child relations across the life course*. New York: Aldine de Gruyter.

Ryff, C. D. (1989). Happiness is everything, or is it?: explorations on the meaning of psychological well-being. *Journal of Personality and Social Psychology*, 57, 1069–81.

Ryff, C. D. (1995). Psychological well-being in adult life. *Current Directions in Psychological Science*, 4, 99–104.

Ryff, C. D., and Essex, M. J. (1992). The interpretation of life experience and well-being: the sample case of relocation. *Psychology and Aging*, 7, 507–17.

Ryff, C. D., and Heidrich, S. M. (1997). Experience and well-being: explorations on domains of life and how they matter. *International Journal of Behavioral Development*, 20, 193–206.

Ryff, C. D., and Keyes, C. L. M. (1995). The structure of psychological well-being revisited. *Journal of Personality and Social Psychology*, 69, 719–27.

Ryff, C. D., Kwan, M. L., and Singer, B. H. (2001). Personality and aging: flourishing agendas and future challenges. In J. E. Birren and K. W.

Schaie (eds.), *Handbook of the Psychology of Aging*, 5th Edition. San Diego: Academic Press, 477–97.

Ryff, C. D., Lee, Y. H., Essex, M. J., and Schmutte, P. S. (1994). My children and me: midlife evaluations of grown children and of self. *Psychology and Aging*, 9, 195–205.

Ryff, C. D., Schmutte, P. S., and Lee, Y. H. (1996). How children turn out: implications for parental self-evaluation. In C. D. Ryff and M. M. Seltzer (eds.), *The parental experience in midlife*. University of Chicago Press, 383–422.

Ryff, C. D., and Seltzer, M. M. (eds.) (1996). *The parental experience in midlife*. University of Chicago Press.

Ryff, C. D., and Singer, B. (2000a). Interpersonal flourishing: a positive health agenda for the new millennium. *Personality and Social Psychology Review*, 4, 30–44.

Ryff, C. D., and Singer, B. (2000b). Biopsychosocial challenges of the new millennium. *Psychotherapy and Psychosomatics*, 69, 170–7.

Ryff, C. D., and Singer, B. (1998a). The contours of positive human health. *Psychological Inquiry*, 9, 1–28.

Ryff, C. D., and Singer, B. (1998b). Human health: new directions for the next millennium. *Psychological Inquiry*, 9, 69–85.

Ryff, C. D., and Singer, B., Love, G. D., and Essex, M. J. (1998). Resilience in adulthood and later life: defining features and dynamic processes. In J. Lomranz (ed.), *Handbook of aging and mental health*. New York: Springer-Verlag, 69–96.

Sarason, I. G., Johnson, J. H., and Siegel, J. M. (1978). Assessing the impact of life changes: development of the Life Experiences Survey. *Journal of Consulting and Clinical Psychology*, 46, 932–46.

Schmutte, P. S., and Ryff, C. D. (1994). Success, social comparison, and self-assessment: parents' midlife evaluations of sons, daughters, and self. *Journal of Adult Development*, 1, 109–26.

Seeman, T. E., and McEwen, B. S. (1996). Impact of social environment characteristics on neuroendocrine regulation. *Psychosomatic Medicine*, 58, 459–71.

Seeman, T. E., McEwen, B. S., Rowe, J. W., and Singer, B. H. (2001). Allostatic load as a marker of cumulative biological risk: MacArthur Studies of Successful Aging. *Proceedings of the National Academy of Sciences*, 98(8):4770–5.

Seeman, T., Singer, B., Rowe, J., Horwitz, R., and McEwen, B. (1997). The price of adaptation: allostatic load and its health consequences: MacArthur Studies of Successful Aging. *Archives of Internal Medicine*, 157, 2259–68.

Seltzer, M. M., Greenberg, J. S., Floyd, F. J., Pettee, Y., Hong, J. (2001). Life course impacts of parenting a child with a disability. *American Journal of Mental Retardation*, 106, 282–303.

Seltzer, M. M., Greenberg, J. S., and Krauss, M. W. (1995). A comparison of coping strategies of aging mothers of adults with mental illness or mental retardation. *Psychology and Aging*, 10, 64–75.

Seltzer, M. M., Krauss, M. W., Choi, S. C., and Hong, J. (1996). Midlife and later life parenting of adult children with mental retardation. In C. D. Ryff, and M. M. Seltzer (eds.), *The parental experience at midlife*. University of Chicago Press, 340–82.

Seltzer, M. M., and Ryff, C. D. (1994). Parenting across the life span: the normative and nonnormative cases. In D. L. Featherman, R. M. Lerner, and M. Perlmutter (eds.), *Life-span development and behavior*. Hillsdale, NJ: Erlbaum Associates, 12, 1–40.

Singer, B., and Ryff, C. D. (in press). Understanding aging via person-centered methods and the integration of numbers and narratives. In R. H. Binstock and L. K. George (eds.), *Handbook of Aging and the Social Sciences*, 5th Edition. San Diego: Academic Press.

Singer, B., Ryff, C. D., Carr, D., and Magee, W. J. (1998). Life histories and mental health: a person-centered strategy. In A. Raftery (ed.), *Sociological Methodology, 1998*. Washington, DC: American Sociological Association, 1–51.

Smider, N. A., Essex, M. J., and Ryff, C. D. (1996). Adaptation to community relocation: the interactive influence of psychological resources and contextual factors. *Psychology and Aging*, 11, 362–71.

Starfield, B., Shapiro, S., Weiss, J., Liang, K. Y., Ra, D., Paige, D., and Wang, X. (1991). Race, family income, and low birth weight. *American Journal of Epidemiology*, 134, 1167–74.

Taylor, S. E., Repetti, R. L., and Seeman, T. (1997). Health psychology: what is an unhealthy environment and how does it get under the skin? *Annual Review of Psychology*, 48, 411–47.

Uchino, B. N., Cacioppo, J. T., and Kiecolt-Glaser, J. K. (1996). The relationship between social support and physiological processes: a review with emphasis on underlying mechanisms and implications for health. *Psychological Bulletin*, 119, 488–531.

Uvnas-Moberg, K. (1997). Physiological and endocrine effects of social contact. *Annals of the New York Academy of Science*, 807, 146–63.

Uvnas-Moberg, K. (1998). Oxytocin may mediate the benefits of positive social interaction and emotions. *Psychoneuroendocrinology*, 23, 819–35.

Van Riper, M., Ryff, C., and Pridham, K. (1992). Parental and family well-being in families of children with Downs syndrome: a comparative study. *Research in Nursing and Health*, 15, 227–35.

Part VI

Personal goals and well-being

13 Individual differences in personal goals in mid-thirties

Lea Pulkkinen, Jari-Erik Nurmi and Katja Kokko

Introduction

Individual motivation and related personal goals play an important role in individuals' lives. People steer their development (Brandtstädter, 1984; Lerner, 1984) by setting personal goals and making responses to developmental challenges (Nurmi, 1993, 1997). They search for personally meaningful and motivating life-trajectories by constructing goals which are based on their interests and motives, but which simultaneously reflect various options available in their environments. Consequently, individuals' goals may reflect both age-graded transitions involving normative demands and developmental tasks typical of their environments (Nurmi, 1992, 1993), and differences in individuals' motives related to personality traits.

Individuals' goals can be represented at various goal levels with different future time perspectives. Heckhausen (1999, p. 105) suggests that a developmental goal on a general level is comparable to "motive" as defined by McClelland, Atkinson, Clark, and Lowell (1953), "unity theme" (Murray, 1938), or "life theme" (Bühler, 1933). A more specific level from the point of view of an individual's engagement or disengagement and life-span coverage is involved in such constructs as "current concerns" (Klinger, 1975), "identity goals" (Gollwitzer, 1987), "personal projects" (Little, 1983), "personal strivings" (Emmons, 1986), "personal goals" (Staub, 1980), and "life tasks" (Cantor and Kihlström, 1987), "possible selves" (Markus and Nurius, 1986), and developmental goals (Heckhausen, 1999).

We defined the concept of 'personal goal' as a construct which stems from a comparison between individuals' motives and their expectations of the opportunities for future actualization (Markus and Wurf, 1987; Nurmi, 1989; Nuttin, 1984). This conceptualization is based on the dual

This chapter was prepared while Lea Pulkkinen was a visitor at St John's College, Cambridge University, UK (1999). The research was supported by the Academy of Finland (Finnish Centre of Excellence Programme No. 40166).

nature of individual motivation as defined by Nuttin (1984) in his relational theory of motivation. He suggested that on the one hand, individual motivation stems from individuals' inner needs and motivational tendencies, such as hunger, sex, sociability, curiosity, and achievement, and individual differences in the strength of this motivation. On the other hand, motives refer to certain objectives, events, or challenges which provide the context for the satisfaction of the individual needs. Consequently, personal goals are often operationalized and analyzed in terms of the "objectives" to which they refer in the real world, such as family and children, intimate relationships, leisure activities, education, and work (Cantor *et al.*, 1991; Little, 1983; Nurmi, 1992). The goals have also been investigated in terms of appraisal dimensions such as importance, progress, accomplishment, stress, and control beliefs (Cantor *et al.*, 1991; Emmons, 1986; Little, 1983). In the present study, goals were investigated with an emphasis on objectives or goal contents.

Constructing personal goals affects the ways in which an individual defines himself or herself as an actor in a particular context (Nurmi, 1997). It has been suggested that a sense of identity emerges as individuals actively cope with various age-graded social demands and developmental challenges, and attempt to make meaningful life choices (Erikson, 1959). According to Marcia (1980, 1988), identity formation typically proceeds by 'bits and pieces': concrete decisions such as whom to date, what education to attend, what job to enter, and who to meet during leisure time, have identity-forming implications. Identity formation has been described in terms of two major processes, exploration of alternatives and commitment to certain decisions and choices (Marcia, 1966), and is closely related to goal construction. Goal construction also presupposes exploratory activities and commitment to certain goals and related activities.

Although several theories have been presented concerning the role of developmental or personal goals in the life-span context (Baltes and Baltes, 1990; Heckhausen, 1999; Nurmi, 1993), and in identity formation (Marcia, 1980, 1988), only a few longitudinal studies have been carried out to investigate the antecedents of personal goals, their associations with people's life situation, and their consequences for individual development. This chapter, which is based on the Jyväskylä Longitudinal Study of Personality and Social Development conducted by Lea Pulkkinen (e.g., 1982, 1996, 1998) for thirty years, will firstly discuss the age-gradedness of personal goals in adulthood, secondly, describe unifying life themes in individuals whose life paths indicate successful or less successful development, and thirdly, study personalized motivation beyond personal goals and the relationships between goal patterns and identity construction.

Age-gradedness of personal goals

Age-normative structures and personal goals

Individuals' agentic behaviors such as goal construction and different age-normative influences interact in human development. People direct their lives in the contexts of different genetically and physiologically determined personal characteristics, and different social, societal, cultural, and institutional structures. As summarized by Heckhausen (1999), biology-related age-gradedness includes "processes of maturation, aging, and age-differential evolutionary selection effects, [whereas society-related age-gradedness can be differentiated] in objectified social institutions of age-gratification, [and] their psychological complements in age-normative conceptions as internalized and shared by the individual members of a given society" (p. 23).

Heckhausen (1999, p. 98) differentiates between two age-graded influences that cut across the biology and social structure of the life-course as well as across age-normative conceptions. These are developmental tasks and critical life events. Developmental tasks represent, according to Havighurst (1948/1974), age-specific goals and developmental challenges resulting from biological changes, transitions into new social roles, and age normative expectations about psychological change (e.g., autonomy). Critical life events (Brim and Ryff, 1980) are major changes in an individual's developmental ecology that present a substantial stress to the individual's well-being and therefore involve major coping responses. Critical events may function as turning points through actively made choices concerning personal goals. The more personal choice the individuals experience at the time of a turning point, the more positively they feel presently and later (Rönkä, Oravala, and Pulkkinen, in press).

Age-normative structures such as developmental tasks and critical life-events provide a basis for the ways in which people construct their personal goals. First, the construction of adaptive personal goals requires a comparison of individuals' motives and opportunities for their actualization (Nurmi, 1993; Nuttin, 1984). Consequently, cultural knowledge about age-graded developmental tasks (Havighurst, 1948/1974), standards (Caspi, 1987), and role transitions (Elder, 1985) provides information about the appropriate ways of actualizing individual interests in different life domains in a certain age period and a certain society. Second, institutional career (Mayer, 1986) and related action opportunities (Grotevant, 1987), provide structures which include behavior modes, models, and related information about how to attain certain goals, and consequently, a basis for constructing adaptive goals. Third, developmental tasks, role transitions, and institutional careers provide a context for evaluating one's success in the goal achievement.

Developmental tasks are not only collective goals for what to attain during a certain life period, but they also include standards for the appropriate time and ways in which they should be reached. Institutional tracks typically include time points for the receipt of feedback concerning success in dealing with the tasks and demands on a particular track. This feedback then provides a basis for goal reconstruction. It has been shown that individuals try to compensate for problems in a certain institutional transition by disengaging from prior goals and constructing new ones which focus on an alternative developmental track (Nurmi and Salmela-Aro, in press). Our study of age-gradedness of personal goals concerned the period of the life-span which can be called late early adulthood, i.e., the time when individuals are in their mid-thirties. Levinson (1986) labels this age from 33 to 40 as the period of Settling Down. It is the time when an individual establishes a niche in society and identifies the steps on the ladder of success in social rank, income, family life, creativity etc. It is preceded and succeeded by transition periods during which an individual reappraises the life structure. In the mid-30s, Western people are generally in good health, they lead intensive family lives with children still at home, and they make progress in their career.

Method

Participants The study was part of the Jyväskylä Longitudinal Study of Personality and Social Development, which began in 1968 with a random sample (N = 369) of 8-year-old school children (b. 1959) and has, since then, continued up to age 36. Interview data at age 36 were collected with 283 participants (77 percent of the original sample). At age 36, most participants (81 percent out of 283) had formed an intimate relationship and lived in their own families, 60 percent were married (4 percent lived in a second marriage), 21 percent cohabited, and 7 percent were divorced. Only 11 percent were single. Living with children was also common: only 10 percent of women and 21 percent of men had no children. The respondents' current health was good according to their self-assessments (good, 43 percent, and rather good, 32 percent; very poor, 0.4 percent). Thirty-six per cent had qualified for university studies, somewhat more women than men (46 percent vs 25 percent). The time of studies typical of early adulthood had passed; only 4 percent of the 36-year-old participants were students. The great majority of the participants (76 percent) were either in full-time employment or self-employed. Eighteen per cent were unemployed. The high unemployment rate was due to economic recession in Finland during the early 1990s. Four per cent of the participants were home mothers. According to Statistics Finland in 1994, these figures were very similar to those for the whole cohort born in Finland in 1959.

Measures Goals are typically studied by asking people to list their personal concerns, projects, strivings, etc., and these are analyzed in terms of the domains of life they concern, such as family and occupation. To study personal goals in mid-adulthood, the following instruments were used in our longitudinal study:

(1) Most important things. The participants were asked in an interview:
  • What is the most important thing in your life at the moment?
  • What, if any, are the second and third most important?
(2) Hopes and fears. The participants were asked in the interview:
  • What kind of hopes do you have when you think about the future?
  • What are your three most important hopes?
  • What things are you afraid of or worried about when you think about the future?
  • Would you mention three fears concerning the future? (Nurmi, 1989)
(3) Life Satisfaction Line (Perho and Korhonen, 1990). The participants were asked if there were any special things or events which had had a special impact on their happiness at the age period from 34 to 36 years.
(4) A Goal Pattern Schedule (Staudinger, 1996) included ten content areas: health, cognitive fitness, hobbies or interests, relations with friends, sexuality, the well-being of family, professional activity, independence, life, and death. The participants were asked to rate on a scale from 1 to 5 how much they thought or did something about each of the topics.

Personal goals in late early adulthood

The most important things, hopes and fears, and the events of the life satisfaction line were coded to 1 of 19 life domain categories created on the basis of the data. The results showed (Table 13.1) that the most frequently mentioned topic as an important thing in people's lives was *family*, including spouse, divorce, and remarriage. More than half of the respondents also mentioned *profession*, for instance, change or loss of job,

Table 13.1 *The most important things, and hopes and fears in people's lives at age 36 (N = 283)*

Domain	Most important things (%)	Hopes (%)	Fears (%)
Family	81	35	11
Profession	55	14	3
Health	29	59	51
Leisure time	24	7	0
Human relationships/friends	23	10	4
Livelihood	10	28	16
Human growth	9	6	3
Lifestyle	8	14	3
Education	6	4	0
Child-rearing	5	30	15
Buying a residence/Property	4	7	1
Religion	3	1	1
Something else	3	3	1
Global problems	1	6	34
Uncertainty about the future	1	4	12
Growing older	0	1	1
Death of a significant other	0	0	18
Change of residence	0	3	0
Travelling	0	7	0

positive or negative aspects of work, unemployment, and promotion in one's career. Health, leisure-time activities covering hobbies and concerns about lack of time for personal use, and human relationships, comprising friends and loneliness, were also domains of great importance for a quarter of the participants.

Hopes were somewhat different from the most important things. Among hopes, health was mentioned by more than half of the respondents, and family and child-rearing by about one-third. Health was also the most often mentioned fear. The second most frequently expressed fear concerned global problems including war, ecological catastrophes, and economic recession.

In the Goal Pattern Schedule, participants reported that they invested the highest amount of time in thinking and acting on the following life domains: family ($M = 4.42$) and profession ($M = 4.02$). The least considered domain was death ($M = 2.39$). Differences between the rest of the domains were rather small varying from health ($M = 3.67$) to leisure time ($M = 3.26$). Our findings were in line with Staudinger's (1996) study, where family was the most invested domain in the age group of 35–54 followed by profession. According to Staudinger's study, investment in the family increases with age, whereas investment towards profession decreases with age.

Overall, the results were in accordance with some major propositions of the life-span theory of personal goals (Heckhausen, 1999; Nurmi, 1993), and also with some earlier findings (Cross and Markus, 1991; Nurmi, 1992). Most of the participants had fulfilled the developmental tasks of young adulthood as described by Havighurst (1948/1974): selecting a mate, learning to live with a partner, starting a family, rearing children, managing a home, getting started in an occupation, taking on civic responsibility, and finding a congenial social group. The participants had goals that focused on dealing with the major developmental tasks of their own age, such as how to satisfactorily handle their marital relationship, how to deal with the issues of career, and, as an anticipation of the future, how to promote one's health. A less frequently mentioned domain was, for instance, education. At this age, most participants were working outside the home, and only 4 percent were studying. Education was not rated highly among goals, as it probably would have been rated at the beginning of early adulthood.

Health is an increasing concern in middle age, and its anticipation was visible in the participants' thinking about their future. In addition, concerns about one's health may reflect anxiety that is caused by global problems and the threat of unemployment among the respondents due to economic recession. The unemployment rate had jumped in Finland from 3 percent up to 18 percent in a few years. World news on wars and ecological issues might also have influenced participants' fears concerning global problems. These results suggest that the ways in which individuals direct their lives in terms of setting personal goals, are closely embedded, both in the major age-normative structures they are currently facing and historical events. As Baltes *et al.* (1980) have remarked, historical events, in addition to normative, age-graded events and non-normative life events, may play an important role in human development.

Unifying life themes and successful development

When asked to list important things in their lives, and hopes and fears associated with the future, as well as the events of the Life Satisfaction Line, most participants mentioned several domains. However, while conducting interviews we formed the impression that several interviewees had a dominating life theme that seemed to integrate their life experiences. For instance, a man was worried about his marriage, because his wife was too preoccupied with her studies and work, and gave too little time and attention to him. He had been happy in his marriage, but he was afraid of the future. His goal was to maintain the marriage, but he found its attainment threatened. This theme arose again and again during this person's interview. Murray (1938) argued that in the life-span perspective, it is possible to reveal themes around which behavior is organized. An individual experiences an integration of the self and the development of a unifying life theme that organizes his or her behavior and directs further development.

Method On the basis of this notion, the interviewers (14 in total) were asked to write down after the semi-structured interview of each person at age 36 what, if any, they perceived was the unifing life theme of the interviewee. Also, what was the topic which the interviewee repeatedly raised, and which was seemingly an important issue to him or her. The interviews lasted from three to five hours and covered several topics such as biographical data, identity status interview, self, health, alcohol consumption, intimate relationships, family and children, work, personality characteristics, and the future. A unifying theme was found in about 80 percent of the interviews.

Individual differences in life themes were studied in the framework of personality styles. Newman and Newman (1984) suggest that during early adulthood, a style of life is established that will serve as a framework for the organization of experience during the rest of adulthood. Styles of life, or personality styles as they are called here, were obtained using a clustering technique (WARD) when the participants were 27 years old (Pulkkinen, 1996), and life themes, nine years later. At age 27, twelve variables were drawn from a large data set by a series of factor analyses in order to reduce the number of variables. They were used as clustering variables, and they comprised personality characteristics (four variables), life orientation (three), and behavioral activities (five).

Successful and unsuccessful development Both women and men fell into two major clusters, one for unsuccessful development (labeled *conflicted*; one-quarter of the participants) and another for successful development. The latter cluster divided into two sub-clusters which were labeled differently for men (*resilient* and *introverted*), and women (*individuated* and *feminine*). Each cluster divided into sub-clusters resulting in seven clusters altogether (see Pulkkinen, 1996). The three most general clusters were compared here (ANOVA and Scheffe's test) in terms of unifying life themes, current life situation, and developmental background factors.

Membership in a certain cluster had roots in an individual's emotional and behavioral regulation from the early school years onward (Pulkkinen, 1996). The *conflicted* individuals had had more problems with self-control of emotions, and consequently, more external and internal problems than the other groups. Compared to the other participants at age 27, the *conflicted* men and women were more neurotic, had been arrested more often, were heavier drinkers, had less cultural interests, were more aggressive, and their life attitudes were more negative.

As regards personal goals, the life themes of these individuals nine years later (Table 13.2) were qualitatively different from the life themes of their more successful counterparts: their life themes more often concerned problems in the accomplishment of age-graded developmental tasks and related personal goals, which manifested themselves in unemployment, conflicts with the spouse, and psychological distress. Women in this cluster mentioned depression, and men mentioned alcohol abuse and suicidal thoughts. The life themes of many *conflicted* women were also focused on children and wishes for family-centered life. Both women and men brought up important life changes, such as (re)marriage.

The life themes of men on the more successful tracks also had unique characteristics. The *resilient* men who had been well-adjusted and socially-skilled since childhood, had life themes which focused on profession, i.e., their own enterprise and work in general, leisure activities (or lack of leisure time), and family. Because of the current economic recession in Finland, many *resilients* had experienced a major life change caused by a financial breakdown, often concerning their own enterprise, such as bankruptcy. These experiences puzzled them and had also forced them to reappraise their values of life. For the *introverted* men who had already been more passive than the *resilients* in childhood, the most characteristic life themes concerned lifestyle, i.e., wishes to experience a quiet life or live day by day without demanding long-term goals. Their life themes were also frequently focused on family, particularly children and their own parents, and health.

Among the successful women (*individuated* and *feminine*), a life theme which emerged more often than among the *conflicted* women, was seeking a balance between work and family life. Typical of Finnish women, most, even the more traditional feminine women, worked full-time outside the home which caused strain in their lives. The two female groups also differed in their life themes. Only the *individuated* women who had distanced themselves from conventional female role expectations and were typically very career-oriented, presented profession as a central life theme. They emphasized independence and efficacy – also found among

Table 13.2 Unifying life themes of individuals on different developmental paths: percentages

Life themes	Unsuccessful path			Succesful paths		
	Conflicted men n = 62	Conflicted women n = 48	Resilient men n = 111	Individuated women n = 101	Introverted men n = 73	Feminine women n = 70
Unemployment	9.7	6.2	0.9	1.0	1.4	1.4
Alcohol abuse	9.7	–	0.9	–	4.1	–
Depression	4.8	6.2	–	–	–	1.4
Suicidal thoughts	4.8	–	–	–	–	–
Spousal conflicts, divorce	14.5	14.6	5.4	5.0	5.5	11.4
Own enterprise	–	2.1	9.0	4.0	–	1.4
Work	6.5	–	9.9	8.9	5.5	–
Independence, efficacy	–	6.2	–	10.9	–	1.4
Leisure time	3.2	–	8.1	–	4.1	–
Life changes	9.7	10.4	11.7	9.9	1.4	2.9
Family	6.5	–	12.6	–	6.8	–
Family-work balance	–	4.2	–	8.9	–	10.0
Children	4.8	10.4	3.6	9.9	11.0	4.3
Quiet life	–	2.1	1.8	2.0	11.0	5.7
Day-by-day	–	4.2	–	–	17.8	11.4
Family centered life	–	12.5	–	5.9	–	15.7
Stress	–	4.2	–	5.0	–	5.7
Religion	–	2.1	1.0	3.0	–	1.4
Health	1.6	–	1.8	–	6.8	–
Family of origin	–	–	1.8	–	5.5	–
Miscellaneous or no life theme	17.3	14.8	31.5	25.6	19.1	25.9
Total	100	100	100	100	100	100

the *conflicted* women – and they had experienced life changes which typically had changed their values towards family-centeredness. Central life
themes of the *feminines* who had accepted the traditional female role with
strong home orientation, were focused on lifestyle and family, i.e., wishes
to live day by day without any demanding projects, and to experience quiet
and family-centered life. The strain was, however, caused by a conflict
between work and family, and also spousal conflicts were raised. Only
women's life themes involved stresses in life.

Conclusions The results presented above showed that about 80 percent
of the participants had a pervasive personal goal which they raised several
times and which seemed to be a kind of unifying life theme. Typically,
these themes focused on conflicts or constraints that limited the attainment of age-graded developmental goals. The content of the themes varied depending on the individuals' personality styles nine years earlier.
Individuals who were on different developmental pathways in their twen-
ties presented somewhat different life themes in their thirties.

Individuals on successful tracks had a capacity to cope with developmental tasks of profession and family in spite of temporary problems. In
late early adulthood, their life themes were tied up with the basic domains.
In spite of critical life events, such as bankruptcy, these inviduals seemed
to be able to cope with challenges and reappraise their values. In contrast,
individuals on unsuccessful tracks were struggling with problems in profession, social relationships, and lifestyles. Their life themes concerned
unsuccessful coping with developmental tasks in work and family, and
low psychological well-being.

Personalized motivation beyond personal goals

Dimensions of individual differences in personal goals

Both the construct of developmental task in Havighurst's (1948/1974)
conceptualization and psychosocial crisis in Erikson's (1963) theory involve the idea that the mastery of the tasks required at later stages of
development depends on the successful acquisition of earlier and sim-
pler tasks. It is not, however, well understood what it means in terms of
individual differences in adulthood if the acquisition of earlier skills has
been unsuccessful. We assumed that differences in individuals' motivation indicated by personal goals would result from different orientations
to age-graded developmental tasks, i.e., that individuals who have accomplished earlier developmental tasks would be more strongly oriented
to current developmental tasks than individuals who have experienced

failures in coping with earlier tasks. We approached this issue by:

(1) analyzing the dimensions of individual differences in personal goals,
(2) extracting patterns of personal goals, and
(3) investigating their developmental backgrounds.

Besides expecting that patterns of personal goals would reflect the attainment of developmental tasks, we assumed that the patterns would differ in identity construction so that patterns indicating the accomplishment of age-graded developmental tasks would be related to advanced identity. In his relational theory of motivation, Nuttin (1984) suggests that an individual's actions are governed through personal, idiosyncratic motivational structures. Nurmi (1993) shares Nuttin's viewpoint and claims that people direct and produce their lives as agents by setting personal goals and constructing related projects. Motivation gives coherence and pattern to people's behavior in terms of the goals that they pursue (Salmela-Aro, 1996).

Four goal factors To study individual differences in personal goals and related intra-individual coherence, we first conducted a principal component analysis with varimax rotation on averaged standardized scores of 19 personal goals (cf. Table 13.1) across important things, goal investments, the events of the life satisfaction line, hopes, and fears. The first goal factor reflected *self concerns* (loaded by goals for, e.g., personal growth .78, lifestyle .67, and human relationships .57); the second factor was interpreted as *basic needs concerns* (e.g., health .70, livelihood .60); the third factor was labeled as *love concerns* (e.g., fear of the death of a significant other .71, child-rearing .52, and family .43), and the fourth factor reflected *global concerns* (e.g., concerns about global issues .77, leisure time activities .65).

Clusters of personal goals

The participants were grouped on the basis of the similarity of their personal goals. This was achieved using a clustering techique (Ward method). Clustering variables were the four factors for goal orientations. Table 13.3 presents the cluster profiles of five clusters which were formed by the four factors. Differences between the clusters in personal goals were examined by:

(1) ANOVA and Scheffe's test in clustering variables and individual goal variables,

Table 13.3 *Clusters for goal orientations*

Clusters and personal goals[1]	Current life situation[2]
Transpersonal-orientation	Long education
Family, occupation,	Married and children
child-rearing, death	Employed
N = 59 (31 women, 28 men), 21%	Enterpreneur
	Cultural activities
	Political interests
Basic needs-orientation	Low education
Health, livelihood,	Financial problems
getting older	Divorce
N = 85 (47 women, 38 men), 30%	Pensioner
Self-orientation	Unmarried
Human growth, lifestyle,	Single parent
human relations	Unstable work career
N = 26 (15 women, 11 men), 9%	Interest in arts
	Depression
	Mental health services
	Frequent drunkenness
Global-orientation	Not employed
Global issues, leisure time	
N = 44 (20 women, 24 men), 16%	
Goalless	Living together + children
Buying a residence	
N = 69 (24 women, 45 men), 24%	

Notes: [1]Personal goals listed for each cluster differed from those for the other clusters (ANOVA and Scheffe's test).
[2]For the variables listed, the frequency was higher than expected by chance (types).

(2) cross-tabulating the clusters with variables describing the life situation of the participants at age 36,

(3) comparing the means of groups using ANOVA and Least-Significant Difference test, and

(4) correlating the summed scores of the most characteristic goal-orientation factor with data on socio-emotional behavior collected at ages 8, 14, 27 and 33 (Pulkkinen, 1996, 1998).

For cross-tabulations, the observed frequencies were compared to expected frequencies occurring by chance. If the observed frequencies were statistically higher, then an interpretation of 'type' was made. Because of a relatively small number of individuals in each cluster, the distributions of the variables did not meet all statistical assumptions. Therefore, the results presented in Table 13.3 should be taken as consistent trends in the background variables differentiating between the clusters.

Five goal clusters The first cluster, which, in comparison to the other clusters, had a higher mean in the goal factor called love concerns, was labeled *Love-orientation* (21 percent of the participants). Compared to the other clusters, the cluster had the highest means in personal goals concerning family, profession, and child-rearing, and in fears concerning the death of a significant other. More often than expected by chance, individuals belonging to this cluster had lengthy education, were married, had children, were employed or self-employed rather than unemployed, and reported several cultural activities and a high interest in politics. The summed score for the love concerns factor correlated with teacher-rated socially active behavior at age 14 and extraversion (NEO-PI) at age 33 for women, but not for men.

The cluster for *Basic Needs-orientation* (30 percent of the participants) had a higher mean than the other clusters in the goal factor called basic needs concerns. The cluster had the highest means, compared to the other clusters, in concerns about health, livelihood, and getting older. Individuals in this cluster had had difficulties in meeting with the developmental tasks of education. They had financial and marital problems. All three young pensioners belonged to this cluster. A summed score for the basic needs concerns factor correlated for men with teacher-rated problems in emotional regulation indicated by aggression in childhood, and with poor school success in adolescence and problem drinking in early adulthood.

The cluster for *Self-orientation* (9 percent of the participants) had a higher mean than the other clusters in the goal factor called self concerns. The cluster had the highest means, compared to the other clusters, in personal goals for human growth, human relationships, and lifestyle. Individuals in this cluster had had difficulties in meeting with the developmental tasks of forming intimate relationships. They were unmarried and single parents more often than could be expected by chance. They were employed on a contract for a specific period of time rather than permanently, which made their careers unstable. They abused alcohol, and were depressed and in need of mental health services more often than by chance. On the positive side, they were interested in arts. Self concerns correlated with openness to experience, agreeableness, and neuroticism at age 33.

The cluster for *Global-orientation* (16 percent of the participants) had a higher mean than the other clusters in the goal factor called global concerns. The cluster had the highest means compared to the other clusters in concerns about global issues, such as war, and in the emphasis on leisure time activities. The only variable for the current life situation in which individuals in this cluster differed from the other clusters was not to be employed in so far as they were unemployed, farmers/self-employed, studying, or on maternity leave. They had distanced themselves from striving for conventional goals for success in career.

The fifth cluster was titled as *Goalless* (24 percent of the participants) because it had low means in all personal goals. It differed from the other clusters only in a materialistic goal, buying a residence. The means were particularly low in goals for human relationships, human growth, and lifestyle. The cluster contained relatively more men than women; in the other clusters the gender distribution was even. This cluster differed from the other clusters in the current life situation only in one respect wherein it was more common among individuals in this cluster to live together and have children without being married.

Summary The analysis of individuals' motivation in goal-orientation revealed that accomplished developmental tasks explained Love-orientation. These developmental tasks concerned education, marital status, childbirth, and employment. Difficulties in the completion of developmental tasks were found in Basic Needs-orientation and Self-orientation. For Basic Needs-orientation, difficulties existed particularly in education, whereas for Self-orientation, difficulties existed in intimate relationships. In both cases, related problems occurred.

Four out of the five clusters resembled the four clusters for human motives obtained by Wicker, Lambert, Richardson, and Kahler (1984) based on goal ratings: Love-orientation for transpersonal orientation, Basic Needs-orientation for security, Self-orientation for personal growth, and Global-orientation for tranquility seeking. The goal patterns extracted also resembled the categories of the need hierarchy introduced by Maslow (1970). Basic Needs-orientation resembles physiological needs, Love-orientation resembles safety, belonginess and love needs, and Self-orientation has links to cognitive and aesthetic needs. Self-orientation is not equal to self-actualization needs. Self-actualizers are high in well-being as described by Maslow, whereas preoccupation with self tends to be related to low well-being (Salmela-Aro and Nurmi, 1997).

The presence of five goal-orientation clusters indicated that there were inter-individual differences as well as intra-individual coherence in the patterns of personal goals and in their associations with various individual characteristics. The results showed that age-graded developmental tasks alone did not explain the kind of goals held by people. In a homogeneous

age group, individual differences in personal goals emerged to form motivated goal orientations which were distinctively related to current life
situation and developmental background.

Goal construction and identity construction

Goal construction and identity construction share common elements
such as exploration of alternatives and commitment to choice. The
present longitudinal study allowed us to investigate parallels in these processes and to compare identity status at ages 27 and 36 for each pattern
of personal goals. Identity formation in relation to the different goal orientations described above was studied by utilizing identity interviews
(cf. Marcia, 1966), conducted at ages 27 and 36, which focused on five
identity domains: religion, political ideology, occupation, intimate relationships, and lifestyle. Data were analysed by focusing on underlying
identity processes across all identity domains: the presence or absence of
exploration and commitment. We estimated each subject's identity status
for each domain by using two criteria: the presence or absence of a period
of exploration and the firmness of personal commitment (Pulkkinen and
Kokko, 2000; Pulkkinen and Rönkä, 1994).

On average, uncertainty about identity goals had diminished from age
27 to 36 as indicated by the increase of commitment and the decrease
of exploration in nine years ($t = -11.76$, $p < .001$ for commitment;
$t = 3.94$, $p < .001$ for exploration). Identity diffusion (no exploration, no
commitment) and moratorium (exploration, but no commitment) tended
to decrease in all clusters for personal goals, whereas foreclosure (commitment, but no exploration) tended to increase in all clusters, and, in addition, identity achievement (both exploration and commitment) tended
to increase in the clusters for Self-orientation and Global-orientation.

The decrease in status of the identity diffusion and moratorium, and
the increase in commitment, evidenced in either foreclosure or identity
achievement, from age 27 to 36, were in accordance with life-span developmental theories. For example, Levinson (1986) assumes that settling
down is typical of individuals in their mid-thirties, whereas openness to
alternatives and their exploration is typical of individuals at a younger
age. By late early adulthood, most individuals had accomplished developmental tasks, such as establishing a family and entering a job. In such
a life situation, a moratorium is no longer adaptive for identity work because options in life are limited by the previous choices to which people
have committed.

The clusters could be grouped at age 36 into three categories according to their identity advancement: (1) Basic Needs-orientation and

Goalless were characterized by identity diffusion at age 36 more often than the other clusters, (2) Love-orientation differed from the other clusters only occassionally, and (3) Self-orientation and Global-orientation were characterized by identity achievement at age 36 more often than the other clusters (Table 13.4). Identity diffusion remained relatively high in individuals whose personal goals concerned basic security and in individuals who belonged to the cluster for Goalless of personal goals. Not confirming our hypothesis, Love-orientation, which most typically demonstrated accomplished developmental tasks, was not more highly characterized by identity achievement than the other clusters. Instead, individuals with goals for personal growth (Self-orientation) or global issues (Global-orientation) were most highly characterized by identity achievement. Consequently, the latter clusters were highest in commitment.

Conclusions

Individuals steer their development by setting goals and making choices as responses to various developmental challenges which they face during their life-span. On the one hand, personal goals reflect major age-graded transitions and normative demands. On the other hand, individual differences in personal goals reflect motivational orientations, such as aiming at personal growth and security seeking, which result in intra-individual coherence in goal patterns. Some personal goals are so pervasive that they characterize individuals' personality styles and long-term successful or unsuccessful development as kinds of life themes. The age-gradedness, coherence, and pervasiveness of personal goals were discussed on the basis of a long-term longitudinal study carried out in Finland.

In their mid-thirties, individuals generally conceptualize their personal goals in terms of family and profession. By definition, personal goals refer to goal construction which involves both individual motives and social opportunity structures for their actualization. This dual nature of personal goals became evident in the analysis of unifying life themes. On the one hand, individuals had personal goals, but on the other, they were aware of constraints that limited their attainment. The latter aspect varied in centrality depending on the successfulness of the individual's developmental track.

Personal goals were investigated with an emphasis on goal content. From the appraisal dimensions, only importance of goals was considered. Other appraisal dimensions such as accomplishment, stress, and control beliefs could only be inferred indirectly. It became evident from

Table 13.4 Personal goals, exploration, and commitment, means and standard deviations

Identity status and process at ages 27 and 36	Clusters for personal goals at age 36					F	p	LSD
	Goalless (n = 69) 1	Love-orientation (n = 59) 2	Basic needs-orientation (n = 85) 3	Global-orientation (n = 44) 4	Self-orientation (n = 26) 5			
	M (SD)	M (SD)	M (SD)	M (SD)	M (SD)			
Diffusion (27)	1.69 (1.42)	1.14 (1.02)	1.67 (1.31)	1.49 (1.37)	0.96 (1.12)	2.651	.034	1, 3 > 5; 1 > 2
Diffusion (36)	1.06 (1.03)	0.82 (0.92)	1.24 (1.13)	0.60 (0.85)	0.46 (0.76)	5.075	.001	1, 3 > 4, 5; 3 > 2
Moratorium (27)	0.92 (1.07)	1.10 (1.07)	0.85 (0.98)	1.05 (1.19)	1.13 (1.15)	0.619	n.s.	
Moratorium (36)	0.22 (0.48)	0.18 (0.58)	0.25 (0.60)	0.35 (0.72)	0.38 (0.64)	0.871	n.s.	
Foreclosure (27)	1.22 (1.15)	1.24 (1.03)	1.24 (1.16)	1.13 (1.06)	1.29 (1.27)	0.100	n.s.	
Foreclosure (36)	2.41 (1.35)	2.25 (1.13)	2.17 (1.17)	2.23 (1.04)	1.77 (1.24)	1.405	n.s.	
Achievement (27)	1.14 (1.26)	1.51 (1.32)	1.23 (1.26)	1.33 (1.36)	1.63 (1.13)	1.029	n.s.	
Achievement (36)	1.29 (1.44)	1.71 (1.26)	1.29 (1.28)	1.81 (1.45)	2.31 (1.38)	4.073	.003	4, 5 > 1, 3
Exploration (27)	2.06 (1.54)	2.61 (1.29)	2.08 (1.40)	2.38 (1.53)	2.75 (1.62)	2.009	.094	
Exploration (36)	1.51 (1.44)	1.89 (1.37)	1.54 (1.34)	2.16 (1.36)	2.69 (1.38)	5.031	.001	4, 5 > 1, 3; 5 > 2
Commitment (27)	2.36 (1.48)	2.76 (1.38)	2.47 (1.44)	2.46 (1.43)	2.92 (1.28)	1.038	n.s.	
Commitment (36)	3.71 (1.21)	3.96 (1.01)	3.45 (1.24)	4.05 (1.09)	4.08 (1.16)	3.097	.016	4, 5 > 3; 2 > 3

the life themes that individuals on successful and unsuccessful developmental paths differed in these dimensions. Successful development was associated with a sense of control over the attainment of personal goals, and on this track, stress was found to be more manageable and more readily compensated for by alternative goals. It is to be noted that the individuals' successful or unsuccessful developmental paths identified nine years earlier were rooted in their personality and socio-emotional characteristics evident in childhood (Pulkkinen, 1996).

The formation of developmental paths is regulated by chains of individuals' conscious or less conscious goal selections within the constraints of the opportunities provided by the environment and the individuals' own resources and successes and failures in the attainment of these goals. Salmela-Aro and Nurmi (1997) have demonstrated a form of a cumulative step-by-step cycle: personal projects that concern major age-graded developmental tasks and demands predict high subjective well-being, which in turn predicts interest in these types of goals. In contrast, low self-esteem predicts interest in self-related projects which again are associated with later low well-being.

Individual differences in motivation were themselves manifested by different goal patterns. As suggested by Nuttin (1984), an individual's actions are governed through personal, idiosyncratic motivational structures. Motivation gives coherence and pattern to people's behavior because it directs the goals that they pursue. Domains that individuals present as important in their present lives reflect either the gratification or deprivation of needs beyond those developmental tasks, which, in late early adulthood, are mainly related to intimate relationships and professional activities.

Goal construction and identity construction were partly parallel as indicated by high identity diffusion and low commitment in the Goalless cluster and the Basic Needs-orientation cluster. For the former, no personal goals were distinctive, and for the latter, difficulties in meeting with developmental tasks emerged. Nevertheless, the Love-orientation cluster which was highest in the accomplishment of developmental tasks was only mediocre in identity achievement and commitment. This is an understandable finding because among adults who have been successful in dealing with major developmental tasks, there is no current need to work with concrete identity issues in terms of active exploration. Kuhl and Fuhrmann (1998) argue that the degree of commitment manifests the amount of volitional efficiency in striving for the goal, and that the two important tasks of volition are maintaining both one's goals and the integrity of one's self. Possibly, both the accomplishment of developmental tasks in, for instance, Love-oriented individuals, and high commitment to goals in, for instance, Self-oriented individuals, may have similar functions in enhancing the integrity of one's self.

REFERENCES

Baltes, P. B., and Baltes, M. M. (1990). Psychological perspectives on successful aging: the model of selective optimization with compensation. In P. B. Baltes and M. M. Baltes (eds.), *Successful aging: Perspectives from the behavioral sciences*. New York: Cambridge University Press, 1–34.

Baltes, P. B., Reese, H. W., Lipsitt, L. P. (1980). Life-span developmental psychology. *Annual Review of Psychology*, 31, 65–110.

Brandtstädter, J. (1984). Personal and social control over development: some implications of an action perspective in life-span developmental psychology. In P. B. Baltes and O. G. Brim, Jr. (eds.), *Life-span development and behavior*. New York: Academic Press, 6,1–32.

Brim, O. G., Jr., and Ryff, C. D. (1980). On the properties of life events. In P. B. Baltes and O. G. Brim, Jr. (eds.), *Life-span development and behavior*. New York: Academic Press, vol. 3, 367–88.

Bühler, C. (1933). *Der menschliche Lebenslauf als psychologisches Problem* [The human life course as a topic of psychology]. Leipzig: Hirzel.

Cantor, N., and Kihlström, J. (1987). *Personality and social intelligence*. New York: Prentice-Hall.

Cantor, N., Norem, J., Langston, C., Zirkel, S., Fleeson, W., and Cook-Flannagan, C. (1991). Life tasks and daily life experience. *Journal of Personality*, 59, 425–51.

Caspi, A. (1987). Personality in the life-course. *Journal of Personality and Social Psychology*, 53, 1203–13.

Cross, S., and Markus, H. (1991). Possible selves across the life span. *Human Development*, 34, 230–55.

Elder, G. H. Jr. (1985). Perspectives on the life course. In G. H. Elder, Jr. (ed.), *Life course dynamics*. Ithaca, NY: Cornell University Press, 23–49.

Emmons, R. A. (1986). Personal strivings: an approach to personality and subjective well-being. *Journal of Personality and Social Psychology*, 51, 1058–68.

Erikson, E. (1963). *Childhood and society*. (2nd edn.) New York: Norton.

Erikson, E. H. (1959). *Identity and the life cycle*. New York: International Universities Press.

Gollwitzer, P. M. (1987). Suchen, Finden und Festigen der eigenen Identität: Unstillbare Zielintentionen [Searching, finding, and consolidating of one's own identity: unsaturatable goal intentions]. In H. Heckhausen, P. M. Gollwitzer, and F. E. Weinert (eds.), *Jenseits des Rubikon: Der wille in den Humanwissenschaften*. Berlin: Springer, 176–89.

Grotevant, H. D. (1987). Toward a process model of identity formation. *Journal of Adolescent Research*, 2, 203–22.

Havighurst, R. J. (1948/1974). *Developmental tasks and education* (3rd edn.). New York: McKay (Original work published 1948).

Heckhausen, J. (1999). *Developmental regulation in adulthood: Age-normative and sociostructural constraints as adaptive challenges*. Cambridge University Press.

Klinger, E. (1975). Consequences of commitment and disengagement from incentives. *Psychological Review*, 82, 1–25.

Kuhl, J., and Fuhrmann, A. (1998). Decomposing self-regulation and self-control: the volitional components inventory. In J. Heckhausen and C. S. Dweck (eds.), *Motivation and self-regulation across the life-span*. Cambridge University Press, 15–49.

Lerner, R. M. (1984). *On the nature of human plasticity*. New York: Cambridge University Press.

Levinson, D. J. (1986). A conception of adult development. *American Psychologist*, 41, 3–13.

Little, B. R. (1983). Personal projects: a rationale and method for investigation. *Environment and Behavior*, 15, 273–309.

Marcia, J. E. (1966). Development and validation of ego identity status. *Journal of Personality and Social Psychology*, 3, 551–8.

Marcia, J. E. (1980). Identity in adolescence. In J. Adelson (ed.), *Handbook of adolescent psychology*. New York: Wiley, 159–87.

Marcia, J. E. (1988). Common processes underlying ego identity, cognitive/moral development, and individuation. In D. K. Lapsley and F. C. Power (eds.), *Ego, self, and identity: Integrative approaches*. New York: Springer, 211–25.

Markus, H., and Nurius, P. (1986). Possible selves. *American Psychologist*, 41, 954–69.

Markus, H., and Wurf, E. (1987). The dynamic self-concept: a social psychological perspective. *Annual Review of Psychology*, 38, 299–337.

Maslow, A. H. (1970). *Motivation and personality* (2nd edn.) New York: Harper & Row.

Mayer, K. U. (1986). Structural constraints on the life course. *Human Development*, 29, 163–70.

McClelland, D. C., Atkinson, J. W., Clark, R. A., and Lowell, E. L. (1953). *The achievement motive*. New York: Appleton-Century-Crofts.

Murray, H. A. (1938). *Explorations in personality*. New York: Oxford University Press.

Newman, B. M., and Newman, P. R. (1984). *Development through life: A psychosocial approach* (3rd edn). Homewood, Ill.: Dorsey.

Nurmi, J.-E. (1989). Adolescents' orientation to the future: development of interests and plans, and related attributions and affects, in the life-span context. *Commentationes Scientiarum Socialium*, vol. 39. Helsinki: Societas Scientiarum Fennica.

Nurmi, J.-E. (1992). Age differences in adult life goals, concerns, and their temporal extension: a life course approach to future-oriented motivation. *International Journal of Behavioral Development*, 15, 487–508.

Nurmi, J.-E. (1993). Adolescent development in an age-graded context: the role of personal beliefs, goals and strategies in the tackling of developmental tasks and standards. *International Journal of Behavioral Development*, 16, 169–89.

Nurmi, J.-E. (1997). Self-definition and mental health during adolescence and young adulthood. In J. Schulenberg, J. L. Maggs, and K. Hurrelmann (eds.), *Health risks and developmental transitions during adolescence*. Cambridge University Press, 395–419.

Nurmi, J.-E., and Salmela-Aro, K. (in press). Goal construction, reconstruction and well-being in a life-span context: A transition from school to work. *Journal of Personality.*

Nuttin, J. (1984). *Motivation, planning, and action: A relational theory of behavior dynamics.* Leuven University Press.

Perho, H., and Korhonen, M. (1993). Elämänvaiheiden onnellisuus ja sisältö keski-iän kynnyksellä. [Happiness of life stages in front of middle age.] *Gerontologia*, 7, 271–85.

Pulkkinen, L. (1982). Self-control and continuity from childhood to adolescence. In B. P. Baltes and O. G. Brim, Jr. (eds.), *Life-span development and behavior.* San Diego: Academic Press, vol. 4, 63–105.

Pulkkinen, L. (1996). Female and male personality styles: a typological and developmental analysis. *Journal of Personality and Social Psychology*, 70, 1288–1306.

Pulkkinen, L. (1998). Levels of longitudinal data differing in complexity and the study of continuity in personality characteristics. In R. B. Cairns, L. R. Bergman, and J. Kagan (eds.), *Methods and models for studying the individual.* Beverly Hills, CA: Sage, 161–84.

Pulkkinen, L., and Kokko, K. (2000). Identity development in adulthood: A longitudinal study. *Journal of Research in Personality*, 34, 445–70.

Pulkkinen, L., and Rönkä, A. (1994). Personal control over development, identity formation, and future orientation as components of life orientation: a developmental approach. *Developmental Psychology*, 30, 260–71.

Rönkä, A., Oravala, S., and Pulkkinen, L. (in press). Turning points in adults' lives: The effects of gender and the amount of choice. *Journal of Adult Development.*

Salmela-Aro, K. (1996). *Personal projects and subjective well-being.* University of Helsinki, Department of Psychology. Research Reports No. 18.

Salmela-Aro, K., and Nurmi, J.-E. (1997). Goal contents, well-being, and life context during transition to university: a longitudinal study. *International Journal of Behavioral Development*, 20, 471–91.

Staub, E. (1980). *Personality: Basic aspects and current research.* Englewood Cliffs, NJ: Prentice-Hall.

Staudinger, U. M. (1996). Psychologische Produktivität und Selbstentfaltung im Alter. In M. Baltes and L. Montada (eds.), *Produktives Leben im Alter.* Frankfurt/Main: Campus, 344–73.

Wicker, F. W., Lambert, F. B., Richardson, F. C., Kahler, J. (1984). Categorical goal hierarchies and classification of human motives. *Journal of Personality*, 52, 285–305.

14   Social production function (SPF) theory as an heuristic for understanding developmental trajectories and outcomes

Johan Ormel

Introduction

This chapter will try to convince you that Social Production Function (SPF) theory provides heuristics that may help the study of developmental trajectories and outcomes. In order to examine social phenomena, such as the dynamics of divorce rates and female labor market participation, as consequences at the collective level of individual behaviors, Lindenberg (1986, 1991) synthesized basic economic, psychological and social insights into what he called Social Production Function theory. SPF theory combines a theory of individual behavior with a theory of goals. In the 1990s the development of SPF theory continued (Lindenberg 1996; Ormel, Lindenberg, Steverink and Verbrugge 1999) and conceptual applications to quality of life and successful aging were developed (Ormel, Lindenberg, Steverink and Von Korff, 1997; Steverink, Lindenberg, and Ormel, 1998). In the same period the first empirical studies guided by the heuristics of SPF theory were undertaken on bereavement (Nieboer, 1998), giving up independent living (Steverink, 1996) and time-spending patterns (Van Eyk, 1997). These experiences have shaped my belief that SPF heuristics are promising for understanding developmental trajectories and outcomes, both at the individual and collective level.

Social Production Function (SPF) theory integrates strengths of relevant psychological theories and economic consumer/household production theories, without their limitations (namely, tradeoffs between satisfaction of different needs are not satisfactorily dealt with in the first, and goals or needs are not in the second). SPF theory identifies two ultimate goals that all humans seek to optimize (physical well-being and social well-being) and five instrumental goals by which the two universal goals are achieved (stimulation, comfort, status, behavioral confirmation, and affection). The core notion of SPF theory is that people choose and substitute instrumental goals so as to optimize the production of their well-being, subject to constraints in available means of production.

In order to arouse your interest in SPF theory and to support my position that SPF theory provides a conceptual framework for the study of developmental trajectories and outcomes, I will describe SPF-theory and apply its heuristics to three rather different phenomena, including subjective well-being, successful aging, and antisocial behavior. Regarding well-being, the leading question will be how person characteristics and life events affect well-being. Successful aging will be conceptualized as resulting from patterned change in resources and goals, followed by a first and very preliminary effort to apply SPF theory to antisocial behavior. In addition I have added a glossary (Appendix 14.1) which describes some critical SPF concepts. This may help the reader to become comfortable with the complexity of ideas and the unfamiliar new concepts.

It should be noted from the outset that this chapter is largely theoretical. Core theoretical constructs of SPF theory have not been measured directly yet, although work on measurement is in progress. The description of SPF theory is largely taken from Ormel *et al.*, 1999.

Social production function (SPF) theory

SPF theory asserts that people produce their own well-being by trying to optimize achievement of universal goals, within the set of resources and constraints they face. Drawing on both psychological and economic theories, humans are seen as active agents who rationally choose cost-effective ways to produce well-being, given that the rational considerations of cost-benefit are constrained by limited information.

Central components of SPF theory are (a) the link between realization of goals and well-being, (b) explicit definitions of universal and first-order instrumental goals, and (c) substitution among instrumental goals according to cost-benefit considerations. The first feature derives from psychological theories; the second, from new household economics theory; and the third, from microeconomic price theory.

Universal and instrumental goals

Although the new household economics distinguishes between universal goals (identical for all human beings) and instrumental goals (individual preferences for the means leading to universal goals), those goals are not well defined. SPF theory identifies both and their relationship to each other. This allows much more specificity about how individuals go about achieving well-being, and it reduces ad hoc statements of needs and wants.

Two universal goals are identified in SPF theory: physical well-being and social well-being:

(1) Physical well-being is attained by two instrumental goals: stimulation (also called activation) and comfort (Table 14.1). Stimulation refers to activities that produce arousal, including mental and sensory stimulation, physical effort, and (competitive) sports. Although humans prefer some degree of activation, prolonged levels of high stimulation become unpleasant (cost exceeds benefit). Thus the association of activation with well-being takes an inverted U shape (Hebb, 1958; Scitovsky, 1976; Wippler, 1987). Comfort is a somatic and psychological state based on absence of thirst, hunger, pain, fatigue, fear, extreme unpredictability, and the like. Activation within the pleasant range, and comfort, are each related to physical well-being in a positive way. In economic terms, these are monotonically increasing production functions with decreasing marginal products. The more physical well-being a person has the less valuable an additional unit of stimulation or comfort is (see Table 1).

(2) Social well-being has been repeatedly claimed to be a crucial universal goal, albeit with different names and labels. "Nature, when she formed man for society, endowed him with an original desire to please, and an original aversion to offend his brethren. She taught him to feel pleasure in their favorable, and pain in their unfavorable regard". Marshall (1920: 14–17) reiterated the importance of social well-being. In modern terms, "the struggle to preserve or enhance feelings of self-worth or prestige marks all men who live above a bare subsistence level" (Krech, *et al.*, 1962: 96). In SPF theory, social well-being is attained by three instrumental goals: status, behavioral confirmation, and affection (Table 14.1). Status refers to relative ranking to other people, based mainly on control over scarce resources. Behavioral confirmation is the feeling one has "done right" in the eyes of relevant others, even when direct reinforcement does not occur. Affection includes love, friendship, and emotional support; it is provided in caring relationships (intimate, family, friendship). All three instrumental goals are assumed to have monotonic increasing relationships with social well-being, with decreasing marginal value for their production.

Others have discussed some of these instrumental needs for social well-being in different conceptual frameworks and terms. Simons (1983) distinguishes three components of psychological need: need for assistance and security, need for intimacy, and need for positive self-esteem. Inability to satisfy them results in, respectively, feelings of insecurity and anxiety, of isolation and loneliness, and of worthlessness and unfulfillment. Simons' conception derives from Weiss' typology of social needs (1974) which includes attachment, social integration, opportunity for nurturing,

Table 14.1 *The universal and first-order goals*

Top level	Utility (or psychological well-being)			
Universal goals	Physical well-being		Social well-being	
First-order instrumental goals	Activation/ Stimulation	External comfort	Internal comfort	Status	Behavioral confirmation	Affection
	(optimal level of arousal)	(pleasant environment)	(absence of physiological needs)	(control over scarce resources)	(what you get from "doing the right thing")	(what you get from others who care about you)

reassurance of worth, sense of reliable alliance, and obtaining guidance. Similar goals are formulated in Brandtstädter and Baltes-Götz (1990) and Rokeach (1973). Omodei and Wearing (1990) state fundamental universal needs that are linked to well-being, such as self-esteem, personal control, purpose, and meaning. The contemporary literature on social support consistently points out the importance of various forms of social support for maintenance and recovery of well-being when people face adversity. Animal research also verifies the importance of attachment and status for primates and rodents' normal behavior and health (e.g. DeKloet *et al.*, 1988; DeKloet, 1994).

There is considerable overlap with Maslow's renowned need hierarchy but there are also important differences (Maslow, 1970; Lindenberg, 1996). The overlap consists of comfort (physiological needs in Maslow's system), affection (belongingness and love needs), and a combination of status and behavioral confirmation (esteem needs). Maslow's system does not consider stimulation but includes safety needs and the need for self-actualization. Lindenberg (1996) has persuasively argued that safety needs can be conceptualized as instrumental goals for comfort and that self-actualization ultimately depends on approval by others. Stimulation was included in the SPF model as a main instrumental goal because there is ample evidence that people do not only seek physical well-being by drive reduction (or comfort), but also by stimulation (Hebb, 1958; Wippler, 1987). This is not meant to say that stimulation and comfort are two sides of the same coin, in that people seek an optimal level of arousal. In that case people would seek stimulation when their arousal level is too low and comfort when it is too high. Consequently, even small substitutions between comfort and stimulation would not be possible. This idea of an optimal level of arousal is too simplistic. Indisputably, extreme levels of arousal are noxious. But within a large range of arousal, people seem to derive pleasure from both reducing and increasing arousal. Thus, within this range, individuals may seek comfort and stimulation at the same time, for instance by watching an exciting movie in a comfortable chair in a warm and pleasant environment.

Hierarchy

In SPF theory, goals are hierarchically arranged with the two ultimate goals at the top, the five first-order instrumental goals just below, and lower-order means of production that serve to produce those five farther down. Production functions specify the factors needed to produce a given goal. Thus, an array of production functions between goals of different levels will show how well-being is generated, maintained, or changed.

To visualize these relationships, consider one example: Utility (U) is achieved through physical well-being (PW) and social well-being (SW); thus $U = f\{PW, SW\}$. In turn, social well-being is produced by status (S), behavioral confirmation (BC), and affection (A); thus $SW = f\{S, BC, A\}$. Each of these is itself a goal that is produced by "second-order" means of production. For example, behavioral confirmation is often generated by membership in groups (I) and conformity to norms (C); thus $BC = f\{I, C\}$. Further, conformity to norms derives from engaging in and abstaining from various activities, depending on the social expectations in the individual's milieu. The lower one goes in the SPF hierarchy, the more context-specific the production functions become.

Resources and constraints

In general, I denote means of production that are available to the person as resources, and those that are not available as constraints. If an individual lacks particular means of production for achieving a first-order instrumental goal (thus there is a constraint), then the production of those means can become an instrumental goal in itself. As soon as these instrumental goals are achieved, they have become resources for the production of instrumental goals at higher levels. For example, a hungry teenager on the way to playing football can stop at a store and buy chocolate to satisfy the hunger, and thereby have sufficient energy for the game. Or, a woman may direct her activities toward making money so that she can renovate her house.

Investment

When there is plenty of time between a resource-gaining activity and its eventual goal, the first is viewed as an investment. The distinction between activities that immediately satisfy a goal and those which increase potential for future production is an important one.

Immediate and delayed satisfactions are intertwined, so that dropping an activity related to the first can have consequences for the second, and vice versa. For example, preventive maintenance of the house (e.g., painting it) is an investment, but it may be accompanied by the desire to gain immediate behavioral confirmation from one's partner and neighbors. Loss or serious illness of the partner and lack of social control in the neighborhood can eliminate motivation for such investment behaviors, with ensuing decline in the quality and yield of social production functions.

Levels of means of production

Resources and constraints play a major role in SPF theory because they determine the relative costs of alternative ways to produce physical and social well-being. Key personal resources are physical and mental health, time, energy, income, education, kin and friend ties, and social skills. Constraints are absence of resources that could help achieve a particular goal; in economic terms, they constitute costs. Besides constraints due to low personal skills, finances, or motivations, there are important environmental constraints in law, social infrastructure, norms, and climate.

Individuals develop social production functions that use existing resources, avoid constraints, and generate new resources. Over the short and long runs, people's activities arise in an ongoing "deliberation" between central instrumental goals on the one hand, and resources and constraints on the other. At a given time, preferred ways of producing well-being stem from both perceived current resources and also personal history of which production functions have been most and least successful to date.

As I said before, resources are means of production a person has at a given time. We can usefully distinguish at least three levels below the first-order means of production (See Figure 14.1; Ormel *et al.*, 1999).

Second-order means of production are activities and endowments that help produce the key instrumental goals. Activities are current behaviors aimed toward a goal, and endowments are statuses and resources as a result of prior activity that enhances its production. For example, bathing regularly helps produce comfort, and long-time good health also enhances it. Satisfying work and marriage represent important endowments in addition to activities. During most of the adult life-span, having work and being married yield by themselves, that is without any activity, status and behavioral confirmation. In addition, satisfying work and good marriage also encompass a variety of (multifunctional) activities that produce stimulation, behavioral confirmation, affection, and comfort (through income). *Third-order* means of production are resources, which are needed for executing activities and obtaining endowments. Examples are basic skills and abilities such as time, effort, and social intuition. These are useful in production functions for many higher-order goals. We note that some resources can operate on goals at several levels in the hierarchy; for example, money confers high status directly, but it also serves at lower levels to give access to activities and reinforce endowments. *Fourth-order* means of production are those that can be mobilized when changes in production capacity require substitution. Such latent resources are analogous to credit or savings. For example, when a partner

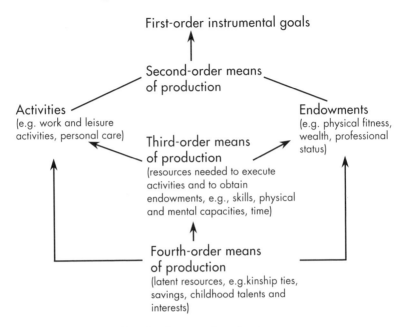

First-order instrumental goals

Second-order means of production

Activities
(e.g. work and leisure
activities, personal care)

Third-order means of production
(resources needed to execute
activities and to obtain
endowments, e.g., skills, physical
and mental capacities, time)

Endowments
(e.g. physical fitness,
wealth, professional
status)

Fourth-order means
of production
(latent resources, e.g.kinship ties,
savings, childhood talents and
interests)

Figure 14.1 Levels of means of production
Source: Ormel *et al.*, 1999.

dies, some of the lost production capacity for affection can be regained by reopening kinship ties that have been dormant for some time.

It is not difficult to envisage how resources and constraints affect the costs of activities and endowments. For individuals who have long working hours and low pay, all activities and endowments that require time and money, will be more costly than for the rich and retired. Likewise, the costs of activities that require much human interaction are much lower for people with strong social skills.

Table 14. 2 provides some examples of lower-order means of production in relation to the first-order instrumental goals.

Substitution

In SPF theory, instrumental goals are substitutable depending on their relative cost. For example, if resources for status achievement decrease, a person may increase production of affection and behavioral confirmation if that appears easier (thus, "cheaper") than status production. Similarly, if someone becomes disabled and can no longer perform sports activities that offered stimulation, s/he may increase alternatives such as reading,

Table 14.2 *Examples of lower-order means of production*

Top level	Utility or psychological well-being					
Universal goals	Physical well-being				Social well-being	
First-order instrumental goals	Activation/ Stimulation	External comfort	Internal comfort	Status	Behavioral confirmation	Affection
Examples of instrumental activities and endowments	Physical and mental activities producing arousal	Appliance, Housing, Security, Social welfare	Absence of pain, fatigue, thirst, and hunger; Vitality	Consumption pattern, Excellence in sports/work, Occupation, Descent	Compliance with external and internal norms, Group membership	Intimate interaction, Providing emotional support, Married
Example of resources	Physical and mental effort	Money	Food, Health care	Education, Social class, Unique skills	Social skills, Competence	Spouse, Empathy, Attractiveness

Source: Ormel *et al.*, 1999

watching television, and telephoning friends. The alternatives open to people who face dissatisfactions, losses, and dilemmas depend heavily on the extent and diversity of their resources. Variety tends to increase over one's life, and high diversity gives not only richness to a current behavioral repertoire but also good chances of alternatives if a particular resource recedes.

Many activities are multifunctional; they achieve several instrumental goals, or they combine immediate production with investment. For example, close social interaction in intimate relationships may produce affection, behavioral confirmation, and stimulation all at the same time, while also serving as an investment for future access to social contact. Such activities are especially efficient in a person's set of social production functions. Losing them can create substitution problems of such magnitude that finding satisfying replacements is impossible or takes a very long time.

Substitution comes into play when valued activities or satisfactions decrease for any reason. For example, close social interactions may decrease sharply when a spouse/partner dies, an intimate friend moves away, or a cherished tie dissolves in conflict. If grief inhibits formation of new ties, people may turn toward more solo activities for a short or long time. Another example is loss of satisfying work. Work not only provides income and status, but it often also encompasses multifunctional activities that produce stimulation and behavioral confirmation. Whether overall utility (U) decreases or is maintained depends on the satisfaction derived from the substituted activities. Some losses are so severe, they surpass a person's ability to substitute and s/he shifts to a lower overall utility level.

Substitutability has limits, at the levels of universal as well as main instrumental goals. For example, people need some level of physical well-being, and no amount of social well-being will suffice to compensate for it (although suicide bombers appear to have been willing to trade physical well-being for social approval). Likewise, people need some degree of physical stimulation, and no realistic level of comfort can compensate that. This can be formally represented by a Cobb-Douglas production function of the form $A = X^a.Y^b.Z^c$, where a, b, c = 1. The outcome A refers to a sought goal, and X, Y, and Z are the lower-order resources used toward it.

Finally, besides the problems of large losses and limited substitutability, cognitive and emotional features can create obstacles to substitution behavior. When an individual is threatened by loss of an important resource for physical or social well-being, considerations of costs and benefits can become one-sided. The potential loss can become so salient that perception of possible gains is void and other goals are temporarily displaced (Kahneman *et al.*, 1982; Kahneman and Tversky, 1984). This process is known as framing. For example, older people who lose a number of valuable resources (work, income, health, siblings, friends) may focus so much on loss, they fail to invest in ways that buttress their future production possibilities (Steverink, 1996). As another example, when one's house is burglarized, a person can become obsessed with security far beyond the amount stolen or likely to be stolen ever again. Framing also occurs when functional or organic mental illness impairs a person's discriminatory capacities. The reason that neurophysiological impairments (cognitive decline, depression, anxiety, pain) produce so much disability and loss of well-being (Ormel *et al.*, 1993; Ormel *et al.*, 1994; Von Korff *et al.*, 1992; Wells *et al.*, 1989) may be because those impairments cause decrements in higher-order mental capacities such as energy, self-regulation of affect, self-confidence, concentration, memory, reasoning, and long-term planning (which we later denote as an important category of third-order means of production). These have profound effects on how well someone selects means of production and engages in them. In all the examples noted above, appraisal does not proceed according to relative price effects. To an outside evaluator, the individual's rationality of appraisals and corresponding actions (given his/her resources and constraints) are non-optimal, i.e., less productive than feasible given the objective constraints.

Substitutability is an essential feature of SPF theory, and stands as such in sharp contrast with Maslow's need hierarchy.

Application 1 – life events, person characteristics and subjective well-being

SPF-heuristics can contribute to the development of a genuine explanatory model of well-being. By genuine I mean a framework that provides heuristics for explaining how well-being rises, falls, or remains stable as people age, events accumulate, and social milieus change. At its best, such a framework should distinguish the importance of stable personal characteristics versus life changes for the production of well-being.

On the side of stable characteristics, personality and social class related variables shape long-term baseline of positive and negative affect (e.g. Costa and McCrae 1980), influence exposure to life changes (e.g. Fergusson and Horwood, 1987), and dampen or amplify effects of life changes on well-being (e.g. Ormel *et al.*, 1988). On the other side, from the stress-vulnerability perspective, the constellation of daily hassles, daily uplifts, and life events are strong factors behind well-being (e.g. Brown and Harris, 1978; Ormel and Wohlfarth, 1991).

Within the framework of SPF theory, stable characteristics are modeled in terms of resources and constraints that facilitate or limit production of well-being and investment in production capacity. Life events affect achievement of first-order instrumental goals by altering the relative costs of their means of production (activities and endowments), and they also affect lower-order means of production and substitution abilities. For instance, being laid off reduces occupational prestige, a major endowment for status, and frequently also leads to loss of income, a major resource for physical well-being. Consequently, production of status, comfort and stimulation become more expensive. A new harmonious intimate relationship is a formidable resource that provides multiple opportunities for activities that produce comfort, affection and behavioral confirmation. Consequently, it becomes 'cheaper' to achieve these main instrumental goals. Likewise, many life changes can be analyzed in terms of their impact on an individual's social production function and resources, although it will be difficult to express these changes in terms of some unit of costs (Ormel et al., 1999).

Several models about the dynamics of subjective well-being (SWB) have been proposed. Headey and Wearing (1989) distinguish four types: the personality model; the adaptation level model; the life event model; and the dynamic equilibrium model.

(1) The personality model assumes that SWB depends mostly on personality, especially the traits of neuroticism and extraversion (e.g., Costa and McCrae, 1980).

(2) The adaptation level model asserts that life events prompt only transient changes in SWB because a person rapidly adapts to the new situation by raising or lowering comparative standards in the direction of the new situation, or adapts by other means (Brickman et al., 1978; Sprangers and Schwartz 1999b). This process minimizes discrepancy between achieved and desired life situation. Personality is involved in this; it can explain why some people persistently experience large discrepancies (unsatisfied) and other small or no discrepancies (satisfied).

(3) The life event model proposes that life changes are exogenous shocks that have significant but transient effects on SWB (e.g., Lawton, 1983).

(4) Empirical evidence strongly suggests a mixed model involving both life events and personality. Headey and Wearing (1989) call this a dynamic equilibrium model, and it is their preference. The essential

feature is that each person has a normal, or equilibrium, pattern of life events and normal level of SWB; both are predictable on the basis of stable personality characteristics. Deviations from the pattern of life events alter SWB, but the change is usually temporary because personality traits act to equilibrate the situation and draw people back to their normal level.

Studies since Headey and Wearing's discussion have provided good support: Ormel and Schaufeli (1991) found that 60 percent of explained variance in distress is due to stable person and environmental characteristics, and 40 percent to life changes. (The 60 percent contain effects of personality mediated by controllable life changes; these could not be separated in the data.) Other twin and longitudinal studies show that stable person characteristics, especially neuroticism, predict exposure to *controllable* undesirable life events and long-term difficulties (Kendler *et al.*, 1993; Kessler *et al.*, 1992; Saudino *et al.*, 1997; Ormel and Wohlfarth, 1991; Plomin, 1994). In sum, these suggest interacting influences of personality and life events on well-being. A good theory of well-being must be able to deal with such interactions.

SPF theory can provide a framework that encompass these findings, that is suitable for dealing with complex interactions between person characteristics and environmental changes, and that permits development of specific hypotheses on the mechanisms through which person characteristics and environmental changes influence well-being. On the first point, the SPF-based explanatory framework readily handles results about small long-term impacts of life events on subjective well-being for most people. In the instance of undesirable events, the cost-effectiveness of all or most current activities is not significantly changed by the events, important resources may not be altered, and effective and rapid substitution occur if they are. In contrast to adaptation level theory, which posits highly reactive changes in personal standards, SPF theory allows for steadiness of those standards in the short run and gradual change in the long run. On the second point, SPF theory views humans as actively shaping and reshaping their activities to attain goals, using all manner of personality and environmental resources at hand. Interactions of stable person characteristics and environmental features are fundamental empirical devices for understanding how people respond to life changes in their social production functions.

At present all knowledge on the 'productivity' of common activities, endowments, and resources is based on common sense; good empirical evidence is lacking. We do not know the productivity of a good marriage and satisfying work or the counter productivity of a poor marriage and dissatisfying work, relative to being single. Neither do we know the marginal utilities of major resources such as income, occupational prestige, friends, and luxury. But if information on relative utilities becomes available, we will have the tools to test a large variety of hypotheses, for instance about why person characteristics such as neuroticism and extraversion are so strongly associated with SWB. It might be that persons with high neuroticism and low extraversion get themselves involved in counter-productive activities; that they have neglected to build up variety in resources, in terms of work skills and relationships; that they lack the resources for effective substitution, such as self-efficacy, competence and control. All this might be involved in the apparent psychosocial vulnerability of some individuals. Likewise, we can deal with important intractable environmental factors such as poverty, social class, and climate.

Application 2 – successful aging

According to SPF-theory, successful development (Ormel *et al.*, 1997) and successful aging in later life (Steverink *et al.*, 1998) depend on:

(1) the ability to select *multi-functional* activities and endowments that yield production *and* investment (such as team sports; a caring spouse; skill learning on the job; leisure activities that build up social capital);
(2) the ability to substitute in ways that are cost-effective in the long term; and
(3) variety in resources for *different* first-order goals (including third- and fourth-order resources).

Steverink and colleagues (1998) argue that variety in resources is the core mechanism for maintaining instrumental goals and resources in old age. The more varied a person's resources, the easier substitution, and the better age-related losses are neutralized or compensated. Important general resources for successful development are probably cognitive and social skills and (social) capital.

Some prototypical substitutions in instrumental goals result from the biological and cultural changes that occur during the life-span and affect the cost ratio of instrumental goals. Status is by far the most sensitive for such age-related changes. Steverink and colleagues (1998) describe some of these prototypical substitutions during the second half of life in Western society (see Figure 14.2). First, they consider status, which in Western societies is largely produced by means of occupational prestige, wealth, and excellence in valued activities. After retirement, their production becomes more difficult. The increase in relative costs of second-order resources for status will motivate older people to give up the production

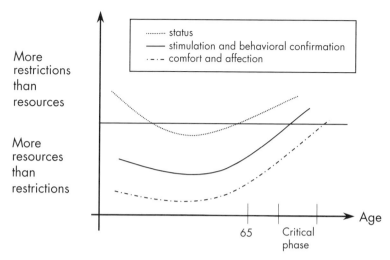

Figure 14.2 Hypothetical course of the relative difficulty of goal realisation for status, stimulation and behavioural confirmation, and comfort and affection across the life span (in a Western society).
Source: Steverink *et al.*, 1998.

of status in favor of affection and behavioral confirmation, since the endowments and resources that achieve affection and behavioral confirmation have become relatively cheaper. The next prototypical substitution when growing older involves stimulation (physically) and behavioral confirmation. They become more expensive with physical decline and loss of social norms and expectations due to the fact that many roles, social structures and formal settings become less pertinent to older people. Consequently, the production of comfort and affection becomes relatively cheaper, and hence comfort and affection tend to replace stimulation and behavioral confirmation. In normal circumstances, affection is relatively easy to produce from early life on into very old age and the resources to achieve comfort are, in Western societies, usually available to old people.

This argumentation led Steverink *et al.* (1998) to the hypothesis that in later life, the goal of behavioral confirmation, and, further down the aging road, the goals of comfort and affection, will gain in relative importance. They also introduced the concept of 'critical phase' in later life. With status, behavioral confirmation and stimulation gone, the production function of older people becomes very vulnerable, since only resources for comfort and affection remain. When additional loss of personal relationships and physical disabilities begin to eliminate the remaining resources for affection and/or comfort, options for substitution at the level of first-order instrumental goals become even more scarce, and hence the older person even more vulnerable. This situation of very poor resources for substitution is what Steverink denotes as the critical phase. She showed that it triggers the frail elderly to undertake or accept rather drastic actions, such as an application to a home for older people or a nursing home (Steverink, 1996). Critical phases, or their perception, may, of course, also occur earlier in life, but this requires rather exceptional circumstances. Successful aging might be viewed as postponement of the critical phase.

The prototypical pattern of age-related shifts in 'popularity' of the first-order instrumental goals (see Figure 14.2) does not take into account individual differences; it describes mean levels of constraints for each instrumental goal at the population level. Large individual differences in timing exist, differences that may well increase with aging. The increase in heterogeneity will occur most strongly at the level of the lower-order means of production, because endowments, activities, and resources become increasingly specific and idiosyncratic when people age. Partly this is due to a lifelong process of cumulative effects (or path dependencies), starting in childhood and gathering momentum in adolescence and young adulthood, the life phase in which educational, professional, marital and friendship tracks begin to solidify. As a result, individual differences in resources and constraints will continue to increase. Steverink and co-authors note that after retirement social norms and institutions have less bearing, causing older people to rely more on personal compared to institutional means of achieving the first-order instrumental goals.

Application 3 – antisocial behavior

At first glance SPF-theory and antisocial behavior (ASB) may seem at odds with one another. In general, i.e. in most circumstances and by most people, antisocial behavior is usually considered abnormal, 'not done.' The very nature of antisocial behavior is norm-breaking behavior. Hence, antisocial behavior is counterproductive, as it will receive negative behavioral confirmation (disapproval) and loss of status from the community at large. Antisocial behavior, in particular criminal forms, carries the risk of severe penalties, even imprisonment, and thus loss of both physical and social well-being. However, the sheer existence of prevalent forms of antisocial behavior – like in Holland, bike stealing, vandalism and aggression in public places – suggests that some people in some circumstances must achieve substantial amounts of physical and/or social well-being by means of antisocial behavior.

What instrumental goals might be produced with ASB depends on the nature of the behavior and the context in which it occurs. Important distinctions of antisocial behaviors involve overt versus covert forms, whether or not aggression is involved, persistence versus transcience, and age of onset (Rutter, Giller and Hagell, 1998). Moffitt (1993) distinguished between adolescence-limited and life-course-persistent antisocial behavior.

Most antisocial behaviors will generally produce physical and social well-being as well. Theft will produce stimulation (the preparation and the act itself), comfort (the stolen goods), but also status and behavioral confirmation (reputation), unless peers are kept entirely in the dark. Public property destruction may yield status in addition to stimulation. Most social well-being (status and behavioral confirmation) will have to be provided by peers, as the community strongly disapproves of overt antisocial behavior.

The diversity of antisocial behavior and the variety of contexts in which antisocial behavior takes place make it difficult to develop SPF-based hypotheses about the etiology of antisocial behavior. If limited to the universal goal of social well-being and antisocial activities in adolescence, we may hypothesize, on the basis of SPF heuristics, that the probability of antisocial activities will increase the more the following four conditions are met:

(1) The lower the level of social well-being currently achieved with 'normal' second-order means, i.e. non-antisocial activities and endowments (the how-much-to-lose consideration). Important normal means of production of social well-being for adolescents include good relationships with parents, teachers and classmates, good friends, good grades, and excellence in popular activities such as sports and dating;

(2) The lower the costs of antisocial behavior (the how-easy-antisocial behavior-is consideration). Costs depend on the availability of opportunities for antisocial behavior and the possession of third-order resources that facilitate the performance of antisocial behavior.

(3) The more productive antisocial behavior is in terms of achievement of status, behavioral confirmation and affection from peers (the yield-per-unit-antisocial behavior consideration).

(4) The more expensive it is to invest in normal resources for the future production of social well-being (the costs-of-normal investment consideration). Costs will be higher with poor cognitive and social skills, with temperamental deviancies like high impulsivity and novelty seeking, and with limited access to opportunities for approved ways of

investment, like education, employment and emotionally stable sexual partners. In particular a short time horizon and poor planning skills may make it difficult to invest in normal resources.

Recently, Rutter *et al.* (1998) have reviewed the literature on risk factors for life-course-persistent antisocial behavior. They distinguished individual characteristics from psychosocial features and society-wide influences. The individual characteristics include genetic influences, behavioral impulsivity, hyperactivity (inattention), sensation seeking, low IQ, distorted social information processing, low automatic reactivity, and disturbed serotonergic functioning. The psychosocial features listed were family discord, hostile parenting, abuse and neglect, poverty, social disadvantage, poor supervision, teenage parenting, parental depression, delinquent peer group participation. Finally, school and area differences, criminal justice features, availability of guns, and mass media were named as society wide influences.

SPF heuristics could contribute to theoretical developments that specify how these risk factors operate, what routes of mediation they follow, and what probabilistic causal chains link distal and proximal risk factors. One way would be to explore how these risk factors influence the four hypotheses listed above. Most of Rutter *et al.*'s psychosocial features will have consequences for the level of social well-being that can be produced with normal means. Many of the individual risk factors will make it harder to invest in normal resources for the future production of social well-being, while they lower the cost of performing antisocial behavior at the same time. In general, the risk of life-course-persistent as compared to adolescence-limited ASB will increase the less there is to lose, the easier ASB is, the higher the yield per unit ASB, and most importantly the higher the costs of 'normal' investment.

Cumulative continuity has been proposed as an important mechanism through which persistence of antisocial behavior is maintained. From a SPF perspective, cumulative continuity could be viewed as the consequence of an ongoing reduction of social well-being achieved by normal means (increasingly less to lose), an ongoing reduction of costs of producing social well-being by means of antisocial acts (cost of antisocial behavior becomes steadily cheaper), ever increasing investment costs for resources needed for normal means of production of social well-being (normal behaviors become ever more expensive), and, perhaps, a steady increase in productivity of antisocial acts (productivity gain), for instance as a result of spending more and more time with deviant peers. All this will erode options for substitution from antisocial to normal ways of producing social well-being. In SPF theory, the term path dependency is used to indicate that particular developmental tracks, or production functions, reduce variety in resources, making it increasingly difficult to change tracks. Many of Rutter's risk factors will also increase the probability of 'lock-in' events, events that glue persons to their tracks and enhance path dependencies. Continuing criminal behaviors may be the prototype of a production function with a very high path dependency.

Discussion and conclusion

The purpose of this chapter was to argue that SPF theory provides heuristics for understanding developmental pathways and outcomes. Three preliminary and exclusively conceptual applications of SPF heuristics were presented, targeting well-being, successful aging, and antisocial behavior, respectively. SPF theory integrates current psychological theories about well-being and goals with economic consumer/household production theories. In this final section I discuss a number of potential problems and limitations of SPF theory.

Natural selection and SPF-theory

Although outside the scope of this chapter, I want to comment briefly on how compatible SPF theory and modern insights of natural selection appear to be. The value of the first-order instrumental goals for what biologists call 'inclusive fitness' (Dawkins, 1976; 1983) seems quite obvious (albeit the ultimate goal that we labeled interchangeably utility and psychological well-being is perhaps better described as inclusive fitness). The significance of the first-order instrumental goals for procreation is most easily seen for the goals of comfort (physically fit) and status (access to the most important resources of food and sexual partners). Both have influenced reproductive opportunities of social animals, and continue to do so. I think that the central assumption of SPF theory – human beings seek to optimize physical and social well-being – is not incompatible with the principles of natural selection and the notion of the selfish gene. As a matter of fact, if a gene influences behavior, it can only remain in the gene pool, if the gene, through behavior, maintains or extends its number of copies in the gene pool of the next generation. My assumption is that the tendency to optimize physical and social well-being results from selective pressures. Combined, high physical and social well-being almost guarantee reproductive success. Because of that, the striving to optimize physical and social well-being probably must have a genetic background, not in the sense that there are genes coding for this striving, but in the sense of genes coding for the neurobiological systems that result in this striving.

One of these systems might be the emotional system. Emotions may provide the motivational basis for the tendency to optimize physical and social well-being. Low levels of physical and social well-being are states that humans try to avoid and ameliorate. By favoring the development of the neurobiological substrate for the emotional system, natural selection may have put into place the hardware for the two universal goals. Natural selection favors behavioral determinants that maximize survival from birth to age 40, thus throughout young adulthood. From the viewpoint of natural selection, a motivational system that inserts a striving for physical and social well-being has obvious advantages for procreation.

Recently, Schultz and Heckhausen (1997) have discussed the role of emotions in the context of their life-span theory of control (Heckhausen and Schultz, 1995). This theory posits a motivation for primary control as a major driving force in both development and survival. Their position is that "humans desire to produce behavior-event contingencies and thus exert primary control over the environment around them throughout their life span" (Schultz and Heckhausen, 1997, p. 188). Primary control targets the external world and attempts to achieve effects in the immediate environment. Besides primary control, they distinguish secondary control, which targets the self and attempts via cognitive processes to achieve changes within the individual.

In Schultz and Heckhausen's innovative and challenging model of emotion and control, emotions serve as the fuel of a regulatory system whose major goal is to maximize the primary control potential of the organism. They present substantial evidence to support their claim, including research on infants. In contrast, SPF theory posits that a major function of emotions is to ensure the optimization of physical and social well-being. How are these two positions related? One possibility might be that the apparent primacy of primary control is an epiphenomenon (unintended consequence) of the universal tendency of human beings to optimize physical and social well-being (and the first-order instrumental goals) in cost-effective ways. If feasible, primary control (i.e. behavior-event contingencies in the form of selecting and modifying the physical and social environment) is undoubtedly an effective way to produce well-being and build up variety in resources for future production of well-being. Thus, if natural selection favors production of physical and social well-being in cost-effective ways, it will also favor behavioral traits that facilitate primary control. Hence, evolutionary evidence for the primacy of primary control can be interpreted equally well as supporting the primacy of the two universal goals. However, a strong case can also be made for the reverse. The apparent tendency to optimize physical and social well-being might be an epiphenomenon of the primacy of primary control.

One way to reconcile both positions is to hypothesize that the behavioral traits that contribute most to inclusive fitness favor optimization of the universal goals and the striving for primary control as well. Given the significance of primary control (i.e. behavior-event contingencies) for all first-order instrumental goals, the saliency of primary control for the cost-effective optimization of the universal goals may indeed be so large, that, in SPF terminology, primary control would become a meta-goal.

Current limitations of SPF-theory

In its current state, SPF theory represents a conceptual framework rather than a tight and refined theory with a coherent set of testable hypotheses. SPF theory needs elaboration and empirical testing, in order to rise above its common sense substance. A first step could be the testing of some straightforward assumptions of the framework. For instance, the assumption that psychological well-being is determined by the level of only two universal goals: physical well-being and social well-being; the important assumption of decreasing marginal utility of the first-order instrumental goals; or, the assumption that social well-being depends on only three first-order instrumental goals: status, behavioral confirmation and affection. It would also be interesting to examine cultural differences in second-order instrumental goals for status and behavioral confirmation, and how these correlate with variation in the cultural emphasis on the individual versus the community (self-esteem and guilt versus balance and shame). A second step could be the development of hypotheses on the differential effects of life events on well-being and the time pattern of effects. Life events are well researched but, with some notable exceptions (e.g. Brown and Harris, 1989; Leenstra et al., 1995), typically without systematically derived hypotheses about the features of life events, the contexts in which they occur, and the social production functions of those exposed to the events that influence the effects of life events on the outcomes of interest.

Not only SPF theory itself needs elaboration, but in order to be productive in understanding developmental trajectories and outcomes, it also needs outcome-specific elaborations and empirical tests. To date, SPF theory does not provide more than just a set of heuristics that, as I have sought to show, can be used to develop explanatory models of a variety of outcomes. Notwithstanding the potential significance of SPF heuristics for *systematic* development of explanatory models, the gap between SPF-theory and truly explanatory models is wide. Bridging it requires not only knowledge of SPF theory but also, most importantly, a thorough understanding of the literature on the outcome at hand.

A necessary condition of elaboration and testing is that reliable and valid measures of the concepts of SPF theory are available. To date, only proxies have been used in the few empirical studies that sought to test SPF assumptions. The extent to which these proxies really measure the concepts as defined in SPF is not clear. This state of affairs seriously hampers the interpretation of the empirical findings, since, in the case of falsification of the hypothesis, it is not clear whether the construct validity of the proxy measure is insufficient or the SPF based hypothesis incorrect. Work on measurement is in progress.

Another problem for SPF theory is cognitive processes. In particular cognitive processes that are directed at the self (self-management) and seek to prevent loss of well-being by means of cognitive strategies such as standard shift, social comparison, illusion or reminiscence. Heckhausen and Schultz (1995) denote the cognitive strategies aimed at protecting the self from loss of well-being without actually targeting the external world secondary control strategies. The problem secondary control posits for SPF theory is that it seems to represent a cost-effective way of producing well-being without actually 'producing' it. According to SPF-theory, secondary control, however, is, when stretched, not without costs.

To be more specific, let me focus on the strategy of standard shift. Standard shift occurs when the standard used by people to rate their subjective well-being changes over time. In the instance of a changing standard, repeated readings of well-being have different meanings. This phenomenon of intra-individual standard shift has been called upon to explain the lack of change in well-being amongst cancer patients (Sprangers and Schwartz, 1999a) and lottery winners (Brickman et al., 1978). Standard shift is typically understood as a powerful adaptive cognitive mechanism to maintain a "normal" level of subjective well-being and is the central mechanism in the adaptation level model of well-being (Brickman et al., 1978). As said before, this model asserts that life events prompt only very transient changes in well-being because a person rapidly adapts to the new situation by raising or lowering comparative standards in the direction of the new situation.

Steverink et al. (1998) have argued, in line with Heckhausen and Schultz's life-span theory of control, that cognitive strategies will only be adaptive in the long run when they help to restore or maintain investment and substitution behavior. If they undermine available or remaining investment and substitution, cognitive strategies carry the risk of becoming non-adaptive. In the terminology of the life-span theory of control, secondary control that is not, at least in part, directed at maintaining or restoring primary control, is non-adaptive. Ormel et al. (1997) have added two possibilities for explaining the robustness of well-being in the face of major adversity without relying on cognitive processes such as standard shift or social comparison. The first possibility is that the loss of means of production caused by the adversity has limited consequences. Due to the non-linear relationship between instrumental goals and universal needs (decreasing marginal utility), the loss of means may only minimally impact the achievement of the universal goals. Marginal utilities are, of course, only small in people with high pre-adversity levels of well-being. The second possibility is that the effects of adversity may quickly erode as substitution is successful.

Prospects

Although much work lies ahead, I think that SPF heuristics have much to offer for understanding developmental pathways and outcomes. They offer a framework to systematically examine how life changes, person characteristics, and social contexts influence well-being. They offer a systematic approach to the study of pro- and antisocial behavior, and to the understanding of why people become involved in criminal activities – be it for shorter or longer periods of time – despite the fact that criminal activities carry substantial risks of penalties, disapproval, and imprisonment. The SPF based work on successful aging contains the seeds for expanding the framework to successful and less successful developmental paths and outcomes across the entire life-span.

Viewed from a general perspective, three clusters of third-order resources seem very important for successful development. The first cluster consists of the cognitive and social skills that determine the ability to select cost-effective and multi-functional behaviors that strike a good balance between production of first-order goals (consumption) and building up resources (investment). I think important components of this ability include good cognitive executive functions, a relatively long planning time horizon, and absence of extreme temperamental deviancies (e.g. high neuroticism and impulsivity). In this context, the overlapping notions of self-regulation (Clark *et al.*, 1991) and primary and secondary control (Heckhausen and Schultz, 1995) are relevant. The second cluster consists of endowments, in part inherited, in part achieved, that provide access to environmental resources. They include good physical and mental health, education, money, and perhaps most importantly, a social network that contains both close, personal relationships as well as ties that give access to other networks, and hence a variety of indirect resources.

Combined, the clusters will ensure optimal substitution, if the need arises, in ways that are cost-effective in the long run, as well as the building up of variety in means of production for future achievement of different first-order goals.

Appendix 14.1: *Glossary*

Concept	Definition/Description
Universal goals	Physical well-being, social well-being (see Table 14.1)
First-order instrumental goals	Stimulation, comfort, status, behavioral confirmation, affection (see Tables 14.1 and 14.2)
Marginal utility	The amount of physical or social well-being produced by one additional unit of first-order instrumental goal. For all first-order instrumental goals, marginal utility decreases with higher levels of achieved first-order instrumental goals.
Hierarchy of goals and means of production	Goals are hierarchically arranged with the two ultimate goals at the top, the five first-order instrumental goals just below, and second-order means of production that serve to produce those five. Two major categories of second-order means are activities and endowments. Production functions specify the factors needed to produce a given goal. Thus, an array of production functions between goals and means of different levels will show how well-being is generated, maintained, or changed.
	Whether a particular level is denoted as goal or a mean of production depends on what level of the hierarchy is selected as the index level. Seen from the index level, levels below are means of production.
Resources	Means of production, at whatever level of the hierarchy, which are available to the individual. Depending what level of the hierarchy is considered the index level in a particular analysis, a resource can also be denoted as an achieved goal.
Constraints	Means of production, at whatever level of the hierarchy, which are *not* available to the individual. If the missing resource is critical for achieving a first-order instrumental goal, achieving it often becomes a goal.
Investment behavior	Achieving a resource without using it immediately for satisfaction of a goal.
Substitution	At all levels of the hierarchy, goals/means are substitutable depending on their relative costs.
Third-order means of production	Resources needed to execute activities and to obtain endowments, e.g., skills, physical and mental capacities, time, money.
Fourth-order means of production	Latent resources, e.g. non-active kinship ties, savings, inactive childhood talents and interests.

REFERENCES

Brandtstädter, J., and Baltes-Götz, B. (1990). Personal control over development and quality of life perspectives in adulthood. In P. B. Baltes and M.M. Baltes (eds.). *Successful aging: perspectives from the behavioral sciences.* Cambridge University Press, 197–224.

Brickman, P., Coates, D., and Janoff-Bulman, R. (1978). Lottery winners and accident victims: is happiness relative? *Journal of Personality and Social Psychology*, 36, 917–27.

Brown, G. W., and Harris, T. (1978). *Social origins of depression. A study of psychiatric disorder in women*. London: Tavistock Publ. Ltd.

Brown, G. W., and Harris, T. O. (1989). *Life events and illness*. London: Unwin Hyman Ltd.

Clark, N. M., Becker, M. H., Janz, N. K., Lorig, K., Rakowski, W., and Anderson, L. (1991). Self-management of chronic disease: a review and questions for research. *Journal of Aging and Health*, 3, 3–27.

Costa, P. T., and McCrae, R. R. (1980). Influence of extraversion and neuroticism on subjective well-being. *Journal of Personality and Social Psychology*, 38, 668–78.

Dawkins, R. (1976). *The selfish gene*. Oxford University Press.

Dawkins, R. (1983). *The extended phenotype: The long reach of the gene*. Oxford University Press.

Van Eyk, L. M. (1997). *Activity and well-being in the elderly*. Thesis. University of Groningen.

Fergusson, D. M., and Horwood, L. J. (1987). Vulnerability to life events exposure. *Psychological Medicine*, 17, 739–49.

Headey, B., and Wearing, A. (1989). Personality, life events, and subjective well-being: Toward a dynamic equilibrium model. *Journal of Personality and Social Psychology*, 57, 731–9.

Hebb, D. O. (1958). *A textbook of psychology*. Philadelphia: W.B. Saunders.

Heckhausen, J., and Schulz, R. (1995). A life-span theory of control. *Psychological Review*, 102, 284–304.

Kahneman, D., Slovic, P., and Tversky, A. (eds.) (1982). *Judgement and uncertainty: heuristics and biases*. Cambridge University Press.

Kahneman, D., and Tversky, A. (1984). Choice, values and frames. *American Psychologist*, 246, 341–50.

Kendler, K. S., Neale, M., Kessler, R., Heath, A., and Eaves, L. (1993). A twin study of recent life events and difficulties. *Archives of General Psychiatry*, 50, 789–96.

Kessler, R. C., Kendler, K. S., Heath, A., Neale, M. C., and Eaves, L. M. (1992). Social support, depressed mood, and adjustment to stress: a genetic-epidemiological investigation. *Journal of Personality and Social Psychology*, 62, 257–72.

Kloet, E. R. de (1994). Stress hormones and brain development. In E. R. de Kloet, and V. M. Wiegant (eds.). *Stress and neuropathology*. Boerhaave Commissie voor Postacademisch Onderwijs, University of Leiden, 7–22.

Kloet, E. R. de, Rosenfeld, P., Eekelen, J. A. M. van, Sutanto, W., and Levine, S. (1988). *Stress, glucocorticoids and brain development. Progress in brain research*. Maarssen: Elsevier Science publ. 101–20.

Krech, D., Crutchfield, R. S., and Ballanchey, E. L. (1962). *Individual in society*. New York: McGraw-Hill.

Lawton, M. P. (1983). Environment and other determinants of well-being in older people. *The Gerontologist*, 23, 349–57.

Leenstra, A. S., Ormel, J., and Giel, R. (1995). Life change and recovery from depression and anxiety in primary care. *British Journal of Psychiatry*, 166, 333–43.

Lindenberg, S. (1986). The paradox of privatization in consumption. In A. Diekmann, and P. Mitter (eds.). *Paradoxical Effects of Social Behavior. Essays in Honor of Anatol Rapoport.* Heidelberg/Wien: Physica-Verlag, 297–310.

Lindenberg, S. (1991). Social approval, fertility and female labour market behaviour. In J. J. Siegers, J. De Jong-Gierveld, and I. Van Imhoff (eds.). *Female labour market behaviour and fertility: a rational choice approach.* Berlin/New York: Springer Verlag, 32–58.

Lindenberg, S. (1996). Continuities in the theory of social production functions. In H. Ganzeboom, and S. Lindenberg (eds.). *Verklarende sociologie; opstellen voor Reinhart Wippler.* Amsterdam: Thesis Publications, 169–84.

Marshall, A. (1920). *Principles of economics: an introductory volume.* 8th edition. London: Macmillan.

Maslow, A. (1970). *Motivation and personality.* New York: Harper.

Moffitt, T. E. (1993). Adolescence-limited and life-course-persistent antisocial behavior: a developmental taxonomy. *Psychological Review*, 100, 674–701.

Nieboer, A. P. (1998). Life events and well-being. PhD thesis, ICS University of Groningen.

Omodei, M. M., and Wearing, A. J. (1990). Need satisfaction and involvement in personal projects: toward an integrative model of subjective well-being. *Journal of Personality and Social Psychology*, 59, 762–9.

Ormel, J., Lindenberg, S., Steverink, N., and Von Korff, M. (1997). Quality of life and social production functions: a framework for understanding health effects. *Social Science and Medicine*, 45, 1051–63.

Ormel, J., Lindenberg, S., Steverink, N., and Verbrugge, L. M. (1999). Subjective well-being and social production functions. *Social Indicators Research*, 46, 61–90.

Ormel, J., Sanderman, R., and Stewart, R. (1988). Personality as modifier of the life event-distress relationship: a longitudinal structural equation model. *Personality and individual differences*, 6, 973–82.

Ormel, J., and Schaufeli, W. (1991). Stability and change of psychological distress and their relationship with self-esteem and locus of control. *Journal of Personality and Social Psychology*, 60, 288–99.

Ormel, J., Von Korff, M., Brink, W. van den, Katon, W., Brilman, E., and Oldehinkel, T. (1993). Depression, anxiety and disability show synchrony of change. *American Journal of Public Health*, 83, 385–90.

Ormel, J., Von Korff, M., Ustun, T. B., Pini, S., Korten, A., and Oldehinkel, A. J. (1994). Common mental disorders and disability across cultures. Results from the WHO Collaborative Primary Care Study. *Journal of the American Medical Association* 272, 1741–8.

Ormel, J., and Wohlfarth, T. D. (1991). How neuroticism, long-term difficulties, and changes in quality of life affect psychological distress: a longitudinal approach. *Journal of Personality and Social Psychology*, 60, 744–55.

Plomin, R. (1994). *Genetics and experience: the interplay between nature and nurture.* London: Sage.

Rokeach, M. (1973). *The nature of human values.* New York: Free Press.

Rutter, M., Giller, H., and Hagell, A. (1998). *Antisocial behaviour by young people.* New York: Cambridge University Press.

Saudino, K. J., McClearn, G. E., and Pedersen, N. L. (1997). Can personality explain genetic influences on life events. *Journal of Personality and Social Psychology*, 72, 196–206.

Schultz, R., and Heckhausen, J. (1997). Emotion and control: a life-span perspective. In K. W. Schaie and M. P. Lawton (eds.). *Annual review of gerontology and geriatrics.* New York: Springer, vol. 17, 185–205.

Scitovsky, T. (1976). *The joyless economy.* Oxford University Press.

Simons, R. L. (1983). Specificity and substitution in the social networks of the elderly. *International Journal of Ageing and Human Development*, 18, 121–39.

Sprangers, M. A., and Schwartz, C. E. (1999a). The challenge of response shift for quality-of-life-based oncology research. *Annals of Oncology*, 10(7), 747–9.

Sprangers, M. A., and Schwartz, C. E. (1999b). Integrating response shift into health-related quality of life research. *Social Science and Medicine*, 48(11), 1507–15.

Steverink, B. J. M. (1996). Succesvol ouder worden: een productiefunctie benadering. *Tijdschrift voor Sociale Gezondheidszorg*, 2: 29–34.

Steverink, B. J. M., Lindenberg, S., and Ormel, J. (1998). Towards understanding successful ageing: patterned change in resources and goals. *Ageing and Society*, 18, 441–67.

Von Korff, M., Ormel, J., Katon, W., and Lin, E. (1992). Disability and depression among high utilizers of health care: a longitudinal analysis. *Archives of General Psychiatry*, 49, 91–100.

Weiss, R. S. (1974). The provisions of social relationships. In Z. Rubin (ed.). *Doing unto others.* Englewood Cliffs, NJ: Prentice Hall, 17–26.

Wells, K. B., Steward, A., and Hays, R. D. (1989). The functioning and well-being of depressed patients: results from the Medical Outcome Study. *Journal of the American Medical Association* 262, 914–19.

Wippler, R. (1987). Kulturelle Ressourcen, Gesellschaftlicher Erfolg und Lebensqualität. In G. Giesen, and H. Haferkamp (eds.). *Soziologie der sozialen Ungleichheit.* Opladen: Westdeutscher Verlag, 221–54.

15 Searching for paths to successful development and aging: integrating developmental and action-theoretical perspectives[1]

Jochen Brandtstädter

Human ontogeny is characterized by a great openness and plasticity: intentionality, choice, and self-cultivation in personal development are made possible, but at the same time are also necessitated, by the modifiability of developmental trajectories across the life-span. We select and construe our developmental paths according to our self-definitions and identity projects, which are themselves developmental outcomes; as soon as we have formed representations of our self and personal development, these representations in turn guide the actions and decisions through which we shape our development and aging (Brandtstädter, 1998; Pulkkinen and Rönkä, 1994).

We begin our life with an infinity of possible developmental paths; at the end, however, we have realized only one. The one path that eventually constitutes our life history is to a large extent the result of our intentional actions and choices, but it also reflects constraints and contingencies that we have not intentionally chosen. The norms, institutions, and knowledge systems that prevail within a given cultural and historical context constrain our action spaces; historical change and cultural evolution continously create and destroy developmental options. The existential fact of a limited life-time already constrains intentional choice, as well as possibilities of undoing the unintended results of intentional choices. These latter restrictions become particularly salient in later life; with advancing age, we may come to realize that some of our goals may remain forever unachieved.

Humans select and shape their developmental paths under conditions of "bounded rationality" (Simon, 1983). The causal and social contexts that mediate actions and effects are partly opaque; furthermore, we live among, and co-develop with, other people who have plans and intentions of their own. A considerable part of our life-activity thus consists in coping with unexpected and undesired effects of our actions and decisions. Even the knowledge that we have of ourselves and of the "inner" context of our actions is limited in principle: neither do we have complete insight into our needs or into the conditions that satisfy them, nor are we able to predict with certainty our future motives and intentional sets (Brandtstädter, 1979; Wilson, 1985). In hindsight, our actions and choices often appear unreasonable or incomprehensible even to ourselves. Obviously then, heteronomous constraints in intentional self-development already arise in part from the developmental openness, and the corresponding lack of coherence and continuity, of our beliefs, interests, and self-definitions over time.

Together with the features of plasticity and selectivity, we thus have to consider *contingency* and *uncertainty* as essential characteristics of human development. This has implications for theoretically modeling optimal development and successful aging; in particular, it follows that attempts to define personal well-being exclusively in terms of efficient goal pursuit are seriously incomplete. Apparently, a comprehensive notion of optimal development and successful aging should also consider the ways in which the person copes with, and comes to terms with, divergences between desired developmental paths and the factual trajectory of his or her life-course.

In this chapter, I will discuss the model of assimilative and accommodative coping (Brandtstädter, 1989; Brandtstädter and Greve, 1994a; Brandtstädter, Wentura, and Rothermund, 1999) as a theoretical framework that centers on two different but complementary modes of achieving a congruence between desired and factual developmental outcomes. This model basically addresses a class of phenomena that have come to be known as "paradoxes of satisfaction": People living under apparently adverse conditions often report high levels of satisfaction. Such "paradoxes" have emerged in many areas; in research on aging, for example, the resilience of the self-system against age-typical losses and constraints is drawing increasing attention (e.g., Brandtstädter, Wentura, and Greve, 1993; Staudinger, Marsiske, and Baltes, 1995). The dual-process model accounts for this resilience in terms of adaptive processes through which goals are adjusted to changing action resources over the life-span, thus integrating action-theoretical and developmental perspectives. According to this theoretical approach, sustaining a positive perspective on self and personal development over the life-span crucially hinges on the balanced interplay between goal pursuit and goal adjustment. Before describing this framework and its empirical applications in more detail, I will provide in the next sections some background about the role of goals in personal development.

Paradoxes of satisfaction: implications for the study of optimal development

The heteronomous constraints that shape our development, as well as our development-related choices and actions, will be experienced as a nuisance only when they endanger the attainment of personal goals. The agent may react to obstacles that impede goal pursuit in two different ways. First, he or she may try to alter the situation and to eliminate the hindrance; this is what theoretical notions of "reactance" (Brehm, 1966; Wortman and Brehm, 1975) would suggest. Second, the person may accommodate to the situation and adjust personal goals accordingly. This latter type of reaction will of course be more likely when the person sees no effective or acceptable way to remove the constraints.

Acceptance of heteronomous constraints enhances, and is enhanced by, disengagement from blocked goals and redeployment of action resources toward new goals. These processes apparently also account for the notorious "paradoxes" of satisfaction (Schwarz and Strack, 1991). Although humans cannot adjust to every kind or degree of adversity, the margins of adjustment seem very wide; it is a common finding that people living under apparently adverse and limiting conditions often report high levels of satisfaction or even happiness. After a period of readjustment, accident victims, physically handicapped people, or people with serious chronic illnesses often report levels of well-being and satisfaction comparable to those found in healthy samples (e.g., Brickman, Coates, and Janoff-Bulman, 1978). In a similar vein, it has been observed that the combined effects of objective indicators such as income, education, and occupational status account for only small portions of variance in measures of well-being and overall life satisfaction (Inglehart and Rabier, 1986).

Whether or not a person feels satisfied with his or her life and developmental prospects obviously depends on the degree to which actualities correspond to personal goals and levels of aspiration. Goals and aspirations, however, tend to adjust to the situation, and they do so in particular when the situation seems resistant to active change and modification. William James (1890) already has stressed the importance of preference adjustments for well-being and satisfaction: "...our self-feeling in this world ... is determined by the ratio of our actualities to our supposed potentialities; a fraction of which our pretensions are the denominator and the numerator our success.... Such a fraction may be increased as well by diminishing the denominator as by increasing the numerator" (James, 1890, 310–11).

The weak predictive relationship between "objective" and "subjective" parameters of well-being renders questionable any attempt to define optimal development or successful aging in terms of external criteria. Unfortunately, "subjective" indicators of well-being have their drawbacks, too. Individual reports of well-being are not simply read-outs of some "internal" state to which the person has privileged access. They are influenced by socially shared beliefs about the "good life" that describe, and prescribe, to what extent one may legitimately be satisfied (or dissatisfied) with one's life and personal development, given one's particular position on dimensions such as income, occupation, educational background, or age. Notions of happiness and well-being, in other words, are social constructs that guide and influence the ways in which people describe, and feel about, themselves and their personal development. Interestingly, these notions have some self-verifying potential: living under conditions that, according to social scripts, should promote happiness or satisfaction – or being aware that one does live under such conditions – may in fact foster a sense of well-being.

Given this backdrop, attempts to define paths of optimal development by general criteria that apply across individuals as well as across cultural and historical contexts should be met with skepticism (see Brandtstädter, 1977). In the following sections, I will focus on the ways in which individuals shape and control their development according to *their own* goals and projections of personal development, and spell out mechanisms through which these normative orientations are adjusted to losses and constraints across the life-course.

Personal goals as sources of sense and meaning

In the regulation of ontogeny, personal goals come into play as soon as the individual has formed representations of current, possible, and desired selves; such self-projections become articulate in the transition to early adulthood. Although self-definitions appear fairly stable across age (cf. Caspi, 1998; McCrae and Costa, 1982; Mortimer, Finch, and Kumka, 1982), they may in principle undergo change at any point in the life-course; even stable self-definitions may translate into different goals in different contexts and segments of the life cycle. In fact, shifts in goals often stabilize and maintain other, more central goals and self-definitions (cf. Brim, 1992).

Personal goals are linked to, and integrated into, more general and overarching life themes and identity projects; these "upward" links are activated when we are asked *why* we pursue a particular goal (Martin and Tesser, 1989). Whether a person can "identify" with his or her actual life and activity, or whether he or she feels dissatisfied and alienated, crucially depends on the extent to which actually pursued goals correspond, and give expression to, personal life themes and identity goals. Goals and projects related to personal development are generally multivalent and overdetermined, that is, they serve a variety of purposes: for example, the occupational goal of becoming a physician may be chosen in order to make money, help people, or acquire social status, or there may be a mixture of several reasons.

In contexts of intentional self-development, personal goals can function as directive forces only to the extent that they are linked to procedural subgoals and means. These "downward" ramifications determine how a given goal can be achieved; they generate "implementation intentions" (Gollwitzer and Moskowitz, 1996) that activate the necessary instrumental behaviors under defined situational conditions. Through procedural specification, goals are translated into a projected developmental path, i.e., a representation of intermediary goals or steps that link the present situation to an intended future outcome. This translation is mediated by semantic, causal, and procedural knowledge.

Semantic knowledge is required insofar as the agent pursuing a particular developmental goal must have some idea what it means, for example, to be a successful manager, scientist, or physician; efficient goal pursuit also presupposes knowledge about the indicators or "recognizer patterns" (Schank and Abelson, 1977) that define the desired developmental outcome. Causal and procedural knowledge, on the other hand, is required for defining the conditions and actions that are relevant for achieving the intended developmental outcome. When goals are in that sense linked to semantic, causal, and procedural knowledge, they are transformed into representational structures that guide and organize goal pursuit (Kruglanski, 1996).

In sum: goals lend meaning, coherence, and structure to intentional self-development, but they do so only insofar as they are charged with motivating valence and representational content through upward ("why") or downward ("how") elaboration. When goals are dissociated from personal life themes and identity projects, commitment to them will be low and tainted with feelings of alienation. This may be the case, for example, when goals are assigned by authorities or when people are forced into particular developmental paths. Goals that are loaded with positive meaning create a stronger commitment, and their pursuit will be experienced as more satisfying. The flip side of the coin, however, is that strong commitments can become sources of frustration and depression when we see no way to reach the pursued goal, or when the goal is rendered infeasible through a loss of action resources. In that case, personal well-being will also crucially depend on whether we are able to neutralize the commitment and to replace it by other options.

Goal elaboration and attainability

The semantic and procedural specifications that translate goals into projected developmental paths constitute a plan (Friedman, Scholnick, and Cocking, 1987; Nuttin, 1984; Smith, 1999). As discussed above, goal specification is mediated by available and contextually accessible knowledge; it may be influenced or supported by social scripts that define, for example, what it means to be "successful" or "competent" in a given role context or occupational field. The specification process has important motivational implications; it enhances a contingent monitoring of goal pursuit, and it provides proximal incentives and reinforcements that help to maintain a commitment to distal goals (cf. Bandura and Schunk, 1981; Harackiewicz and Sansone, 1991; Locke and Latham, 1990).

Attainability of goals depends on internal and contextual factors. Insufficient semantic and procedural elaboration may block the enactment of a goal at an early stage so that the formation of goal-related intentions remains fragmentary. Such "degenerated intentions" (Kuhl and Helle, 1986) can induce feelings of helplessness and depression, and will do so in particular when the person is unable to disengage from the blocked goal and to replace it with other, more feasible ones. Procedural elaboration of the goal is a necessary condition of efficient goal achievement, but it is of course not a sufficient one. External obstacles, conflicts, distractions, or a lack or loss of action resources may thwart even the most elaborate plan.

Divergence between an actual developmental course and an intended one usually generates dissatisfaction and distress. When the discrepancy appears to be irreversible and beyond personal control, such aversive feelings are particularly strong, and may eventually turn into depression. People harboring self-percepts of high control over personal development are more confident in that regard, and they will usually be more persistent in their efforts to overcome obstacles and constraints (Bandura, 1981; Skinner, 1995). Thus, the expectation of having control over personal development appears to be one critical ingredient of subjective life quality (see also Baltes and Baltes, 1990). Indeed, people scoring high in measures of perceived control look toward their future with competence and optimism, and they feel proud and satisfied when looking back on past achievements, whereas self-beliefs of low control over development are related to despondence and depression (Brandtstädter, 1992).

These affective consequences, however, are modulated by goal importance. Differences in goal attainability have a stronger effect on personal well-being when the person's commitment to the goal is high (see also

Brunstein, Schultheiss, and Maier, 1999). Trivial as it may seem, this observation has important implications for the study of well-being and successful aging; it suggests that downgrading the personal importance of goals that have become infeasible can be an important source of resilience in later life.

Developmental paths: open and closed

Sequences of subgoals and instrumental behaviors that lead toward the attainment of an intended developmental outcome constitute a closed developmental path (Raynor, 1982). Successful completion of a projected developmental path generally gives rise to feelings of satisfaction and joy; such "consummatory" emotions may be particularly strong when goal attainment was very demanding and difficult, so that visions of failure were highly accessible during goal pursuit (see Kahneman and Miller, 1986). People appear, however, to overestimate systematically the duration of positive affects related to future goal attainment (Gilbert, Pinel, Wilson, Blumberg, and Wheatley, 1998). Goal attainment can even result in disorientation and loss of meaning, at least as long as new and attractive commitments are not in view (see Baumeister, 1986; Brim, 1992). Obviously then, dissolving prior attachments may become a problem even in cases of successful goal attainment; this is all the more true as desired goal states, when they come true, often fall short of expectations.

The emotional quality of personal developmental prospects thus seems crucially to hinge on the extent to which the person succeeds in creating new and meaningful commitments after concluding a particular path (see also Raynor, 1982). To some extent, the orientation toward new and meaningful goals is enhanced by cultural scripts of the life-course that define a temporal sequence of developmental tasks. It should also be noted that there are types of goals that are not attainable through a finite sequence of instrumental steps. For example, identity goals such as behaving honestly toward others or being a dependable person constitute "chronic" intentional sets that may guide action and self-development throughout life (see Gollwitzer, Bayer, Scherer, and Seifert, 1999). Such goals, which define general maxims and principles rather than specific outcomes of personal development, constitute open developmental paths that can provide a continuing source of meaning and motivation. Likewise, complex competence goals such as professional expertise, artistic creativity, and social commitment may be constantly redefined and filled with new meanings, thus fostering a sense of personal continuity through the life course.

Compatibility of goals: intra- and interpersonal

Goal selection and definition usually involve a holistic perspective encompassing the whole system of personal goals, or at least larger segments of it: the attractiveness of a goal, and its attainability as well, generally depends on its compatibility within a larger array of personal projects and strivings. In most cases, the choice of a particular developmental path is a "package deal" (Bratman, 1987) that involves gains as well as losses and often compromises between different personal strivings.

Problems of goal compatibility arise because people generally strive for a variety of goals in different domains of life and often pursue more than one goal at a time. Although we try to ensure the compatibility of our strivings, we are not always capable of doing so. Untoward side effects often become apparent only in later phases of goal pursuit; furthermore, goal compatibility may be affected by inadvertent changes in personal and contextual and action resources. Sometimes the pursuit of particular goals can be postponed in order to channel resources to goals that do not permit delay, but this sequential, focalizing strategy is not always viable. Pursuing goals that mutually impede each other creates psychological and physiological strain and is often associated with reduced physical and psychological well-being (see Emmons and King, 1988). Furthermore, the commitment to a particular goal is diluted when other goals are activated at the same time, and this effect is of course particularly strong when goals pull in divergent directions (Shah and Kruglanski, in press).

People generally prefer, and tend to select, settings that minimize intra- and interpersonal goal conflicts, and that allow them to use their capacities at the highest and most differentiated level. This tendency is a basic motive of "proactive person-environment-transactions" (Caspi, 1998), and it is expressed in domains such as in mate selection, friendship formation, and occupational preferences. Well-being over the life-span critically hinges on the extent to which developmental ecologies are congruent with, and responsive to, a person's developmental potentials and interests. By the same token, environments that do not afford the requisite variety of developmental paths through which people can express and actualize their competences and identity goals tend to create boredom, anxiety, or even depression (see also Csikszentmihalyi and Rathunde, 1998).

Compatibility between goals critically depends on the physical, cognitive, material, and temporal resources that are available and accessible to a given agent in a given context at a given time. Time pressure and heavy attention load, for example, are factors that reduce the capacity for pursuing multiple goals simultaneously. Under such constraints, resources will often have to be channeled to one particular goal at the expense of other worthwhile strivings. To some extent, breadth and depth of information processing are automatically adjusted to available capacities (cf. Neumann, 1996). Action resources vary across situations, and they are subject to ontogenetic change. From a developmental point of view, *time* is of particular interest as an action resource. Time is required for implementing goals and life plans. In addition, it is a medium for resolving goal conflicts, as goals that cannot be simultaneously achieved may become compatible when pursued sequentially. Time pressure creates conflicts between time-bound goals (Dörner, 1984), forcing us to set priorities and eventually to disengage from some goals in order to attain others.

Most important, the age-inherent shrinking of residual life time reduces the maneuvering space for resolving goal conflicts through temporal sequencing. Whereas for the younger person, two time-consuming goals such as writing a book and building a house may be attempted sequentially, the same goals may exclude each other in late life. As a consequence, allocation and efficient use of reduced temporal and physical resources become increasingly urgent concerns with advancing age. With the fading of life time reserves, the basic motivational vectors of intentional self-development shift from self-actualization and expansion of resources toward maintenance of competences, compensation for losses, and consolidation of past achievements (cf. Baltes and Baltes, 1990; Cross and Markus, 1991; Nurmi, 1992; Ogilvie and Rose, 1995). At the same time, the ability or readiness to disengage from blocked goals and to adjust goals to resources becomes an important asset of resiliency (Brandtstädter and Renner, 1990; Brandtstädter and Wentura, 1995).

Substitutability of goals

Goals can often be reached in several ways. Availability of multiple, functionally equivalent means enhances compatibility between goals; goal conflicts may be resolved when new and different routes are adopted. Accessibility of different paths toward a goal also implies that the blocking of one particular path can easily be compensated. Maintaining one's self-esteem, for example, is a goal that may be reached in different ways, so that a setback in a particular self-relevant domain may be compensated by making salient some other positive facet of the self (cf. Kruglanski, 1996; Steele, 1988; Tesser, Martin, and Cornell, 1996). Generally, agents will less readily be forced to disengage from goals that can be attained through a variety of paths.

We have to distinguish between the substitution of means toward a goal from the substitution between goals (which of course may be means toward other goals). Both aspects are interdependent; substitution on the level of goals becomes an issue when all paths toward a goal are blocked. Goals (like subgoals or means) are substitutable or functionally equivalent to the extent that they serve similar instrumental or expressive purposes. Equivalent substitutions are generally less easily found for goals (subgoals, means) that are instrumental to the attainment of a multitude of other goals; goals that are related to the protection or preservation of resources such as health, time, money, social status, or social support may be considered as examples. As the blocking of such multifinal goals threatens many developmental options, it is particularly likely to create emotional strain (Hobfoll, 1989). Availability of functional equivalents also depends on the "phrasing level" (Little, 1989) of a goal; generally, highly abstract goals (such as, e.g., "occupational success") can be attained in a greater variety of ways than more specific goals that impose specific constraints (such as, e.g., "becoming a successful lawyer"). Even the most abstract goals have to be implemented in concrete ways, however; as soon as the person has taken a particular path to the goal, alternative routes may no longer be accessible: for example, the longer one has followed a particular occupational career, the lower tend to be the chances to achieve "occupational success" through some alternative path. Accessibility of alternative goals having comparable instrumental and incentive value enhances disengagement and reorientation when a particular goal is definitively blocked and all means to reach it seem exhausted. This may explain why people with low "self-complexity", whose identity projects are centered on one central, monolithic goal or life theme, seem to be more vulnerable to depression when facing a loss or setback (Linville, 1987).

Goal pursuit and adjustment: assimilative and accommodative processes

The considerations so far suggest that any personal or contextual factor that enhances the attainability of goals, as well as compatibility and substitutability within the individual's goal structure, is a developmental asset that fosters well-being, self-esteem, and personal efficacy. The field of forces that constrains the definition, choice, and implementation of goals and projected developmental paths, however, changes on ontogenetic and historical levels, and these changes affect the feasibility, compatibility, and substitutability of personal goals. When goals drift out of the feasible range, they turn from sources of positive meaning into sources of distress; problems of depression and alienation typically arise when the person believes that he or she can no longer be or become what he or she wants to be (Smedslund, 1988).

Against this backdrop, subjective life quality and well-being through the life-span seem to depend on the interplay of two quite different types of adaptive processes: first, on activities through which personal development is brought into congruence with individual goals, identity projects, and life themes; and second, on the adjustment of goals, identity projects, and life themes to changes in constraints and resources.

We have denoted these two adaptive modes as *assimilative* and *accommodative*, respectively (Brandtstädter, 1998; Brandtstädter and Greve, 1994a; Brandtstädter and Renner, 1990; Brandtstädter *et al.*, 1999; Brandtstädter and Rothermund, in press). Both modes reduce discrepancies between a desired developmental path and the actual course of personal development. They involve, however, opposed adaptive tendencies of the self-system: in the *assimilative* mode, the actual self (or, more precisely, the situation to which the corresponding self-representations refer) is adjusted to the desired self. In the *accommodative* mode, by contrast, desired self-projections are adjusted to the actual self.[2]

Assimilation and accommodation are inherently antagonistic regulatory processes; people will not relinquish goals or downgrade aspirations as long as they consider them attainable. Despite this antagonistic relation, assimilative and accommodative processes may complement each other in coping episodes and synergistically enhance problem solving and emotional readjustment. This paradoxical integration in part reflects the complexity of factual coping episodes. Problems such as bereavement, divorce, or coping with chronic illness usually involve a diversity of adaptive tasks, some of which may call for assimilative persistence, whereas others may benefit more from accommodative flexibility. On the dispositional level, there are stable individual differences in the tendency to employ assimilative or accommodative modes of coping that express themselves in characteristic styles of coping, and these styles may be differently suited to different types of problems (Rothermund, Dillmann, and Brandtstädter, 1994). In later life, accommodative patterns of coping become increasingly important for dealing with uncontrollable and irreversible loss; I will present pertinent evidence for this assumption below.

The functional antagonism between accommodative and assimilative processes points to a basic dilemma in action regulation: the tension between tenaciously maintaining goals even against obstacles, and of adjusting goals to irreversible constraints. These tensions become particularly salient when goal-related efforts approach capacity limits so that the tendency to continue the pursuit of the goal competes with a tendency to dissolve the commitment. In this situation, the person will eventually select or create alternative and more effective routes to the goal or engage the help of others; in other words, he or she may try to resolve the conflict through substitution or compensation. If this strategy does not solve the problem, accommodative tendencies may eventually gain the upper hand, so that previous commitments are dissolved and action resources are channeled to new goals.

Assimilative activities

In the assimilative mode, the person tries to alter the situation and to adjust the course of personal development so that it converges with personal goals and projected paths. The older person, for example, may engage in preventive or compensatory activities to alleviate developmental loss, select particular social contacts to find emotional closeness and security, and so on. The is-ought discrepancy that induces assimilative efforts may be self-initiated, for example when the person sets some ambitious goal for his or her future development. Discrepancies may also be imposed by external circumstances, for example when obstacles or losses threaten the attainment of desired outcomes (see also Bandura, 1989).

In the assimilative mode, the person adheres to his or her goals and self-projections and responds to obstacles with increased effort. The strength and persistence of assimilative tendencies depend on action-outcome-expectancies as well as on the personal value of intended outcomes. Assimilative efforts dominate as long as the person sees a chance to attain the desired outcome; other things equal, the agent will persist longer in the assimilative mode if the goals at stake are of high personal importance. Even the use of means of questionable efficiency may be a rational option in cases where the intended outcomes are of utmost personal importance and no other means are available; in such cases, the dividing line between rational choice and superstition becomes blurred.

When established action patterns no longer seem sufficient to attain some goal or maintain some desired performance standard, the intentional focus of assimilative activities may shift toward preventive, corrective, or optimizing objectives such as acquiring new skills or reallocating resources (Baltes and Baltes, 1990), and eventually to mediated or collective forms of control in which external help (professional experts, support systems) is engaged to achieve the desired outcome. As intimated above, compensatory activities presuppose an "equifinality" structure (Kruglanski and Shah, 1997) in which goals are connected to several means. In the performance domain, most tasks involve a multitude of component skills, so that a low level of proficiency in one component function may be counterbalanced through strengthening or intensified use of another component skill (Bäckman and Dixon, 1992). For example, an older tennis player may compensate for losses in speed or power by strengthening certain strategic elements of her play. She may also engage in intensified athletic training or choose more sophisticated equipment. As already mentioned, complex goals and activity domains often offer more scope for finding equifinal substitutes; the older university professor who has passed his zenith of creative productivity may put a stronger emphasis on mentorship tasks, on administrative and management duties, and the like (such shifts may already involve elements of goal adjustment or accommodation, however).

Compensatory objectives become urgent concerns when action resources decline; this fact explains why this type of assimilative activity has received much attention in the study of successful aging (e.g., Bäckman and Dixon, 1992; Baltes and Baltes, 1990). Compensatory activities, however, themselves use, and depend on, resources. When functional losses are progressive, compensatory efforts yield diminishing returns and may eventually reach a limit where costs outweigh benefits. In some athletic domains, for example, age-related loss may be counteracted for a while through intensified training; this extra effort, however, may become increasingly taxing. When growing portions of time, money, or energy are invested into one particular goal domain, the opportunity costs of neglecting other worthwhile projects increase. In functional areas where losses and constraints cumulate, compensatory efforts should thus exhibit a curvilinear (inverted u-shape) regression on age, reaching a maximum when losses are already distinct but still appear reversible, and declining thereafter (for supporting evidence, see Brandtstädter and Rothermund, in press).

When assimilative and compensatory efforts to pursue some developmental goal or maintain some desired level of performance approach a limit and yield diminishing returns, a situation arises that, according to traditional control-theoretical formulations (e.g., Alloy, 1988; Ingram, 1990) should precipitate depression and distress. According to the dual-process model, however, this is the critical point where accommodative tendencies come into play. Our aging tennis champ, for example, may perhaps become depressed as long as she retains her earlier ambitions or standards, but eventually she will adjust her aspirations, select comparison standards that make losses less salient (for example, playing with senior partners), or shift to another type of leisure pursuit. Accommodative shifts in preferences and self-evaluative standards help to stabilize and protect a sense of worth, efficacy, and personal continuity against experiences of loss and constraints. People harboring high self-percepts of control will generally less easily shift from assimilative to accommodative modes of coping; this resistance may put them at a disadvantage when they are confronted with factually irreversible losses and changes. Researchers are becoming increasingly sensitized to the potential drawbacks and negative side effects of strong self-percepts of control (e.g., Thompson, Cheek, and Graham, 1988); although it does not negate the adaptive value of perceived control as a coping resource, the dual-process model provides a rationale for such reservations.

Accommodative mechanisms

In the accommodative mode, goal discrepancies are neutralized by adjusting preferences to situational constraints and by downgrading the commitment to blocked goals. This mode is activated when goals are definitively blocked, so that the discrepancy cannot be eliminated through instrumental actions, but only mentally through neutralizing previous intentions and preferences. Assimilative activities are fueled by the hedonic differential between the pursued goal and the actual state, and they are enhanced by making this difference cognitively salient. Accommodative processes, by contrast, deconstrue this hedonic differential through increasing the availability of arguments and cognitions that render the blocked goal less attractive and the present situation less aversive. Note that this situation differs from the case where a goal is relinquished in favor of some more attractive option; in the case of blocked goals, new attractive options must be found or construed post hoc.

Examples of accommodative processes include disengaging from blocked goals, downgrading ambitions, reanchoring self-evaluative standards, or shifting comparison perspectives. Like assimilative activities, accommodative processes depend on personal and contextual factors. Accommodation is enhanced in particular when personal goals and resources are highly differentiated so that equivalent substitutes for a blocked goal may be more easily accessible. The biography of Robert Schumann provides an example: after suffering a paralysis of his left hand, Schumann had to abandon his plans to become a virtuoso pianist; he was able to overcome his desperate situation, however, by redefining his life design and becoming a composer (see also Brandtstädter and Greve, 1994b).

Accommodative shifts in preferences adjust goals and strivings to action resources. In contrast to assimilative actions, however, accommodative processes cannot be intentionally originated. We cannot disengage from blocked goals, downscale our aspirations, or dissolve attachments simply by an act of will; such a decision, if it occurred, would already be the outcome of an accommodative process (see also Brandtstädter, 1998). This draws attention to the automatisms of information processing that underlie accommodation.

In the assimilative mode, the cognitive system is tuned toward the pursuit of goals and the specification of action paths; the ongoing course of action is shielded from distractive stimuli and competing action tendencies (see also Kuhl, 1987). Generally, goal pursuit in the assimilative mode is characterized by a cognitive tendency to ward off information that would undermine the perceived attainability and attractiveness of the goal; beliefs concerning personal control over the goal may even be positively biased. As the system shifts toward the accommodative mode, this "implementative mind set" (Gollwitzer, 1990) is neutralized or reversed. The range of attention widens, responsiveness to task-unrelated stimuli that have been warded off as distractors in the assimilative phase increases again, and a divergent, defocused mode of processing comes to supersede the focalized mode of processing that dominates during goal pursuit (Brandtstädter and Rothermund, in press; Rothermund, 1998). Accommodative processes are further enhanced by a tendency of the cognitive system to withdraw attention from problems that have become insoluble, and to gravitate toward conclusions that mitigate aversive emotional states (Brandtstädter and Renner, 1990). In line with these assumptions, experimental findings point to an increased availability of cognitions that enhance a positive reappraisal of an initially aversive situation in the accommodative mode (cf. Wentura, 1995).

Figure 15.1 summarizes the considerations so far. Along with the basic facets and mechanisms of assimilation and accommodation, the figure lists conditions that differentially affect the dominance of these two adaptive modes. As intimated above, self percepts of control and contextual resources of action support and motivate assimilative activities that enhance the perceived attainability of goals. On the other hand, high self-complexity enhances accommodative processes through fostering goal substitutability. Furthermore, there are dispositional differences in the preference for assimilative or accommodative modes of coping; the concepts of assimilative persistence and accommodative flexibility refer to these differential constraints. Corresponding to the antagonism between assimilative and accommodative processes, factors that activate or enhance the former processes tend to inhibit the latter, and vice versa. Through the balanced interplay of assimilative and accommodative processes, the self-system resolves the basic dilemma between maintaining a stable course of action and adapting goals to losses and constraints. Figure 15.1 also points to conditions that impede this adaptive

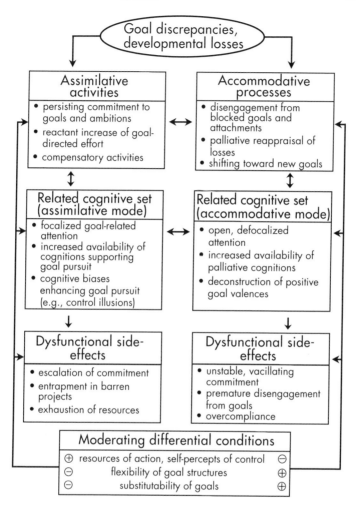

Figure 15.1 Assimilative and accommodative processes: related cognitive sets, possible dysfunctional side effects, and differential conditions ("+" and "−" signs indicate enhancing or inhibiting effects, respectively).

interplay. In the extreme, assimilative persistence may foster dysfunctional escalation of commitment to barren projects; on the other hand, accommodative flexibility may degenerate into a fluctuating, unstable commitment and a premature abandonment of projects in the face of difficulty.

Accommodative modes of coping as a resource in later life[3]

In the following, I will discuss some findings that highlight the particular importance of accommodation as a protective resource in later life. A focus on accommodation seems justified because this adaptive mode is seriously underresearched and often interpreted in misleading ways. As I have argued, accommodative processes are important resources of coping throughout life which, however, become particularly important developmental assets in adapting to later life. Over the last years, findings from questionnaire studies as well as from experiments and interviews with elderly people have lent growing support for this assumption.

In questionnaire studies, dispositional differences in assimilative persistence and accommodative flexibility (see above, Figure 15.1) have been assessed by the scales of Tenacious Goal Pursuit (*TGP*) and Flexible Goal Adjustment (*FGA*) (Brandtstädter and Renner, 1990).[4] These measures do not form a bipolar dimension, but constitute orthogonal facets of coping competence; both scales show substantial associations with indicators of well-being and subjective life quality (Becker, 1995; Brandtstädter and Renner, 1990). Despite these convergent relations, *TGP* and *FGA* exhibit opposite regressions on chronological age, indicating an increasing preference for accommodative over active-assimilative modes of coping with advancing age (Brandtstädter, 1992). Considering the cumulation of irreversible losses and the curtailment of action resources in later life (e.g., Seligman and Elder, 1986), this pattern corresponds with theoretical expectations, and it points to the importance of accommodative processes as a resource of resiliency in later life.

To preview, accommodative flexibility (*FGA*) shows two intriguing effects: first, in "flexible" subjects, dissatisfaction with respect to particular domains of life and function seems to spread or generalize less easily to a global sense of well-being. Second, accommodative flexibility appears to buffer the negative effects of age-typical losses and constraints. Experimental studies furthermore hint that accommodative flexibility enhances the availability of uplifting cognitions in situations of loss or threat. Converging with these observations, interview studies with elderly people suggest that they consider accommodation of goals and aspirations to be an important ingredient of successful aging; content analyses do reveal that participants who emphasize an accommodative stance report greater satisfaction with their aging.

Interactive buffering effects of accommodative flexibility: implications for well-being and perceived control

For reasons already discussed, successful goal attainment does not always bring about lasting satisfaction; nevertheless, when people *believe* that attainment of a particular goal will make them happy, failure to attain this goal will make them unhappy (McIntosh and Martin, 1992). This should in particular hold for goals that, through "upward connections" in the sense given earlier, are linked to central identity projects and strongly charged with positive meaning. The dual-process model posits that accommodative mechanisms should deconstrue these links when goals are unattainable, so that failures and setbacks in particular goal domains are taken more lightly and affect satisfaction and well-being to a lesser degree.

In our panel studies with adult samples, individual differences in well-being and satisfaction were assessed on global and domain-specific levels (e.g., Brandtstädter and Baltes-Götz, 1990). Domain-specific ratings positively predict global measures of well-being, but high accommodative flexibility moderates this relationship in the theoretically expected way. For example, for people scoring high in the *FGA* scale, perceived developmental deficits in particular goals domains (e.g., health, social recognition, physical fitness, personal independence) are less predicitive of global life satisfaction (as measured by the *LSI* scale; Neugarten, Havighurst, and Tobin, 1961). Figure 15.2 exemplifies the corresponding interaction pattern for the goal domain "prosperity, comfortable standard of living." The conditional regressions for high $(+1z)$ and low $(-1z)$ flexibility were derived from a moderated multiple regression involving life satisfaction as the outcome measure; as predictors, goal distance ratings, accommodative flexibility (*FGA*), plus the product of distance ratings and *FGA* were included in the regression function (Cohen and Cohen, 1983). The data were obtained from a sample of 800 participants in the age range from 62 to 86 years.

Similar buffering effects have emerged over a broad range of predictors and outcome measures. In married couples, for example, high accommodative flexibility tends to dampen the negative impact of marital problems on general life satisfaction (Brandtstädter and Felser, 2000). In older samples, health problems, impairments, and chronic pain generally predict depression and low life satisfaction; these relationships appear mitigated in people scoring high in *FGA* (see Brandtstädter, Rothermund, and Schmitz, 1998; Schmitz, Saile, and Nilges, 1996). Noticeably, such buffering effects are generally weaker or absent for the Tenacity scale.

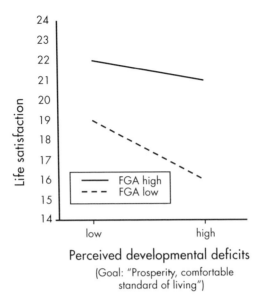

Figure 15.2 General well-being and perceived developmental deficits: buffering effects of accommodative flexibility.

Accommodation theory also provides an explanation for the astounding stability of perceived control in later life that has been noted in many studies (e.g., Gatz and Karel, 1993; Lachman, 1986; Rodin, 1987). If we assume that the degree to which losses of control in particular goal domains affect a general sense of control depends on the personal importance of that domain, a general sense of self-efficacy should be protected through adjusting goals and priorities to the feasible range. These theoretical predictions are borne out by findings from a longitudinal study involving a core sample of 735 adults in the initial age range from 30 to 59 years. With respect to a list of 17 goals (e.g., physical fitness, intellectual efficiency, personal independence, comfortable standard of living, social recognition), participants rated the degree of perceived control over each goal, as well as the personal importance of the goal. The analysis of longitudinal change scores over an eight-year interval revealed that decreases in domain-linked measures of control had a weaker impact on the person's global sense of control when the importance of the domain was downgraded during the longitudinal interval. This interaction effect was highly consistent across the different goal domains considered (Brandtstädter and Rothermund, 1994).

Availability of palliative cognitions and accommodative flexibility

As intimated above, accommodative processes basically involve a decon-
strual of negative meanings and a positive reappraisal of initially aversive
situations. We have used techniques of semantic priming to analyze these
mechanisms more closely (Wentura, Rothermund and Brandtstädter,
1995). In one series of experiments that involved 120 participants in
the age range 56 to 80 years, subjects read descriptions of a stressful
episode. The vignettes ended with a phrase that comprised threatening
as well as comforting elements (e.g., "...caring for yourself is becoming
increasingly burdensome. Your children offer to move you into an apartment in their new house. Leaving your familiar surroundings is difficult
for you, but you enjoy the prospect of being close to your children").
Speed of recognition and frequency of recognition errors for positive and
negative text elements were used to assess the cognitive accessibility of
the corresponding contents (e.g.,"familiar surroundings," "close to your
children"). Persons scoring high in the *FGA* measure should enhanced
access to positive or palliative contents. This effect, that becomes more
pronounced with increasing age, is further intensified when a short phrase
epitomizing the aversive episode (in the given example, "apartment") is
presented as a prime before the target phrases (Figure 15.3). Apparently,
accommodative flexibility enhances palliative associative links between
aversive contents and positive situational aspects in episodic memory,
thus dampening or neutralizing negative emotional responses in situations of threat or loss.

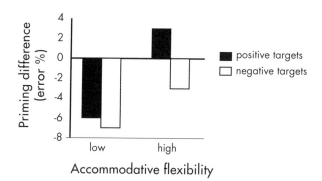

Figure 15.3 Associative dominance of palliative vs. aversive content:
moderating effects of accommodative flexibility (positive priming differences indicate enhanced recognition for the respective target).

Accommodative contents in biographical narratives:
observations from interview studies

In interviews with elderly people, we tried to gauge personal experiences and general expectations related to the process of aging. Within a semistructured format, the interviews focused on a differentiated assessment of various facets of accommodation such as a tendency to adjust goals to age-typical constraints, the absence of rumination about the past, acceptance of irrevocable changes, or drawing of positive meaning from adversities (see Dillmann, Steinleitner, and Brandtstädter, 1994; Schmitz, 1998). The interviews involved 60 participants (30 male, 30 female) in the age range from 55 to 79 years (mean age: 67 years).

Typical statements that illustrate how accommodative tendencies manifest themselves in a biographical narrative include the following (see also Brandtstädter *et al.*, 1998; Schmitz, 1998):

When you're younger, you try to perfect your natural talents and abilities. I think that is both healthy and proper. But that feeling goes away bit by bit. You don't want to, maybe because you can't, but maybe too because it doesn't seem to make all that much sense anymore. (*62 years, female*)

You regret the fact you're getting old, that your body's getting old, that you, well, don't look very attractive in a bikini anymore. But somehow, after a certain amount of time, you come to terms with it, because other things are always happening, which are nice and have little to do with your appearance. (*57 years, female*)

You have to accept…now that doesn't mean that for instance you should give yourself over to fate, rather I'm trying to say you have to be humble enough to say, You aren't 40 anymore! Taking a break is normal! It's normal that you get more tired on some days. (*63 years, male*)

Things that I can't change – I don't worry about them that much. Because if I moped about, the wrinkles would get worse (*laughs*). And when I don't think about it, then it just follows its natural course, but I don't do anything to worsen it. (*73 years, female*)

These quotations highlight that accommodative thinking is by no means akin to resignation or depression. Rather, they give an impression of calmness, perhaps even wisdom, and of a positive attitude toward life. Consistent with such impressions, content analyses reveal significant associations between the relative frequency of statements coded as "accommodative" and indicators of well-being and satisfaction. Participants who expressed accommodative tendencies were more likely to describe themselves as satisfied with their actual situation ($r = .35$, $p < .05$) and with their aging ($r = .55$, $p < .01$), and they reported a more positive attitude toward the course of their life in general ($r = .47$, $p < .01$). In hindsight, they experienced more continuity ($r = .36$, $p < .05$) and found more meaning ($r = .36$, $p < .05$) in their personal development.

Although focally concerned with accommodative modes of coping, the interviews also addressed assimilative strategies such as prevention and compensation. The dual process model posits that assimilative efforts are enhanced by expectations of control (see above, Figure 15.1). Content-analytic findings clearly converge with this assumption. Participants ascribing to themselves a high degree of control in managing their aging tended to express more assimilative tenacity in pursuing personal goals ($r = .27$, $p < .05$), whereas "accommodative" arguments were linked with the mention of uncontrollable factors in the aging process. Many participants emphasized the importance of preventive and compensatory efforts for successful aging; this emphasis was associated in particular with future-related expectations of control ($r = .33$, $p < .05$), and with indications of a higher satisfaction with their own aging ($r = .28$, $p < .10$). In comparison to accommodative modes, however, relations between assimilative tendencies and expressions of well-being and subjective quality of life appeared less clear-cut. It should be noted, however, that preventive or compensatory efforts involve positive as well as negative expectations about aging: they are jointly motivated by initial expectations of loss and by the "revised" expectancy that losses can be avoided or postponed through corrective action. This dissociation between generalized and personal expectations about aging may explain why, in our interview data, assimilative tendencies do not clearly indicate positive attitudes toward aging. This explanation finds some support in the observation of a stronger congruence between personal and generalized views about aging among participants emphasizing accommodative attitudes (see Schmitz, 1998).

Summary and conclusion

There is no single path to "optimal" development and "successful" aging, but there is a constant search for it throughout life and at any branching point of the life-course. Individuals strive to control and optimize their development in order to strike a favorable balance of gain and loss across the life-span. They do so, however, within developmental ecologies that are partly opaque and beyond their control. Notions of optimal development or successful aging thus cannot focus exclusively on the successful pursuit of goals, but must likewise consider the processes that enhance disengagement from barren developmental paths and the adjustment of goals to changing resources of action.

Focusing on personal goals and their translation into developmental paths, I have highlighted some critical conditions that contribute to the quality of life and personal development, such as: the extent to which chosen developmental paths are planfully elaborated; the degree to which they are linked to, and compatible with, one's basic life themes and identity goals; or the degree to which goals conform with action resources and developmental potentials. Personal goals lend structure and meaning to life and personal development; they can become a source of frustration and depression, however, when they are not adjusted to available action resources.

I have discussed the model of assimilative and accommodative coping (Brandtstädter, 1989; Brandtstädter and Renner, 1990; Brandtstädter and Greve, 1994a) as a framework that integrates these aspects. Drawing together action-theoretical and developmental perspectives, the dual-process model focuses on the interplay of intentional activities through which personal development is brought into congruence with personal goals and self-projections, and of processes through which goals and self-projections are adjusted to changes in control potentials and developmental reserves. Theories of coping and successful aging have given short shrift in particular to the latter, accommodative type of process, thus missing an essential dimension of life management. In the final part of this chapter, I have reviewed findings from various lines of research that suggest that accommodative modes of coping become particularly important when we focus on development in later life.

NOTES

1 This chapter was prepared while Jochen Brandtstädter was a Fellow at the Center for Advanced Study in the Behavioral Sciences, Stanford (1998/99); the financial support by the German-American Academic Council is gratefully acknowledged.

2 Note that our use of terms differs from Piagetian terminology, where assimilation and accommodation refer to the application and adjustment of sensorimotor or cognitive schemata.

3 The research reported in this section was supported by grants from the German Research Foundation (DFG).

4 Sample items: "The harder a goal is to achieve, the more appeal it has to me"; "When faced with obstacles, I usually double my efforts"; "Even when things seem hopeless, I keep on fighting to reach my goals" (Tenacious Goal Pursuit); "I find it easy to see something positive even in a serious mishap"; "In general, I am not upset very long about an opportunity passed up"; "I adapt quite easily to changes in plans or circumstances" (Flexible Goal Adjustment).

REFERENCES

Alloy, L. B. (ed.). (1988). *Cognitive processes in depression.* New York: Guilford Press.

Bäckman, L., and Dixon, R. A. (1992). Psychological compensation: a theoretical framework. *Psychological Bulletin,* 112, 259–83.

Baltes, P. B., and Baltes, M. M. (1990). Psychological perspectives on successful aging: the model of selective optimization with compensation. In P. B. Baltes and M. M. Baltes (eds.), *Successful aging: perspectives from the behavioral sciences.* New York: Cambridge University Press, 31–34.

Bandura, A. (1981). Self-referent thought: a developmental analysis of self-efficacy. In J. H. Flavell and L. Ross (eds.), *Social cognitive development. Frontiers and possible futures.* Cambridge University Press, 200–39.

Bandura, A. (1989). Self-regulation of motivation and action through internal standards and goal systems. In L. A. Pervin (ed.), *Goal concepts in personality and social psychology.* Hillsdale, NJ: Erlbaum, 19–85.

Bandura, A., and Schunk, D. H. (1981). Cultivating competence, self-efficacy and intrinsic interest through proximal self-motivation. *Journal of Personality and Social Psychology,* 41, 586–98.

Baumeister, R. F. (1986). *Identity. Cultural change and the struggle for self.* New York: Oxford University Press.

Becker, P. (1995). *Seelische Gesundheit und Verhaltenskontrolle.* Göttingen: Hogrefe.

Brandtstädter, J. (1977). Gedanken zu einem psychologischen Modell optimaler Entwicklung. In J. Schneider and M. Schneider-Düker (Hrsg.), *Interpretationen der Wirklichkeit.* Saarbrücken: ssip-Schriften, 117–42.

Brandtstädter, J. (1979). Bedürfnisse, Werte und das Problem optimaler Entwicklung. In H. Klages and P. Kmieciak (Hrsg.), *Wertwandel und gesellschaftlicher Wandel.* Frankfurt a.M.: Campus, 556–72.

Brandtstädter, J. (1989). Personal self-regulation of development: cross-sequential analyses of development-related control beliefs and emotions. *Developmental Psychology,* 25, 96–108.

Brandtstädter, J. (1992). Personal control over development: some developmental implications of self-efficacy. In R. Schwarzer (ed.), *Self-efficacy: Thought control of action.* New York: Hemisphere, 127–45.

Brandtstädter, J. (1998). Action perspectives on human development. In W. Damon (Editor-in-Chief) and R. M. Lerner (Vol. Ed.), *Handbook of child psychology* (5th edn.), vol. 1: *Theoretical models of human development,* 807–63. New York: Wiley.

Brandtstädter, J., and Baltes-Götz, B. (1990). Personal control over development and quality of life perspectives in adulthood. In P. B. Baltes and M. M. Baltes (eds.), *Successful aging. Perspectives from the behavioral sciences.* New York: Cambridge University Press, 197–224.

Brandtstädter, J., and Felser, G. (2000). *Entwicklung und Stabilität in Partnerschaften: Projektbericht der Forschungsgruppe Trier, Dezember 1999.* (Berichte aus der Arbeitsgruppe "Entwicklung und Handeln", Nr. 75). Trier: Universität Trier.

Brandtstädter, J., and Greve, W. (1994a). The aging self: stabilizing and protective processes. *Developmental Review,* 14, 52–80.

Brandtstädter, J., and Greve, W. (1994b). Explaining the resilience of the aging self: reply to Carstensen and Freund. *Developmental Review*, 14, 93–102.

Brandtstädter, J., and Renner, G. (1990). Tenacious goal pursuit and flexible goal adjustment: explication and age-related analysis of assimilative and accommodative strategies of coping. *Psychology and Aging*, 5, 58–67.

Brandtstädter, J., and Rothermund, K. (1994). Self-percepts of control in middle and later adulthood: buffering losses by rescaling goals. *Psychology and Aging*, 9, 265–73.

Brandtstädter, J., and Rothermund, K. (in press). Intentional self-development: exploring the interfaces between development, intentionality, and the self. In L. J. Crockett (ed.), *Motivation, agency, and the life course* (Nebraska Symposium on Motivation, vol. 47). Lincoln, NE: University of Nebraska Press.

Brandtstädter, J., Rothermund, K., and Schmitz, U. (1998). Maintaining self-integrity and self-efficacy through adulthood and later life: the adaptive functions of assimilative persistence and accommodative flexibility. In J. Heckhausen and C. S. Dweck (eds.), *Motivation and self-regulation across the life span*. New York: Cambridge University Press, 365–88.

Brandtstädter, J., and Wentura, D. (1995). Adjustment to shifting possibility frontiers in later life: complementary adaptive modes. In R. A. Dixon and L. Bäckman (eds.), *Compensating for psychological deficits and declines: Managing losses and promoting gains*. Mahwah, NJ: Erlbaum, 83–106.

Brandtstädter, J., Wentura, D., and Greve, W. (1993). Adaptive resources of the aging self: outlines of an emergent perspective. *International Journal of Behavioral Development*, 16, 323–49.

Brandtstädter, J., Wentura, D., and Rothermund, K. (1999). Intentional self-development through adulthood and later life: tenacious pursuit and flexible adjustment of goals. In J. Brandtstädter and R. M. Lerner (eds.), *Action and self-development: Theory and research through the life-span*. Thousand Oaks, CA: Sage, 373–400.

Bratman, M. E. (1987). *Intentions, plans, and practical reason*. University of Stanford Press.

Brehm, J. W. (1966). *A theory of psychological reactance*. New York: Academic Press.

Brickman, P., Coates, D., and Janoff-Bulman, R. (1978). Lottery winners and accident victims: is happiness relative? *Journal of Personality and Social Psychology*, 36, 917–27.

Brim, G. (1992). *Ambition. How we manage success and failure throughout our lives*. New York: Basic Books.

Brunstein, J. C., Schultheiss, O. C., and Maier, G. W. (1999). The pursuit of personal goals: a motivational approach to well-being and life adjustment. In J. Brandtstädter and R. M. Lerner (eds.), *Action and self-development: Theory and research through the life span*. Thousand Oaks, CA: Sage, 169–96.

Caspi, A. (1998). Personality development across the life course. In W. Damon (Editor-in-Chief) and N. Eisenberg (Vol. Ed.), *Handbook of child psychology* (5th edn.), vol. 3: *Social, emotional and personality development*, 311–88. New York: Wiley.

Cohen, J., and Cohen, P. (1983). *Applied multiple regression/correlation analysis for the behavioral sciences* (2nd edn.). Hillsdale, NJ: Erlbaum.

Cross, S., and Markus, H. (1991). Possible selves across the life span. *Human Development*, 34, 230–55.

Csikszentmihalyi, M., and Rathunde, K. (1998). The development of the person: an experiential perspective on the ontogenesis of psychological complexity. In W. Damon (Editor-in-Chief) and R. M. Lerner (Vol. Ed.), *Handbook of child psychology* (5th edn.), vol. 1: *Theoretical models of human development*, 635–84. New York: Wiley.

Dillmann, U., Steinleitner, C., and Brandtstädter, J. (1994). *Veränderung von Bewältigungsprozessen und subjektive Lebensqualität im höheren Alter: Entwicklung eines Codierschemas zur inhaltsanalytischen Auswertung der Interviewstudie* (Berichte aus der Arbeitsgruppe "Entwicklung und Handeln", Nr. 52). Trier: Universität Trier.

Dörner, O. (1984). Denken und Handeln in Unbestimmtheit und Komplexität. In P. Wapnewski (Hrsg.), *Wissenschaftskolleg zu Berlin – Jahrbuch 1982/83*. Berlin: Siedler, 97–118.

Emmons, R. A., and King, L. A. (1988). Conflict among personal strivings: immediate and long-term implications for psychological and physical well-being. *Journal of Personality and Social Psychology*, 54, 1040–8.

Friedman, S. L., Scholnick, E. K., and Cocking, R. R. (eds.). (1987). *Blueprints for thinking: the role of planning in cognitive development*. Cambridge University Press.

Gatz, M., and Karel, M. J. (1993). Individual change in perceived control over 20 years. *International Journal of Behavioral Development*, 16, 305–22.

Gilbert, D. T., Pinel, E. C., Wilson, T. D., Blumberg, S. J., and Wheatley, T. P. (1998). Immune neglect: a source of durability bias in affective forecasting. *Journal of Personality and Social Psychology*, 75, 617–38.

Gollwitzer, P. M. (1990). Action phases and mind-sets. In E. T. Higgins and R. M. Sorrentino (eds.), *Handbook of motivation and cognition: Foundations of social behavior*. New York: Guilford Press. 2, 53–92.

Gollwitzer, P. M., Bayer, U., Scherer, M., and Seifert, A. E. (1999). A motivational-volitional perspective on identity development. In J. Brandtstädter and R. M. Lerner (eds.), *Action and self-development: Theory and research through the life span*. Thousand Oaks, CA: Sage, 283–314.

Gollwitzer, P. M., and Moskowitz, G. B. (1996). Goal effects on action and cognition. In E. T. Higgins and A. W. Kruglanski (eds.), *Social psychology: Handbook of basic principles*. New York: Guilford, 361–99.

Harackiewicz, J. M., and Sansone, L. (1991). Goals and intrinsic motivation: you can get there from here. In M. L. Maehr and P. R. Pintrich (eds.), *Advances in motivation and achievement*. Greenwich, CT: JAI Press. 7, 21–49.

Hobfoll, S. E. (1989). Conservation of resources: a new attempt at conceptualizing stress. *American Psychologist*, 44, 513–24.

Inglehart, R., and Rabier, J.-R. (1986). Aspirations adapt to situations – but why are the Belgians so much happier than the French? A cross-cultural analysis of the subjective quality of life. In F. M. Andrews (ed.), *Research on the quality of life*. Ann Arbor, MI: University of Michigan, 1–56.

Ingram, R. E. (ed.) (1990). *Contemporary psychological approaches to depression.* New York: Plenum.

James, W. (1890). *The principles of psychology.* New York: Holt.

Kahneman, D., and Miller, D. T. (1986). Norm theory: comparing reality to its alternatives. *Psychological Review*, 93, 136–53.

Kruglanski, A. W. (1996). Goals as knowledge structures. In P. M. Gollwitzer and J. A. Bargh (eds.), *The psychology of action: Linking cognition and motivation to behavior.* New York: Guilford Press, 599–618.

Kruglanski, A. W., and Shah, J. Y. (1997). *Means to an end: goals-network theory and principles of activity engagement.* Paper presented at the Symposium on "Principles of Activity Engagement", Meeting of the Society for Experimental Social Psychology, 23–25 October, 1997, Toronto, Canada.

Kuhl, J. (1987). Action control: the maintenance of motivational states. In F. Halisch and J. Kuhl (eds.), *Motivation, intention and volition.* Berlin: Springer, 279–91.

Kuhl, J., and Helle, P. (1986). Motivational and volitional determinants of depression: the degenerated-intention hypothesis. *Journal of Abnormal Psychology*, 95, 247–51.

Lachman, M. E. (1986). Personal control in later life: stability, change, and cognitive correlates. In M. M. Baltes and P. B. Baltes (eds.), *The psychology of control and aging.* Hillsdale, NJ: Erlbaum, 207–36.

Linville, P. W. (1987). Self-complexity as a cognitive buffer against stress-related illness and depression. *Journal of Personality and Social Psychology*, 52, 663–76.

Little, B. R. (1989). Personal projects analyses: trivial pursuits, magnificent obsessions and the search for coherence. In D. M. Buss and N. Cantor (eds.), *Personality psychology: Recent trends and emerging directions.* New York: Springer, 15–31.

Locke, E. A., and Latham, G. P. (1990). *A theory of goal setting and task performance.* Englewood Cliffs, NJ: Prentice-Hall.

Martin, L. L., and Tesser, A. (1989). Toward a motivational and structural theory of ruminative thought. In J. S. Uleman and J. A. Bargh (eds.), *Unintended thought.* New York: Guilford Press, 306–26.

McCrae, R. R., and Costa, P. T. (1982). Self-concept and the stability of personality: cross-sectional comparisons of self-reports and ratings. *Journal of Personality and Social Psychology*, 43, 1282–92.

McIntosh, W. D., and Martin, L. L. (1992). The cybernetics of happiness: the relation between goal attainment, rumination, and affect. In M. S. Clark (ed.), *Review of personality and social psychology.* Newbury Park, CA: Sage. 14, 222–46.

Mortimer, J. F., Finch, M. D., and Kumka, D. (1982). Persistance and change in development: the multidimensional self-concept. In P. B. Baltes and O. G. Brim, Jr. (eds.), *Life-span development and behavior.* New York: Academic Press. vol. 4, 263–313.

Neugarten, B. L., Havighurst, R. J., and Tobin, S. S. (1961). The measurement of life satisfaction. *Journal of Gerontology*, 16, 134–43.

Neumann, O. (1996). Theories of attention. In O. Neumann and A. F. Sanders (eds.), *Handbook of perception and action*. London: Academic Press. 3, 389–446.

Nurmi, J.-E. (1992). Age differences in adult life goals, concerns, and their temporal extension: a life course approach to future-oriented motivation. *International Journal of Behavioral Development*, 15, 487–508.

Nuttin, J. R. (1984). *Motivation, planning, and action: A relational theory of behavior dynamics*. Hillsdale, NJ: Erlbaum.

Ogilvie, D. M., and Rose, K. M. (1995). Self-with-other representations and a taxonomy of motives: two approaches to study persons. *Journal of Personality*, 63, 643–79.

Pulkkinen, L., and Rönkä, A. (1994). Personal control over development, identity formation, and future orientation as components of life orientation: a developmental approach. *Developmental Psychology*, 30, 260–71.

Raynor, J. O. (1982). A theory of personality functioning and change. In J. O. Raynor and E. E. Entin (eds.), *Motivation, career striving, and aging*. Washington: Hemisphere, 249–302.

Rodin, J. (1987). Personal control through the life course. In R. P. Abeles (ed.), *Life-span perspective and social psychology*. Hillsdale, NJ: Erlbaum, 103–19.

Rothermund, K. (1998). *Persistenz und Neuorientierung: Mechanismen der Aufrechterhaltung und Auflösung zielbezogener kognitiver Einstellungen* (unpublished doctoral dissertation). Trier: Universität Trier.

Rothermund, K., Dillmann, U., and Brandtstädter, J. (1994). Belastende Lebenssituationen im mittleren und höheren Erwachsenenalter: zur differentiellen Wirksamkeit assimilativer und akkommodativer Bewältigung. *Zeitschrift für Gesundheitspsychologie*, 2, 245–68.

Schank, R., and Abelson, R. P. (1977). *Scripts, plans, goals and understanding*. Hillsdale, NJ: Erlbaum.

Schmitz, U. (1998). *Entwicklungserleben älterer Menschen. Eine Interviewstudie zur Wahrnehmung und Bewältigung von Entwicklungsproblemen im höheren Alter*. Regensburg: Roderer.

Schmitz, U., Saile, H., and Nilges, P. (1996). Coping with chronic pain: flexible goal adjustment as an interactive buffer against pain-related distress. *Pain*, 67, 41–51.

Schwarz, N., and Strack, F. (1991). Evaluating one's life: a judgment model of subjective well-being. In F. Strack, M. Argyle, and N. Schwarz (eds.), *Subjective well-being. An interdisciplinary perspective*. Oxford: Pergamon Press, 22–47.

Seligman, M. E. P., and Elder, G. (1986). Learned helplessness and life-span development. In A. B. Sorensen, F. E. Weinert, and L. R. Sherrod (eds.), *Human development and the life course: Multidisciplinary perspectives*. Hillsdale, NJ: Erlbaum, 377–428.

Shah, J. Y., and Kruglanski, A. W. (in press). Priming against your will: how goal pursuit is affected by accessible alternatives. *Journal of Experimental Social Psychology*.

Simon, H. A. (1983). *Reason in human affairs*. Oxford: Basil Blackwell.

Skinner, E. A. (1995). *Perceived control, motivation, and coping*. Thousand Oaks, CA: Sage.

Smedslund, J. (1988). *Psycho-Logic*. Berlin: Springer.

Smith, J. (1999). Life planning: anticipating future life goals and managing personal development. In J. Brandtstädter and R. M. Lerner (eds.), *Action and self-development: Theory and research through the life span*. Thousand Oaks, CA: Sage, 223–55.

Staudinger, U. M., Marsiske, M., and Baltes, P. B. (1995). Resilience and reserve capacity in later adulthood: potentials and limits of development across the life span. In D. Cicchetti and D. J. Cohen (eds.), *Developmental psychopathology. II: Risk, disorder, and adaptation*. New York: Wiley, 801–47.

Steele, C. M. (1988). The psychology of self-affirmation: sustaining the integrity of the self. In L. Berkowitz (ed.), *Advances in experimental social psychology*. vol. 21: *Social psychological studies of the self: perspectives and programs*. New York: Academic Press, 261–302.

Tesser, A., Martin, L. L., and Cornell, D. P. (1996). On the substitutability of self-protective mechanisms. In P. M. Gollwitzer and J. A. Bargh (eds.), *The psychology of action: Linking cognition and motivation to behavior*. New York: Guilford Press, 48–68.

Thompson, S. C., Cheek, P. R., and Graham, M. A. (1988). The other side of perceived control: disadvantages and negative effects. In S. Spacapan and S. Oskamp (eds.), *The social psychology of health*. Newbury Park: Sage, 69–93.

Wentura, D. (1995). *Verfügbarkeit entlastender Kognitionen. Zur Verarbeitung negativer Lebenssituationen*. Weinheim: Psychologie Verlags Union.

Wentura, D., Rothermund, K., and Brandtstädter, J. (1995). Experimentelle Analysen zur Verarbeitung belastender Informationen: differential- und alternspsychologische Aspekte. *Zeitschrift für Experimentelle Psychologie*, 42, 152–75.

Wilson, T. D. (1985). Strangers to ourselves: the origins and accuracy of beliefs about one's own mental states. In J. H. Harvey and G. Weary (eds.), *Attribution: Basic issues and applications*. Orlando: Academic Press, 9–36.

Wortman, C. B., and Brehm, J. W. (1975). Responses to uncontrollable outcomes: an integration of reactance theory and the learned helplessness model. In L. Berkowitz (ed.), *Advances in experimental social psychology*. New York: Academic Press. 8, 278–336.

Index